After-Images of the City

After-Images of the City

Edited by
Joan Ramon Resina
and Dieter Ingenschay

Cornell University Press

Ithaca and London

First published 2003 by Cornell University Press
First printing, Cornell Paperbacks, 2003

Printed in the United States of America

Library of Congress Cataloging-in-Publication Data

After-Images of the city / edited by Joan Ramon Resina and Dieter Ingenschay.
   p. cm.
   ISBN 0-8014-4021-1 (cloth : alk. paper) — ISBN 0-8014-8789-7 (ppk. : alk. paper)
   1. City and town life in literature.   2. City and town life in art.   3. City and town life.
4. Cities and towns—Study and teaching.   5. Sociology, Urban—Study and teaching.
6. Intellectual life.   I. Resina, Joan Ramon.   II. Ingenschay, Dieter.   III. Title.
PN56.C55 A34 2003
809´.93321732—dc21

                                                                            2002012579

Cornell University Press strives to use environmentally responsible suppliers and materials to the fullest extent possible in the publishing of its books. Such materials include vegetable-based, low-VOC inks and acid-free papers that are recycled, totally chlorine-free, or partly composed of nonwood fibers. For further information, visit our website at www.cornellpress.cornell.edu.

Cloth printing   10 9 8 7 6 5 4 3 2 1
Paperback printing   10 9 8 7 6 5 4 3 2 1

Contents

Illustrations

Acknowledgments

The editors wish to thank Paz Sufrategui and El Deseo for their kind permission to use an image from Pedro Almodóvar's film *All about My Mother* on the book's cover. We are obliged to Antoni Ribas and Produccions El Balneari for facilitating the reproduction of an image from his film *La ciutat cremada*. Further thanks go to Maria Mena of the Arxiu Fotogràfic of the City of Barcelona for her kind assistance; to Anthony Montoya, director of the Paul Strand Archives; to Sarah Greenough, curator of photography in the National Gallery of Art; to Janice Madhu, archivist at the George Eastman House; and to William G. Staffeld in the Visual Resources Collection at the Cornell College of Architecture, Art, and Planning. We are especially grateful to the Thyssen Foundation for a grant that made possible the preparation of the manuscript of this book.

We would like to thank the University of Minnesota Press for permission to reprint "Tijuana: Shadowtext for the Future" from *Border Women: Writing from La Frontera*, edited by Debra A. Castillo and Socorro Tabuenca Córdoba.

Preface

Dieter Ingenschay and Joan Ramon Resina

Rien ne peut m'empêcher de reconnaître la multiple présence
des simulacres dans l'exemple de l'image multiple. . . . On ne
peut pas supposer la signification par elle-même des états dis-
tincts de l'image en dehors de la notion du temps.

—Salvador Dalí

    The genesis of *After-Images of the City* began several years ago with dis-
cussions between the coeditors of this volume regarding the ways in which
knowledge and public "views" of the city are formed, mediated, destabilized, superseded, and sometimes reactivated. We were interested in a
broadly cultural rather than technical approach to the subject. Because
we belonged to the field of literary studies and were interested in the role
literary discourses have played and continue to play in shaping the urban
imaginary, we wished to trace the points of contact between such discourses and other venues for empirical and representational knowledge
of the city. We therefore formed a discussion group that includes scholars
working on or around the border between literary and visual studies, or in
the fields of the history of architecture, cultural theory, and urban geography. These scholars were invited to test the concept of "after-image" in
their own areas of expertise, to see how this concept could be developed
inductively as a valid analytical tool rather than simply expostulated, as
theoretical neologisms often are, without great concern about the means
to descend from the laboratory of formalization to the mill of cultural interpretation.

    What is an "after-image"? And why is it pertinent to urban studies? We
hyphenate the word "after-image" to signify an area of meaning controlled to some extent by the denotation of the nonhyphenated term—
namely, a sensation that lingers after the visual stimulus has disap-

peared—but also, more importantly, a theoretical domain influenced by other semantic forces tending to destabilize the notion of image. Some of these forces underscore the ideas of temporal displacement, sequentiality, supersession, and engagement. It is important to note that we do not conceive "image" in a narrowly optic sense but in the general sense of "visuality," which includes tropes, mental arrangements of spatial information, and the effects of perceptual organization that may well entail, as Tom Conley argues in his essay, the vanishing of "the real." Even if "material" images are at the origin of our "prehension" of cities, the knowledge thus obtained depends as much on the cultural agency of the intellect as on the psychological one of the mind for its private and public senses.

The pertinence of the concept of after-image to our understanding of cities becomes clear when we consider the direction taken by urban studies in recent decades, as analysts have de-emphasized the city as a bounded physical reality in favor of the city-as-process. David Harvey has argued that it is incumbent on the urban critic to keep in mind the dialectical relation between "the urbanising process and this thing called the city." Furthermore, he claims that "the ways that particular 'thing-like structures' . . . precipitate out of fluid social processes and the fixed forms these things then assume have a powerful influence upon the way that social processes can operate." (Harvey 21) If we translate this thought into visual terms, we see that "image-like structures," that is, the ordinary conception of an image as a fixed structure of visibility, are momentary precipitates from social and historical "solutions." In this way, the social "fluid" temporarily hardens into well-defined and, for that reason, meaningful dispositions, which, in turn, affect the process of image formation. An urban image, we contend, insofar as it is always the result of a social process, must be analyzed in terms of the dialectic between form and process, since it reveals its full sense only as the (provisional) end product of the ongoing dispute regarding the definition of (social) meaning.

The connection between city and after-image is foundational in the sense that the concept of after-image was elaborated in the context of discussions about urban representations held in spring 1996 in the center of Berlin, a city whose divided image (so replete with visible mementos of the 1930s and 1940s) was just then undergoing a vast mutation at all levels: most obviously, in the rearrangement of the city limits and districts and in the massive public and private works projects that were well under way in that year, but also in more abstract ways involving Berlin's new symbolic function as national capital and its decline as a refuge for alternative lifestyles and aesthetics in the staunchly capitalist and politically conservative Federal Republic of Germany. Already a half-voiced, diffident nostalgia for the communist past was perceptible among those alienated by the display of Western arrogance and careerism. Yet the question of whether the after-image could have emerged in a rural setting and in relation to a nonurban object, that is, whether the relation between city and after-image is contingent, is no trifling matter. If we remember that people have been fascinated with decoding urban images as far back as the period of industrial concentration, when the traditional communities where individuals possessed a relatively secure identity and a life knowable in its regular and regulated stages dissolved—the period that gave rise to a welter of urban representations characterized by confusion, disorientation, the masking of appearances, and social and individual strategies against these forms of anomie—then it appears that the concern with the city's legibility was stimulated by one of the most dramatic transitions in the historical image of the city.

If traces of a bygone transparency haunted the eerily empty streets photographed by Eugène Atget in nineteenth-century Paris, or if the mature Walter Benjamin, by tracking the echo of his footsteps in the streets of Berlin, was able to "read off" and thus narrativize the memories of his childhood, it is largely because the city itself had become the external measure of the shift from transparency to opacity. From then on, it could function as a surface for inscribing images that no longer corresponded to the residents' experience; images that no longer communicated in a clear, shared idiom, that interfered with one another and even evoked the interference.

The novelty and analytical range of the concept of after-image requires a theoretical foundation, which Joan Ramon Resina provides in chapter 1. Emphasizing the temporality and mutability of iconic constructions, he develops the concept in reference to Walter Benjamin's evocation of the instability of the image and to Roland Barthes's elucidation of how images are semantically invested. Claiming that the power of images depends on the ontological gap between perception and representation, Resina shows that the efficacy of the after-image as a medium is that it "opens up a space for reflection not just on the cultural meditation of what is perceived but on the image's mnemonic character." To illustrate some of the ways this concept operates in city representations, Resina first refers to proleptic city images in films such as *Blade Runner* and *Metropolis*, where there is a reversal of causality. In these films, he claims, the image, mistaken for an object perceived, engenders an illusory sequence and a fake ontology. What is seen will have happened. But since the imaginary of the modern city has been largely constructed through discourse, Resina reviews urban theories from Georg Simmel to Richard Sennett and to Marc Augé's nonplace (which he considers "the contemporary paradigm of city after-images") in an attempt to locate the intersection between such theories and the cultural paradigms of perception. Nevertheless, the concept of after-image must be validated through its usefulness in concrete case analyses, and this is the task undertaken in the following chapters.

Balzac's treatment of Paris may be the first great example in literature of a deliberate, systematic devising of city images. In this sense, his narrative may be regarded as foundational. In chapter 2, David Harvey looks at "Balzac's cartographic imagination," primarily in the author's early trilogy, *History of the Thirteen*. Harvey not only examines the utopian Balzac, who contributed so decisively to the popular image of the French capital, and the Balzac who depicted the constellation of class forces, but also analyzes how memory combines with desire to generate hope. The extent to which Balzac's Paris is related to the concept of after-image becomes clear in the comparison with Haussmann. Whereas the reformer's intention was to create a new urban order by implementing a distinctive class project, the writer's "obsessive personal quest" gives rise to a vision of the city "devoid of morals," by supplementing a spatial pattern of "infamous" and "noble" streets linked to a subjective moral order. His quasi-anthropological interest in Paris leads him to an "anthropologized" image of the city as a correlative for spatiality ("as materiality, as representation, and as lived experience").

Whereas Harvey discusses the anachronistic quality of the image in "City Future in City Past," Jürgen Schlaeger sketches "future images of the past." And just as Harvey interprets Balzac's "cartographic efforts . . . as a power play in a high stakes game," Schlaeger detects in the official projects for London's Millennium Dome a "massive reinvention operation." Although this experiment in urban reinvention failed (in spite of a huge propaganda campaign), a spate of novels succeeded in reinventing the city as "a score for multiple self-projections, a space teeming with endless signification, a poly-palimpsestuous site." Here again, the after-image is at work. Iain Sinclair, one of the authors whose texts on London Schlaeger analyzes, is accompanied in his work by photographer Marc Atkins, who finds "no physical London to explore street by street," but only fragments "encrusted with layers of myths, episodes, histories, remembered impressions." Considering the "postmodern" paradigm in London novels of the last twenty-five years, Schlaeger not only establishes the "after-images of dreams, visions, books, films, artworks," but also uses them as "an energy source, a starting point for embarking again and again on the endless journey of rewriting and reimagining the city."

Berlin, a city for which Hitler envisioned an entirely different image (to the point of renaming it "Germania"), has undergone enormous physical changes since the end of World War II, and again, with renewed intensity, in the last decade. The closing years of the twentieth century yielded copious after-images in this most palimpsestic of cities. In chapter 4, Mark Seltzer tracks the waves of demolition, redemolition and reconstruction in Berlin. He obtains his after-images from the city's "anti-architecture," which turns Berlin into a "theme park of the uncanny" but also refers to the "event" culture of the Love Parade and to "new" architectural attempts at reimagining and remodeling the past, such as the Reichstag Dome or the Holocaust memorial being designed by Richard Serra and Peter Eisenmann. In addition to focusing on postcommunist architecture, event culture, and art, Seltzer's outline of Berlin as the image of an empty place connects the city as "crime scene" to wound culture and to those ersatz models of reality that display images of authenticity "in rehearsals of violence and violation as markers of 'the real,'" where, in the form of so-called Reality TV, image and after-image oscillate and interpenetrate.

In the following chapter, Joan Ramon Resina explores the symbolic consequences of spatial practices as they affect the formation of conceptual images and the rise of tropes that mediate the public understanding of cities. He contends that visual tropes may conceal the process by which space is produced. Space, he claims, is grasped and put to use through the power of images, which are the locus of an ideological struggle to determine the uses of space. In this view, the image is not the unproblematic record of a state of things. Rather, it reveals a symbolic effort to subsume and occlude social conflict into visual coherence. For this reason, says Resina, an image of social space is always an after-image, in the double sense of lingering impression of a past event and pattern superimposed on previous patterns whose outlines can still be discerned in the socially dominant image. He illustrates this thesis by relating the dominant images of modern Barcelona to the history of civilian contestation: the repeated revolts against the state's restrictive definition of the physical perimeter of the city. Tracking an entire century of physical and symbolic strife by focusing on three crucial revolutionary moments, Resina underscores the decisive influence of the state on the outcome of such struggles.

In chapter 6, Dieter Ingenschay applies the concept of after-image to postmodern Madrid literature. Postfrancoist after-images have redrawn the city map as a semiotic field, or as a sum of non-places that expose the visitor to the fascination of the marginal. Although these after-images differ from Camilo José Cela's paradigmatic novel, *The Hive*, they return to the same central metaphor by means of a significant displacement. Ingenschay discusses four *post-movida* texts, all of which renounce the traditional ideological model for literary representations of Madrid since the nineteenth century: the dichotomy between the "two Spains" of authoritarian conservatism and liberal democracy. These recent novels, however, not only question such traditional models but also move beyond them, abandoning the discussion of the past. Still, they oscillate between nostalgia for a bygone image and the celebration of its postmodern refashioning.

In his programmatic first chapter, Joan Ramon Resina discusses the retinal constitution of images and its importance for the concept of the after-image. Ottmar Ette's chapter on city images and after-images in Albert Cohen's novels deals specifically with the retinal response. Ette's digression into Goethe's *Farbenlehre* (Treatise on colors) proves that the after-image "is much more than merely a literary process." Rather, it is part of an archive of images stored long ago and possibly transcending personal experience, which are reactivated in different forms of mental activity. He illustrates the processes of image fixation and storage through Cohen's (after-)images of European cities. Even though these images are often nonspecific, they leave deep traces in a European Jew traumatized by the experiences of the Holocaust.

Tijuana, a town Néstor García Canclini has called a "laboratory of postmodernity," is the subject of Debra Castillo's chapter. As a site of experiences shaped by post- and neocolonial practices, Tijuana has recently become an icon of borderline culture. Castillo considers this city's otherness from a dual perspective: from the north, as an exotic (and yet familiar) Mexican Disneyland where North Americans satiate their touristic appetites, and from the south, Mexico City, as a neutralized forecourt of U.S. pseudocivilization. In her interpretation, Tijuana "becomes the realm of fearful possibility and of rejected affinities." Its borderline location endows it with the character of an after-image, where the historical memory of colonization overlaps the present-day north/south cultural conflict. And if the images of recent Mexican and Chicano culture cannot step outside the dominant culture of each of the two countries, at least they are able to shake up conventional attributions.

In chapter 9, Mary Woods analyzes a uniquely U.S. aesthetic emerging from the way U.S. photographers and filmmakers in Alfred Stieglitz's circle recorded the era of the skyscrapers and the vertical city created in Manhattan. Synthesizing traditional ideas of U.S. identity and spirituality with European modernism (from James Whistler to Marcel Duchamp), these photographers capture experiences and expressions of modernity that Woods understands as engaging after-images of the "new" New York that continue to resonate in painting, photography, film, architecture, and popular culture.

Where the stadium was once one of the functional centers of cities, and strollers, joggers, and marathon participants *knew* the city as a space through which the body *moved*, where cities and their sport clubs were once united by a common fate, everything has now changed with the prevalence of televised sport events. In the last chapter of this book, Tom Conley reflects on how the city—New York in this case—is featured on commercial TV and, specifically, in sports broadcasting. The new mediation of the city image invites a retrospective look at former paradigms of the city's imaging: the bird's eye-view design of early modern city settings, then the Foucault-inspired "panopticism" of many postmodern approaches. The after-image he develops goes beyond those models: strange icons, Budweiser and Nike signs, turn New York into "a function of advertisement, as would any other city view in the emblematic configuration heralding each of the sections of the telecast."

We believe that, in their thematic and methodological range, these ten essays provide a useful starting point for urban analyses that take into account the intrinsic instability of the image. Focusing on the moment (and movement) between the provisional "freezes" in which an urban image comes to "rest," each essay reveals how the city becomes a fetishized object for a gaze that is caught in the symbolic conventions of cultural or ideological consumption.

CHAPTER ONE

The Concept of After-Image and the Scopic Apprehension of the City

Joan Ramon Resina

Several years ago I coined the term "after-image" in an effort to express a concept that had emerged as the editors of the present volume were discussing new ways to approach the subject of cities from a broad cultural point of view.[1] A great deal of published work on cities deals with images (both pictorial and conceptual), modes of representation, and perceptual strategies, and this suggested a fresh approach that would take stock of this epistemological tradition and at the same time avoid at least some of the problems inherent in an unquestioned notion of imaginary representation.

Our approach differs from classic image-of-the-city studies not because it chooses iconoclasm over postmodern iconolatry, but because it takes stock of the limitations involved in a static or simply seriatim scrutiny of images. Because we were aware of these limitations and of those involved in merely critiquing the concept of image, we did not give in to the temptation, in an age of proliferating posts-, to add one more to the ever-expanding list. Instead we preferred to explore the semantic wealth of the prefix "after" in the context of visual metaphors and urban representations.[2]

Detached from the presumed transcendence implied by "post-," the hyphenated term "after-image" retains the full sense of its constituents as well as the meaning of the nonhyphenated form. It denotes a visual sensation that lingers after the stimulus that provoked it has disappeared, and opens the idea of "image" to a cluster of theoretical possibilities based on temporal displacement, sequentiality, supersession, and engagement. Unlike "post-image," however, the concept of after-image does not suggest that one transcends and leaves behind the imaginary. The image is fully retained, but is now a temporalized, unstable, complex image brimming with the history of its production.[3]

A clarification is in order. The image is not to be conceived in a narrowly optic sense but in a larger visual one. We do not know the city only through our eyes and through the media: cartography, photography, film, virtuality. Even though the "material image" (an oxymoron) subtends much of what we know or think we know about cities, we always turn to our mental apparatus to grasp and decode the external organization of stimuli; we turn, that is, not only to our faculties of apprehension but also to the (private or public) imaginary within which the after-image is an image, but no longer an empirical one, a processed bit of knowledge that would be very difficult to isolate from more abstract forms of the image, such as the concept or the metaphor.

Perception psychology has shown that postperceptual processes are at work in fixing and storing images. The time elapsed between perception and decoding, and between retention and retrieval, is an eventful time. The term "eventful time" is redundant, of course, but the point should be clear: the image is not a timeless Platonic entity, nor is it a concurrence of presences linking the subject to the object. The retinal response, based on a physiological mechanism, is not a metaphor or an index but the very model for the formation and persistence of mental images. "How can we have failed to grasp," Paul Virilio asks, "that the discovery of retinal retention that made the development of Marey's chronotopography and the cinematography of the Lumière brothers possible, also propelled us into the totally different province of the mental retention of images?" (Virilio 60–61).

Between the prolepsis of the impression—a "fore-sight"—and the analepsis of recognition, seeing organizes, and, in a sense, creates, perception. Seeing, then, consists of the time intervening between impression and fixation, or rather, of the event or sum of events allowing us to focus on a fragment of the visual field. But since this activity begins in the past and fully holds that past in the present of vision, it comprises not only the memory function but also a subliminal harmonization of the differential moments in the visual take. In other words, seeing implies a certain tension within and a resolution of the image.

Once this is understood, image resolution can no longer be conceived spatially, through static terms and concepts, but must be seen temporally, as the provisional stabilization of visual effect through mental or technical editing. "Let's not forget, either," says Virilio, "that there is no such thing as 'fixed sight,' or that the physiology of sight depends on the eye's movements, which are simultaneously incessant and unconscious (motility) and constant and conscious (mobility)" (61).

The nonsynchronous occurrence of impression and perception can also take another form, when the after-image involves temporal extrapolation. By this I mean that the formation of the image can produce a misadjustment of temporality through an illusory reversal of the cause-effect relation. The image, that is, may literally come *after* the event it represents, altering its documentary value. Under such circumstances it appears to follow the future perfect temporality of the *"postmodern"* as defined by Jean-François Lyotard: "The paradox of the future (post) anterior (modo)" (Lyotard 81), the time of what will have been.

We find an example of an after-image in this sense in the postmodern cult film *Blade Runner* (1982) by British director Ridley Scott. In the scene, Rachel (a female human simulacrum called a "Replicant") answers Deckard's suspicions of her counterfeit nature by appealing to her childhood memories. Deckard, who works as a Replicant-exterminating agent, refutes this subjective proof by pointing out that those memories were implanted into her genetically engineered body. The past that a Replicant can call forth, then, is a programmed synthesis of nonlived experience, or possibly a transplant of vicariously lived experiences, as Deckard suggests: "Those aren't your memories, they're someone else's."

The purpose of a synthetic past is to promote libidinal cathexes and subjective projection, thus making Replicants easy to control through the manipulation of their libidinal anchors. As Tyrell the Replicant builder remarks: "If we give them a past, we create a cushion or pillow for their emotions, and consequently, we can control them better." Visibly touched by the threat to her subjectivity, Rachel advances one last confirmation of her humanness: a photograph of herself as a child with her mother. What is interesting in this scene is not that images can be tinkered with but that, as a consequence, they reverse the testimonial order, designing memories to suit the affections. Whereas the documentary authority of photography was based on the synchronicity between the image and the event it "captured," the images of Replicants (and images as replicas) turn out to be postfactual, they come *after* the event they evoke without having witnessed it.

The scene is compelling insofar as it defines nonsynchronicity as the very "essence" of images. If they "speak" about anything, it is about the gap between themselves and their authentic other, about themselves as gap. Their act of signification is itself an index of the displacement of action from the event in itself to the event *in* the image. Through its own dynamic, the image, like the Replicants in Scott's film, is capable of fulfilling the requirements of the eventful. It fulfills them not by making something happen—although that possibility cannot be ruled out—but rather by making it necessary that something has already happened. Rachel's photograph is performative, establishing her past in Lyotard's postmodern fashion, as that which will have been by virtue of the image.

Scott's film establishes a similar relation between image and event through its proleptic viewing of a Los Angeles existing in 2019. The issue here is not that the film produces the city as a simulacrum on the same ontological level as its Replicants, but that the imagery is essentially rhetorical and nostalgic, that it yearns for a history not of the city but of city images that properly belong to the history of film. Scott himself declared that *Blade Runner* is "a 40-year-old film set forty years in the future" (quoted in Doel and Clarke 142). And Mike Davis, commenting on the film's failure to activate a vision of the real Los Angeles "as it socially and physically erodes into the 21st century," declares that *Blade Runner* "remains yet another edition of [a] core modernist vision . . . of the future metropolis as Monster Manhattan." Indeed, after one removes "the overlays of 'Yellow Peril' . . . and 'Noir' . . . as well as a lot of high-tech plumbing retrofitted to street-level urban decay, what remains is recognizably the same vista of urban gigantism that Fritz Lang celebrated in *Metropolis*" (Davis, "Beyond *Blade Runner*" 1–2; quoted in Doel and Clarke 145).

In this regard, it is immaterial whether *Blade Runner*, like Rachel's photograph, thereby creates a false genealogy, whether, that is, it merely "*appears* to reflect something of capitalism, subjectivity, history, and the real" as "so many false mirrors—so many hauntings or spectral manifestations," as Marcus A. Doel and David B. Clarke assert (146). Either as mirror or as false mirror, the image defines the event: what will have happened or what will simply appear to have happened reverses the logic of *post hoc propter hoc*. Through this reversal, causality is downgraded to sequentiality: the cause of the vision (the image) engenders an illusory sequence and a fake ontology: I show it, therefore it happened.

My own awareness of the inherent complexity and contradiction in the images we entertain about cities began many years ago. This can be best illustrated by referring to a city of which I have relatively little *direct* experience (which does not mean I have few or insignificant experiences of it). I underscore the word "direct" to suggest how problematic the notion is that one can have unmediated experiences of such thoroughly cultural realities as cities. More distinctly than any of the cities in which I have lived, Madrid is for me a mediated "place." I never set foot in it as long as it was "Franco's city." When I finally arrived there in the summer of 1976, I went to see, first, not the Plaza Mayor, the Castellana, or the Prado Museum, but the warped mirrors in the calle de Alvarez Gato. I had read about them in Valle-Inclán's expressionist play *Luces de Bohemia* (1924) and was not sure they would still be there. They intrigued me more than anything else in Madrid because they were the objectual metaphor or objective correlative for a new aesthetic, a new art of creating images: one that was developed theoretically in the process of producing a counterimage or, in our terms, an after-image of that very city.

The mirrors were, in fact, still in the alley, modest witnesses to an image that, like themselves, contained the residue of a spent gaze. By 1976 Madrid had perfected its image as the symbolic center of a sinister exercise of power, a power that was still discernible in the familiarity and, in some instances, in the devotion with which people spoke about Franco and his military aides in bars and cafés. Yet careful inspection of some still-inconspicuous details revealed to the outside observer that the city was ready to leap toward a new cultural image. In 1976 these two images met in a kind of interzone strongly imprinted with the past, but a past already worn around the edges. And it was at the edges that the dissolve was taking place. At the time, however, the two images remained separate and dissonant, as if reflected in the two warped mirrors in the calle de Alvarez Gato. Only much later did I realize that those images were complementary, not just because both partook of the same social imaginary, but because they were intimately related, two versions or moments in a lengthy and ongoing effort to determine the symbolic status of that "place."

The notion of urban image entails several assumptions. The first and most obvious is that the city is primarily a visual object, that it is grasped above all through sight ("La ville s'appréhende avant tout par le regard" [Bofill and Véron 127]). Another is that a synthetic faculty exists by means of which city dwellers convert their sensory impressions into functional eidetic representations of their environment. For those who share this hypothesis, "the image of the city can be grasped in its totality as a 'figure' in a differential relationship with a 'surrounding'" (Mazzoleni 293). Kevin Lynch, theorizing such an image-building faculty, posited a convergence between epistemic and everyday living practices. In hindsight, however, such a perspective seems naive, especially in reference to modern conurbations.

Before the development of the nineteenth-century metropolis, cities could be measured by walkers and grasped as visual totalities when observed from outside the limits of the urban area. The very structure of the city transmitted important information about the population's lifestyle and conditions, even though the city's symbolic dimension (still perceptible to the Renaissance observer) had gradually become unrecognizable. Today those inclusive images are no longer available, except as virtual compositions in the urban imaginary. As J. B. Jackson notes, "the image of the contemporary city, the sign or logo which all of us know how to interpret, is a blend of cartographic abstraction and aerial view" (Jackson 55).

The perceptual change does not mean simply that a previously dominant architectural image has been displaced by a more abstract aviator's view. A downward-looking, remote perspective has not taken the place of an upward-looking, more absorbed one. The mutation, rather, is that architecture has become obsolete as the sole or even primary medium for visualizing the city. The image of the contemporary city is not only mediated by a variety of communications media but actually emerges from them. Increasingly, it is generated by the techniques of mechanical reproduction and manipulation in the service of urban marketers. One consequence of this appropriation is to further distance use and aesthetic values, a process that was already noticeable in the modernist city, and which gives rise to a semiotic dislocation in which, according to Kevin Robins, "the image of the city floats free from the 'reality' of the built environment" (306). As one critic of Barcelona's renovation pointed out in the mid-1980s, a large number of the spaces that were planned or reconverted were designed to be photographed (quoted in McDonogh 363).

While official discourse pandered to the need to respect and enhance the distinct life of the neighborhoods, much of the acclaim for the renovations undertaken by the socialist teams at city hall was an international response to the promotion of the planning and architectural work in glossy brochures, magazines, and lavishly illustrated books. Not only will the pictures retain their postmodern glamour longer than the buildings and city furnishings, but, as enduring dissatisfaction in certain districts suggests, the gap between experience and promotion, between those who collectively make up the city and use it and those responsible for its soaring image (and real estate prices), confirms the inadequacy of Lynch's idea of the city image as the meeting place for epistemic and everyday practices, or, in social terms, as the conjunction between the experience of residents and the goals of planners.

More fundamentally, comprehensive city images are no longer possible because, after the successive modern expansions and assimilations of neighboring municipalities, the metropolitan area has replaced the city. Where it still exists as a social and not just an administrative circumscription, the city can no longer be demarcated except, as Thomas Sieverts claims, through a collection of visually unobservable features. The new delimiting marks are arbitrary statistical thresholds regarding density of population, labor relations, the labor market, consumption patterns, rates of criminality, and so on (Sieverts 88). The totality once represented by the city image now reappears synthetically as an average, which can be graphically displayed but nonetheless remains an average image or, more exactly, the image of an average (Sieverts 94). Qualitative relations disappear from the picture; henceforth only easily quantifiable features are deemed relevant or even practicable by city planners, analysts, and authorities. What is left out constitutes a fundamental area of experience that was presupposed in Lynch's concept of imagibility: the area of direct observation by the participants in city life.

If quantitative relations fall within the purview of urban pragmatics and planning, the qualitative area associated with participatory consciousness seems to partake of the poetic imaginary, which Bachelard linked to a condition of not knowing and to the piecemeal association of images (Bachelard xxix). In its freedom from cultural mediations and ordinary perception (xx), Bachelard's poetic image differs from city images and after-images. Nevertheless, it embodies a distinction between the totalizing images of planning and the composite images produced ad hoc by the anonymous agents of city life. Still, the distinction should not be conceived categorically as that between seeing and not seeing or image and nonimage. Michel de Certeau contrasts observation from the ground to the scopic power of the planning god, the perspective of urban ants to King Kong's perspective. It remains true nonetheless that grounded, participatory observation (however residual or anachronistic) invests the strivings for urban totalizations by those in power with a content. Observation, as Chris Jenks points out, "is no longer regarded as the empirical exercise of the optic senses" (145); yet this exercise remains a foundational metaphor for the subtler, because abstracter (and thus potentially more arbitrary) methods in modern sociocultural analysis.

Sight as metaphor sustains Certeau's anthropomorphic formulation of modern planning and control epistemologies. In a celebrated passage from *The Practice of Everyday Life*, he evokes the viewpoint from the top of the World Trade Center. Up there one is a voyeur, a nonparticipant. Distance from the street allows the viewer to "read" the city (but in which urban code and in relation to what urban textuality?) or, more properly, to look down on it in a thoroughly objectifying—scientific or semiological—way. As Certeau recognizes, "the fiction of knowledge is related to this lust to be a viewpoint and nothing more" (92). The distance of 1,370 feet above street level (a visual metaphor for the godlike distance of pure knowledge and now, as the events of September 11, 2001 have shown, for the terrorist's lethal emotional distance from his victims) transmutes the city into a semic surface, unrolls it like a map under the pressure of the panoramic view, and supports the fiction of readability, which, in Certeau's accurate phrase, "immobilizes [the city's] opaque mobility in a transparent text" (Certeau, *Practice* 92).

Immobile transparency of a text or message (but are texts truly immobile?) also defines the fully semiotized image that the concept of after-image calls into question. The modern city is still organized by the scopic drive that created the medieval and Renaissance perspectival representations, but the desire to immobilize the city in an encompassing image is contested by a multiplicity of participatory viewpoints, which amount to so many perspectives. Certeau, who is clearly aware of this particularity, also declares: "The panorama-city is a 'theoretical' (that is, visual) simulacrum, in short a picture, whose condition of possibility is an oblivion and a misunderstanding of practices" (*Practice* 93).

Certeau's theoretical simulacrum refers to an actual technology for the spectacularization of the city and is therefore a belated theoretical deployment of the effects produced by a new visual contrivance. In 1791 Robert Barker inaugurated a sensational 360-degree painting medium, the panorama, which he introduced to the public in Leicester Square in London. While the pseudo-Greek term "panorama" added scientific glamour to the invention, its original name, "View-at-a-Glance," suggested the speed and inclusiveness of the gaze experienced in the panorama—in other words, the spectator's control over the object on display, an object which, in that first showing as in most later programs, was a cityscape. The appeal of the simulacrum lay, obviously, in its spectacular effect, due in large part to the initial shock of immediacy and also to the reversal of inside and outside, whereby the city appeared spread out inside a building. Yet the publicity stressed above all the power of the illusion to substitute itself for the referent and thus to dispense with the actual experience of place.

When Barker's panorama opened in the autumn of 1791, the advertisement for the "view-at-a-glance of the Cities of London and Westminster" promised visitors they would be "deceived as to suppose themselves on the Albion Mills from which the view was taken" (D'Arcy Wood 112). Since the simulated view was virtually the same as the original, there was no need to position oneself at the physical site to enjoy the perspective. After visiting Pierre Prévost's Panorama of Athens, shown in Paris in 1821, Quatremère de Quincy declared: "The precious remains of antiquity of the city were rendered with a verisimilitude that seemed to dispense with the need to actually see the originals" (quoted in D'Arcy Wood 103).

Certeau can contrast the panoramic view to the obliterated practices *in* the city, and especially, to walking, because practices, the assorted social forms of dealing with objects and with the world as object, are superseded in the illusion of instant availability to the eye. Since the first of all practices is to physically go to meet the object, the panorama spectator's deception regarding location implied not only the disappearance of the object (the vanishing of the city into its image) but also the inauguration of a social dysfunction. Henceforth, the acting subject is seduced into passively consuming a synecdochic relation to the fetishized environment. The panorama induces voyeurism as the characteristically modern approach to the city; *flânerie*, so often invoked in connection to movement in the street, is, in view of the flâneur's objective detachment in his ritual scopism, less a practice than a liturgy of social self-removal (from the crowd and everything it stands for) and control through the eye—in short, a means of spectacularizing the social world while dispensing with the need to acknowledge one's position in it.

It is precisely practices that the concept of after-image evokes, by emphasizing the tension-ridden, mutation-oriented, and temporally determined character of an otherwise flat and static iconic construction. By connecting theory with its etymon "viewing," Certeau implicitly concedes the static nature of theoretical discourse. Theory hankers after representation. Even if it strenuously avoids mimetic strategies, it operates by stabilizing and imaging a shifting reality. In M. Christine Boyer's words, "Every discourse sets up a spatial order, a frozen image that captures the manner in which the transitory present is perceived. Momentarily arresting disruptive and energetic forces, representational forms become succinct records of what we consider to be present reality. These aesthetic models transform our sense of the real, for the image of the city is an abstracted concept, an imaginary constructed form" (32).

Visual simulacrum and frozen image, however, are not inescapably linked to inscrutability and blindness. The experience of cities, in other words, need not be expressed by the dialectic between removed demiurgic seeing and eyeless involvement. What can one make, then, of Certeau's assertion that practices are embedded in an opaque atmosphere far below the threshold of visibility? How much credit should we lend to the claim that the practices constituting the city are blind, or that the networks woven by those practices do not presuppose an author or spectators and are themselves incongruous with representation? (Certeau, *Practice* 93) Are these anything but concessions to a poststructuralist predilection for the fragmentary, the disturbing, the incomprehensible? Do they amount to more than a radicalization of the Marxist idea of a false consciousness (which reads, but necessarily in the wrong code) and of the psychoanalytical motif of an instinctual language (which not only lacks a univocal interpretive science but also a detached, transference-free analyst)?

I would say yes. In the passage under consideration, Certeau provides an eloquent description of the image-forming and image-displacing processes. The spatial recital of previsual activities in the interstices of the city skyline serves as a description for the inter- and suprasubjective processes of image formation. Certeau's almighty seer from above is obviously a metaphor for the detached contemplation of the planner who turns the city into a spectacle based on the concealment of practices. The events of September 11, however, have shown how sudden flares can emerge from the obscure world of practices and turn the city into a spectacle of its own disappearance (see chap. 5). By yielding the most stunning, the most unpredictable images, these bursts of eradicating energy momentarily expose what planning and the social order had objectified in the seeming atemporality of the image. What scopic power conceals—and what the terrorist's fleeting appropriation of that privileged viewpoint on the city reveals—is, above all, the history of the production of its images.

As Hubert Damisch observes, bird's-eye views long preceded the invention of the airplane, confounding the image of the city with its relief map. But it was in the nineteenth century that architects multiplied panoramic views and opened perspectives in the core of the old cities. "It is as though, at the moment when the great city, the metropolis, the *Grossstadt*, was beginning to call for an image of agglomeration other than a strictly architectural one, it seemed indispensable to preserve its visibility" (Damisch 12). Indeed, it would seem that the very images in which the modern city has sought to recognize itself were visual rejoinders to a newly forming image that had to be kept below the threshold of visibility, at the level of the opaque experience Certeau calls practices. In nineteenth-century Paris, the newly perfected camera made the ritual of "walking in the city" a self-conscious representation on Haussmann's new perspectival stage (Burgin 14). Walking on the boulevards lost the opacity of traditional street-level mobility in favor of a self-seeing participation in the production of the vanishing point. Still, could the restrictions on the use of the camera in public places—finally lifted in 1890—have obeyed a logic of concealment? Might they have been intended to keep from public recognition, and thus from the city's image, those aspects that Haussmann's perspectivism helped obscure and displace? In practice, the newfangled image of Paris resulted from a power differential among urban players, all with stakes in a risky game of visibility/invisibility.

We must be careful, however, not to anthropomorphize the city and invest it with mythical self-reflexivity. The city does not look upon itself; it does not manage its images with the fabled intelligence and blind rationality of the market. There is no invisible visibility, no remote urban god responsible for the formation of city images. There is, however, as James Donald notes, a historically specific mode of seeing that arises with cities and allows us to conceive of the city as "a structure of visibility" (Donald, "The City" 92). The city produces novel modes of perception, poetic metaphors, and conceptual categories, and is, therefore, deeply implicated in the epistemology of the image. The concept of after-image could only have emerged in an environment where, in Georg Simmel's memorable words, "the rapid telescoping of changing images" (325) forces the mind not only to adapt to the accelerating changes but also to reflect on change itself, on the relation between the images and temporality.

For a long time, it has been generally believed that the image is a stable representation, and one, moreover, that offers itself up to spontaneous decoding or that requires no decoding (the case of radical mimesis). The dictum, "a picture is worth more than a thousand words," reveals as much about the cultural bias in favor of visual "eloquence" as it does about the widespread sense that the power of the image does not depend on meaning but on its capacity to expose. On the other hand, attention to historicity, to process, and to diegesis brings out the relevance of the image, raising the question of whether it was ever an adequate means for the cognitive apprehension of the city. Skeptical about the efficacy of the image, Richard Sennett points out that the principle of mutation underlying urban processes drains the meaning from unchanging representations of a place (219). Sennett's remark, warranted by the accelerated pace of change in today's urban environment, brings to the fore ideas that were implicit in the observations of early sociologists. Modernity and its urban stage, the metropolis, featured two new qualities: abstractness and an accelerated rhythm of encounters. A desire to understand these new aspects led to sophisticated analyses of the relations between mobile perception and the exposure of realities ordinarily hidden to the static viewpoint.

Around 1900 it became clear that "the image would have to incorporate the element of temporality, a sense not only of newness but also of accelerated rhythm. The multiplication of perspectives [by the cubists] was a way of acknowledging the existence of simultaneous realities and also the condensation and intensification of time in the street, the automobile and the train" (Donald, "The City" 84). With the rise of the dynamic image and of images-in-succession in film, the city manifested itself as a process with the force of self-revelation. In Benjamin's characteristically sculpted phrase, "by the dynamite of the tenth of a second," film burst open the buildings, rooms, and streets of metropolitan reality, expanding their dimensions by temporally extending the subject's perceptions of ordinary reality ("The Work of Art" 236).

The symphony films of the 1920s multiplied perspectives, subjecting them to the rhythm of urban activities while vastly enlarging the field of perception for the city dweller. Furthermore, the emphasis on machinery and the technical conditioning of daily routines seemed to refute Benjamin's observation that film's mimetic illusion depends on the erasure of the technological infrastructure subtending modern reality and its images ("The Work of Art" 233). With the development of montage, it became clear that the semantic gunpowder of the image flared up at contact with other images, that the power of an image to signify depended on the other images with which it came in contact and on the speed of the transition from one image to the next. Film not only temporalized the photograph, subjecting it to rhythm; more important, it turned the still photograph into a site for dialectical encounters.

It was film, more than Proust's *mémoire involontaire* (which often gets the credit), that inspired Benjamin's "dialectical image," that is, an image that, according to Graeme Gilloch, "seeks to capture historical movement, the changing visage of the metropolis in a textual freeze-frame" (114). Certainly, the concept is linked to forgetfulness and to recovery, or, in more explicitly Freudian terms, to repression and disclosure. In "The

Work of Art in the Age of Mechanical Reproduction," Benjamin emphasized alienated visual memory, but he did so in relation to the discoveries of the camera. Like the stream of memories unlocked by Proust's madeleine, in cinema a whole chain of previously inaccessible images could be triggered by an external object that aided the body's sensorium. "The camera," wrote Benjamin, "introduces us to unconscious optics as does psychoanalysis to unconscious impulses" ("The Work of Art" 237). But it was film's articulation of vision in the movement between different stills that produced a new form of awareness in the instant of the object's vanishing.

This cinematic rendering of urban life draws on Simmel's 1903 essay, "The Metropolis and Mental Life." Simmel anticipated the idea that intensified flows of stimuli, typical of the environment of the modern city, can overwhelm the human sensorium. "Man," said Simmel, "is a creature whose existence is dependent on differences, i.e., his mind is stimulated by the difference between present impressions and those which have preceded" (325). Perception and the meaning of the objects perceived were seen to depend more on the transitions between impressions than on the discreet impressions themselves. But impressions could be too intense and, above all, too densely packed and too diverse to be smoothly integrated into consciousness. "The rapid telescoping of changing images, pronounced differences within what is grasped at a single glance, and the unexpectedness of violent stimuli" (325) demanded the development of new strategies of perception.

Years later, Benjamin would consider those strategies formally established by film (Donald, *Imagining* 74). For him, film extended the range of the visible, just as the city did for Simmel. Unsurprisingly, it was the city that Benjamin identified as the privileged stage for the operation of film, so that the "far-flung ruins and debris" of the old visual world exploded by the camera were in effect the fragments of "our taverns and our metropolitan streets, our offices and furnished rooms, our railroad stations and our factories" ("The Work of Art" 236). In short, those debris were fragments of a closed and static image that film had forced open as an "unexpected field of action" ("The Work of Art" 236).

Benjamin was exploring ways for the historian to shake the accumulated and fossilized memories of the past. The historical materialist was engaged in "blasting open" history's continuum ("Theses" 262), just as the camera "burst asunder" the "prison-world" of traditional city images ("The Work of Art" 236). Through its systematic use of the shock experience produced by the modern metropolis and the arrival of new technologies of motion (Schivelbusch, *The Railway Journey* 160), film was able to create discontinuities in perception that favored attention to previously unremarked details, relations, or objects. It provided an epistemic model for the fleeting, the marginal, and the suppressed, which could then reappear under pressure from the tension packed in the moment of attention—what Benjamin calls the "moment of danger," in the "Theses on the Philosophy of History" (255). It is in this text that he asserts most explicitly the instability of the image, its resemblance to a trace: "The true picture of the past flits by. The past can be seized only as an image which flashes up at the instant when it can be recognized and is never seen again" (255). The past, that is, cannot be grasped or retained; it appears only in the recognition of its disappearance, as an image that comes in its own wake: an after-image. Such an image takes shape momentarily in the counterreflection with which the historical materialist "brush[es] history against the grain" and, in doing so, redeems the genuine historical image from the static images that make up the continuum of history into which the oppressor inscribes his relation to the past ("Theses" 257).

A century of visual education in the intrinsic dynamism of images should have dispelled the pictorial conventions that have organized the apprehension of cities in the West. But, as Grady Clay points out, recent books on cities continue to deal with their subject in the obsolete terms of order and unity, scale and space, light and shadow, and color and texture, which no longer respond to contemporary urban reality (29). Our way of looking, he claims, is culturally conditioned; it responds to centuries-old conventions that cause us to apprehend the familiar at the expense of all that escapes established ways of looking. We are "stuck to an old constraint," which holds our perceptions at an earlier historical stage (23). Of these premodern conventions, he finds perspectivism the most pervasive; it confines the world in "a kind of tunnel vision" (23). The claim may or may not be true (cubism and futurism, for example, challenged the monoperspectival tradition), but it is indisputable that our long-ingrained pictorial mode of looking supports the idea of stable images, and of a perceiving subject who acts as a pivot for the world's symmetry and intrinsic order.

Images that are controlled by a univocal perspective are steadfast and ahistorical. They are fertile ground for the rhetoricity that Roland Barthes associated with ideological messages. Incidentally, it is the assumption of a stable visual order—an order that would allow the reliable coding of images—that has given rise to the idea of the city as text, an idea that, if it has any sense at all, presupposes a stable meaning that can be accessed at different times by a community of "readers."

Barthes raises urgent questions about the semantic status of the image: "How does meaning get into the image? Where does it end? And if it ends, what is there *beyond?*" ("Rhetoric of the Image" 32). In attempting to answer these questions, he finds that the image contains a triad of messages, that it deploys a threefold sphere of communication. The first of these messages is explicitly linguistic. In the case of the city, it would include all linguistic signs, from neon advertisements to noniconic traffic signs, and the whole array of inviting, tempting, informing, forbidding, or warning messages that keep step with a walker's meandering path through a city. In this category are the journalistic, the literary, the political, the artistic, the economicist, and all texts generated by and addressed to the city as a community of textually initiated residents. At this level, the image is anchored by the linguistic message, which selects some signifieds and excludes others. In contrast, the two messages that arise at the iconic level constitute the image proper.

The second and third messages, Barthes argues, are not discreet and can only be distinguished analytically. One refers us to the image as coded icon and the other to the same image as uncoded, that is, to the confusion of the object with its image in naive perception. Insofar as images function ideologically, they aim to establish themselves at this third level of the message, pretending to be message-free, or rather, to be their own message. Ideological images seem to be fragments of nature that can be perceptually appropriated without reference to any given code. It is this lack of coding or, more exactly, an automatic decoding below the threshold of awareness, that allows images to disguise intentionality and pass for universal statements of fact.

In an important sense, images depend on a reflexive doubling of perception; they depend, that is, on an awareness of the ontological gap between perception and representation. As W. J. T. Mitchell remarks, "an image cannot be seen *as such* without a paradoxical trick of consciousness, an ability to see something as 'there' and 'not there' at the same time" (17). Implicit in this trick is an answer to Barthes's question: "What is beyond the image?" Once it is understood, the trompe l'oeil effect intrinsic to every image discloses the fact that the image is *always already* beyond itself. It can only be grasped in the absence (and in the awareness of the absence) of a referent: object, idea, emotion, or, in short, the meaning it would re-present. In other words, an image is always *after* itself, in the sense that it tries to catch up to its referent, but also in the sense that a gap, whether physical, psychological, or cultural (or a combination of all three), always separates the sensation from its resolution and verification. Through this gap, meanings enter (or come out of) the image by virtue of a process of hermeneutic amplification. Such a process is often unreflective. Acculturated interpretive dispositions and previously internalized cognitive patterns are fired by the image, which is thus connoted, turned into a visual aid for meanings that precede it in the social field.

The gap between naive and acculturated perception has an analytical correlative in the concept of after-image, since the latter opens a temporal hiatus within the image that is more than the neutral delay associated with retinal retention. Implicit in many studies about the cultural production of images is the assumption that cultural tinkering affects merely the ideologizable components of visuality, such as viewpoint or interpretation, while the images themselves are the optical resolution (and thus the objective presence) of that which is "sighted." In contrast, the concept of after-image opens a space for reflection not just on the cultural mediation of what is perceived but on the mnemonic character of the image, on its intervisuality. Such a space cannot be sutured by referring to the given character of the visual, nor by a hermeneutics that would naturalize (and neutralize) the relations between figure and discourse. If, as Mitchell says, "the image is the sign that pretends not to be a sign," and the word is "its 'other'" (43), then it follows that the dichotomy can, and often will, be enlisted to release the tension between the two components in favor of the illusion that the image, and the image alone, can retrieve the univocal truth of nature; or conversely, that it can restore us to the perceptual paradise where (Adamic) naming was redundant, since it merged with the fullness of the entities named.

To Barthes's question, "how does meaning enter into the image?" we can reply without hesitation: by importing time, consciousness, and history into its formal patterns. And perhaps guilt as well, the weight of culturally accumulated violence. The image, in any case, is never univocal. All images are, as Barthes declares, polysemous. Under the ice block of signifiers flows a throng of signifieds, some of which are hermeneutically netted while others swim past the conventional nets of meaning ("Rhetoric of the Image" 39). Furthermore, images brim with the history of their own production and with the conflicts and traumas of their emergence. The prefix "after-" has a slight connotation of exhaustion and spent energies, a touch of "aftermath," "the day after," or even, "after the battle." Beyond the commonplace that images provoke skepticism and thus a conflict of interpretations (which are in fact a form of verbal supplement), the concept of after-image uncovers a previous (and precariously settled) conflict of intentions.

As used in this book, the term "after-image" applies to the interpretation of both visual and linguistic messages, thus implicating the image in the postvisual process of cultural extension and decoding. Whether these messages are deemed ancillary to the phenomenological image or intrinsic to the symbolic status of images, whether they are strictly perceptual or installed in a textual imaginary, they are always coded, always culturally mediated. Much of the thematic material in this book includes not only discursive references to images in so-called visual media but also linguistic images of the city. Hence the question arises: does attention to the text elide the iconic status of the image? Does the textualization of the image demand its metaphorization? In other words, are linguistic images only rhetorical and not real? I would claim that this is not the case, and for good reason, namely, because the notion of "real images" is rendered suspect by the intrinsic rhetoricity of the image and by the after-image status of decoded visual messages. While the media shape images differently depending on the technologies employed, the borderline between empirical reality and rhetoricity is as thin as that between Barthes's second and third messages within the image's range of communication.

If we now turn to the city, it becomes easy to discern that the textual dimension of the after-image underlies, and in a crucial sense, constitutes, the information structure of urban icons. The text ought not to be omitted (in a strict sense, it cannot be) from the analysis of modern after-images, for the important reason that purely sensorial, language-free icons are unavailable in a modern urban context. As Barthes reminds us, "in order to find images without words, it is doubtless necessary to go back to partially illiterate societies, to a sort of pictographic state of the image" ("Rhetoric of the Image" 38). The "pure image" or the resolutely "material image" yearns for a premodern state of innocence, as "imaginary" for preindustrial societies (consider, for example, the doubly coded—scripturally and pictographically—postCortesian Mexican codex Mendoza which combines pre-Colombian techniques such as the ideogram with text in Spanish) as it is for modern urban culture. In this anthropological sense as well, our images are most decidedly after-images, images fallen from the paradise of sensorial candor and semantic immediacy.

Barthes distinguished two functions in the linguistic component of the image: anchorage and relay. Anchorage directs the receiver's attention toward a preempted meaning; it preselects the signifieds that will become available. Through this function, the text controls the consumption of the image, cordoning off potentially destabilizing readings and favoring semantic permanence. Relay is a function of complementarity between text and icon: "The words, in the same way as the images, are fragments of a more general syntagm and the unity of the message is realized at a higher level, that of the story, the anecdote, the diegesis" ("Rhetoric of the Image" 41). In relay the accent falls on temporality and narrative tension, as meaning travels like a current along the sytagma while negotiating the status of the image. Although Barthes acknowledged that both anchorage and relay can be active within the same icon, he considered the prevalence of one or the other decisive in defining the character and uses of a particular image. Thus, anchorage is typical of press photographs and advertisements, while relay is found in comic strips and, above all, in film, where dialogue does not comment on the images but introduces an extrinsic semantic dimension that is nonetheless inseparable from the movement of the photograms.

These two functions of the linguistic component are at work in the after-image. Cultural conventions depend on anchorage to promote the fixity of the image and, at their limit, to conceal the presence of the controlling text. Anchorage sustains the illusion by satisfying ingrained expectations; thus it helps conceal the synthetic character of the image. The image of a city, for example, is anchored in our general assumptions and limited knowledge about that city; or, in the case of cities we know well, it rests on hegemonic meanings that, because they have been successfully socialized, seem more legitimate than privately acquired ones. Hence, even if the experience of a city acquired through practices such as walking produces not a unified image but a series of images linked by a movement that is as contingent as the perspectives it yields, Lynch's observation remains true to some extent: city dwellers and visitors strive to compose a synthetic image merging the disparate fragments of their experience, and this will to make an overall meaning often gives rise to a manipulation of the visual order to produce images for consumption.

If they are to override our private memories of segmented space and juxtaposed urban fragments, such synthetic wholes must be anchored in widely accepted ideas. At the same time, these ideas must not call attention to themselves or their role as a framing device if the totalization they foster is to get the better of our perceptual wisdom. According to Barthes, images are structured around a set of connotative relations that stand for culture and a denotative syntagma that inserts the image into nature ("Rhetoric of the Image" 51). It is easy to recognize the two conventionally structuralist chains of linguistic relations in this dyad; but, in spite of its conventionality, this model of "ideological looking" may prove useful for disclosing the tensions repressed within stabilized or naturalized images, those which, according to Wittgenstein, hold us captive by virtue of their linguistic embeddedness (48).

The inexorable repetition of a picture tangled up in linguistic signification (and in the allure of mechanical reproducibility) is illustrated by the early history of print. Discussing the information value of pictures, E. H. Gombrich explains that medieval and Renaissance drawings were unconcerned with the relation between image and caption. In Hartmann Schedel's *Nuremberg Chronicle*, a book graced with woodcuts by Dürer's teacher Wolgemut, an image of a medieval city is used repeatedly with different captions to represent Damascus, Ferrara, Milan, and Mantua. Gombrich comments: "Unless we are prepared to believe these cities were as indistinguishable from one another as their suburbs may be today, we must conclude that neither the publisher nor the public minded whether the captions told the truth. All they were expected to do was to bring home to the reader that these names stood for cities" (69). It would seem that, in early print culture, artists and their audiences were indifferent to the relation between the linguistic and iconic levels of the image. What counted was the plausibility of the image rather than its specificity. Unlike today's victim of urban advertising, the medieval reader would have been fully aware of the arbitrary link between image and text. In a curious nominalist turn the caption or nomenclator, not the idealized image, rendered the referent specific. The caption, in other words, did not function as an identifying tag; on the contrary, it was the picture that gave conceptual content—that of "cityness"—to an otherwise meaningless name. Like a road sign, or like an icon on a tourist map, the image functioned as a universal coding device, oblivious to the peculiarities of the actual site.

One reason for this absolute supremacy of anchorage may be that, as Gombrich points out, detailed pictures and a firsthand acquaintance with different cities were still rare in the Renaissance (68). Anchored in a culturally familiar topography, the city image served the purpose of categorical representation, controlling, through abstraction, the scope of the referents denoted by different captions. In this way, the picture contained the potentially boundless range of connotations of the linguistic message.

Notwithstanding its literalism, the image of the city presented by Schedel's "Nuremberg Chronicle" did not constitute a denoted image in Barthes's sense, and for a reason diametrically opposed to his explanation. According to Barthes, it is unlikely that "readers" will remain at the literal level of signification because "everyone from a real society always disposes of a knowledge superior to the merely anthropological and perceives more than just the letter" ("Rhetoric of the Image" 42). Yet, as we have seen, the earliest printed icons of cities were dutifully literal, to the point of taking over the denotative function entrusted to their captions. Most people's knowledge of foreign cities did not rise above the information transmitted by the image qua image. In order to raise the stakes of connotation and to reintroduce into the image the discontinuities between sign and meaning, readers had to become travelers, had to test images against the touchstone of their own experience. In other words, they had to ground their recognition of cities in their own experience of motion and contingency.

That condition of *having-been-there*, which Barthes considered specific to the photograph ("Rhetoric of the Image" 44), eventually led to the destruction of the aura and, along with it, of the belief in "true icons." Originally a guarantee of the authenticity of the visual citation of reality, having-been-there gave way to the synthetic illusion of presence and the annihilation of distance (and consequently, of time as well), which Benjamin discerned as the deepest desire of the masses. In due course, the iconoclasm of modernity formalized its skepticism toward representation by inventing semiology. At the same time, however, modern skepsis and the attendant requirement of *having-been-there* gave birth to realism, the illusion that images are, if not presences, at least documents (from Latin *docere*, to teach, to show, related to the Greek *dokein*, to appear, to seem). It is an illusion induced by a technically contrived overlap of present(ed) meaning and witnessed meaning—meaning procured by spatiotemporal displacement, by *going there* or *having-been-there*.

The spatiotemporal displacement implicit in the *having-been-there* of realistic images exposes *in nuce* the workings of the prefix "after-" at the heart of the image. With the rise of realism, images no longer usurped the denotative function of captions, but rather sought to complement it, supplying, along with a plethora of referential detail, information about their own aesthetic status. Thus, they replaced auratic presence with potentially endless strings of visual allusions intended to guarantee the faithfulness of the image to its referent. With the rise of the connoted image (and realism proved to be the strongest possible connoter), the coding and decoding of the messages became more laborious, since connoted images stress the relay function, subordinating linguistic and visual semes to higher units of signification.

One way of achieving this was for the semes to act as morphological stimuli encouraging the articulation of more complex meanings. Subordinating the units of signification into larger connoted structures was paramount in the development of realism. As Gombrich points out, it is not wealth of detail that produces the mimetic effect, since the amount of information packed into the picture may actually hinder its illusory power. Mimesis is achieved less by overstatement than by the painter's capacity to enlist the viewer's projective faculties (221). Realism is always connoted; it rests on the beholder's willingness to replace sensory impressions with information originating at the eidetic level. In Barthes's terms, with the emergence of realism information became "costlier," more demanding.

Simultaneously, with the sharpening of the gaze, the image became open to self-reflexivity and self-supersession, inescapably so because, under the increasingly semiotic conditions of European culture, the image was prey to an ever more acute consciousness of its inadequacy as a facsimile. Gradually, this self-induced "unhappiness of the image" pushed realism to ever greater feats of precision, leading eventually to its self-defeat through the systematic frustration of its conventions. The hopeless race against the referent quickened the obsolescence of images, contributing to their proliferation and incessant replacement and to a heightened sense of their historicity.

By "self-supersession" and "incessant replacement" I do not mean—at least not primarily—the different readings to which the image is susceptible by virtue of the various forms of knowledge that can be brought to bear on its interpretation. I refer, rather, to the destabilization caused by these very forms of knowledge. The image was destabilized when lexicons were multiplied and an ever greater competence was required to apprehend the visual message. Under these conditions, images were increasingly surrogates for other images, and the accelerating tempo of dislocation made the transference of meaning perceptible not just between but also within images. Even so, images often endure beyond their lifespan, creating the impression that the historical course of an image is blazed by the previous images that track on its tail. Such optical relics invade the range of their epigones, causing a perceptual overlap and corresponding interpretive tensions. This loitering of the image, the delayed effect caused by its disappearance, is evidence that images spawn, engage with, discipline, and combat one another.

Claiming that the denotative syntagma was responsible for naturalizing the rhetoric of the image, Barthes defined that rhetoric as "the signifying aspect of ideology" ("Rhetoric of the Image" 49). One could also describe this naturalizing mechanism as the takeover of denotation by the cultural (connoted) elements of the image, a process we saw naively (but not innocently) at work in Schedel's "Nuremberg Chronicle." Less naively, denotation was again overlaid with rhetorical codes when cinema produced city images. Here, however, the effects were the opposite of those achieved by the Renaissance woodcuts. Fritz Lang's image of "Metropolis" may have been inspired by New York, but, as Siegfried Kracauer reminds us, it was produced in the studio by the Shuftan process, using small models to represent massive architectural forms (*From Caligari* 149). Rhetoric was eminently at work in turning allusion into illusion.

Like Wolgemut some four centuries earlier, Lang designed a city inspired by an idea of what a contemporary city looked or should look like, but, unlike his predecessor, he did not match this model to any given city. Abstaining from making mimetic claims and giving up topographic references, he futurized the image, placing it squarely in the realm of possibility. With its U.S. skyline, its baroque pleasure gardens, its Gothic cathedral, and its early Christian catacombs, Metropolis is as reminiscent of dadaist photomontages and of the industrial and urban landscape paintings of *Neue Sachlichkeit* (Huyssen 67–68) as it is of an unworldly city (Telotte 51).

By neutralizing and rendering anachronistic the embedded preindustrial images through a sleek technological *Aufhebung*, Metropolis furnished capitalism with the urban image of its bogus universality. Seduced by this non-place (history and crises are, as we know, pushed down into the catacombs), planners have since disseminated its image over the entire surface of the world. Supported by the master narrative of modernity, Metropolis appropriated the captions of actual topographic locations, which, unlike the cities denoted by Wolgemut's woodcuts, could now be readily tested for agreement between image and referent.

Shall we conclude, then, that the non-place is the contemporary "caption" for city after-images? There is some justification for this conclusion. The non-place not only depletes the connotative resources of the referent, thus revalidating the purpose of the early Renaissance image; it also "sublates" the historicity of the city into the image of the so-called global city: the delocalized, dis-located after-city. As Marc Augé defines it, the non-place is not so much the lack of place as its negation, a kind of antiplace. Whereas place is historical and concerned with identity—both are attributes of early modernity—the non-place has nothing to do with topographic temporalities and specificities. It is an outgrowth of supermodernity (Augé, *Non-Places* 77–78). These new spaces of global intercourse are defined not by the relations they structure, or rather fail to structure, but by their instrumentality and the ends they serve: travel, transit, commerce, administration, leisure. Unlike places, which build the webs of the social, non-places create "solitary contractuality" (*Non-Places* 94). Of special interest is Augé's remark that place "is never completely erased," while the non-place "is never totally completed." One supervenes the other and wrests its meaning or nonmeaning from the previously existing symbolic determinations. In fact, says Augé, "they are like palimpsests on which the scrambled game of identity and relations is ceaselessly rewritten" (*Non-Places* 79).

If we seek to replace the textual metaphor of the palimpsest with a visual one, we immediately come upon the after-image: graphic superimposition on the one hand, but, on the other, preservation of the occluded image, which is and is not there, which is neutralized by supervening images but also determines them just as a background determines its figure. The after-image refers to an optic realm where outlines and relations are ceaselessly debated and hierarchies of meaning reversed. Thus, the proliferation of non-places stimulates the fabrication of place, a sort of city camp in the era of telecommunications and the high-speed travel that guts the inner life of cities and turns mid-sized towns into casual stopping areas along the routes by which we desert historical places. Augé explains: "Every town or village not of recent origin lays public claim to its history, displaying it to the passing motorist on a series of signboards which add up to a sort of 'business card.' Making the historical context explicit in this way, which in fact is quite a recent practice, coincides with a reorganization of space (the creation of bypasses and main motorway routes avoiding towns) that tends, inversely, to short-circuit the historical context by avoiding the monuments that embody it" (*Non-Places* 68). As Augé remarks, this touristic strategy is effective only to the degree that motorists have a taste for history and for rooted identities, a taste he claims has become a distinctive French trait over the past twenty years, that is, over the period of expansion of the European non-places of supermodernity.

In Augé's account of newly emerging signs of local identity, it is possible to discern the reappearance of the Renaissance practice of invoking urban specificity through the caption, while dissolving that specificity in figurative homology. Today, as non-places multiply, the images of disappearing places must be advertised—and semioticized—to be perceived at all. The consequence of resemiotization is, paradoxically, to reinscribe the palimpsest, creating a visual overlay that calls into question the correlation between locality and authenticity. From now on, the historical imagination is stimulated by quotation—that is, by reference to the traces of that which can no longer be retrieved. Genuine monuments, and sometimes counterfeit or reconstructed ones, are consumed as so many tokens of the past, but, just as no reader of the "Nuremberg Chronicle" became any wiser about what Damascus, Ferrara, Milan, or Mantua *really* looked like, so today's cultural tourist, having plunged into history, gets back on the road without the promised experience of authenticity. As Augé puts it, "a gap is opened up between the landscape's present and the past to which it alludes" (*Non-Places* 69).

The temporal dislocation of places can also be expressed as a failure of denotation, as a breakdown of the narratives that naturalize the image of place. More positively, it might be seen as a resistance to the commodification that historical places display, paradoxically, through their imperviousness to the images of themselves produced by heritage promoters. "The sites from which every blink of an image is extracted," says McKenzie Wark, "are a reservoir of past events. . . . Sites like the Brandenburger Gate and the Potsdamer Platz are story accumulators, storage sites for stories about events that can never totally be commodified, packaged, and sold" (77). By pitting memory against the image, historical places upset every effort to freeze meaning in space. Memory is strongly connoted, and connotation opens a temporal gap in the surface of even the sleekest of images. Rushing in through this gap, stories and, above all, the story of the production of the image burst into the image. That gap is signified by the hyphen in the term "after-image." More a semantic placeholder than a place, the hyphen also expresses the gap in the after-image, itself a non-place, but one that re-places the image, restores it to place by infusing it with time and change.

CHAPTER TWO

City Future in City Past:
Balzac's Cartographic Imagination

David Harvey

Time present and time past
Are both perhaps present in time future,
And time future contained in time past.
If all time is eternally present
All time is unredeemable
— T. S. Eliot

THE POLITICS OF CULTURAL LABORS

In his *Prison Notebooks* Antonio Gramsci complains that when "political questions are disguised as cultural ones" they "become insoluble" (Gramsci 149). It is useful to reflect on this statement given the powerful "cultural turn" that has taken place in the thought of "traditional intellectuals" (as Gramsci would doubtless categorize most academics). Indeed, it is undeniable that this cultural turn has been accompanied by a certain depoliticization of academia in recent times.

Gramsci does not hold that cultural questions are irrelevant, diversionary, or superficial, but he does imply that if we take such questions seriously we have to do the hard work of excavating their meanings in relation to political projects. When Raymond Williams, Stuart Hall, Fredric Jameson, and many others of a "leftist" persuasion opened cultural questions to scrutiny, they certainly did not intend a diversion from politics. They oriented their inquiry toward deepening political-economic arguments by exploring their roots in cultural life and their manifestations within and through cultural forms. Much closer attention had to be paid, in their

My reading of *History of the Thirteen* is indebted to a course on "The City in Literature" I team-taught with Neil Hertz. Many of my interpretations rest on his insights.

view, to what Karl Marx called those "legal, political, religious, artistic or philosophic—in short ideological forms in which men become conscious of (conflict) and fight it out" (*A Contribution* 21). In particular, the role artistic production and creativity play in defining alternatives, in leading the way toward some alternative future, needed to be both carefully studied and cultivated.

Novels have had a particularly important role in this regard. They are, it is said, "possible worlds" (Ronan). They have inspired the imagination, influenced conceptions of, for example, the city, and thereby affected material processes of urbanization. Sometimes the influence is direct, as when Ebenezer Howard was inspired by Edward Bellamy's novel *Looking Backward* to launch the "new towns" movement (Fishman 33). But literary works more often permeate thought in more subtle ways, helping to create a climate of opinion or some "consensus of the imagination" in which certain kinds of political-economic action suddenly seem both possible and desirable.

As far as possible, we need to "unpack" the complex dialectic between literary representations and the guiding visions deployed in the tangible work of city building. Robert Park provides an interesting line of argument:

> The city and the urban environment represent man's most consistent and, on the whole, his most successful attempt to remake the world he lives in more after his heart's desire. But if the city is the world which man created, it is the world in which he is henceforth condemned to live. Thus, indirectly, and without any clear sense of the nature of his task, in making the city man has remade himself. (3)

The parallel with Marx's conception of the labor process is striking. We change ourselves, says Marx, only by acting on the external world and changing it. But

> we presuppose labour in a form that stamps it as exclusively human. A spider conducts operations that resemble those of a weaver and a bee puts to shame many an architect in the construction of her cells. But what distinguishes the worst architect from the best of bees is this, that the architect raises his structure in imagination before he erects it in reality. (*Capital* 177–78)

The architectural imagination provides a space in which alternative urban possibilities can be formulated and, perhaps, acted upon. The architect creates spaces so as to give them social utility as well as human and aesthetic/symbolic meanings; shapes and preserves long-term social memories and strives to give material form to the longings and desires of individuals and collectivities; and struggles to open spaces for new possibilities, for future forms of social life. But the architect is not an isolated monad. The architectural imagination operates under all kinds of constraints (some of them extremely harsh). Indeed, a case can be made that the figure of the architect provides a lucid metaphor for all forms of constructive activity, making us all, in our own ways, architects of our fates and fortunes as we struggle to make our history and geography, though never under historical and geographical conditions of our own choosing (Karatani; Harvey *Spaces* part 4).

Two decades ago, when I was working on the processes of urbanization in Second Empire Paris (Harvey *Consciousness*), it became clear to me that the novelists of the period had played an undefined but nevertheless crucial role in representing and imagining the city. Paris in the first half of the nineteenth century was already undergoing major changes in its physical and social forms. Urbanization and city life were evolving rapidly under the various impulsions of capitalism, industrialization, and modernization, spiraling beyond the reach of thought or practice, beyond their ability to capture and tame them. The rapid growth and seemingly chaotic forms arising in early nineteenth-century cities posed serious dilemmas for interpretation, to say nothing of social control under the threat of revolution. Finding how to represent the city, how to capture its seemingly chaotic unfolding was a difficult enough task. Beyond that, however, there were accumulating pressures to fracture any sense of the city as an organic totality or even as a graspable entity (a "body politic") of any kind. Capital, T.J. Clark remarks, did not want the city to have an image precisely because capital needed to see it as a tabula rasa for the extended and, it was hoped, perpetual accumulation of capital through the speculative pulverization and reconstruction of urban spaces (Clark 36).

The responses to this trend were as fiercely political as they were personal and subjective. Utopian alternatives were all the rage (Louis-Auguste Blanqui, Henri Saint-Simon, Charles Fourier, Etienne Cabet, Pierre-Joseph Proudhon). Social inquiries into the state of urban life were common (Taylor; Rabinow). And there were innumerable manifestations within Paris of a desire to return to an Enlightenment tradition of rational urban planning, well before Georges Haussmann took the city in hand with his own version of rational planning to foster capital accumulation and control the "dangerous" and restive classes. Several writers, M. Christine Boyer records, made extensive plans in the early 1840s for a "new representational order" that "drew the totality together" in such a way that it both respected historical memory and inspired the citizenry "to be rational and orderly in their public affairs" (Boyer 14; Marcus, chap. 1).

The novelists of the period, Honoré de Balzac in particular, participated directly in this process. They provided countless acute observations on urban life (a documentary source of some importance, however dubious it may be as a record of facts). They recorded much about their material world and the social processes (desires, motivations, activities, collusion, and coercion) flowing around them. They explored different ways to represent that world and helped shape the popular imagination regarding what the city was and might be about. They considered alternatives and possibilities, sometimes didactically (Eugène Sue, for example), more often indirectly, by evoking the play of human desires in relation to social forms, institutions, and conventions. They helped make the city legible and provided ways to grasp, represent, and mold seemingly inchoate and often disruptive processes of urbanization to human wants, needs, and desires.

It would be far-fetched, of course, to think that Haussmann drew directly from, for example, Balzac as he set about his transformative work in Second Empire Paris. He could appeal to his own engineering tradition. But Balzac's representations, set out in that formidable body of work known as the *Comédie humaine,* are not entirely inconsistent with Haussmann's actions. Balzac may well have fostered a climate of public opinion that could better understand (and even accept, though unwittingly or regretfully) the political economy of urban transformation in Second Empire Paris. And insofar as Balzac reveals much about the psychological underpinnings of his own representations, he may provide insights into the murkier plays of desire that tend to get lost in the lifeless documents in the city archives.

Balzac was not alone in his endeavors, but he inspired a vision of the city as a dynamic whole while acknowledging its multiplicity, its complexities, and its contingent unpredictability. The depth and nuances of Balzac's understanding of Parisian life give his work an unusual richness. He provides a far stronger historical materialist grounding for understanding the urban problematic than many of his contemporaries. Consequently, Marx developed a far stronger affinity for Balzac than for the utopian socialists or reformist writers such as Sue (Prawer 181; 318). Such an affinity may appear strange given Balzac's overt and violent contempt for revolutionary socialism and his polemical support for a conservativism in which the noblesse oblige of the traditional aristocracy played such a prominent role. But there is a reason for Marx's fascination. Balzac not only found a way to represent the city as a constellation of class forces but, in so doing, he opened new perspectives on what the city was and could become.

BALZAC'S UTOPIAN MOMENT

For Balzac, the "only solid foundation for a well-regulated society" is the proper exercise of power by an aristocracy based on private property, "whether it be real estate or capital" (Balzac, *History* 182). What Fredric Jameson calls "the still point" of Balzac's churning world comes into focus here:

The Balzacian dwelling invites the awakening of a longing for possessions, of the mild and warming fantasy of landed property as the tangible figure of a Utopian wish fulfillment. A peace released from the competitive dynamism of Paris and of metropolitan business struggles, yet still imaginable in some existent backwater of concrete social history. (*The Political* 157)

This is, of course, the utopian sensibility that frequently reemerges in the history of urbanism as a nostalgia for a genteel aristocratic world (now populated with "urban villages") within a secure social order. It is what Boyer calls a "pastoral model in which the leader positively ensured, sustained, and improved the life of each individual." But this in turn implied that "a ruler must have sufficient knowledge to judge wisely and must know the needs of the subjects and the state of the nation, its markets and trade, its territory and property." And this required subjects who "were educated, obedient, and acted responsibly so that they partook of the art of governance" (Boyer 13). For Balzac, leadership devolved on a properly constituted aristocratic class capable of realizing such a dream:

Those who wish to remain at the head of a country must always be worthy of leading it; they must constitute its mind and soul in order to control the activity of its hands. But how can a people be led except by those who possess the qualities of leadership. . . . Art, science and wealth form the social triangle within which is inscribed the shield of power and from which modern aristocracy must emerge. (*History* 179)

Balzac tries his best to ward off nostalgia, recognizing that "means of action lie in positive strength and not in historic memories." He admires the English aristocracy because it recognized that "institutions have their climacteric years when terms change their meaning, when ideas put on a new garb and the conditions of political life assume a totally new form without the basic substance being affected" (*History* 182–84). This last notion—that the substance is unaffected—returns us, however, to the still point of Balzac's pastoral utopianism. Interestingly, this utopianism does not abolish class distinctions or class conflict: "An aristocracy in some sense represents the thought of a society, just as the middle and working classes are the organic and active side of it. Hence there are different centres of operation for these forces, and from the apparent antagonism between them there results a seeming antipathy produced by a diversity of movement which nevertheless works for a common aim" (*History* 179). Here Balzac is following Heraclitus's maxim that "the finest harmony is born from difference." The problem is not, then, the existence of social differences and class distinctions. It is entirely possible for "the different types contributing to the physiognomy" of the city to "harmonize admirably with the character of the ensemble" (*History* 112): "Harmony is

27

the poetry of order and all peoples feel an imperious need for order. Now is not the cooperation of all things with one another, unity in a word, the simplest expression of order?" (*History* 180) The working classes, he maintains, are "drawn towards an orderly and industrious way of life." It is simply sad to observe how they are so often "thrust back into the mire by society" (*History* 58). Paris and all Parisians have fallen victim to the illusions of the age: "The more our laws aim at an impossible equality, the more we shall swerve from it by our way of living. In consequence rich people in France are becoming more exclusive in their tastes and their attachment to their personal belongings than they were thirty years ago" (*History* 82). The result is "a fanatical craving for self-expression." "Equality may perhaps be accepted as a *right*, but no power on earth will convert it into a *fact*. It would be well for the happiness of France if this truth could be brought home to the people" (*History* 180).

The pursuit of money, sex, and power has become an elaborate and farcical but nevertheless destructive game. Speculation and the senseless pursuit of money and pleasure wreak havoc on the social order. A weak-willed and corrupt aristocracy is failing in its historic mission, while the bourgeoisie, the central focus of Balzac's rage, has no civilized alternative to offer.

How, then, is it possible to conjure something positive out of this dyspeptic account and the reactionary utopian vision that fuels it? There is, I would argue, something else in Balzac that is much more positive and enlightening than might be deduced from his undoubtedly conservative, even reactionary standpoint. And that "something else" has a resonance that encompasses the possibilities that exist for constructing and reconstructing the social order and its urban forms. The difficulty is that this "something else" exists in a close dialectical relationship with his utopian conservativism and pastoral vision. We cannot, therefore, merely banish the latter and claim that Balzac truly was on the side of the revolutionaries without knowing it, as Victor Hugo proclaimed in his funeral oration (Shattuck 164). The task is rather to understand how Balzac's standpoint gave him the power to discern and dissect the social situation and its alternatives to such devastating effect.

"HOPE IS A MEMORY THAT DESIRES"

A casual observation by Balzac provides a crucial clue as to how his standpoint operates and why it is both productive and problematic at the same time. "Hope," wrote Balzac, "is a memory that desires" (quoted in Poulet 126). That matching of memory with desire warrants careful reflection. What, exactly, does he mean by "memory"? The term was as fraught then as it is now. Considering Balzac's meaning might clarify a host of contemporary questions.

Most of Balzac's novels are historical in the sense that they pay close attention to processes of social change, primarily in the period after 1814, which saw the Restoration of the monarchy. The novels resonate with failure, the failure to achieve a "real" restoration of progressive aristocratic, Catholic, and monarchical power after the catastrophic end of the Napoleonic regime. But Balzac fights nobly against nostalgia for a lost era. While it may reasonably be claimed that he lost that battle, he cannot be accused of failing to recognize the problem. His memory is colored by historicism because he sees the failure of the Restoration as a point of no return. He invokes the memory of a restoration that might have been in order to vigorously lament a restoration that now can never be. It is from this class standpoint that he offers his perceptive observations on the nature and structure of French society.

Balzac loses his battle with nostalgia on the terrain of his pastoral utopianism. But this raises issues of more general interest because almost all utopian schemes and representations are riddled with nostalgia. Escaping what Boyer calls "the stench of nostalgia" turns out to be one of the most troubling of all problems in conceptualizing alternative urban forms (consider how the ideology of the "new urbanism" now sweeping the United States idolizes a small-town America that never existed) (Boyer 67; Harvey, *Spaces*, chap. 8). City future has the awkward habit of not only being constrained by city past but also of being contained in it. Balzac's failings here are generic. Marx saw the problem clearly. His vigorous objections to utopianism were derived in part from the fact that it invariably looked backward rather than forward. Looking backward for inspiration from revolutionary moments was likely to have deleterious consequences. As Marx put it in the *Eighteenth Brumaire*:

> The tradition of all the dead generations weighs like a nightmare on the brain of the living. And just when they seem engaged in revolutionizing themselves and things, in creating something that never existed, precisely in such periods of revolutionary crisis they anxiously conjure up the spirits of the past to their service and borrow from them names, battle cries and costumes in order to present the new scene of world history in this time-honoured disguise and this borrowed language. . . . The social revolution of the nineteenth century cannot draw its poetry from the past, but only from the future. It cannot begin with itself before it has stripped off all superstition in regard to the past. (*Eighteenth Brumaire* 15–16)

This, however, is easier said than done. While Marx acknowledged that we can never hope to make history outside the historical conditions actually prevailing, he never escaped the conundrum of the role of memory and the imagination in the pursuit of alternatives. How could he reconcile the idea that revolutionaries must freely create a poetry of the future, loose their imaginations to construct the world, when he also held that the real foundations of consciousness lay in the material conditions of daily life as it actually existed?

While I do not think the conundrum is insoluble (*Spaces* part 4), the exact role to be given to history and memory needs more careful analysis. Marx (and even more certainly, the Marxist movement) failed to eliminate the possibility of a restoration of the past in the name of a progressive future. Events in Russia and Eastern Europe since the collapse of communism have hammered home the dark message that history and memory can exercise an incredible power over the future.

The incipient power and wisdom behind Balzac's formulation then comes into view. His general approach to the problem admits of a distinction between history and memory that Maurice Halbwachs and Boyer have since emphasized. But he pays very little direct attention to the idea of collective memory, even though the representation of the city he arrives at is itself arguably the foundation for a kind of collective memory. Consider this parallel with Aldo Rossi:

> One can say that the city itself is the collective memory of its people, and like memory it is associated with objects and places. The city is the *locus* of the collective memory. This relationship between the *locus* and the citizenry then becomes the city's predominant image, both of architecture and of landscape, and as certain artifacts become part of its memory, new ones emerge. In this entirely positive sense great ideas flow through the history of the city and give shape to it. (Rossi 130)

Balzac works this connection from another direction. By giving a distinctive image to the city, he constructs a distinctive *locus* in the imagination for collective memory. He adds to and augments the flow of great ideas through the history of the city simply by making the image of the city so memorable.

Nevertheless, it would be wrong to put only a positive spin on this activity. Memory, like history, is the art of selective forgetting, selective erasure, and Balzac certainly does his share of both. Benjamin's attack on a historicism that culminates in universal history and positions itself within an ideology of progression "through homogeneous empty time," forcefully applies to Balzac's historicism. "To write history therefore means to quote history," says Benjamin, which implies "that any given historical object must be ripped out of its context." We should always be aware, writes Boyer in her gloss of Benjamin, that history "is in need of redemption from a conformism that is about to overpower it in order to erase its differences and turn it into an accepted narration" (Boyer 377). Balzac's conformism, manifested as conventional narrative, operates in a negative manner. Benjamin has an answer to the Marxian dilemma of how to accomplish that dialectical and revolutionary leap into "the open air of history" while acknowledging the power of history and memory. To begin with, "history is the subject of a structure whose site is not homogeneous, empty time but time filled by the presence of the now." Time past is, as it were, contained in time present. But in that case, "the past can be seized only as an image which flashes up at the instant when it can be recognized and is never seen again." Benjamin continues: "To articulate the past historically does not mean to recognize it 'the way it really was' (Ranke). It means to seize hold of a memory as it flashes up at a moment of danger" (Benjamin, "Theses" 255). Time past "flashes up" into time present.

The implication, as many commentators have since noted, is that "memory, as opposed to history, responds more than it records, it bursts upon the scene in an unexpected manner, demanding an alteration of established traditions. Operating only in fragments, memory is an art that connects disparate events; it is formed on the tactics of surprise, ruptures, and overturnings that reveal its true power." Memory of this sort is not only the great destabilizer. In Benjamin's world, writes Boyer, "memory springing from the natural chains of tradition should be like an epiphany, flashing up in ephemeral moments of crisis, searching to exhibit at that particular time the way of the world in order to direct one's pathway toward the future" (Boyer 68; 130). Time future is illuminated by memory constructed out of time past.

Some credence must be given to Benjamin's views given that his opinion is so frequently invoked in the vast literature on the general problem of memory, but also given the enormous energy given over to controlling, co-opting, corrupting, staging, deflating, and constructing both history and memory as key tools in political struggle, primarily (though by no means exclusively) on the part of the dominant powers. There are, therefore, those who now claim that we suffer not from an absence of memory (collective amnesia) but from a surfeit. Charles Maier writes:

> The surfeit of memory is a sign not of historical confidence but of a retreat from transformative politics. It testifies to the loss of a future orientation, of progress towards civic enfranchisement and growing equality. It reflects a new focus on narrow ethnicity as a replacement for encompassing communities based on constitutions, legislation and widening attributes of citizenship. The program for this new ethnicity is as symbolic as it is substantive. It aspires preeminently to the recognition by other groups of its own suffering and victimhood. Finally, it cathects to landscape and territory because territoriality has been abandoned as a physical arena for civic action and is nurtured instead as an enclave of historicism. (Maier 150)

While the specific referent is unmistakable, the issue posed is more general. Exactly how can memory "flash up" to become a progressive agent of change when it is so frequently "dumbed down" or manipulated for purposes of social control or political mobilization of any sort (often of a narrowly nationalist if not downright reactionary complexion)? The hope, to which most fans of Benjamin cling, is that there is something uncontrollable about memory and that it will destabilize and transgress all attempts to control it come what may. But that, too, is inadequate according to Balzac's dictum, since it is not hope that should guide memory but memory that generates hope when it connects with desire. In Balzac's work, memory "flashes up" everywhere. But it does so not at moments of social revolution but at moments of personal desire. The fact that it so often leads to the frustration of that desire shows how frequently memory "weighs like a nightmare on the brain of the living" in personal as well as political life. Exactly how does memory connect with desire to generate hope in Balzac's work? This brings us to the thorny question of how Balzac understands desire.

INTERIORITY AND THE FEAR OF INTIMACY

As Sharon Marcus points out, interiors have a very distinctive role to play in Balzac's novels. The inevitable porosity between exteriors and interiors and the traffic that necessarily flows across boundaries to sustain life in the city in no way diminish the fierce struggle to limit access and to protect interiors from the penetration (the sexual connotations of that word are all too apt here) by unwanted others into interior spaces. The vulnerability of apartment dwelling in this regard, as Marcus correctly points out, provides an appropriate material ground on which such relations can be depicted. Balzac's technique, as many commentators have observed, is to start with exteriors (as in *Old Goriot*) and then move to the interiors of dwellings before entering the person to reveal the deep interior concealed behind all these defensive barriers.

Despite the danger, a simplification is warranted here: Balzac has a mortal fear of intimacy, and intimacy and interiority are related. Much of the action in Balzac's novels is fueled by attempts to protect oneself physically and emotionally from the threat of intimacy in a world where others are perpetually striving to penetrate, colonize, and overwhelm one's interior life. The outcome of any successful penetration is invariably death, a final resting place in the cemetery where all threat of intimacy is eliminated. Those (primarily women) who willingly give in to real love and intimacy suffer mortal consequences (sometimes sacrificially and even beatifically, like the reformed harlot, Lucien's lover, in *A Harlot High and Low*).

The desire for intimacy perpetually confronts the mortal fear of its deadly consequences.

This is, of course, Balzac's personal problem, and projecting it on the world around him, as he so uniformly does, hardly makes for good sociology or even adequate social commentary. If Balzac has one central criticism of the bourgeoisie, for example, it is that it is incapable of intimacy or even feelings because it has reduced everything to the cold calculus and egoism of financial value, the market, and the pursuit for profit. Crevel, the crassest of Balzac's bourgeois figures, makes a gambit to procure the affections of his son's mother-in-law at the beginning of *Cousin Bette;* when he is finally offered that affection by Adeline, however, who has been reduced to chronic indebtedness by her husband's licentious profligacy, Crevel callously refuses, after elaborately, and to Adeline's face, adding up the loss of rents on his capital that such a gesture would entail. But imputations of this sort, and the way they reflect a chronic fear of real intimacy, may make for perceptive psychology. If so, the overwhelming fear of intimacy that Balzac exhibits warrants some deeper investigation into the social setting.

Consider, for example, one of Balzac's early and more extraordinary stories, "The Girl with the Golden Eyes." Henri de Marsay is struck by the great beauty of a woman he sees in the Tuileries. He pursues her ardently through protective walls and overcomes all manner of social and human barriers to gain access to her. Led blindfold through mysterious corridors, he earns Paquita's love and passion in her remote boudoir. In that intimate space he unravels her mystery, experiences "indescribable transports of delight," and even himself becomes "tender, kind, communicative" as "he [loses] himself in those limbos of delight which common people so stupidly call 'imaginary space.' " But she knows she is doomed. "There was the terror of death in the frenzy with which she strained him to her bosom." She even tells him: "I am sure now that you will be the cause of my death." Henri, appalled when he discovers she is attached to someone else, returns, intending to extract her from that interior space, but finds her stabbed to death after a violent struggle with her woman lover, who turns out to be Henri's long-lost half-sister. Paquita's "whole body, slashed by the dagger thrusts of her executioner, showed how fiercely she had fought to save the life which Henri had made so dear to her" (*History* 370–89).

In "The Duchesse de Langeais" (also in *History of the Thirteen*), the plot moves in the opposite direction but with similar results. Women protect themselves from the damaging effects of intimacy by resorting to evasions, flirtations, calculated relationships, and strategic marriages. General Montriveau is outraged at the way the duchesse (who is married) trifles with his passions. He abducts her from a public space (a ball in progress)

33

and conveys her to his inner sanctum, which has all the Gothic aura of a monk's cell. There, in his own intimate space, he threatens to brand the duchesse, to place the sign of the convict on her forehead (a fire flickers in the background and ominous-sounding bellows are heard from an adjacent cell). The abducted duchesse gives in and declares her love as a soul in bondage—"a woman who loves always brands herself," she says. After returning to the ball, the emotionally branded duchesse ends up fleeing to a remote chapel on a Mediterranean island. This dramatic conversion of a flirtation into sublime love, through a series of accidents in timing,) fails to be realized except in a transmuted form many years later. Montriveau, after finally tracking down his lost love, listens to a sublime rendering of the *Te Deum* on an organ in the chapel. It is the duchesse, long lost to the world as Sister Terese, having given herself to God, who is playing. Montriveau's plan to abduct the nun succeeds perfectly but it is only her dead body that is retrieved, leaving him to contemplate a corpse "resplendent with the sublime beauty which the calm of death sometimes bestows on mortal remains" (*History* 253–70; 304–5).

It may seem from these examples that Balzac's main subject is relations between men and women. But he develops the theme of intimacy in all directions. In a short piece called *The Unknown Masterpiece*, a celebrated painter takes a talented student (Poussin) as an apprentice. Admitted to the inner studio of another painter, they find him surrounded by works of genius but doting on a masterwork that is an empty canvas. When Poussin blurts out that there is nothing there, the genius grows angry. He then dies, having burned all his canvases during the night.[1] And, in two of Balzac's last major works, the theme becomes even more universal and explicit. *Cousin Pons* features a man who has only one identity in life, that of a collector of bric-a-brac. His collection, which turns out, unbeknownst to him, to be immensely valuable, is all that matters to him and he fiercely protects it in the interior of his apartment. Penetration into this inner sanctum by a coalition of forces (the woman concierge who purports to look after him plays a very instrumental role) brings about Pons's death. A Jewish dealer in antiquities (who keeps his own collection, together with his daughter, under lock and key, surrounded by guard dogs in a secure hotel rather than an open apartment) is poised to gain illegal entry into Pons's apartment. Balzac comments that "this was tantamount to introducing the enemy into the heart of the citadel and plunging a dagger into Pons's heart." On entering, the dealer experienced "the same delight" that a "connoisseur" of women would feel if he managed to steal into the boudoir of a friend's beautiful and jealously secluded mistress" (*Pons* 148; see also Marcus chap. 2). In *Cousin Bette*, the same theme recurs, but this time it is a scheming peasant cousin who inserts herself as the intimate and angelic companion to the women in an aristocratic household, only to destroy them. Again and again, the surrender to intimacy and the penetration into the interior have destructive consequences, no matter what the circumstances or the social situation.

Why, then, pursue intimacy in the face of such potent dangers? Why castigate women for their preference for the superficial and the social when to risk intimacy is to be branded with love or to embrace death? Why mock the bourgeoisie so mercilessly for avoiding intimacy at any cost? It is difficult even to speculate on the answers. Perhaps for Balzac it is the memory of some long-lost intimacy that "flashes up" to constitute moments of exhilarating danger. Perhaps he sees intimacy as a human quality we can never do without. Perhaps it is linked to Balzac's utopianism, which postulates a secure and pastoral place with a settled life of intimacy and comfort secluded from the rough-and-tumble world. This may have been Balzac's dream, destined, like Montriveau's and the duchesse's love, to remain unfulfilled, which suggests that Balzac fears what he most desires.

Such a possibility is broached directly in *Cousin Pons.* Madame Cibot, the concierge who leads the way into the interior of Pons's apartment with such fatal consequences, dreams of using her ill-gotten wealth to retire to the peace of country life. But this she dares not do because the fortune-teller she consults warns her that she will suffer a violent death there. She lives out her days in Paris. Does this signal the death of Balzac's utopian dream in his last years? Or does it signify that pastoral utopianism was all along understood as unrealizable, as a signifier without a referent, as a form of quiet intimacy that could be nothing more in practice than a living death? It is therefore understandable why women would do everything in their power to protect themselves from intimacy, given what characters like Henri de Marsay (and probably Balzac himself) would do with it. The bourgeoisie stand condemned not because they avoid intimacy but because they are indifferent to it and incapable of it even as a momentary event that "flashes up" dangerously, only to be immediately lost. In any case, Balzac's own way of establishing intimacy with his characters as he purports to penetrate to the very core of their being invariably has devastating effects.

Whatever the answers, the search for intimacy and the fear of its consequences perpetually force Balzac away from the still point of his pastoral utopianism. In "The Girl with the Golden Eyes" this compulsion is understood in very masculine terms: "To a man who has just been sated with pleasure there comes an inclination to forgetfulness, a measure of ingratitude, a desire for freedom, an urge to escape, a tinge of scorn, even perhaps of contempt, for the idol he has worshipped; in short a medley of inexplicable sentiment, which reduce him to baseness and ignobility" (*History* 371).

Yet there is also something else at work that explains the incredible drawinog power of intimacy:

> Paquita responded to the craving which all truly great men feel for the infinite, that mysterious passion so dramatically expressed in Faust, so poetically translated in Manfred, which urged Don Juan to probe deep into the heart of women, hoping to find in them that infinite ideal for which so many pursuers of phantoms have searched; scientists believe they can find it in science, mystics find it in God alone. (*History* 382)

Where does Balzac find it? Does he flee the intimacy of interior spaces into some wider exterior world or does he experience, through intimacy, some kind of sublime moment of ecstasy, which the common people stupidly call "imaginary space"? Balzac, as the contrasting pair of passages from "The Girl with the Golden Eyes" indicates, oscillates between the two possibilities.

THE ANNIHILATION OF SPACE AND TIME

"In the whole work of Balzac," remarks Georges Poulet, "nothing recurs so frequently as the proclamation of the annihilation of space-time by the act of mind." Balzac writes: "I already had in my power the most immense faith, that faith of which Christ spoke, that boundless will with which one moves mountains, that great might by the help of which we can abolish the laws of space and time" (quoted in Poulet 106). Whatever else may be said about this theme, Balzac plainly believed himself capable of internalizing everything within himself and thereby empowering himself to express the totality through a supreme act of mind. He could live "only by the strength of those interior senses that . . . constitute a double being within man." Even though "exhausted by this profound intuition of things," the soul could nevertheless aspire to be, "in Leibniz's magnificent phrase, a concentric mirror of the universe" or could condense "in a small space the appalling accumulation of a whole world of thoughts." (Balzac, quoted in Chevalier 176; see also Poulet 109). And this is precisely how Balzac constitutes his interiors. Pons's interior is precious in the double sense that it is not only his but a concentric mirror of a European universe of artistic production. He has filled it by traveling in Europe and ceaselessly searching the boulevards for special objects. Paquita's boudoir exerts its fascination because it is redolent of the exoticism associated with the Orient, the Indies, the slave girl, and the colonized woman. Montriveau's room, to which the Duchesse de Langeais is forcibly abducted, internalizes the ascetic sense of purity associated with a medieval monk's cell. The interior spaces all mirror an external world.

The "annihilation of space and time" was a familiar enough theme in Balzac's time. The expression may have been taken from a couplet by Alexander Pope: "Ye Gods! annihilate but space and time / And make two lovers happy" (quoted in Marx, *Machine* 164). Goethe deployed the metaphor to great effect in *Faust* and by the 1830s and 1840s the idea was more broadly associated with the arrival of the railroads. The phrase then had widespread currency in both the United States and Europe among a whole range of thinkers contemplating the consequences and possibilities of a world reconstructed by new transport and communication technologies (everything from the canals and railroads to the daily newspaper, which Hegel had already characterized as a substitute for morning prayer). Interestingly, the same concept can be found in Marx (implicitly in the *Communist Manifesto* and explicitly in the *Grundrisse*). Marx uses it to signify the revolutionary qualities of the capitalist penchant for geographical expansion and acceleration in the circulation of capital. It refers directly to the penchant for periodic bouts of what I call "time-space compression."[2]

In Balzac, however, the idea usually refers to a sublime moment outside time and space in which all the forces of the world become internalized within the mind and being of a monadic individual. That moment "flashes up" as an intense revelation, the religious overtones of which are hard to miss (Balzac's dalliance with religion, mysticism, and the powers of the occult is frequently in evidence). It is the moment of the sublime (a favorite word of Balzac's). But it is not a passive moment. The blinding insight that comes with the annihilation of space and time allows for a certain kind of action in the world. Consider, for example, how Balzac uses the idea in *The Quest of the Absolute*, when Marguerite, after a furious argument with her father, reacts:

> When he had gone, Marguerite stood for a while in dull bewilderment; it seemed as if her whole world had slipped from her. She was no longer in the familiar parlour; she was no longer conscious of her physical existence; her soul had taken wings and soared to a world where thought annihilates time and space, where the veil drawn across the future is lifted by some divine power. It seemed to her she lived through whole days between each sound of her father's footsteps on the staircase; and when she heard him moving above in his room, a cold shudder went through her. A sudden warning vision flashed like lightning through her brain; she fled noiselessly up the dark staircase with the speed of an arrow, and saw her father pointing a pistol at his head. (*Quest* 173–74)

A sublime moment of revelation outside space and time allows one both to grasp the world as a totality and to act decisively in it. Its connection to sexual passion and possession of "the other" (a lover, the city, nature,

God) is unmistakable (as indicated in the original Pope couplet). But it allows Balzac a certain conceptual power, without which his synoptic vision of the city would be impossible. It also allows him to "lift the veil" on the future.

In Balzac's view, we need in some sense to be "outside of space and time" to have any alternative vision at all. This raises the tantalizing (though speculative) thought that such a psychological positioning is always implicated in the search for alternatives, for some future that is not already contained in time past. While it would be easy to dismiss this, too, as some utopian fantasy on Balzac's part (which operates dialectically in relation to his nostalgic pastoralism), I think it warrants further consideration since it could be a crucial insight into how alternative futures of any sort are freely imagined and acted on (the visionary William Blake provides parallel evidence of how such a mode of thinking might work). The theory of revolution it might generate is well represented, for example, in the work of Henri Lefebvre.

The perpetual bourgeois desire to reduce and eliminate all spatial and temporal barriers would then appear as a secular version of this desire. Balzac is well aware of this secular dimension. He observes, for example, how "the crowd of lawyers, doctors, barristers, business men, bankers, traders on the grand scale" are ruled by time. They must "devour time, squeeze time" because "time is their tyrant; they need more, it slips away from them, they can neither stretch nor shrink it" (*History* 316–17). As Balzac writes:

> Man possesses the exorbitant faculty of annihilating, in relation to himself, space which exists only in relation to himself; of utterly isolating himself from the milieu in which he resides, and of crossing, by virtue of an almost infinite locomotive power, the enormous distances of physical nature.
>
> I am here and I have the power to be elsewhere! I am dependent upon neither time, nor space, nor distance. The world is my servant. (quoted in Poulet 103–5)

Is Balzac, through his appeal to the ideal of an annihilation of space and time, providing us with some hints about how the distinctively capitalistic and bourgeois version of the sublime (making the world one's servant) is being constituted in both thought and practice? This standpoint will later emerge in the reconstruction of the spatiotemporal world of Second Empire Paris, if not in the whole bourgeois project of constructing the world market through what we now call globalization.[3] The conquest of space and time and the mastery of the world (of mother earth) appears as the displaced but sublime expression of sexual desire in innumerable capitalistic fantasies (including, most recently, the construction of cyber-space). This displaced search may have a significant psychic role in the historical geography of capitalism.

For Balzac, the collapse of time future and time past into time present is precisely the moment at which hope, memory, and desire converge. "The culminating instants of passion are those in which the actual emotion is charged and swollen with a double weight of memories and hopes," writes Poulet. Then, citing Balzac himself, "one triples present felicity with aspi-ration for the future and recollections of the past" (Poulet 126). This is the supreme moment of personal revelation and social revolution, a sublime moment Balzac loves and fears.

BALZAC'S SYNOPTIC VISION

Through the fantasy of a momentary annihilation of space and time, Balzac constructs some Archimedean or visionary position from which to survey and understand the world, if not to change it. He imagines himself "riding across the world, disposing all in it to my liking. . . . I possess the world effortlessly, and the world hasn't the slightest hold upon me" (quoted in Poulet 100).

The imperial gaze is overt: "I was measuring how long a thought needs in order to develop itself; and compass in hand, standing upon a high crag, a hundred fathoms above the ocean, whose billows were sporting among the breakers, I was surveying my future, furnishing it with works of art, just as an engineer, upon an empty terrain, lays out fortresses and palaces" (quoted in Poulet 99). The echo of Descartes's engineer and of Goethe's Faust is unmistakable (see Berman chap. 1). From this perspec-tive, the dialectical relations between motion and stasis, between flow and movement, between interior and exterior, between space and place, be-tween town and country, can all be investigated and represented.

For the most part, however, Balzac is out to possess Paris. But he wants to do more than merely dominate it His desire to appropriate is not a de-sire to destroy or diminish. He respects and needs the city far too much as a sentient being that feeds him images, thoughts, and feelings to want to turn it into a dead object (as Haussmann and Gustave Flaubert later did in their own ways). Paris has a personality and a body—it is often depicted as a woman.

> Paris is the most delightful of monsters; here a pretty woman, farther off a poverty-stricken hag; here as freshly minted as the coin of a new reign, and in another corner of the town as elegant as a lady of fashion. (*History* 32)

Or:

> For the devotees, Paris is sad or gay, ugly or beautiful, living or dead; for them
> Paris is a sentient being; every individual, every bit of a house is a lobe in the
> cellular tissue of that great harlot whose head, heart and unpredictable be-
> haviour are perfectly familiar to them. (*History* 33)

But, as a cerebral entity, it takes on a masculine personality:

> Paris is the intellectual centre of the globe, a brain teeming with genius which
> marches in the van of civilization; a great man, a ceaseless creative artist, a po-
> litical thinker with second sight. (*History* 324)

The end product is a synoptic vision, encapsulated in extraordinary descriptions of the physiognomy and personality of the city (such as those
that open "The Girl with the Golden Eyes"). Again and again, we are
urged to see the city as a totality and graspable as such. Consider this passage from *Ferragus*:

> Paris again with its streets, shop signs, industries and mansions as seen
> through diminishing spectacles: a microscopic Paris reduced to the tiny di-
> mensions of shades, ghosts, dead people. . . . Jules perceived at his feet, in the
> long valley of the Seine, between the slopes of Vaugirard and Meudon, those
> of Belleville and Montmartre, the real Paris, wrapped in the dirty blue veil en-
> gendered by its smoke, at that moment diaphanous in the sunlight. He threw
> a furtive glance over its forty thousand habitations and said, sweeping his arm
> over the space between the column of the Place Vendome and the gilded
> cupola of the Invalides: "there it is that she was stolen from me, thanks to the
> baneful inquisitiveness of this crowd of people which mills and mulls about
> for the mere pleasure of milling and mulling about." (*History* 147)

Rastignac, at the end of *Old Goriot*, standing in that same cemetery,

> saw Paris spread out below on both banks of the winding Seine. Lights were
> beginning to twinkle here and there. His gaze fixed almost avidly upon the
> space that lay between the Column of the Place Vendome and the Dome of
> the Invalides; there lay the splendid world that he wished to conquer. He eyed
> that humming hive with a look that foretold of its despoliation, as if he al-
> ready felt on his lips the sweetness of the honey, and said with superb defi-
> ance: "it's war, between us two." (*Goriot* 304)

This synoptic vision is repeated throughout the century. Haussmann,
armed with balloons and triangulation towers, likewise appropriated Paris
in his imagination as he set out to reshape it on the ground (perhaps even
muttering "it's war, between us two" as he did so). In Haussmann's case,

however, there is an important difference. Whereas Balzac is on an almost obsessive personal quest to command, penetrate, dissect, and internalize everything about the sentient being of the city within himself, Haussmann converts that fantastic urge into a distinctive class project in which the state and the financiers will take the lead in both representation and action. Haussmann's achievement, in Clark's eyes, was "to provide a framework in which another order of urban life—an order without an imagery—would be allowed its own existence" (Clark 36). Haussmann produced a totalizing vision of the city as a cadaver to be dissected at will.

PARIS PRODUCT: MONEY AND PLEASURE

The processes that Haussmann later mobilized to achieve a specific kind of transformation in the Parisian built environment and in its political economy, state administration, and cultures were all quite evident to Balzac. He understands that Paris is being produced by constellations and clashes of class forces and that the production of Paris is at the mercy of these processes. It is part of Balzac's mission to understand these forces and he sets out a whole series of daring theses on the motives and dynamics of historical/geographical change.

Paris, says Balzac, is a "vast metropolitan workshop for the manufacture of enjoyment." It is a city "devoid of morals, principles and genuine feeling" but within which all feelings, principles, and morals have their beginning and end:

> No sentiment can stand against the swirling torrent of events; their onrush and the effort to swim against the current lessens the intensity of passion. Love is reduced to desire, hate to whimsy . . . in the salon as in the street no one is *de trop*, no one is absolutely indispensable or absolutely noxious. . . . In Paris there is toleration for everything: the government, the guillotine, the Church, cholera. You will always be welcome in Parisian society, but if you are not there no one will miss you. *(History* 309–11)

To find out how Paris works, says Balzac, you have "to break open the body to find therein the soul" (quoted in Poulet 137). The dominant forces at work are interpreted in various ways. But at the heart of it all lie gold and pleasure, filtered through class perspectives. "Take these two words as a guiding light" and all will be revealed, because "not a cog fails to fit into its groove and everything stimulates the upward march of money" *(History* 311). "In Paris people of all social statures, small, medium and great, run and leap and caper under the whip of a pitiless goddess, Necessity: the necessity for money, glory or amusement" *(History* 325).

"The monster we call Speculation" takes over. *Eugenie Grandet* records a key historical moment of conversion: the miser who hoards gold becomes the rentier who speculates in interest-bearing notes, coming to equate self-interest with monetary interest. It is reminiscent of a passage from Marx: "The boundless greed after riches, this passionate chase after exchange value, is common to the capitalist and the miser; but while the miser is merely a capitalist gone mad, the capitalist is a rational miser" (Marx, *Capital* 1, 153).

So it is with Grandet himself. But it is speculation of all sorts that rules. The working classes speculate as "they wear themselves out to win the gold which keeps them spellbound" and will even take to revolution, "which it always interprets as a promise of gold and pleasure!" The "bustling, scheming, speculating" members of the lower middle classes assess demand in Paris and reckon to cater for it." They forage the world for commodities, "discount bills of exchange, circulate and cash all sorts of securities" while making "provision for the fantasies of children," spying out "the whims of vices of grown-ups" and squeezing out "dividends from their diseases." The "stomach of Paris in which the interests of the city are digested and compressed into a form which goes by the name of *affaires*" gives rise to "more causes of physical and moral destruction than anywhere else" (*History* 312–18). It is here that the entrepreneurial lust for "creative destruction" is most in evidence. Throughout his works, Balzac is keenly aware of how, when money "becomes the community" (as Marx would have it), all passion becomes "resolved into two terms: gold and pleasure," and of how incredibly destructive such a resolution can be (Schumpeter; Marx *Grundrisse* 221–24). The aristocracy and the artists can only bow down before these same forces. Rendered impotent, condemned to a hollow existence, a perpetual waiting for pleasure that never comes, the aristocrats acquire "pasteboard faces" in which "only gold is mirrored and from which intelligence has fled" (*History* 324).

Speculation reshapes the city:

> During that period Paris had a building mania. Paris may be a monster, but it is the most monomaniacal of monsters. It falls for a thousand fantasies. At one moment it takes to brick-laying like a lord enamoured of the trowel. . . . Then it falls into the slough of despond, goes bankrupt, sells up and files its petition. But a few days later, it puts its affairs in order, sallies forth in holiday and dancing mood. . . . It has its day to day manias, but also its manias for the month, the season, the year. Accordingly, at that moment, the whole population was demolishing or rebuilding something or other, somehow or other. (*History* 64)

"Such a picture of Paris," Balzac concludes, writing from the perspective of class divisions, habits, and moral aspirations "proves that physically speaking, Paris could not be other than it is." In that way, the "kaleidoscopic" experience and "cadaverous physiognomy" of the city are understood and the forces that compel its transformation laid bare (*History* 57; 324–29).

THE CITY AS A SPATIAL PATTERN AND A MORAL ORDER

Paris understood merely as an undifferentiated sentient being would be incoherent. Balzac has to dissect and map it if he is to come to terms with it. Social distinctions of gender, class, status, and provincial origin are, of course, everywhere in evidence. Their seeming rigidity is softened by the rapid shifts that occur in individuals in the high stakes pursuit of money, sex, and power. Lucien, for example, returns to his provincial origins, penniless, powerless, and disgraced at the end of *Lost Illusions,* only to reappear in Paris reempowered by his association with the arch-criminal Vautrin and his liaison with a woman in *A Harlot High and Low.* These aspects of Balzac's world are well known and need no further elaboration here.

What has been less remarked is the way the spatial order of the city, as Balzac maps it, secures so much of the social positioning. The principle is clearly stated. In every zone of Paris "there is a mode of being which reveals what you are, what you do, where you come from, and what you are after" (*A Harlot* 19). The physical distances that separate classes are understood as "a material consecration of the moral distance which ought to separate them" (*History* 181); they are "lobes in the cellular tissue of that great harlot." The separation of social classes creates a vertical segregation as well as different sociospatial zones. Paris has "its head in the garrets, inhabited by men of science and genius; the first floors house the well-filled stomachs; on the ground floor are the shops, the legs and feet, since the busy trot of trade goes in and out of them" (*History* 31).

But Balzac toys with our curiosity about the innumerable hidden spaces, turns them into mysteries that pique our interest. "One is loath to tell a story to a public for whom local colour is a closed book," he says coyly (*History* 34). But he immediately opens the book to reveal a whole world of spatiality and its representations:

In Paris there are certain streets which are in as much disrepute as any man branded with infamy can be. There are also noble streets; then there are streets which are just simply decent, and, so to speak, adolescent streets about whose morality the public has not yet formed an opinion. There are murderous streets; streets which are more aged than aged dowagers; respectable streets; streets which are always clean, streets which are always dirty; working class, industrious mercantile streets. In short, the streets of Paris have human qualities and such a physiognomy as leaves us with the impressions against which we can put up no resistance. (*History* 31)

This spatial pattern enforces a moral order. In *Ferragus*, anyone and everyone who transgresses the spatial strictures dies. Characters out of place disturb the ecological harmonies, pollute the moral order, and must pay the price. Madame Jules, a pure and perfect creature, ventures, out of filial devotion, into a part of Paris inconsistent with her social status. "This woman is lost," declares Balzac, because she has strayed outside the bounds that define the Parisian moral order. Contaminated by entry into an odious space, she finally dies of "some moral complication which has gone very far and which makes the physical condition more complex" (*History* 34; 128). Auguste, Madame Jules's admirer, is likewise ordained to die because, "for his future misfortune, he scrutinized every storey of the building" that is Madame Jules's secret destination.

Ferragus, the father, is, however, one of the secret band of the thirteen, who, equipped with wings, were able "to soar over society in its heights and depths, and disdained to occupy any place in it because they had unlimited power over it" (*History* 26–27; 105). Their secret power resides precisely in the inability to locate them in either a spatiotemporal or a social sense. They are outside space and time and derive their special powers from that condition. Ferragus's location, sought by both Auguste and Jules (as well as by the police), is never found. There is, Jules complains, "no means of knowing in what quarter of Paris this extraordinary man lives." He appears only when and where he wants. Even as the tragedy concludes, Ferragus, desolate with grief at having lost his daughter, ends up in a "nameless spot" where "Paris has no sex or gender," where "Paris has ceased to be; and yet Paris is still there" (*History* 151). Balzac's cartography in *Ferragus* is, clearly, an intensely spatial and moral statement.

Early in the twentieth century, Robert Park wrote a suggestive essay on the city as a spatial pattern and a moral order (Park chap. 4). Park observed how social relations were inscribed in the spaces of the city in such a way as to make the spatial pattern both a reflection of, but also an active moment in, the reproduction of the moral order. This idea plays itself out directly in Balzac's fiction: "In every phase of history the Paris of the upper classes and the nobility has its own centre, just as the plebeian Paris will always have its own special quarter. This separatism with its periodic variations offers ample material for reflection to those desirous of studying or depicting the different social zones, and perhaps we ought to research into causes" (*History* 178).

There is, however, an evolution in this perspective in Balzac's work. The spatial rigidities that play such a determinant, almost deterministic role in *History of the Thirteen* become more porous and malleable in later works.

As Marcus perceptively observes, the concierge's effect on Pons is lethal because she can use the resources of the spatial ecology of the city, construct a web of intrigue (using the concierge network) within which a disparate coalition of conspirators can trap the unsuspecting Pons. The concierge not only has command over the place where Pons resides, she also deploys "an abstract power that extends into a diffuse space" by circulating through the space of the city, gaining entry into all manner of other spaces and thereby producing new space relations (Marcus 74). The capacity to command and produce space in this way is recognized as a hidden power through which even the lowliest of people in society can subvert the spatial pattern and the moral order. This capacity and power, which belongs solely to the thirteen in Balzac's earlier stories, mutates into a more tangible force primarily through the commanding figure of Vautrin, the arch-criminal turned police chief, who uses his knowledge of the spatial ecology of the city and his capacity to command, control, and construct it to his own ends. The spatiality of the city is increasingly appreciated as dialectical, constructed, and consequential rather than passive or merely reflective. Balzac's novels, read as essays on the production of space (as materiality, as representation, and as lived experience, in Lefebvre's terms) take on an extraordinary luminescence as the product of a distinctively urban cartographical and geographical imagination.

URBAN VISIONS AND CARTOGRAPHIC POWERS

Cartography, writes Harley in one of his seminal essays, is a form of knowledge and power. "Maps are a way of conceiving, articulating, and structuring the human world which is biased towards, promoted by, and exerts influence upon particular sets of social relations." In Harley's judgment, however, maps are rarely about protest. The "social history of maps, unlike that of literature, art or music, appears to have few genuinely popular, alternative, or subversive modes of expression" (Harley 278–79; 297). Haussmann's use of the map as a weapon of class power (to say nothing of the whole history of colonization and mapping) supports Harley's view. But this leaves open the question of Balzac's cartographic imagination. In particular, it poses the question of whether the cartographic sensibilities that pervade Balzac's work are as potent a weapon of social change as the formal maps used by planners, administrators, and engineers.

From this standpoint, Balzac's cartographic efforts can be seen as a power play in a high stakes game. The referent is Paris in the full flood of its social, political, and spatial transformation under the twin impulsions of compulsive capital accumulation and the commodification of everything, including pleasure, status, and power. Balzac actively constructs a map of the city's terrain and evokes its qualities as a sentient being. He is his own cartographer. He puts a signature on that map, his own. He thereby establishes his power within and over the city. Yet he also renders the city legible for us in a very distinctive way.

This last is, in itself, no mean achievement. As Kevin Lynch points out, the building of an adequate image of a city is fundamental to understanding behavior (of administrators, industrialists, developers, and financiers as well as ordinary citizens) with respect to the city.[4] The formation of that image allows, as Rossi suggests, ideals of the city to circulate as collective memories. The qualities of the cartographic image then become significant. Balzac's cartography has a "still point" of utopian longing, a distinctive perspective, and a particular mechanics of projection from on high (outside space and time). Like any map, it conceals as much as it reveals, distorts in certain dimensions while holding to a microscopic accuracy of detail in others. There are times when the map seems unduly static. Balzac's perspective may be judged warped, his positioning inappropriate, and his utopianism anachronistic. But we also see the naked power that resides in the sort of cartographic imagination he cultivated. Power of that sort is necessary in any attempt to change the world. A premonition of a future permeates Balzac's depictions of time present and time past. But what kind of future?

Marx, according to his son-in-law Paul Lafargue, considered Balzac "not only as the historian of his time, but also as the prophetic creator of characters that were still in embryo in the days of Louis Philippe and did not fully develop until after his death, under Napoleon III" (Prawer 181). Balzac was, as Baudelaire declared, a "passionate visionary" (quoted in Shattuck 163). This vision, Jameson avers, played a role in "a properly bourgeois cultural revolution—that immense process of transformation whereby populations whose life habits were formed by other, now archaic, modes of production are effectively reprogrammed for life and work in the new world of market capitalism" (*Political* 152). Balzac's "new kind of objectivity"—however critical its orientation and intent—in this sense helped produce the very situation it described and deplored.

But Balzac's cartography was also a conscious attempt to depict, intervene in, and, if possible, resist that bourgeois future and to undermine the processes that supported it. What makes Balzac's own account peculiarly compelling, however, is that he persistently urges his readers to follow his example. He casts himself as one of those "few devotees, people who never walk along in heedless inattention," who "sip and savour their Paris and are so familiar with its physiognomy that they know its every wart, every spot or blotch on its face" (*History* 330). Balzac produced an image of the city as a moral entity and a sentient being, available, in principle, to all. Check the city out, he often advises, and figure things out for your-selves. You, too, can become one of those devotees who can "sip and savour" the city if you wish. "Could you really grudge," he asks, "spending a few minutes watching the dramas, disasters, tableaux, picturesque inci-dents which arrest your attention in the heart of this restless queen of cities?" "Look around you," he urges, as you "make your way through that huge stucco cage, that human beehive with black runnels marking its sec-tions, and follow the ramifications of the idea which moves, stirs and fer-ments inside it" (*History* 311). We, too, become explorers, with Balzac act-ing as guide. His cartography is a far from passionless affair in which dead spaces are manipulated to some greater purpose. The attraction of Balzac's mapping rests precisely on his passionate commitments. His hope, like ours, is shaped from a memory that desires.

Balzac constructs the kind of geographical knowledge necessary to shape the city to human desires. The totalizing vision, the search for the sublime in the midst of those ordinary employments that, as Adam Smith put it, so "corrupt the courage of our minds," the clear recognition of the forces of change that must be tamed or harnessed, the understanding that the production of space is a constitutive moment in the transformation of social and moral orders, and the need to mobilize utopian desires and dreams—for Balzac, these are all necessary elements in any embrace of fu-ture possibilities. That these became (or already were) exclusive powers of the bourgeoisie, of the capitalist class in alliance with the state, was a con-dition against which Balzac resolutely though hopelessly fought.

Sadly, as Balzac himself presciently observed, "when a literature has no general system to support it lacks solidity and fades out with the age to which it belongs" (*History* 190). Because capital did not want the city to have an image, as Clark suggests, Balzacian fantasy and its democratizing cartographic power also had to be effaced. But we are always free to ex-hume Balzac's cartographic vision. And there is something subversive about Balzac's technique. It runs against the grain of ordinary and more passive forms of cartographic manipulation. Figures like the arch-criminal Vautrin or even the pedestrian concierge Madame Cibot manipulate and construct spaces for alternative ends. At the same time, Balzac reveals the secret cartographic passions of the ruling classes, captures their totalizing vision, their own warped quest for the sublime through speculation, the pursuit of gold and the annihilation of space and time. In spite of his aris-tocratic preferences, there is something fundamentally democratic and accessible about Balzac's cartographic objectivism. Balzac does a remark-able job of penetrating the inner sanctums of bourgeois values, thoughts, and fears. He may unwittingly have written, out of his own monadic in-sights, an appropriate epitaph for that time future when the bourgeois era of seemingly endless capital accumulation and the magic of interest come to a crashing halt: "Thus I envelop the world with my thought, I mold it, I fashion it, I penetrate it, I comprehend it or think I comprehend it; but suddenly I wake up alone and find myself in the midst of the depths of a dark light" (quoted in Poulet 110). If we use Balzac's thought as a concentric mirror of the bourgeois universe and rephrase it accordingly, we might one day say of the whole history of the capitalist bourgeois era: "They enveloped the world with their thoughts, molded it, fashioned it, penetrated it, comprehended it—or thought they comprehended it; but suddenly they woke up alone and found themselves in the midst of the depths of a dark light."

CHAPTER THREE

London: Tomorrow's Yesterday, Future Images of the Past

Jürgen Schlaeger

When Iain Sinclair's *Lights Out for the Territory* appeared in 1997 it caused a stir in the already densely populated market of books about London. The reviewers reacted enthusiastically.[1] They described it as "a riot of a book on London," as the effusions of a "sublime archaeologist of the present," as "one of the most remarkable books ever written on London." Although most of the pieces it contained had already been published separately, their cumulative effect was tremendous.

Indeed, Sinclair's book is more than just another critical investigation of established city realities or discourses, more than just another literary appropriation of London from an East End point of view. It is not a work of fiction, at least not ostensibly so. Superficially, it is a journal with notes, thoughts, pictures of walks around London, of visits to a large number of places in different areas; it contains reminiscences of films and reviews of poems, fragments of autobiography and of character studies of individuals as diverse as Lord Archer and the Kray brothers. The actual experience of walking the city is only loosely and intermittently interwoven with the imaginary journeys undertaken, so to speak, along the road. References to films and poems about the city, to biographical and autobiographical episodes of city life, are never introduced as mere additions to or illustrations of a main text because there is no main text—only an assortment of subtexts barely held together by what Sinclair calls his "quest."

As a text, the book is hybrid, a fractal composition of different discourses strung together by the author's determination to go through with it, however multidirectional, endless, and ultimately aimless it may seem. For Sinclair and his photographer companion, Marc Atkins, there is no physical London to explore street by street. Everything they encounter is already encrusted with layers of myths, episodes, histories, remembered impressions, stories, texts, and pictorial superpositions such as graffiti, paintings, and films. Thus the two city explorers move about, not as in a physical reality, but in ever-changing configurations of imaginary constructs. Implicitly, Sinclair claims to convey in this manner what no urbanistic discourse is able to communicate. In a sense, he thereby takes Clifford Geertz's "to-know-a-city-is-to-know-its-streets approach to things" (Geertz, *Local Knowledge* 167). The text thus presents itself as a contribution to an entirely new type of city literature, defined as a "topographics" by the series of books published by Reaktion Books—a series in which Sinclair's next book, *Liquid City*, would appear. Reaktion Books defines its project as follows:

Topographics features new writing about place. Embracing both the cultural and the natural, the city and the wilderness, it appraises the geographies people inhabit, visit, defend, destroy—and overlook. The reverse of travel literature, the books in this series do not depend on a journey to supply a plot. Instead they mingle analysis with anecdote, criticism with original expressive writing, to explore the creative collision between physical space and the human mind. (Atkins and Sinclair book jacket)

Liquid City contains a selection of the photographs Marc Atkins took during their walks in London and new texts by Iain Sinclair.

In terms of London discourses, Sinclair's strategy can be defined as a special kind of intertextual and intericonographic practice, a thick description without the professional anthropologist's desire to be exact, systematic, and explanatory.[2] Crucial to this practice is a reversal of the direction of meaning assignment. Already existing discourses are not only alluded to, added to, discussed, rejected, extended, and arranged around a piece of city reality to make that piece more visible, more plausible, historically profound, or personally significant, but they also provide the raw material for his reinterpretations of the city. This process is so insistent that the physical reality of the city never materializes or, when Sinclair feels that he has to insist on its physicality, he describes it as a phantasmagoric aberration from the true realities of city life, which are mythogenic, imaginary, and visionary.

Lights Out for the Territory is not an exercise in topographical analysis, not a sophisticated mimesis, but, to use Kevin Lynch's key concept, a practice of multiple "imageabilities." Contrary to Lynch's claim, however, its readability does not depend on the ideal of a city that guarantees security and order, but rather lies in its character as an endless process of signification.[3]

The concept of a complex intertextual and intericonographic practice sounds like a contradiction in terms, since such practices are by definition highly self-reflexive, that is, they imply a stance above the matter dealt with; they are highly artificial, that is, removed from experience and not practical at all. Therefore, the implication that there may be something deeply empirical about Sinclair's total immersion in signifying practices is in need of some explanation.

Let me deal with this problem by taking a little detour. I will begin with Jonathan Raban's *Soft City,* continue on to the New Labour project to re-brand Britain and the role the Millennium Dome in that project, then head back to Patrick Wright's *A Journey through Ruins* (1991), and from there proceed to Geoff Nicholson's *Bleeding London* (1997), before return-ing to Iain Sinclair's extraordinary *Lights Out.*

Lights Out did not come out of the blue. In more than one sense, it is the climax of a development in the writings about London, which began with Jonathan Raban's *Soft City—What Cities Do to Us and How They Change the Way We Live, Think, Feel* (1974). In this study Raban tried to rescue the city from the hands of heritage mongers and tourist authorities, from soci-ologists, urban theorists, historians of architecture, and political scientists. He softened the so-called hard evidence of their reconstructions and dis-sections of the city and opened it both to a sympathetic ethnographic in-spection and to the lived experience peculiar to large cities. In England, Raban's book marked a turning point in the literature about cities in gen-eral and about London in particular. As David Harvey has observed, "It was also written at that cusp in intellectual and cultural history when something called 'postmodernism' emerged from its chrysalis of the anti-modern to establish itself as a cultural aesthetic in its own right" (Harvey, *The Condition* 3).

Unlike most of the critical writings about urban life in the 1960s, Raban, following Simmel, directs our attention to the psychological and phenom-enological particularities of cities, of his city of London as a great force for liberating human potential (see Simmel, "The Metropolis"). He is not in-terested in adding "to the already fat dossier on the evils of urban life" or in repeating the endless list of housing projects, slum clearance projects, and road improvements gone wrong; nor does he engage in speculations about the logic of capitalism and the pressures of the market that are to blame for the urban disasters. Rather, he concentrates on the concrete conditions of living in a big city (Raban 3). His implicit claim is that, if you forget who is to blame and how terrible it all is, the true fascination of city life and the opportunity it holds for the individual will reveal itself. Al-ready, one can see this is a much more radically subversive approach than many of the blatant and blunt social criticisms of his time.

At such moments of revelation, he writes, "the city goes soft; it awaits the imprint of an identity. For better or worse, it invites you to remake it, to consolidate it into a shape you can live in." For him, "cities are plastic by nature" (Raban 3).

> We mould them in our images: they, in their turn, shape us by the resistance they offer when we try to impose our own personal form on them. In this sense, it seems to me that living in cities is an art, and we need the vocabulary of art, of style, to describe the particular relationship between man and material that exists in the continual creative play of urban living. The city, as we imagine it, the soft city of illusion, myth, aspiration, nightmare, is as real, maybe more real, than the hard city one can locate on maps, in statistics, in monographs on urban sociology and demography and architecture. (Raban 3)

Ideally, you can live such a city, but you can only do so by writing it. Raban pointed the way for such a possibility, but his program had to wait for others to carry it out more radically, those who would collapse the distinction between living and writing once and for all.

Raban predates postmodernist insights into the constructedness of reality, and he gives city experience a creative twist. He understands it as an enhancement of the range of opportunities city dwellers have to take charge of their own lives. His city dwellers are active and creative. Their city, his soft city, is more real than the material city we find represented on maps and graphs, the statistical evidence produced by urban sociologists and demographers, frozen structures of abstract townscapes in blueprints for urban renewal. His city dweller is continually shaping his own surroundings against the dry facts of city professionals and against the image tinkering of the tourist trade.

If the authorities responsible for shaping and changing cities had taken Raban's reasonings seriously, their policies might have moved the city much closer to its utopian promise as a stage for human creativity than they actually have. But there was massive resistance. Thus far, the proclaimed shift from the tyranny of so-called social truths to the freedom of signifying practices has failed to bring about a significant change in urban public policies. On the contrary, these public policies have increasingly taken advantage of the dramatically increased opportunities for visual propaganda. Manipulation of perceptions of any kind, the staging of illusions, the grand gestures of representational activities are now easier than ever to carry out. This is obvious from the way politics increasingly uses the new freedom to invent, construct, and revisualize realities to manipulate our perceptions for the politicians' own benefit.

While the literature of London became increasingly diversified, multi-voiced, its descriptions thicker (in Geertz's sense), official London engaged in a massive reinvention operation of its own. As a result, the space of signification is today more congested and contested than ever. The de-

Figure 3.1 London's Millennium Dome. Courtesy of QA Photos Ltd.

bates about the progressive gentrification of run-down quarters, about the Docklands, and especially about the Millennium Dome are typical of such ideologically loaded manipulations of London.

The political establishment, in conjunction with city planners, architects, and other professionals, saw the approach of the millennium as a "once-in-a-lifetime opportunity": "We have for the first time in generations the chance to generate a sufficient critical mass of architectural projects, festivals, exhibitions and celebrations to re-introduce the Thames into the lives of Londoners" (Rogers 142–43).

The plan to create a new vision of London, "to make the whole greater than the sum of its parts" was prominent on Richard Rogers's political agenda. "With its immense cultural, political and social resources," he claimed, "London could become the city to visit in the year 2000. It should host a year-long millennium celebration of unrivaled quality and diversity at Greenwich and throughout the capital."

> This approach to celebrating the millennium would leave a functioning river bus service and river banks revitalised with parks, promenades, piers, floating restaurants and boardwalks. The Thames restored to the people and the linking of London's public spaces should be the physical legacy of the city's millennium celebrations—a thriving public domain that strings together our national monuments and places, past and future.
>
> London has the opportunity to become a cultured, balanced and sustainable city. It is up to Londoners to demand an elected strategic body to deliver its full potential. (Rogers 142–43)

The elected body is now in place, but, with the benefit of hindsight, one can see that the Millennium Dome and other millennium projects in London have completely failed to change for the better people's lives in this city.

The new Labour government immediately recognized the possibilities of such projects for its own postmodern concept of selling its policies. Peter Mandelson, then minister without portfolio and the brains behind the think tanks and advisory committees of the spin doctors credited with Labour's tremendous election success, was put in charge of everything, particularly the most conspicuous project: the Millennium Dome at Greenwich, designed by Richard Rogers and built at a cost of a billion dollars. One of the first things Mandelson did was to travel to Orlando to see how best to plan and execute attractive illusions and sensational gimmicks for the Dome. The government propaganda machine was set in motion and the Dome was praised as the best Britain had to offer in the sciences, technology, natural resources management, and so on. Concurrently, another think tank produced a visionary project aimed at the heart of British self-perceptions, traditions, and heritage. It is described in a booklet issued by Demos and composed by Mark Leonard.

Like Rogers, Leonard was convinced that the millennium provided a unique opportunity for projecting a new image of Britain to the world, presenting new stories, events, buildings, and exhibitions. He proposed to redesign "airports and train stations, and entrance points such as the Channel Tunnel, to provide visitors with a stunning welcome to the country and immediate contact with the best contemporary art and design." He also proposed to develop "the world's most impressive web sites to provide an introduction to Britain linked in with web sites for the major cities and including not only public information, but also discussion groups, arts, listings and tourism information." He was receptive to the idea that the new Labour government had put its weight behind the construction of a "model" living museum of the future—a real global village or "Millennium City" in Greenwich to act as a showcase for the future of health, learning, retailing, and democracy, and to situate the U.K. as a laboratory of future ways of living (see Leonard 11–12).

In short, there is overwhelming evidence that the grandiose rhetoric of fundamental renewal has now failed to achieve what it set out to do. The theme park vision of rebuilding the image of London has made no difference in people's lives in the metropolis. It will merely leave London pockmarked with another set of phantom limbs to remind everyone of another short-lived and very expensive fit of metropolitan megalomania.

As Sinclair put it, "The art of the Thatcher/Major (bingo millennialist) era was, . . . the art of the proposal. . . . An industry grew up for describing things that hadn't quite happened, epiphanies for empty rooms." The Labour government has intensified and accelerated the drive for spectacular images, for impressive imageabilities, by constructing "a mental landscape for a culture of compulsory leisure," which masquerades as the quintessence of core values with which not only Londoners but also the British people as a whole are expected to identify (Sinclair, *Lights Out* 217, 210; see also Sinclair, *Sorry Meniscus*).

In comparison, the world of London we enter when we begin reading Wright, Nicholson, and Sinclair is unrecognizable. Their London does not consist of history trails, improvement zones, conspicuous landmarks, monuments, decorative greenery, and a clearly defined grid that separates public from private, major from minor, central from peripheral, and marks touristic attractions wherever you turn It is territory in the sense Huck Finn uses the term when threatened by Aunt Sally's idea of an orderly life and a decent upbringing.

Their London does not consist of the bird's-eye view of town planners, the zoning graphs of demographers, or the arrow maze of the traffic statisticians; they do not fly over it, pore over maps, or move imaginary masses about. Rather they explore known and unknown territory in which literally everything—a house, a door, a scrap, a sign on the wall, even absences behind the presences—can trigger complex memories, metaphoric transpositions, and associations to stories, events, and people. The city thus becomes a score for multiple self-projections, a space teeming with endless signification, a poly-palimpsestuous site inviting endless discoveries, mythopoetic activities in every possible direction. Living in the city means realizing to the fullest its immense potential.

A first step in this direction is taken by Patrick Wright in his *A Journey through Ruins* (1991). His object of study, Dalston Lane, is for him "an open archeological site in which the story of the nation's post-war history can be traced out in unexpected detail," and it is from it that he has "read the signs of the time" (Wright 46). These signs point to a growing fluidity of the "border-lines between fact and fiction" (35).

55

But Wright does not go all the way. He only dives deep into thick description to bring some representative, paradigmatic meaning to the surface. Dalston Lane is for him a case study and his approach suppresses the immediacy and impact of the concreteness and particularity of his finds at the very moment when these finds might begin to have an effect. For Sinclair, who has cooperated with Wright on various occasions, Dalston Lane and its "hobbled spurt" labors "gamely under the burden of cultural significance imposed upon it" by him (Sinclair, *Lights Out* 15).

This passage reveals one of the many differences between Wright's book and those of Sinclair: Sinclair refuses to abstract. His text does not point beyond itself, it does not probe external meanings, general implications, critical summaries, but it embodies the city as a poly-palimpsestuous site.

Wright's book is a kind of cultural anagnorisis in action. Geoff Nicholson's *Bleeding London* is a novel—a novel that faces the problem that, in most city novels, the city appears already mapped, physically stable at least in part, a setting for human action, a prop for a drawn-out *comédie humaine*. Leaving aside the ambiguity of the title, we can describe *Bleeding London* as an attempt to undermine the idea that maps provide reliable information about large cities. From the point of view of his protagonists and their highly individualized projects, the existing maps of London are uninteresting or a nuisance, to say the least.

Mick, one of the protagonists whose story is told, comes to London on a mission of revenge. He thinks that his stripper girlfriend has been gang-raped by six "rich, stuck-up, posh bastards." And he has come all the way from Sheffield to find them and teach them a lesson. At first, he is completely disoriented. He refuses to use the available means of transportation to find the hotel in Hackney that a friend has recommended to him. As a result, he wanders more or less aimlessly. Eventually, he finds a map shop—but his hopes for finding directions are dashed immediately when he discovers that the shop assistant looks Japanese, exotic, not like somebody likely to know the city and to be of help to him. He discovers, however, that she is perfectly able to speak his language, and is, in fact, a Londoner. She asks him if he wants to purchase a guidebook.

He said, "Maybe." And she directed him to the modern guide book section where he was duly baffled. "Any recommendations?"

"How about this one?" she said. She handed him a book called *Complete London*. "Complete?" he queried. "Yes."

He looked puzzled and doubtful. "Well, how can it be?" he said. "If it was really complete it'd have to contain all the information in all these other books wouldn't it? In fact, it would have to contain all the information in all the books in the whole shop. Right?" "I suppose that's true," she admitted graciously.

"And all the information in all the books on London that you *don't* have in the shop. The book'd have to be bigger than the shop. In fact the book would probably have to be bigger than London itself, wouldn't it?"

"I'd never thought about it in quite that way," she said.

"Well, think about it," he said. (Nicholson 22)

Mick's deliberate literalism and naïveté take us to the center of the problematic of the book: maps and their representational claims. Mick finally settles for a guide called *Unreliable London* and that, I suppose, is an epistemologically sound decision.

While Mick maplessly pursues his mission to beat up and expose the official London embodied in the persons of his victims, the two other protagonists, Judy Tanaka and Stuart London, pursue their obsession to radically remap London according to their own, highly idiosyncratic projects.

Stuart has set up a successful business that provides thematic walks for tourists: the Architectural Walk, The Mob Walk, The Sculpture Walk, a range of options he later diversifies to include a Shakespeare Walk, a Royal Walk, a Rock n' Roll Walk; he then adds the Beatles' London, Virginia Woolf's London, Pepys's London, Hogarth's London, the Henry VIII Walk, the Jack the Ripper Walk, the Thomas Middelton Walk, the Post-Modernist Walk, and finally, the Anarchist's Walk and the Lesbian Walk—the last proving to be one of the most popular tours for a time (see 71–75).

The more of London he appropriates in this way, the less interested he is in his business. Finally, he leaves all practical business to his efficient wife, Anita Walker, and withdraws to the Museum of London, the Victoria and Albert, and the British Museum, where he can enjoy London without being forced to impose any structure or timetable on its exploration. But these museums only provide short respites from his obsessions with walks, streets, and maps. An ideé fixe grows within him, the idea of an ultimate walk, a walk that would involve walking every single street in the *A to Z Map of London*. He does so, blackening out the streets on the map as he goes along. In the course of this mission, it becomes clear to him that, by walking London out of existence street by street, he also walks himself out of life (after all, he is called London). He is, in a word, engaged on a suicide mission and thus becomes an allegorical figure for the futility of using maps to orient oneself in the metropolis.

Judy Tanaka adopts an entirely different plan. Her project is not fueled by a refusal to recognize London as structured by tube lines, bus routes, or maps, or to eradicate it by walking it into nonexistence, but rather by a desire to remap it as she likes. In her studio apartment she hangs a map of London covered with black crosses indicating all the places she has had sex. Her life's quest is to mark as many public places as possible with her sexual desire. In the process, she makes many converts and collects the transparent plastic sheets her lovers have given her to prove they have played their part in her mission. In a final act, she places all those transparencies on top of one another over a map of London, which, with each added plastic sheet, becomes more opaque and finally disappears under the starlike density of black markings. "They were not distributed evenly or symmetrically or representatively, but they certainly showed how geographically promiscuous she had been" (343). In a final radical twist she remaps London on her body and shows "the map made flesh" (345) to her female therapist, who tenderly fingers the tattooed River Thames and then says quietly: "I can see, we may need more sessions than I first thought" (345).

In the end, all protagonists get entangled in their problematic mappings. Mick discovers he was set up and that the gang rape never happened. Stuart fails to commit suicide and disappears. Judy transforms herself into a map of London, a map of her own desires written on an exotic body. With it, the final triumph of the protagonists' missions and their personalized images of the metropolis over its established representations is complete. It is to such a soft, mapless city that Mick later returns of his own free will.

As a novel about remapping and de-mapping, *Bleeding London* takes its readers constantly beyond the concreteness of the action and the characters into a more abstract discursive field. The novel's problematic always has to be read parallel to its story.

Sinclair's *Lights Out for the Territory* also begins as a series of walks:

> The notion was to cut a crude V into the sprawl of the city, to vandalize dormant energies by an act of ambulant sign making. To walk from Hackney to Greenwich Hill, and back along the River Lea to Clingford Mount, recording and retrieving the usages on walls, lampposts, door jambs: the spites and spasms of an increasingly deranged populace. . . .
>
> Armed with a cheap notebook, and accompanied by the photographer Marc Atkins, I would transcribe all the pictographs of venom that decorated our near-arbitrary route. The messages were, in truth, unimportant. Urban graffiti is all too often a signature without a document, an anonymous autograph. (Sinclair, *Lights Out* 1)

These messages are "a mere parody of the corporate tags," which are nothing more than "the marginalia of corporate tribalism" (Sinclair, *Lights Out* 1).

"First, fragments of London are perceived as Polaroid epiphanies; signed and abandoned" (2). But the failure of this quest to gather deep significance from recordings of these "meaningless" and often "minimal adjustments to the psychic skin of the city" (3) brings about a rebirth of a new type of city stalker, a "born-again *flâneur*" as "a stubborn creature, less interested in texture and fabric" or in "eavesdropping on philosophical conversation pieces than in noticing *everything*":

> Alignments of telephone kiosks, maps made from moss on the slopes of Victorian sepulchres, collections of prostitutes' cards, torn and defaced promotional bills for cancelled events at York Hall, visits to the homes of dead writers, bronze casts on war memorials, plaster dogs, beer mats, concentrations of used condoms, the crystalline patterns of glass shards surrounding an imploded BMW quarter-light window, meditations on the relationship between the brain damage suffered by the super-middleweight boxer Gerald McClellan (lights out in the Royal London Hospital, Whitechapel) and the simultaneous collapse of Barings, bankers to the Queen. Walking, moving across a retreating townscape, stitches it all together: The illicit cocktail of bodily exhaustion and a raging carbon monoxide high. (4)

Sinclair's strategies are designed to deconstruct time and space as principles of order. He is not moving in a physical environment that then produces and organizes meaning or beckons for interpretations; rather, he moves in a highly complex and chaotic continuum of meanings, pictures, voices, and memories, which he randomly strings together and attaches to observations, occurrences, and physical details along his journey. No principle of selection, no system of priorities can be discovered.

During this quest the past becomes an optional landscape (208). The future cannot be called on "to describe the geography of a present divorced from its memory traces" (65). There is no fixing "the future to rewrite the past" (77). In the territory, such clean divisions of labor between past, present, and future do not exist and do not make sense. For Sinclair, in a sense, the past is as present as the future. There is a level playing field of time in his book, which refuses to be structured in any simple, linear way. If there are connecting networks, they are subterraneous, out of sight, magical, shamanistic, grids of forces beyond rational comprehension. "We were convinced," he writes, that London "was mapped by cued lines of energy, connecting buildings with natural geological and geographical forms; making paths available down which the more tedious laws of time could be aborted. Now there was another, wilder system in play: the improvisations of the dog. The retreats, spurts, galloping loops and pounces of the stalker" (85).

The energy fields underlying the city are erased by architectural incrustations of inhuman rationality. The flow of energy must be set free again. In a sense, one could argue that Sinclair would like to sing the city into existence again, like the aborigines in Chatwin's songlines (see Sinclair on Rimbaud 146, 154, and on Aidan Dun 155).

At stake here is what Sinclair calls the "psychogeography" of the city, that is, a geography in which the after-images of dreams, visions, books,

films, and artworks are not presented as separate from the physical presence of everything the city holds.

> By now we are cruising past the accommodation address . . . of that mysteri-
> ous and fugitive publication, the *Newsletter* of the London *Psychogeographical
> Association.*
>   . . . This anonymous, unsponsored, irregular, single-sheet squib is prob-
> ably the most useful of all London's neighbourhood tabloids. And certainly
> the most entertaining. It has no fixed cover prize and no distribution. If you
> need it, it finds you. It writes itself. It invents the rumours that it purports to
> discover. The deranged geniality of its prose offers the only accurate temper-
> ature chart of the city's fevers: reality as an infinitely accommodating sub-
> stance. A fictional documentary, a retrospective prophecy. The *Newsletter* is
> unembarrassed by the knowledge that news is whatever you want to make it.
> News has no present tense. It's dead when you read it. Much better to trust
> fantasies that become fact through the sheer energy of the prose. (25)

Consequently,

> The matter of London, the re-fleshing of Lud's withered hide, is exposed by
> doctored maps, speculative alignments, black propaganda. The revenge of
> the disenfranchised. Improvisations on history that are capable of making ad-
> justments in the present time. Prophecy as news. News as the purest form of
> fiction. Subversion in splash headlines. The most corrupt of all forms, the
> tabloid, can be "turned." The psychogeographers are operating an equivalent
> of James Elroy's novel *American Tabloid*, freebasing among archetypes and
> video clips, speeding through the image bank. A paranoid poetic whose lies
> are so spectacular that they have become a new form of truth. (26)

The psychogeographer's dream, which is obviously also Sinclair's dream,
is achieved by reading all manner of texts back into the city. Phone numbers, poems, newspaper clips, and books become scores for playing the
psychogeographical tune. After-images are not that which remains and
which has to be compared to actual experience, but they form an energy
source, a starting point for embarking again and again on the endless
journey of rewriting and reimagining the city. Not the result, but the process, is what makes the city what it is. No outside point of view can reveal
its truth: only living it and writing it will bring readers close to what it
means to live the city today.

CHAPTER FOUR

Berlin 2000: "The Image of an Empty Place"

Mark Seltzer

The technology of public belief and popular memory called "reality TV" is one of the most conspicuous signs of the interactive compulsion in contemporary culture. And one of the most visible markers of reality TV—both in its true confession format and in its true crime format—is the interaction of stranger intimacy and stranger violence. That is, the public spectacle of torn and private bodies and torn and private persons is also the spectacle of a style of sociality that has become inseparable from the mass exhibition and mass witnessing, the endlessly reproducible display, of wounded bodies and wounded minds in public. Hence the trauma a priori that has burgeoned in recent popular and academic culture. Hence the lurid, albeit transient and quasi-anonymous, celebrity of the spokesvictims of contemporary wound culture. Hence too the manner in which crime, mass-mediated interiority, and publicness have been drawn into an absolute proximity.

In these pages, I will be concerned with these two intricated scenes of a wound culture: the public scene and the site of violence, the scene of the crime. I will be concerned, more exactly, with some of the ways that the scenes of crime and of publicness have become, since the late nineteenth century, two ways of saying, or imaging, the same thing. My examples, for the moment, will be drawn from the volatile and phantasmic cityscapes that provide the social and cultural and psychic conditions of these linked experiences of violence and publicness: first, the surreal estate of the city of Berlin, its demolition, redemolition, and reconstruction; second, and collaterally, the more general woundscapes and scenes of the crime—the

For S.H.

forensic scene and the forensic aesthetic—where these experiences become legible.

Hence the intent here will be to put in place some of the landmarks of place and identity (the forms of place-identity) that make up a wound culture: that make up, that is, what I have been describing in a series of studies and across a series of scenes, as the pathological public sphere (see Seltzer, *Serial Killers*). The intent, finally, will be to test out the forms of urban legibility and urban credibility that make up something like the reality show, the idioms of public and popular belief and memory, of the torn and reconstructed city itself.

WOUND CULTURE

The beauty of Berlin, if one can describe in that way a city whose essence is destruction, is its emptiness. That emptiness is in large part a matter of wound and memory, violence and loss: the city's scarred identity as wound landscape and as the scene of the crime. But it is also more than that.

For the architect Rem Koolhaas, for instance, this emptiness is a matter of the city's "efficiency": how "entirely missing urban presences or entirely erased architectural entities nevertheless generate what can be called an urban condition." For one thing, there are the hypervisible modes of efficiency in the city: the everyday openness of the city of Berlin to its own infrastructure, its own nervous system. There is a basic difference between urban emptiness as a loss that can be filled or replaced by architecture—even an architecture that monumentalizes loss or emptiness—and a postarchitectural city, one that cultivates its emptiness. The beauty of Berlin is, or was, then at least in part its *antiarchitecture*: its vast quasi-occupied areas of nothingness. In this view, the promise of Berlin, as "the most avant-garde European city," was the promise of the "post-architectural city," an empty-center city (see Koolhaas, "Current Urban").

The promise was inseparable from destruction, and not least in that destruction itself was experienced as a precursor to, or even as a form of, urban planning. If Haussmann was Paris's "artist in demolition," total war was Berlin's. What urban planners represented, and embraced, as "the mechanical decongestant of bombing and the final battle"—the annihilation, or de-densification, of the center of the city—was something like the technical production of Berlin's "newest rubble architecture" (see Schivelbusch, *Cold Crater* 14–15; Kittler 324).[1] For this reason, it was possible to maintain that "total war must be seen not only as the end of the Third Reich, but also as the precursor to reconstruction" (Durth 15). Or, as Friedrich Kittler has argued (by way of Thomas Pynchon's total war novel, *Gravity's Rainbow*), the carpet bombings of the city belonged to the same

Figure 4.1 Berlin. Photo by S. Herfurth.

secret history of urban design: "each shockwave plotted in advance to bring *precisely tonight's wreck* into being . . . it is in working order" (Kittler 325; Pynchon 520–21; see also Davis, "Berlin's Skeleton" and Colquhoun et al.).

The reconstruction of the last decade or so reworks these relays of devastation and preservation. The reconstructed city tends toward, on one side, an erasure of the past in the world-corporate architecture of the posthistorical city unimpressed by time. It tends, on the other, toward a mechanical self-preservation, "the result of a gigantic attempt to make it the museum of its own past, a museum not of originals but of *Blade-Runner*-like replicated reality." In the narrow interim between reconstruction and reoccupation as the new capital, empty-centered city has appeared at times as a "brand-new ghost town": for an interval, a Brasilia at the heart of the new Europe (see Schivelbusch, "Cold Crater" 186).

That emptiness, in short, is now being reoccupied at an astonishing pace. The large areas of openness that have defined the cratered and divided postwar city are disappearing, as Berlin is being torn apart and reconstructed to take over as the synthetic capital and ersatz representation of the newly reunified Germany in the twenty-first century.

A look at the situation of Berlin, its empty places and lethal spaces, can, then, begin to indicate some of the relays between scene and crime, space and wound, place and identity, that will occupy me here. For what has the

open or empty space of the city—the romance of an antiarchitecture—
come to mean? And what exactly does it mean for these empty spaces, for
empty space generally, to disappear? "The architecture of redevelop-
ment," the critic Rosalyn Deutsche observes, "constructs the built environment as a medium, one we literally inhabit, that monopolizes popular
memory by controlling the representation of its own history. It is truly an
evicting architecture" (Deutsche, "Architecture" 176; see also Deutsche,
Evictions). But what, more precisely, is being evicted here? And what re-
places it?

THE LOVE PARADE

One of the annual events that takes place in Berlin, each July, in the
years since the reunification, is a mass gathering called the "Love Parade"
(an event that has now spread to several other European capitals). Nomi-
nally a political event—the city picks up the trash—hundreds of thousands
of people move to, and gather at, and fill the vacant center of the city to
the rhythmic, sampled machine beat of techno. The vast massing of the
population without a clear object—unlike the nationalist Bastille Day and
the retro-nationalist World Cup massings that took place in Paris around
the same time as the 1998 parade—seems in Berlin to be a demonstration
of something strange and, perhaps, something new: a demonstration of
the very possibility of a mass gathering without a clear national or political
referent. That is to say, a resolutely peaceful and festive massing of the
public that *seems to hold the place of the very possibility of "the public" itself.*

Things are of course more complex. In the few years since the first small
populist Love Parade, corporate sponsorship of the event has moved in.
The slogan of the 1998 parade, for instance—"One World, One Future"—
might be read as the new corporate logo of the world-corporation city
under construction: the new federal architecture rivaled and mirrored by
corporate monuments such as the Sony Center and the Daimler building
near the razed and reoccupied Potsdamer Platz.

The slogan of unity itself has powerful resonances in this place: the
writer François Mauriac memorably remarked that he loved Germany so
much he was glad there were two of them. For half a century there has
been an unrelaxed insistence on rewriting "Deutschland über alles" as (in
Hans Magnus Enzensberger's alternative slogan) "Germany, Germany—
among other things." But if the Love Parade gathering has perhaps acquired some of the markers of corporate publicity or (in Stuart Hall's
phrase) "authoritarian populism," it may, beyond that, tell us a bit more
about the status of public spaces, their opening and their appropriation
(see Hall).

Figure 4.2 Berlin. Photo by S. Herfurth.

The "One World, One Future" captioning of the Love Parade might be taken, alternatively, as an emblem of what the political philosopher Claude Lefort calls "the loving grip of the good society." For Lefort, this is the *negative* formula for the retreat of the political and the *lapsing* of a democratic politics. This is because "the important point is that democracy is instituted and sustained by the *dissolution of the markers of certainty*. It inaugurates a history in which people experience a fundamental indeterminacy as to the basis of power, law and knowledge, and as to the basis of relations between *self* and *other*" (Lefort, "Question of Democracy" 19). The radical mutation inaugurated in the form of society that Alexis de Tocqueville called "the democratic invention" was the elaboration of a social order that structures itself by itself. According to this logic, there is nothing deeper than the "groundless ground" of a strictly indwelling network of relations of power and knowledge. This is a society "without a body . . . a society which undermines the representation of an organic totality": as the by-now default and quasi-automatic refrain goes, "radically open, contingent, incomplete" (Lefort, "Question of Democracy" 18; Deutsche, *Evictions* 303). Without basis or foundation, "groundless ground," disembodied, undermined: this is the idiom of an antiarchitecture. Its image is not that of the loving grip of the good society. It is instead what Lefort calls "the image of an empty place" ("Logic of Totalitarianism" 279).

The ghostly or phantom-like character of the public and of the public sphere is, in this view, precisely the point. It is not something to be exorcised, congealed into a fixed place, or coerced into an organic identity: it is the phantom condition of the public as such.[2]

There are two risks here, both of which, it will be seen in a moment, are mapped in high relief on the Berlin landscape. The first entails an unequivocal identification ("One World, One Future," for instance), which gives rise to an identity politics. The second—in effect an endorsement of equivocation, an abiding in ambivalence, openness, contingency, and incompletion tout court—is that no name whatsover can be given either to the political or to the subject.[3] If the first risk threatens to make Berlin into a sort of Architecture-of-Democracy Mall, the second promises to make of it something like a Theme Park of the Uncanny. This deadlock— the compulsive pas de deux between a corporatism operating in the name of democracy and a self-evacuating style of postmodernism—has become familiar enough. It is nowhere more visible than in the projects for reconstructing Berlin.

DEMOCRATIC SOCIAL SPACE

Consider the debate about a "representative" architecture for the city. This is not merely a debate about what this architecture should represent, what an editor of *Der Spiegel* called "the dream of representative buildings" (Schreiber 203). It is a debate about whether places, including empty ones, mean or represent anything at all, about, in the architect Bernard Tschumi's words, "the idea of a meaning immanent in architectural structures" (quoted in Hollier xi). The dream of representative buildings is countered by a dream of emptying structures of significance.

The relentlessly self-effacing architecture of the interim capital, Bonn, resisted not merely a particular symbolic style but the imposition of any symbolism as such. Hence it is argued in the reconstruction debates that "architecture in a democracy need not be faceless"; that "symbolism in architecture need not be synonymous with the Third Reich" (quoted in Wise 37, 61). What becomes visible is what Deleuze and Guattari have called "the face-system" and its "face-landscape correlations": "Architecture positions its ensembles—houses, towns, or cities, monuments or factories, to function like faces in the landscape they transform" (Deleuze and Guattari 172). The face-system that correlates place and identity— that produces what might be called place-identity—gothicizes space and personates place.

It is not difficult to see how these debates restage two related fallacies or fantasies: first, the genetic fallacy, and second, the republican fantasy. The

Figure 4.3 Berlin. Photo by S. Herfurth.

genetic fallacy is the notion that where things come from can tell us what they are or what they mean—the fallacy at the bottom of identity studies and its complement, trauma studies. Its counterside, the republican fantasy, is the desire to come from nowhere, to give birth to oneself. I have traced these tendencies at some length elsewhere (see *Serial Killers*, esp. chap. 4). For now, we may note that, at its most reductive, one rediscovers in these debates a resistance to meaning-as-such as a resistance to power-as-such—a kind of pop-Foucauldianism that also has become familiar.

Here is a brief sampling of how place-identity functions across these sites. The dream of representative buildings has meant, most visibly, drawing on expanses of transparent glass to express openness and accessibility: the glass wall as an emblem of democratic transparency. This is in part carried over from the insistently understated and self-effacing federal architecture of the interim capital, Bonn, an architecture that, in erasing the fascist period, referred back to a prefascist and exiled Bauhaus style—even as a "Bauhaus-inspired modernism had become the house style for corporate America in the late 1950s and 1960s" (Wise 29). The glass wall also functions as a response to the emphatically paradoxical situation of the free city, for decades entirely encircled by, and defined by, an imprisoning dead wall. The appeal is to a direct equivalence between transparent facades and democratic public space: an exorcism of the ghosts of fascism through the construction, for example, of a new type of dome on the Reichstag—a glass lighthouse for democracy redesigned by the British (i.e., not German) architect Sir Norman Foster.

One difficulty is that such crystal palaces have for more than a century served as the architecture of commercialism and have more recently come to represent a self-referential, self-reflective corporatism. Another is the counterassociations of a politics of transparency: for instance, the Casa del Fascio (House of Fascism) built for Mussolini by Giuseppi Terragni: "a glass house in which everyone can peer, giving rise to the architecture that is the complement of this idea: no encumbrance, no barrier, no obstacle between the political hierarchy and the people" (quoted in Schumacher 48). In Manfredo Tafuri's terms, "Glass—[is] the synthesis of matter and the immaterial, the symbol of the transparency of the subject with respect to collectivity"—that is, the spatial projection of a sheer identification of the people and the state (Tafuri, "U.S.S.R.—Berlin 1922" 131).

There are further difficulties of a different order. The Berlin architecture of democracy-made-visible has a hyper-explicitness about it, suspending the very belief it posits. As one urban designer puts it, "We want to create the impression that we have nothing to hide"; and, as another says, the intent is to create "only a feeling of openness" (Walter Karschies, quoted in Wise 85). For the glass-walled federal building in Bonn, too small to accommodate a gallery, bleachers were erected so that citizens could view their representatives at work in their name through the glass.

For the new capital buildings, bulletproof glass is incorporated into the designs. The glass dome set on top the reconstructed Reichstag is filled with a pair of spiral viewing ramps, open to visitors when the Bundestag is in session. This is see-through democracy in several senses: democracy made visible and public space as spectacle, in effect, as safe zone from the public it at once represents, images, and evicts.

The public/private divide, in all its normalcy and in all its incoherence, is what is at issue, what trembles, in these proliferating designs. There is, for one thing, a relentless proliferation of pseudo-public, or privatized public, spaces: the overlit atrium of the gathering population epitomized by the privatized public space of the mall (see Davis, "Urban Renaissance" 87; Morris; Deutsche, *Evictions*, esp. "Agoraphobia" 269–327).

Writing on that peculiar institution, the hotel lobby, Siegfried Kracauer observes that the determining togetherness of this social space means that the guests are "guests in space tout court—a space that encompasses them and has no function other than to encompass them." It posits a stranger-intimacy that "signifies only its own emptiness," the "inessential foundation" of an abstract and formal equality. In this model of democracy as the image of an empty place, the individual is "reduced to a 'member of society as such' who stands superfluously off to the side" (Kracauer, "The Hotel Lobby" 173–85).

This space seems to be a rehearsal for the symbolic architecture I have been imaging. The Reichstag's interior was gutted but the exterior was preserved in a way that, as its architect Foster expressed it, left the structure "present but void." At the center of the Sony Center, still under construction when I saw it in March 2000, there is, suspended inside the impressive atrium, an enormous empty sphere: in effect, the monumentalization of an encompassing but voided space. This is, I have been suggesting, a paramnesic symptom of the democratic idea: that is, its image and its disavowal.

There is one final "turn" in the proliferation of such images of an empty place in Berlin. Throughout the wounded city, one rediscovers projects that attempt a localization of memory through memorialization, the erasure of history in its monumentalization. These are attempts, as Michael Wise has written, to "heal the wounds" of the city as a way to heal its inhabitants of "the malady of being German": ways of constructing a "final solution to Germany's memorial problem" (Wise 154). One project, initially rejected as a central memorial to the victims of the Reich, was the scheme designed by Richard Serra and Peter Eisenman. It consisted of four thousand wall-like concrete slabs, arranged like a vast burial ground. If the erasure of what had been erased consists of an erasure of the past in the name of history, this project was seen as the permanent creation of what former chancellor Kohl called an "open wound in central Berlin," a wound, in effect, as its own monument.

THE MIMESIS OF PUBLICNESS, OR COMMISERATION

The common places of a wound culture could not be more visible and more explicit than here, in the excruciated and self-excavating debates about Berlin's reconstruction. In the contemporary pathological public sphere, pain, trauma, damage, and the wound have become the self-authorizing indexes of the real, both historical and psychic. But it is not difficult to detect how these collective probings of the wound are, by now, a

Figure 4.4 Berlin. Photo by S. Herfurth.

little *too* self-evident, as if deferring belief in what is at the same time affirmed, as if serving as a sort of placeholder for something else.

That something else is the contemporary form of the public sphere, in which publicness and pathology have become indissociable. It is not merely that the mourning thing—the trauma apriori—has emerged as something like an infomercial for the psychic order, or, at the least, for the modern soul. The wound and its strange attractions have come to function as a relay point of the psychic and the social orders, a way of locating and cathecting social space. This is a public sphere bound to shock, trauma, and damage: an opening or gaping toward others as the principle of (psychical) relation to an other and (social) relation to others.

That in modernity public and private communicate in the wound may by now be a commonplace. But that communication remains to be specified. For Benjamin, for example, following Simmel and Freud, the modernist experience is an experience at once of mechanical reproducibility and of shock or trauma: trauma, by extension, is something like mechanical reproducibility housed in persons. Along these lines, the recent turn to the trauma apriori serves as a proxy for the absence of a compelling idiom by which public and private, the historical and the psychical, might find their point of contact in contemporary culture.

I have taken up this line of inquiry elsewhere (see *Serial Killers*, esp. part

4, "Wound Culture: Trauma in the Pathological Public Sphere"). Here my concerns are somewhat different. The decline of the "aura" in machine culture, for Benjamin, is, more exactly, its "ultimate retrenchment" in the "fleeting expression of the human face." The face is the "focal point" of early photography. For Benjamin, this gives way, around 1900, to another photographic image: the exhibition of eerily empty or deserted city streets. Instancing Atget's photographs, Benjamin observes, we recall, that "it has justly been said of him that he photographed them like scenes of the crime. The scene of the crime, too, is deserted; it is photographed for the purpose of establishing evidence." No doubt there is a policial aspect to these images. But what surfaces here is perhaps something more, something like a resemblance between the face and the scene of the crime. "No face is surrealistic to the same degree," Benjamin notes elsewhere, "than the true face of a city." The disturbance in the relations between personality and space—the condition of the torn and open subject of the pathological public sphere—is nowhere clearer than in the image of an empty place as both the scene of the crime and of a wounded sociality (Benjamin, "Work of Art" 226; "Surrealism" 182).

Hence what I have been tracing, by way of the situation of Berlin, are in effect two versions of the urban after-image, which are also, and crucially, two versions of the condition of publicness today: the traumatic and the forensic. I want to conclude by unpacking somewhat these versions of the sociality of the wound and by making a bit clearer how notions of urban credibility—that is, the credibility of collective life—are relayed by torn scenes such as the city of Berlin.

The trauma apriori should by now be clear enough. One might say that the repressive hypothesis (by which the entire culture, according to Michel Foucault, turned to the confession of sex) has been given over to the trauma hypothesis (by which the entire culture has turned to the confession of wounds and victimhood). What has been described as the emergence of a "new victim" order, an order that proceeds under the sign of an ecumenical pathos, amounts to the positing of the sociality of the wound: *collectivity in commiseration.*[4] Hence the by-now compulsively repeated commonplaces about, for example, "the ghosts of Berlin," its "haunted" character, and the debates about how a "building or monument might be able to display the wounds of Berlin's past" (see Ladd 235).

The forensic apriori proceeds along somewhat different lines. The forensic appeals as well to the afterwardsness of violation and to the "aftermath" character and the "always already" foreclosure of scene and event (It is as if the deconstructive logo—déjà toujours—were something of a placeholder for both the traumatic and the forensic turns.) Beyond that, the forensic way of seeing pathologizes, or criminalizes, public space. The term "forensic" is itself derived from "forum," with its implications of

public meeting and collective exchange: forensic realism couples publicness and crime in a generalized fantasy of surveillance. It posits the everyday openness of every body to detection and places every area of urban
life under suspicion. It operates, that is to say, in the film noir idiom of an
"ecology of fear": the urban scene as crime scene.

Consider, for example, the 1997 Los Angeles exhibition of California
art called "The Scene of the Crime." Instancing what Ralph Rugoff, the
curator of the exhibition, calls an "aesthetic of aftermath," this forensic
art updates Atget's deserted city streets as the scene of the crime, with its
multiplication of deteriorated, defaced, and abandoned architecture; de-
populated and evacuated interiors; emptied places and torn spaces. This
is the imaging of the forensic—public scene and crime scene—in the
image of an empty place (see Rugoff, "Introduction" and "More Than
Meets the Eye").

It is not difficult to detect what such after-images look like and what, in
turn, they make visible. For one thing, one may detect here a becoming-
visible of something like the radical ("new") historicist, or culturalist, conviction that there is nothing more to the interiority of the subject than its
formation from the outside—the subject produced and evacuated at once,
such that the socialization of the subject and its traumatization, are two
ways of saying the same thing. The at once solid and emptied spatial interiors that define, for example, the extraordinary work of the British sculp-
tor Rachel Whiteread—the solidification of vacated interiors, the congealing of negative space—provide an exact counterpart to the psychotechnic
modeling of place and identity, both individual and collective.

But it is just this congealing of democracy-as-empty-place into an image
that returns us to the problem of the newly renovated "synthetic" metropolis as replica or theme park or reality show, returns us to social symbolic
space as, in effect, a ready-made. The synthetic metropolis distributes
across its landscapes ready-made versions of intimacy and publicness, putting in place, here and there, interactive replicas of its own condition, a
perpetual reality show. The ready-made has been seen to "ratify the self-
sufficiency of reality and the definitive repudiation, by reality itself, of all
representation" (Tafuri, "Toward a Critique of Architectural Ideology"
18). But it may also be seen to ratify just the reverse, the definitive repudiation, in the self-sufficiency of representation itself, of all reality. For if the
reality show, from one point of view, represents nothing but a drive to re-
stock the depleted hunting grounds of the real with artificial game, it represents, from another, "the true ambition of the Metropolis": "to create a
world totally fabricated by man, i.e., to live *inside* fantasy."[5]

The synthetic metropolis responds to the fear of not getting enough reality with ersatz models of authenticity—not least, rehearsals of violence
and violation as markers of "the real." It responds to the fear of not getting

Figure 4.5 Berlin. Photo by S. Herfurth.

enough pleasure with models of surrogate or referred intimacy. In short, it responds to the incredulity with respect to the reality of any social bond or collective life with the public reality show and its interactive compulsions.

In the mimesis of publicness, the citizens of the synthetic metropolis are guests in space tout court, a space in which the entire population can play the part of extras. It is difficult not to see the glass house architecture of the Reichstag dome in terms of such a mimesis of publicness. But the point not to be missed is how such public spaces at the same time resonantly and evocatively function as placeholders of the democratic invention.

The contemporary pathological public sphere posits precisely *the sociality of the wound* in the *public and collective gathering* around trauma, crime, and damage. Along these lines, the "Scene of the Crime" exhibition in Los Angeles might be seen in relation to other urban shock shows such as Saatchi's "Sensation" or the 1998 exhibition at the Moderna Museet in Stockholm called "Wounds: Between Democracy and Redemption in Contemporary Art."[6] Here too, torn and opened bodies and torn and open spaces relay—on the model of referred pain—the referred intimacies and referred beliefs that are the condition of urban collectivity and urban credibility today.[7]

There is a good deal more to be said about such *Stimmungsarchitektur* (mood architecture) of democracy and about such social and cultural scenes in which an unremitting scarring and a perpetual state of emergency are experienced as communality (see, for example, Elsaesser 145–83). But let me conclude with one last small example. In fall 2000 the exhibition organized by the Moderna Museet of post-1989 art by artists of formerly Communist Eastern Europe, "After the Wall: Art and Culture in Post-Communist Europe," was to have as its final destination the Hamburger Bahnhof in Berlin. What this after-image will look like, in a city unremittingly referred back to itself and its wounded premises, remains to be seen.

CHAPTER FIVE

From Rose of Fire to City of Ivory

Joan Ramon Resina

When they wish to spread the rumor of an approaching revolution in Spain, they begin to say it will break out in Barcelona,
or that it is about to break out there, or that it has already broken out there.

Edmundo de Amicis

In Barcelona one does not "prepare" Revolution, for the
simple reason that it is always "prepared." It shows up in the
street every day; if the environment is not ripe, it turns back; if
it is, Revolution sets in.

Angel Ossorio y Gallardo*

Beautiful marble city of the external world,
made gold-like by a loving gaze!

Guerau de Liost**

I will start with the assumption that cities are apprehended through
acts of imagination, so much so that they are sometimes conceived as de-
ployments of an ideal form or Gestalt. But beyond the utopias of planning, historical cities are the outcome of multiple and often conflicting efforts to render urban life visible. The ancient city was conceived as an
imago mundi, a representation of the cosmos. Its foundation was the closing act of an order-creating struggle envisioned in the epic, the poem that
spoke of origins and the institution or revalidation of centers. "Envi-

---

* En Barcelona, la revolución no 'se prepara,' por la sencilla razón de que está
'preparada' siempre. Asoma a la calle todos los días; si no hay ambiente para su desarrollo,
retrocede; si hay ambiente, cuaja (13).

** Bella ciutat de marbre del món exterior, esdevinguda aurífica dins un esguard
d'amor! (331)

sioned" is the key word. Historically, the eye has been the privileged organ for the perception and conceptualization of the city in Western experience. Vision furthers abstract apprehension and, aided by spatial techniques ranging from cartography to blueprints, facilitates the illusion of total appropriation. In his classic study, *The Image of the City*, Kevin Lynch proposed the idea of "imageability" as a goal for planners. He believed that the production of images on a massive scale served the urban dwellers' need to build mental images of the city they inhabit (7). Of course, an image is also a rhetorical tool, a trope, that facilitates the transfer from the visual to the legible, translating the city image from sensory impression to coded sign. Since the eighteenth century, texts have been an important means to create and establish lingering images of the city. These images come easily to mind: Daniel Defoe's London, Honoré de Balzac's Paris, Mariano José de Larra's Madrid, James Joyce's Dublin, Joseph Roth's Vienna, and so on. Textually transmitted urban images have such a powerful hold on the mind that, on visiting the cities to which they refer, one is always surprised by their evanescence. Inevitably, a rush of impressions supersedes them, keeping the visitor from ever conjuring up again the cultural image in its pristine state.

In a philosophical sense, to ask about the formation and replacement of city images is to ask about the production of social space. In a celebrated work, called, precisely, *The Production of Space*, Henri Lefebvre discusses the difference between works and products. Works are the result of spontaneous or freely creative activity, while products stem from repetitive, programmatic action. This distinction corresponds to a more fundamental one between "representations of space" and "representational spaces." The former are tied to the relations of production and to the "order" those relations impose, and hence to signs and codes that subtend knowledge. "Spaces of representation" embody complex symbolic systems "linked to the clandestine or underground side of social life" (Lefebvre, *Production* 33). In a sense, Lefebvre's distinction between "representations of space" and "spaces of representation" characterizes the opposition between the two images, the "rose of fire" and the "city of ivory," in the title of this essay. Not only is space produced, but the spaces that result from the planned development of our living environment are increasingly visual in character. "They are made with the visual in mind," says Lefebvre (75). This does not mean simply that the visual may conceal the process by which space is produced,[1] that it may perform an ideological function, but, more crucially, that space is becoming increasingly perceptual, that it is grasped and used through the power of images and that these images are the locus of an ideological struggle to determine the uses of space. The visual objectification of space is especially marked in the city, so much so that the city has been defined "as a historically specific mode of seeing" (Donald, "The City, the Cinema" 92). Although it would be an oversimplification to claim that in each historical period the city is attended by a recognizable "structure of visibility," it is true that in each period one can find struggles for dominance between modes of seeing and also between the symbolic images produced by these modes.

The outcome of such struggles and the ensuing configuration of a given space is not a linear process based on univocal causation. In the first place, as James Donald remarks, "The past exists as the projection backwards of present concerns" (*Imagining the Modern City* 123). This means that disputes over the cultural definition of place modify the spaces of memory and the memory of spaces, so that our historical understanding of urban processes is suffused with the processes in which we ourselves are inserted. In the second place, even if one holds to an evolutionary idea of urban change, one should not conclude that the visual identity of the city is simply the result of the accrual of signs on the urban palimpsest. An adequate understanding of the urban imaginary must include mediations and mediators: the social groups that dispute among themselves the nature of the space they produce, the cultural workers who project images, the media that broadcast and disseminate them, and the institutions that foster them and contribute toward stabilizing them. This means that knowledge of a specific social space must include the social relations accompanying its appearance, as well as the cognitive factors, genuine or ideological, that contribute to the image whereby this space is apprehended as a social fact.

Considered in this way, the image is hardly straightforward. Even when offered to immediate apprehension, it is in the first place not transparent but factitious. It displays a striving for a pattern, a symbolic effort to subsume social conflict under visual coherence. For this reason, an image of social space is always an after-image, in two senses: a lingering impression and a pattern superposed on previous ones whose outlines can still be traced in the new image. In this second sense, city images—and perhaps all images of space—are inherently historical. Like the doors to the houses of Saumur in *Eugénie Grandet*, such images beg to be decoded, thereby offering themselves to a different apprehension from that allowed either by mediated representations or by the pragmatic interaction between self and place. Although the relation between the historical and city images seems axiomatic, it may itself be historical and may no longer apply to recent spatial configurations. This would be the case with the non-places of "supermodernity" studied by Marc Augé. Non-places are non-identitary locations that do without (or do away with) the traces of history. As the paradigmatic loci of supermodernity (Augé's term for the contemporary world), non-places are narrowly associated with images, to the point that, according to Augé, we are becoming accustomed to limiting our relation to the world to that which can be accessed through images (*Anthropology* 122). The association of images with supermodernity does not contradict my assertion that non-places evade the logic of the after-image. Super-modernity is characterized by the disappearance of the social, understood as the relational dimension of human action; non-places do not symbolize this dimension. Furthermore, the image world Augé speaks of—"perhaps the only world that we can speak of today" (*Anthropology* 122)—is the world of the immediate present, a one-dimensional world devoid of tem-porality and flattened onto the superscreens of the society of the specta-cle.

Augé is aware, of course, of the intrinsic complexity of the image. He acknowledges that "the image also functions as memory, reference point, imaginative creation or re-creation; in this way, the world of the image, like that of the individual, is more like a dimension or a compo-nent" (*Anthropology* 108). And this is precisely what I try to convey with the term "after-image." But, in linking the image to spaces that deny temporality and to the city-as-spectacle, Augé alerts us to the possibility that after-images themselves may be residual components of a super-seded way of looking, traces of a structure of visibility tied to modernity and conceptualized at dusk, when scholarly owls exercise their retro-spective vision. In any case, I am concerned with the dialectics of the image of a historical place as it comes into modernity, though my con-clusion raises the question of whether the globalization of this modern image does not entail its entry into the world of the spectacle. There-fore, I end with the question of whether Barcelona, like other so-called global cities, has ceased to be a place and has inaugurated its existence as a posthistorical non-place.

Modern Barcelona, that is, the image of the place bearing that name that emerged in the early twentieth century, is inseparable from the growth of the city after the demolition of its surrounding wall in 1855, the growth not only of the city's layout but also of the means of production and the essential mediations: political institutions, urban planning, and a cultural apparatus supplied by the modern art movement. An archaeol-ogy of this image would have to trace the modernizing impulse to a key moment a few years earlier. In 1843, during one of the many popular re-volts for which Barcelona came to be known, citizens armed with crow-bars and pickaxes tried to demolish the city walls. They were fighting for living space. A population of 150,000 was confined inside the medieval perimeter of the city and prevented by the authorities from building within two kilometers of the walls, the range of the cannons. Two years earlier, Pere Felip Monlau had published a reasoned plea for the demoli-tion, *Abajo las murallas. Memoria sobre las ventajas que reportaría a Barcelona y especialmente a su industria la demolición de sus murallas que circundan la ciu-*

dad (1841). Monlau describes an untenable situation presenting serious health and social hazards. This may be one of the few cases in modern history when a failure of city planning provoked an uprising and led to the formation of a revolutionary junta to administer the city's affairs (Trillo 10). The rebellion was quickly suppressed by the troops and citizens were forced to rebuild the wall.

Let us pause for a moment on this image. Barcelona: a town captive within its walls and policed from a citadel almost the size of the civilian area. This internal fortress, planned by the Flemish engineer J. B. van Verboom after the fall of Barcelona to the Castilian army in 1714, inscribed repression in the spatial structure of the city. From the citadel, and from the fort perched on top of Montjuïc on the opposite side of the harbor, the army could easily bombard the city. In 1843 General Van Halen fired over one thousand projectiles at the city, setting the price for civil disobedience at more than four hundred destroyed houses—a small price compared to the twelve hundred houses razed in 1714 in the Ribera district to make room for the citadel. In 1856, General Juan Zapatero again bombarded the city, though somewhat more selectively. He rubbled *only* the working-class neighborhoods of Sants and Barceloneta, leaving the center undamaged.

Authorization to bring down the walls finally came from Madrid in 1854. In the next thirty years over sixty thousand buildings were erected and, on April 20, 1897, a royal decree formalized the incorporation of the surrounding municipalities already swallowed up by the metropolitan spread. The annexation added 174,000 to Barcelona's almost 334,000 inhabitants; the number reached 533,000 in 1900. By 1905 the city covered more than 14,826 acres of land, about four times the area of Madrid and three-fourths that of Paris. This race for space, fueled by demographic growth and increased consumption—despite a very high rate of illiteracy among workers, Barcelona had one sixth of all the bookstores in Spain—made liberalization and a degree of political autonomy indispensable. Yet Spain's municipal laws constrained Barcelona to the same administrative dependency on Madrid as that applied to provincial capitals of fifteen thousand. To change this state of affairs, Barcelona's oligarchy organized a reform party known as the Regionalist League. Under the league's aegis the city became a modern ideal and Barcelona Spain's chief modern city. From the turn of the century to the late 1920s Barcelona rose to the level of urban myth. In addition to performing other ideological services, this myth accommodated the bourgeoisie's conception of the city as a platform for political action. Texts from this period make numerous appeals for Barcelona to become "a great metropolitan capital," "the instrument of a renascent people," "the new Paris of the South," and so on (Solà-Morales 143).[2] Another purpose of the myth was to dispel Barcelona's notoriety as a rebellious city, a reputation frankly exploited by Madrid's politicians to justify their tight grip on Barcelona's life and finances.

Thus, before considering the struggle between these two images of urban space—the city as revolutionary battleground and as a rostrum for social virtues—we need to establish what these two conceptions had in common and what was lost or forgotten in the gap between their two irreconcilable fetishes, the bonfire and the sculpture. Caught in the grip of reciprocal fear and hatred, both the reformist bourgeoisie and the revolutionary working class lost sight of the power that thwarted their conflicting aspirations. Above the Catalan social classes but defining the political arena in which they clashed, the state deployed its own logic, without regard for the urban fabric of coexistence. It was an absolutist logic or, in Lefebvre's translation, the logic of absolute space, an abstraction, certainly, but one that commands the highest cathexis as the fetish of fetishes, since it is "the locus and medium of Power" (Lefebvre, *Production* 94).

A SHORT HISTORY OF THE GRID

Historically, absolute space emerged in the wake of the conquest of the Americas. The same monotheistic conception that justified the subjection of peoples in the name of the universal spirit of Christianity subtended the discoverers' claim to the "new" lands in the name of Christian monarchies. Unlike medieval acts of conquest, which were vindicated as spoils in the struggle for the "true" faith, taking possession of the New World involved an act of erasure prior to the actual conquest. Claiming ownership of previously unknown lands proceeded under the assumption that these territories were a "virgin" extension of the known world and were therefore subsumed under the universal law instituted by the Christian God's original act of creation. Thus, to lay claim to a land in the name of the Christian monarchy was an act of creation ex nihilo, or more precisely, it derived its power from that originating act. If the newly discovered lands happened to be already occupied by bodies, then these were regarded as a mere aspect of space, exactly like rivers and mountains, and like the flora and fauna of the New World. Through baptism, those bodies could be re-created and integrated into a boundless spatiality and temporality (marked by God's attributes of infinity and eternity), the universal empire that Castilian functionaries and ecclesiastical figures had envisioned since the middle of the sixteenth century. This act of cosmological violence inaugurated the disappearance of place and its replacement by space. If Aristotle, in accord with the ancient world, assumed the essential heterogeneity and particular "power" of places, modern thinkers from Descartes to Leibniz completely disregarded the nongeometric meaning of location. By the middle of the seventeenth century, William Gilbert could haughtily affirm that "place is nothing, does not exist, has no strength." But, as Edward Casey remarks, "it has no strength (*vim*) and does not exist precisely because it has been denied existence and power by those who prefer to locate strength in space" (Casey 135). In 1687 the penetration of physics by theocratic principles culminated in Newton's *Philosophiae naturalis principia mathematica*, in which the author dubbed "absolute space" the modern space of conquest and infinite expansion. Throughout this space, which Newton describes as "an emanent effect of God" (quoted in Casey 148), the same physical and metaphysical laws can be found at work, just as each colonial mission and viceroyalty contains the symbols of the same imperial power.

Rather than collapsing with the breakdown of the empire, the logic of absolute space pervaded the modern conception of the state both in its Hegelian form, as manifestation of the universal idea, and in the related claim that the state is the only plausible (and even legitimate) agency of universalization. Whether as destroyer or as sponsor, the state is a powerful producer of urban images. In 1860, shortly after General Zapatero shelled the working-class districts of Barcelona, a royal decree decided the future shape of this city by imposing the project of a civil engineer, Ildefons Cerdà, on a reluctant City Hall (fig. 5.1). In November of the previous year, the city council had selected an altogether different plan drafted by the architect Antoni Rovira i Trias (fig. 5.2).

Government interference in municipal affairs was by no means rare, but the question that arises is why did the government favor Cerdà's plan? A possible answer is that Cerdà was able to take advantage of his political connections. As a previous member of the state's Cuerpo de Ingenieros (Engineer Corps) and a former deputy in the Spanish Cortes in 1851, he could have appealed to well-placed Madrid friends. Yet this explanation (which has been given), however plausible, is misleading. There is no evidence that Cerdà ever solicited official intervention on behalf on his project, or, for that matter, that the government supported Barcelona's expansion. In a strange departure from the usual practices, the topographical survey of the large area outside the old ramparts, the Pla de Barcelona, was not undertaken (or financed) by the government but by Cerdà himself (Roca 158–59). Then why did the government prefer Cerdà's project to the others? The answer lies in bureaucratic thinking. Cerdà's plan may have found favor because it reflected officialdom's predilection for a particular division of space, one that is easily surveyed and facilitates administrative control as well as rapid military maneuvering. Its topographical organization was, in any case, familiar to Spanish legislators.

Since 1513 the grid had been systematically deployed in all new Span-

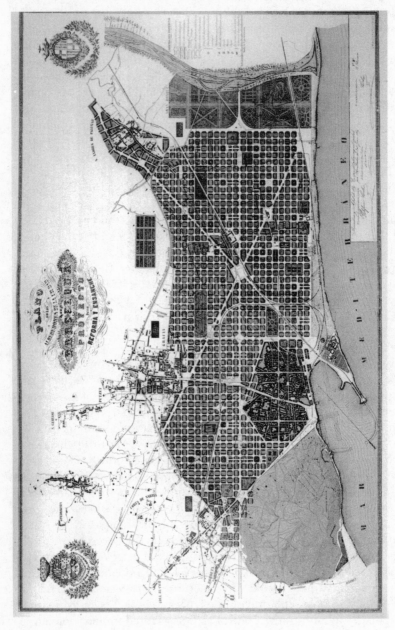

Figure 5.1 Blueprint of the project for Barcelona's Expansion (*Eixample*) by Ildefons Cerdà (1859). Ajuntament de Barcelona-Urbanisme.

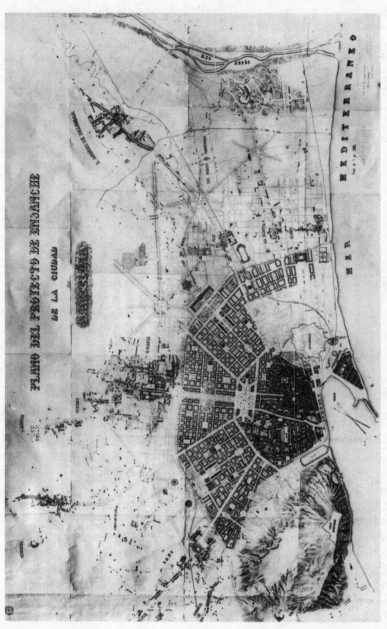

Figure 5.2 Project for Barcelona's Expansion (*Eixample*) by Rovira i Trias (1859). Ajuntament de Barcelona-Urbanisme.

ish-American towns following royal instructions, later published in the *Orders for Discovery and Settlement* (1573). In these colonial settlements the town was laid out on a grid extending from the central square, or Plaza Mayor. Its space was arranged hierarchically in terms of proximity to the center, but otherwise appeared homogeneous. In this way, the town's configuration allowed for potentially endless expansion in a form that disregarded geographic or tectonic conditions, preparing the way for the sprawl of modern urban development. Charles V's 1526 decree anticipated the pattern of forced urbanization that has characterized modernization throughout the world. Spanish settlements in the New World were to be rationalized so that "even if the population increases greatly, [the town] can be extended and expanded in the same manner." And growth was to be promoted through forced resettlement of the subject population: "Let them be settled by Indians and natives" (quoted in Trillo 13). Although Lefebvre warns against generalizing from the concrete conditions of the creation of urban space in Spanish America, pointing out, for example, the different function of the grid in the transformation of New York City after 1810, it is possible to draw a historical link as well as a functional analogy between these precedents and the case under consideration. In North America as well, the development of grid cities erased the physical and cultural spaces that preceded them, even if, as Richard Sennett points out, in the North this erasure eliminated rather than colonized preexisting space.

In the Hispanic world, colonization meant that spatial neutrality (as produced by the grid) was punctuated by auratic sites of power, the sees of spiritual and material orientation. In this respect, Sennett's observation that gridded space "subdues those who must live in the space, but [by] disorienting their ability to see and to evaluate relationships" (60) is not borne out by the colonial gridwork that characterizes the Spanish mode of neutralizing difference. There is, however, no denying the efficacy with which this kind of space modulates the experience of those trapped within it. It was the efficiency of the grid as a spatial-administrative machine that made it attractive to the absolute monarchy. Soon, what had proved effective in the colonies was redeployed on the Iberian peninsula with a view to enhancing the Crown's control over the ancient kingdoms. In this way, colonial forms of domination were reflected in peninsular territory. These ranged from the enactment of language laws modeled on the decrees for the eradication of the indigenous American languages (Lüdtke 142),[3] to the deployment of the provincial grid on formerly diverse political spaces in order to homogenize them and, in the process, nullify the centuries-old guarantees of the Iberian peoples, the *fueros*.

It would be wrong to infer from this history of authoritarian space that Cerdà was complicitous with Spain's centralizing bureaucracy. Biographical evidence points in the opposite direction, showing, for example, that during the short-lived federal republic of 1873, Cerdà, then vice president of Barcelona's Diputació, threw his lot with the federalists. There is no question that an egalitarian view of society underlies his geometric plan, which may in turn be seen as the foundational image of a democratic city (Roca 161). It is well known that Cerdà conceived his project to combat the massing of workers in the poorest districts of the old city, where lack of space and poor hygienic conditions resulted in a life expectancy of only 25.7 years for Barcelonans in 1855 (today Catalonia boasts Europe's highest life expectancy). Furthermore, there is now general agreement that Cerdà's plan forestalled the emergence of problems—like automobile traffic—that would have proved intractable with the realization of Rovira i Trias's project. But it is also true that Cerdà's ideal of equality was based on an extreme rationalization that entailed the abstract leveling of all social conditions; on an ideal, therefore, that could easily merge with the ideology of centralization. His abstract idea of social justice depended on the elimination of irregularities to the point of boredom. Thus, in his *Teoría de la viabilidad urbana y reforma de la de Madrid* (1861), he valorized monotony in the terms of a democratizing ethics: "Justice requires, demands, imposes that uniformity and equality that fools call *monotony*. Justice is always equal and uniform for everybody. In this sense there is no greater monotony in the world than equality before the law."[4] (*Las cinco bases* 130). One obvious problem with this universalizing principle is that it not only posits absolute equality before the law, but the validity of only one law, which thus becomes absolute and ahistorical.

Cerdà's rationalistic project partook of nineteenth-century social ideals. Nonetheless, if his *Teoría general de la urbanización y aplicación de sus principios y doctrinas a la reforma y ensanche de Barcelona* (1867) took stock of hygienic conditions and sought a balance between urbanized space and human pressure on the land (the Eixample was intended to have a low density, 250 people per 2.5 acres), the application of the theory to Barcelona's expansion soon fell prey to the profit motive. The potential for this perversion was inscribed in the plan itself: regular geometric divisions invited further subdivision, expanding the limits of density tolerance. After all, Barcelonans had been living in cramped quarters for several centuries and had no taste for the airy, garden-like quadrangles flanked by two rows of buildings that Cerdà placed at the core of each new block. Even if we take into account its frustrated utopian dimension, the grid set the stage for a historical dislocation, for a city ensconced in the ideology of growth, an ideology based on the rationalization of progress, whose clock always keeps modernity time. Cerdà considered himself a progressive, even a socialist. But his fascination with new technologies and his concern for a livable city with hygienic conditions for all went beyond the progressive's wish to overcome traditional limitations. In contrast to his humanist defense of the autonomy of the home and his faith in its socially regenerating potential (*Teoría general de la urbanización* 406), he conceived a completely penetrable city connected to a network of mobility, with homes as mere stopping places in world traffic (*Teoría general* 272). In this way, he anticipated the insertion of Barcelona into the network of global cities in a world that had yet to come into being. The underside of his city plan, however, also announced new forms of subjection through central planning and the "rational" use of space. History—the history of capitalist speculation—has resolved the tension between humanist ideals of individual freedom and the modern requirement for greater social control by reducing the autonomy of the home to its minimal expression in the stacked apartment boxes that cover large tracts of modern cities, and by sealing up the city by funneling traffic through toll roads and hyperpoliced airport gates, whose regulation falls to the state or to the agencies to which the state delegates this function.

Space produced according to the dictates of power achieves only reproduction. Despite his faith in progress, Cerdà created a homogeneous space in the image of the centrally administered territory that all of Spain had become after its organization into provinces in 1833. While geometrically divisible space generated enormous profits, it also tended to erase historical references by subjugating locality to extension. This result was in tune with the state's conception of the territory as an abstract administrative domain. The city was thus literally caught in the tension between its old historical core and the modernity of the grid. Efforts to harmonize the two by reforming the center, as proposed in the Baixeras project of 1881, came to nothing, partly because of the resistance of owner associations and partly because of a lack of governmental support (Sánchez de Juan 15). Cerdà himself made no concession to history and wasted no thought on how the old city might dovetail into the new.

Unlike Rovira i Trias's plan, which would have preserved a spatial image of the city's growth by inscribing the bourgeoisie's expansive perspective in a fanlike structure of boulevards originating at the historic center, Cerdà's Eixample, consisting of twelve hundred blocks 436 feet on each side, gives the impression of a city without beginning or end, infinitely expandable as long as land is made available for speculation. Rationalized even more radically than the Paris of Napoleon III, Barcelona thus expanded in an inexorably regular manner, as a "checkerboard" stretching toward the outlying villages and interrupted only by the two rivers flanking the city on its north-south axis, and by Europe's longest avenue, the "Diagonal," on its east-west one. Fittingly named for its purely geometrical character, this boulevard became the backbone for the spread of reproducible quadrangles with no limits other than the impassable orography of hills and rivers and the proximity of historical settlements, which could, nevertheless, be absorbed by the metropolitan integuments.

Toward the end of the century, with only one third of the Eixample actually completed, dissatisfaction with the monotony of the grid and its lack of relation to the historical city gathered strength. Soon architecture challenged the indifferent quality of the space constructed with the help of a ruler, and architects such as Gaudí, Doménech i Montaner, and Puig i Cadafalch fought horizontal boredom with their imaginative use of the facade, or by introducing monumental structures such as Doménech's new Hospital de Sant Pau, Gaudí's Sagrada Família, or the new Industrial University, which break up the regularity of the plan and produce their own insular spaces. Another way of resisting the leveling effect of the grid was to turn it into a repository for local memory. In 1864, Víctor Balaguer, a leading historian of reemerging Catalan culture, proposed using the new streets of the Eixample as a surface of inscription for the key persons, places, and episodes of Catalan history, with the objective, as he put it, "of creating a historical and harmonious general setting or plan" (quoted in Llobera 339). Accepting his proposal, city hall assigned historical names (rather than numbers, as in rationalized Manhattan, or the names of trades, as in old Barcelona) to the streets of the Eixample, turning the latter into a compendium of Catalonian history, from its medieval expansion and annexations to its modern struggles, including its distinctive political institutions, literary, philosophical, and scientific luminaries, military and political leaders, and the principal areas for the country's entrepreneurial activity: Commerce, Navigation, and Industry. Balaguer's intention was clearly to reestablish mnemonically the historical continuity of the city map that the grid had broken.

SUN, BULLS, AND FIRE

A more emphatic contestation of public space emerged during revolutionary episodes, with the adoption of spatial tactics, such as throwing up barricades, blocking streets, and disrupting communications. During these revolutionary interludes a radical attempt to change the image of the city was made by setting religious buildings on fire. These incidents recurred so frequently and were so widespread that they seemed programmatic, as if the revolutionaries, by deleting certain architectural phrases, hoped to turn the city into a different text. The tensions between the rationality of planning and the "intrusions" of various forms of resistance ultimately meant that the public image of modern Barcelona became inseparable from civic struggles against the dominance of absolute space.

From the turn of the century to the mid-1930s, two images vied for the status of Barcelona's "public image." One celebrated the rationality of the grid, while the other resisted it, although both turned their backs on the past. Lynch defines the city's public image as one that condenses the fragmentary perspectives of city dwellers (46). Nonetheless, it can also be conceived as a dominant "icon" resulting from a protracted struggle for representation. Insofar as it issues from an effort to resolve discrete perceptions and ideological needs, such an image enjoys the status of a myth. In this sense, the city image is not the mental or chemical imprint of a perceived object but an after-image. In other words, the public image of a social space is not on the order of representation but of mediation. It does not reveal a natural morphology but a synthetic resolution, and, as we will see with the *noucentista* city, its ideological value is predicated on this very synthetic power.

Underneath the city's fungible appearance, Lefebvre perceives a system that consumes enormous amounts of energy; for him, the city "is in effect a constantly burning, blazing bonfire" (*Production* 93). Although this is a felicitous metaphor for the urban process in general, the bonfire became so closely associated with Barcelona at a literal level that the image reached a second degree of lyricism when this city became known as "the Rose of Fire" in the early twentieth century. It is no exaggeration to say that Barcelona owes its modern image to its quarrelsomeness. In modern times this city has been Spain's foremost stage for the class struggle and for the struggle against the centralized state (indeed, against the idea of the state). Engels remarked that Barcelona's history counted more barricade battles than any other city in the world (481). Few other cities have destroyed as much architectural patrimony during revolutionary upheavals (or in speculative ventures, for that matter).[5] Such cycles of destruction permanently altered the look of the city. Where religious architecture was once prominent, now only a few monuments stand stranded in secular space.

In Barcelona the second half of July is a hazardous time. Occasionally, the sultry heat combines with political turbulence, setting off colossal potlatches,[6] as in the notorious mid-summer weeks of 1835, 1909, and 1936. Three times in the span of a century, Barcelonans offered fellow citizens the spectacle of a burning city, gutting scores of Church buildings in a nugatory effort to overthrow the social matrix.[7] Each of these explosions of the underlying social antagonism indelibly etched Barcelona's revolutionary image, while contributing, paradoxically, to the European look that for many visitors distinguishes this city from other Spanish towns. In 1873 Edmundo de Amicis wrote that "Barcelona is, in appearance, the least Spanish city of Spain" (12). Many other travelers, before and after, have made similar remarks. In 1840, after an extensive tour of Spain, Théophile Gautier found that "Barcelona resembles Marseilles in its aspect, and the Spanish type is hardly more visible here." He observed, however, the oppressiveness of the walls: "Barcelona feels a little stiff, a little tense, like all cities girdled too closely by a jacket of fortifications" (374).[8] In 1929 Henry de Montherlant exclaimed: "On leaving these stifling and stifled cities . . . a great city, finally! the only one in Spain!" (39).[9] One reason for this impression may be precisely the impact of the fires on a city that was never distinguished for its monumentality. As a result of the architectural losses, the city became more lively and populist; it exchanged the aura of the religious and artistic patrimony for commercial conveniences such as shops, markets, arcades, and hotels, and popular pleasures like cafés and theaters.[10] Its most popular promenade, the Rambles, took on its cheerful aspect in the years after the first round of convent burnings. It is possible, of course, that the urban inscription of cultural difference is not primarily the product of nineteenth-century upheavals but a *longue durée* phenomenon. The Spanish historian Luis García Valdeavellano, in his *Sobre los burgos y los burgueses en la España medieval* (Madrid 1960), maintains that "in Spain, Catalonia is probably the territory in which the formation and development of the towns, of urban life and of bourgeois social groups in the Middle Ages is most similar in its evolution to the formation and development of towns and of the bourgeoisie in other European countries" (quoted in Sobrequés 82). That being the case, the history of Catalan towns, and of Barcelona in particular, may explain not only the physical aspect of urban space but also the nineteenth- and twentieth-century revolutionary interludes by embedding them in a long genealogy of struggles for civilian control of the city.

It is useful to distinguish, following Michel de Certeau, between a tactic and a strategy as discrete approaches to concerted action. The tactic necessarily operates in the space organized by an alien law, while the strategy develops on its own terrain. By holding and even defining the territory, the strategy may introduce panoptic practices to control the image (Certeau, *Practice* 35–37). Although a tactic is discontinuous and "takes advantage of 'opportunities'" (Certeau, *Practice* 37), each attack on Barcelona churches contained traces of the previous one. Without exactly being a repetition, each revolutionary moment seemed to incorporate a memory of the preceding one, taking up the struggle again at the scene of a drama that had once seemed a revolutionary triumph. Each of these events lingered as an after-image in the social memory. The concept of "after-image" can thus be refined to include, along with the idea of dialectical image, the notion of the trace, of the delayed effect of impressions in the social consciousness, much as retinal impressions endure beyond the time of exposure.

By claiming a direct relation between a long cycle of popular upheavals and the modernization of the city's aspect and "feel," I do not mean to imply that the assaults on religious buildings obeyed a conscious plan to redesign the cityscape. Nevertheless, if, as Victor Hugo claimed in *Notre Dame de Paris*, architecture, and especially medieval architecture like the cathedral, was a preprint form of writing (Pike 52), then the summer events in Barcelona might be understood as a form of counterwriting. Although the participants had no overall strategy other than to combat the reaction in what they considered its headquarters, they were tactically destroying the visible symbols of the system of duties and prohibitions imposed on the working class. Like their forerunners taking the Bastille in 1789 or setting fire to the Braunschweig Palace in 1830 (and later the Tuileries and Paris town hall during the Commune in 1870–71) (Beyme 40), time and again the Barcelona populace capped the first stage of revolutionary violence by setting fire to a symbol of repression. Yet, on each of these occasions, recourse to this highly symbolic and scarcely effective form of subversion seemed contingent on impulses of the moment (and on socially inherited models of action) rather than being articulated in a long-term plan for political struggle. In this too, the revolutionaries showed themselves incapable of mastering the logic of calculation and exhibited their inherent weakness in the deployment of symbolic violence with an intensity that was proportional to their lack of hold on the time of strategic dispositions, a time that alone could have guaranteed the minimal chance for a revolutionary claim on the future.

On Saint James's Day in 1835, in the midst of a dynastic war, Barcelona's populace attacked the regular orders. A popular song from the period blames the mutiny on a disappointing afternoon at the bullfight:

On Saint James's Day—of the year thirty-five
there was great jesting—in the bull pen;
seven bulls came out—none of them brave:
this was the reason—why the convents burned.[11]

Although the turbulence that eventually focused on the convents began in the bull ring, the bullfight itself was merely tinder for the explosive mood in the city. Earlier that month, there had been rumors of a conspiracy by the monks, who were deeply implicated in the civil war, fighting on the side of the absolutist pretender, Charles V. On the twenty-second, in the town of Reus, some sixty-five miles south of Barcelona, a group of militiamen had been waylaid and killed by Carlists. A militiaman was said to have been crucified and his eyes pulled out by a friar in the Carlists' company. The rumor prompted an assault on the convents of that city, two of which were set on fire, while the populace killed as many friars as it could lay its hands on (Tasis 316). Whether tradition is right to blame a disappointing bullfight or whether the "federal principle, always active," according to the conservative Marquis of Miraflores, explains Barcelona's riots in 1835 (Anguera 45), one thing is certain: the clergy had become an object of popular hatred for Barcelona's lower classes, who amply belied Richard Ford's confident assertion about Catalans: "These fierce republicans and defiers of the sceptre have ever bowed abjectedly to the cowl and crosier" (2: 692).[12] Whatever the long-term civil relation to clericalism, the clergy's support of the absolutist camp during the Carlist war goes a long way toward explaining the people's delight at the sight of crumbling vaults and arches and their lack of compunction about murdering friars. A journalist of the time, Joaquín del Castillo y Mayone, bore witness to the mood on July 25, 1835:

> Amidst this confusion the city was calm: all the house tops were crowded with spectators, neighbors chatted gaily from the balconies, at shop entrances and in the streets themselves. Those who were more curious placidly visited the burned places, celebrating the horrid fracas of the crashing vaults, considering that this was the only way to get rid of the gnawing plague of cloistered monks, who have been the bane of humankind. Men, women, and children with smiling faces turned back home, satisfied with the thought that from then on there would be no more friars. (Castillo 13)[13]

Watching the religious city disappear, these citizens believed that the newly secularized space would inevitably become liberalism's own. Their hope was fulfilled to some extent, for, as historian Jaume Vicens i Vives explains, that night of destructive frenzy decided Catalonia's future: "By deepening the rift between Carlists and liberals, [this crisis] left the bourgeoisie on the side of the latter, sharing . . . the joy of 'seeing the monastic institutions suppressed'" (232–33).[14] The bourgeoisie had practical reasons for casting its lot with the liberal cause and looking with pleasure at the outcome of the uprising, if not at "the violent means used for the purpose" (Pi i Arimon, quoted by Vicens i Vives 233).[15] Not only did the bourgeoisie fail to protect the convents, but, as Vicens i Vives remarks, at a time when the textile industry was expanding in Barcelona, each industrialist had his eye on a convent where he dreamed of installing his loom (Vicens i Vives 232). There are indications that the revolt was less the doing of a crowd infuriated by a boring bullfight than a timely episode prompted by a complex mixture of passions and interests backed by the popular demand for disentailment of the large monastic properties. Another contemporary, Josep Coroleu, wrote in his *Memorias de un menestral de Barcelona (1792–1864)* that the insurrection was characterized by the regularity and deliberateness of the destructive work, which proceeded as if those who executed it were following a plan laid out in advance (Tasis 317–18).

The scene of burning convents heightens the connection between the definition of space and the consumption of images. As some economists have pointed out, the upheaval had the perhaps unintended effect of clearing space in a walled city that had reached its saturation point. Subsequently, the comparatively large plots of land occupied by the convents could be employed to increase the number of residences or to install the industrial plants that were transforming Barcelona into Spain's industrial spearhead. Notwithstanding the eventual uses of secularized space, the momentary fascination with the spectacle of destruction transcended bourgeois aesthetic categories. The crowd, though calm and cheerful, was not immersed in disinterested contemplation, nor was it spellbound by a sublime experience. The pleasure it felt stemmed from the consumption of an image that was a consuming image, one that exhausts itself and leaves a void behind. Something was no more, and the image of its cessation captured a moment of freedom: freedom to imagine, to anticipate another image that would be illuminated by revolutionary fires—an afterimage.

DANSE MACABRE

In 1909 the circumstances were different but the fascination was the same. The social dynamite had been piling up throughout the spring and summer in the form of labor unrest, but the spark was the embarkation of reserve soldiers for Morocco, where the colonial army had suffered a serious defeat. Most of these soldiers were factory workers with families to support. Discontent mounted by the hour after the troops began to embark on July 9. On the twenty-sixth the protest against what many in Barcelona called "the Bankers' War" reached insurrection proportions, turning into armed rebellion when workers of the Gràcia district fired on soldiers and began to build barricades. Ensconced in their homes during the long week, the upper classes anxiously deciphered the meaning of every shot and every rumbling, cheering when a cannon discharged because the implications were unequivocal. At no point did they attempt to stop the arsonists or to defend the convents, as spokesmen for the religious orders bitterly noted. The dominant posture was simply to look on. Throughout the city people watched the fires with an apprehensiveness that did not rule out festivity. In the Eixample, someone played the Marseillaise and people applauded from the balconies (Coromines 77).[16] Even the soldiers sometimes turned into fascinated spectators. After General Santiago escorted the Piarist fathers from their residence, his detachment positioned itself on the other side of the street to watch the entire block burn (Ullman 209).

Attitudes on site were quite different. Bystanders generally applauded the arsonists, and in some neighborhoods residents prevented firemen from putting out the fires (Coromines 78). By midnight of the second day of the rebellion, twenty-three churches and convents had burned in the heart of Barcelona, where troops had been concentrated, while in the un-patrolled suburbs only eight convents were attacked (fig. 5.3). By the end of the week, twenty-one of fifty-eight churches and thirty of seventy-five convents were ashes and rubble (Romero 515).[17] The distribution of the fires is instructive. Although they occurred in suburban areas such as the residential Les Corts and Sant Gervasi, and in the industrial districts of Sant Andreu, Clot, and Sant Martí de Provençals,[18] they were clustered downtown, above all in the historical area and in the upper-class zone of the grid. While this distribution is consistent with the higher density of re-ligious buildings in the center, it also suggests an effort to alter Barcelona's image by scarring its core districts. Then as now, Barcelonans regarded the urban core as the city's most symbolic space and, conse-quently, as the site where action could readily have symbolic implications.

On July 18, 1936, action converged again in the center, with most of the heavy fighting taking place in Plaça de Catalunya, in the Drassanes bar-racks at the lower end of the Rambles, and in the area around the univer-sity. The concentration of the fighting in and around the plaza was moti-vated by the tactical importance of this open area. It was here that F. Theo Rogers, a British reporter, saw the workers charging army positions and noticed the military significance of controlling the plaza's tall buildings, which dominated the old town and the passage to the newer part of the city (Cortada 4). Again churches burned throughout the city as people watched from balconies or from the street (fig. 5.4). But this time there was no pleasure in the spectacle. There seemed to be little point in the re-production of an image that had become grossly pretextual. It was not that it seemed trivial or ineffectual; rather, it seemed belated, dislocated, or out of focus. In 1835 the burning convents had gratified a crowd of all ages. During the Tragic Week the same sight had furnished entertainment while people waited for the troops to put down a revolt. By 1936, in the midst of a workers' revolutionary clash with a military putsch, the scene had no intrinsic sense. It drifted into the present like an after-image of by-gone struggles. In his memoirs, architect Oriol Bohigas recalls watching the spectacle of Barcelona consuming itself from the balcony of his fam-ily's apartment, and remarks that, at the time, that vision shook many an ideological conviction (*Combat* 85). The image of patrimonial destruction was now atavistic and politically counterproductive; it no longer coincided with the revolutionary cause or even with political awareness. The Tragic Week had exhausted itself in a pointless attack on Church property, while the rebels neglected to occupy the factories and the centers of govern-

Figure 5.3 Burning religious buildings during the Tragic Week. Partial view from the slope of Montjüic (1909). Courtesy of the Arxiu Fotogràfic de Barcelona.

ment, finance, and the military. In 1936 the workers avoided the second mistake but could not prevent a relapse into anticlericalism—such was the power of the image in which the revolution recognized itself.

When we speak of social space, it is important to ask who produces it, what agents alter or reinforce its meanings. Who were the incendiaries in 1909? The reports mention groups of youngsters, as well as working women and prostitutes. Pere Coromines mentions groups of eight to ten people who gathered at the sound of whistles and chimes. In most cases, the arsonists were lightly armed, yet they were almost never disturbed in their action. Their political motivation was vague. Anticlericalism was certainly ingrained in the lower classes, but circumstances in July 1909 did not justify its exacerbation. Even after the fires had started, many religious communities did not believe they would be targeted. A stupefied priest declared: "In 1835 we deserved it, but I can't understand the present burnings" (Llates 162, quoted in Romero 534). There was a manifest lack of political direction behind an uprising that began as a protest against the conscription of workers for an unpopular colonial war and veered into Church bashing. This development supports the hypothesis that the ideological mainstays of organized labor, anarchism, and Catalan republicanism had not yet deeply penetrated the working class. Instead, the rebels' behavior was consistent with the anticlerical slogans of Alejandro Ler-

Figure 5.4 Church of Belem in the Rambles on July 19, 1936. Photo by Pérez de Rozas.

roux, professional agitator and leader of the Radical Republican party (Romero 539).

Because architecture, like urban planning, inscribes social controls in space, each flaming church revealed an effort to change society by altering its spatial referents. Churches and convents displayed the hierarchy that ordered urban life. Hence, in razing these emblems of ideological domination, the revolutionaries hoped to undo that very hierarchy. Yet there was something carnivalesque about this drama, as if the insurgents knew it could not last. Their grim fascination with the exhumed corpses of religious women became an index of despair about a freedom they knew to be ephemeral (fig. 5.5). Breaking religious taboos, like breaking the surfaces of streets, merely suspended the ordinary distribution of space. Burning churches attested to a trespassing on hallowed ground, while cobblestones, torn up and piled high in parapets and barricades, hindered the traffic they had once facilitated. Spatial relations prescribing movement and orientation were radically altered. A barricade thrown across a street or a sniper on a rooftop instantly changed the spatial code. A collapsing church altered the meaning of a district.

What is the relation between cobblestones and cadavers, between the urban and the gruesome? One possible answer is that, while tearing up the pavement challenges the organization of space, the macabre, for its part, upsets the division of space between the dead and the living. The Tragic Week was, at face value, a spontaneous reaction to the social distribution of the duty to die *elsewhere* for certain consecrated causes: king, honor, fatherland. There was nothing extraordinary in this challenge. Revolution is inherently profane: it subverts the most general and unquestioned assumptions, calling into question the principles that regulate society in order to expose the arbitrariness of even the most fundamental prohibitions. As Bruce Lincoln observes, "The rule of respect for the dead is a social construction propagated by the members of society for the good of society but still transgressible by those who define themselves as standing outside and in revolt against the established social order" (114). With the collapse of the urban and moral orders, the idea of death mediated by the chief social institutions is likely to break down as well. Or conversely, the rituals of exhumation, unequivocally restricted to the exposure of religious corpses, clearly aimed to shake the pillars of social morality, which in Spain were inseparable from the centuries-old Catholic dominance on all matters of secular comportment.

Yet the secular idea of social struggle fails to fully account for the shocking spectacle of exposed cadavers in a modern metropolis. The shudder that ran through the Spanish middle classes as they learned of this turn of events can only be compared to the horror inspired by the democratizing Dance of Death in the Middle Ages. In the visual representations of the

Figure 5.5 Exposed corpses of nuns. Tragic Week (1909). Courtesy of the Arxiu Fotografic de Barcelona.

danse macabre Ursula Link-Heer notes a proclivity to critique the social order, to display cynicism, and to engage in the burlesque and the obscene. Hence, these representations abandon the sphere of the sacred, lifting the repression of laughter before the image of death and opening the floodgate to excess (Link-Heer 89). Unlike the massacre of monks in 1835 and the assassination of priests and religious persons in 1936, in the summer of 1909 anticlericalism took on a sensational rather than a homicidal dimension. It extended into the modern era those medieval images of dancing skeletons that had threatened the gloomy severity of death installed at the center of the social order. There was nothing casual about this "analepsis." Spain's backward-looking Catholicism, still hegemonic in a country that was staging its modernity, made such outbursts of medievalizing excesses not only possible but inevitable.

Every broken taboo lowers the status of the sacred. When that happens, the transgression endures in the social imaginary as an after-image of powerlessness rendered fleetingly triumphant by the tottering social order. Powerlessness is, so to speak, temporarily reversed, as the dominated combat the auratic images that mediate their subjugation. It is difficult to agree with Lincoln when he asserts that no act of iconoclasm is ever

carried out with the intention of destroying an icon's power, that iconoclasts act with the assurance that the icon is powerless or even that there is
no such thing as sacred power. Here again, the secular standpoint proves
exceedingly limited. Sacred images are vested with social power and it is
precisely this power that iconoclasts defy when they attack its symbolic
concentration in the image. Lincoln comes very close to accurately describing the dialectic of the image when he explains that "it is [the iconoclasts'] intent to demonstrate dramatically and in public the *powerlessness*
of the image and thereby to inflict a double disgrace on its champions,
first by exposing the bankruptcy of their vaunted symbols and, second,
their impotence in the face of attack" (120). Iconoclasts may well be nom-
inalists, but without the certainty of the image's power they would not
make an attempt against it. Ineffectual representations do not inspire hatred. An image is defiled not because it is felt to be symbolically impotent
but in order to render it so. Iconoclasm is performative. Like consecration, it relies on the concurrence of certain conditions of validity. The act
of disgracing a symbol does not merely enunciate the disgrace; it brings it
about.

Often, however, the social inversion lasts only as long as the "rituals of
collective obscenity"—to use Lincoln's apt phrase—which, like all rituals
of inversion, actually display powerlessness in the fleeting view of a society
upside down (see Turner 168). Perhaps for this reason the most ghastly
images of the Tragic Week were provided by women and a simpleton. The
scene began when a woman claimed that her sister had been martyred in
the convent of the Hieronymite Nuns. Incited by this tale, a group of
women entered the convent and opened fifteen tombs. After finding
corpses of nuns tied hand and foot, they believed they had uncovered tor-
ture practices within the religious orders, and in an effort to persuade the
authorities to intervene against such practices, they conveyed the caskets
to city hall. Some of the women dragged corpses to a barricade on Carme
Street. There, in a spell of black humor, the men holding that position decided to carry the cadavers to the homes of Eusebi Güell and the marquis
of Comillas, patricians who owned shares in the Rif iron mines, for the
benefit of which the war was being waged. While the gruesome cortege
proceeded along the Rambles, Ramón Clemente García, a twenty-two-
year-old collier, earned fatal notoriety by dancing with the corpse of a
nun. On October 4, he stood before a firing squad.

The execution of rebels brought a sharp end to the carnival spirit and
reinstated the taboos. It was now the bourgeoisie's turn to reimagine the
city. Soon everything was back in place: the churches rebuilt, the streets
repaved. Idealism grew like new skin over the wounds of the city, casting
a new image. Outlined against a smokeless sky, a city of marble and
golden domes appeared like a vision. Reclaimed for the Logos, a classical

city conceived as the embodiment of rationality now took over the scene. But before one image tipped over into the other, a third image fleetingly mediated between the memory of destruction and the brutally reconstituted idealism. In this suspended image we catch a glimpse of an elsewhere, of a metaphysical space lodged in the fractures and wounds of the physical city.

The ashes from the fires were still smoldering when the poet Joan Maragall endeavored to turn the image of the burned church into an emblem of reconciliation and a space for healing. He hoped to hush the clamor for heavy-handed repression, but, beyond that, he resorted to an urban icon marked by conservative piety *and* revolutionary passion. In doing so, he was proposing a new public image of Barcelona. With the irruption of the class Other, recent events had exposed the condition that Rob Lapsley, following Heidegger, calls the inevitable ruinance of city life (186). Maragall strove to suture the rent symbolic order by appealing to an Other of the Other and inviting the city to recognize itself in the ruins. Beyond destruction there was love, he asserted, and yesterday's revolutionaries could become tomorrow's builders if they were allowed to rebuild after their fashion. Substituting the language of otherness for the language of class identity, he tried to mediate between the antagonists by evoking the burned church as an image of the unified social subject. Certainly, this subject was idealistic, but it was not utopian. Its site was never in doubt. In the eviscerated church, on the altar exposed to sun and rain under the crater of the fallen vault, the two cities could be reconciled. In his vision, the sooty temple became the stage for social catharsis. Though a fervent Catholic and a respected member of the bourgeoisie, Maragall discomfited the *bien pensant* readers of the Regionalist League's paper, *La Veu de Catalunya*, by criticizing the Church as a class institution. Worse yet, he compared anarchism to primitive Christianity, asserting that, by rights, the temple belonged to the very people who had wrecked it. Inert and soporific, the old church had resonated with vague, unintelligible words; it had sent out an exclusionary message. Now, doorless and gaping, windy, and full of flies, the church was once more Christ's "natural Church," a place for social communion. Maragall admonished his fellow bourgeois citizens not to rebuild it in the old image:

Do not take [the Church] away from them by rebuilding it; do not raise stronger walls or build a tighter vault, do not place iron-clad doors on the hinges. These things are not its best defence . . . and you would lull yourselves to sleep once more. Nor should you ask the state to protect your church. In some respects it already looked too much like an office in the eyes of the people. And do not take too much money from the wealthy in order to rebuild it, lest the poor think it belongs to the other side and mistrust the donation. Let them rebuild it themselves, if they want it: in this way it will be after their liking and only then will they love it. ("L'església cremada," quoted in Benet 200–201)[19]

To this vision the Church responded by armoring itself. After the Tragic Week, many temples had their doors reinforced with iron. Convents imitated defense architecture by opening portholes and embrasures in their walls (Coromines 154). Maragall's mediation failed. The city of anarchy and the city of order succeeded each other the way a hangover follows a binge. After the debauchery of destruction came the debauchery of repression: thousands of detentions, over two thousand courts-martial, confinement or exile for many. And, beyond the individual punishments, the entire left-wing press was shut down and 150 lay schools and civic centers were closed by a civil governor newly appointed to crack down on the rebellious city.

If life had been difficult while the city, cordoned off and deprived of power and services, turned eagerly to the spectacle of its own destruction, it became unbearable a week after the resumption of order. A privileged witness, Pere Coromines, notes that, in a city of six hundred thousand, no one asked for clemency when the first death sentence fell (quoted in Benet 129). This observation is inaccurate. In another article, "La ciutat del perdó" (The city of forgiveness), Maragall beseeched the bourgeoisie to be merciful. But Coromines could not have known about the article, because *La Veu de Catalunya* had declined to print it.

Neither this attitude nor this social vision of the city was new to Maragall. Eight years earlier, in "La ciudad," he had already visualized compassion as a force lighting up and unifying opposite images of the city. Compassion permitted a phenomenological synthesis by bracketing the perceived social divide through the intervention of an eidetic form stemming from the Christian imaginary. "It [the city] has districts where, behind a picturesque poverty, throbs a destructive hatred; and others in which frivolity luxuriates comfortably with a disdainful insolence. And all of a sudden you see a glimmer of piety making both [sides] shudder and turning them into brothers" (Maragall 269).[20] Extrapolating from the Christian terminology, we may ask: what is this energetic flicker of emotion that bridges social difference and unifies the city? The answer must be: the intuition of a common need for a spatially situated community to protect itself from brutal depredation by the state. Maragall's perception of a fraternizing energy is nothing but the affirmation of a primordial, and thus sacred, local structure of habitation. Since the state accrues its power by eroding local power, it instigates internal conflict to undermine the civic network of relations on which municipal power depends:

A political state may rule and combine [the cities] well or badly and for more or less general purposes; but their inner life is sacred and inviolate, because it is the live spirit of a world that is both older and higher than the state and all its external combinations.

For this reason any action that, originating outside the city and its spirit, tries to direct its inner life is a profanation; and its instrument must be rejected as an alien and harmful element. Everything inside the city that serves those external combinations and sacrifices its spirit is a treason that must be denounced and punished. Everything inside that means hatred, personal selfishness or the germ of barren destruction must be uprooted and cast away. (270) [21]

In 1909 history put Maragall's vision to the test, and the city's spirit, which, like a talisman, should have preserved Barcelona from the external combinations of power, failed to materialize. Was this civic spirit a sentimental idealization of a reality that had always been riddled with conflict and fragmentation? Yes, if idealization is taken to mean the utopian desire for a seamless community of interests and a perfectly socialized urban space. Emphatically no, if it implies that Maragall was oblivious to class stratification and the social encoding of space. In this article he anticipated, albeit in vague terms, the events of 1909:

At times the city becomes congested, breaks out in a mutiny that shouts horribly: hot hatred clashes with cold, savage force, terror spreads and blood runs in the gutter of the agitated streets . . . ; and when the shadows darken this or that finally empty square, people stroll peacefully along the streets that were a battlefield just then, as if suddenly sobered of their recent hatred. Oblivious to everything, they head for the brightly lit pleasure palaces, in whose depths the germs of terrible catastrophes are already working. (269–270) [22]

"Ah! Barcelona . . . ," the first of the three articles written in response to the Tragic Week, explicitly discusses the city as successful or hindered sociality. Maragall perceives Barcelona as an imperfect, unrealized city, at odds with a similarly underrealized state whose only effective branch is the repressive apparatus. Many citizens would have agreed with the poet thus far. But that was not all he had to say. Rather than a reified organization of space, he saw the city as a massive confluence of energies in need of suitable expenditure. "Here we have a huge concentration of individual energies which have not been able to create a social organism commensurate to its mass" (quoted in Benet, 104). [23]

Under the influence of a certain kind of organicism, Maragall conceives the city as an aggregate of simple beings in the throes of developing a superior organization. A milieu is created within an ill-defined enclosure through the accumulation of anomic energies that do not find release in socially complex functions. As Lefebvre observes apropos of living organisms, it is the nature of energy that it be expended. "In effect—he says—energy must be *wasted*; and the explosive waste of energy is indistinguishable from its productive use" (*Production* 177). Discharged energy alters the nature of space. Whether one regards its effect as constructive or desublimating depends on the ratio between energy and its available channels. In short, it depends on the differentiation and diversification of social functions.

Maragall knew the ambivalent potential of human energies massed in urban space. For him, destructiveness is merely another name for frustrated creative impulses: "Bombs and blasphemy are one and the same thing: a destructive release of the incapacity to create" (Benet 104).[24] Beyond the principles of production and accumulation subtending the industrial city, the poet discerns a different principle at work: namely, gratuitous expenditure, denial of asceticism, excess. If economic rationality controls energy consumption and reproduction, Maragall, for his part, affirms the existence of an irrational economy surpassing both the satisfaction of need and the calculation of cost. Implicit in his vision of Barcelona is a theory of gratuitous expenditure. Dangerous and transgressive when arbitrarily obstructed, "civic enthusiasm" fires the irrational consumption and self-consumption that Maragall considers the fundamental social drive. "That which in life's unhappiness is hatred and in contentment egotism: it's all the same, lack of love; and love is the first social reason, the generator of organisms, and the only power" (Benet 104).[25]

Like many intellectuals at the turn of the twentieth century, Maragall was confronted with the phenomenon of the urban masses. Still reeling from the impact of the July events, the bourgeois press harped on the negative connotations of "masses," making use of the pejorative term "mob." Maragall took this term from the conservative press and turned it on its head, exposing the shallowness of current social analyses. At the very moment when the lower class was being morally lynched, he referred to the bourgeoisie as "the other . . . the conservative mob" (quoted in Benet 114).[26] By extending the concept of "mob" to include both sides of the class equation, Maragall alters its conventional association with plebeian unruliness to connote the enticements of anomy that impede the apprehension of the city as a meshing of mutually dependent parts. When this understanding fails, first the city, then the entire nation, are degraded to an abstract aggregation of elements.

If this were the lasting image elicited by the Tragic Week, then the nature of the city's social space would not offer any problem to the observer. "Seeing Barcelona deserted, Catalonia wasted, any traveller could say: Maybe there was a large population here, but certainly there never was a people" (quoted in Benet 105).[27] Urging the bourgeoisie to reflect on the causes of the outbreak of social violence, the most distinguished *modernista* poet was inevitably led to question the aptness of current concepts to define the collective body that had been shaken by the recent events. As it happens, concepts such as "people," "crowd," "mass," in both their Spanish and Catalan versions, were, as Hans Ulrich Gumbrecht claims, "symptoms for the impossibility of experiencing the new social realities from the perspective of the traditional intellectual roles" (877).[28] Maragall stipulates a meaning for *poble* (people) that clearly evades the traditional "vague reference to the lower classes" and points in the direction of "the new thought of 'people as sovereign'" (Gumbrecht 877),[29] so much so that his distinction between a mass of individuals and a people hinges on the availability of human forces capable of producing an advanced social space.

The paradigm for such a space is the city, which the poet considers a more concrete and consequential reality than the state. Yet the city, by which Maragall unequivocally means the modern city, is not the only concrete form of organized sociality. To the extent that it resolves the tendency to fragmentation and ruinance through a creative articulation of energies, the city unfolds a higher form of interdependence: the nation. Incidentally, Benedict Anderson's definition of the nation as an "imagined community" is meaningful only in a literal sense, namely, that the nation is inextricable from images, first and foremost images of social space. But if the term is taken—as it often has been—to mean that nations are figments of the imagination and have nothing more than an ideological status, then it becomes trivial and even false. Anderson does in fact infer the nation's imaginary existence from the truism that it can never be intuited in its totality. But this applies equally to most social constructions, including the city. Hence Lynch's insistence on its imageability, its need for a Gestalt. Are we therefore entitled to say that the city is an imagined community? Most emphatically, yes, if by that we mean that it is objectively apprehended through piecemeal interactions and discrete acts of perception, recollection, and anticipation, and that it is subjectively appropriated through totalizing images from various sources: art, philosophy, urbanism, politics, etc.

Maragall's image of the burned temple is one instance of imagined community. By opening up imaginary space, it makes room for the obscene, for that which escapes conventional representation. As an image of love—which is socially unrepresentable and thus a constant challenge to representation—the ravaged church was an attempt to mediate between a revolutionary image that struck at society's metaphysical underpinnings and a prescriptive image monumentalized by the champions of authority. But the time was not ripe for this kind of double exposure.

THE CANON OF SOCIAL BEAUTY

Turning a conservative page on the history of Catalan modernism, an emerging group of writers and artists, the *noucentistes*, vowed to reestablish the Logos in space. With them, aesthetics came to the aid of administration. *Noucentista* aesthetics was formally classic but methodologically baroque, since it was visualized through concept and allegory. In practice this meant that, in order to found the city of reason, the *noucentistes* had to reinvent abstract space. More accurately, they had to produce space abstractly. Consequently, they appropriated many of the city's materials, actors, functions, and relations, but the image they produced erased the discontinuities among those elements. And, with the loss of contrast, the fragments of experience faded into the icon of a city reimagined through the nostalgia for order.

Curiously, this yearning for restraint—the obverse of the bourgeois fear of the mob—did not appreciably alter the city's physical layout. In the end, Barcelona was transformed more profoundly by speculation than by preemptive planning against revolts. Instead of being redesigned for repressive purposes or pacified through a rehabilitation of the old districts and the defusing of the immediate causes of rebellion, the city was, above all, fetishized. Its new image, if not its reality, seemed to transcend the crisis exposed by turn-of-the-century anarchist bombs and by the Tragic Week. But magical transcendence is deceptive. An allegory of order is not order itself, nor is civility a police matter. And the *noucentista* city, confirmed in its ideality, failed to mediate between antithetical images. Eugeni d'Ors, *noucentisme*'s chief theoretician, had already sidestepped Maragall's warning against social anomie by confidently announcing that "throngs, no longer the image of Chaos, will be definitely organized, or even better, *vertebrated* into a City" ("*Les multituds* d'en Casellas," *Obra Catalana* 86).[30]

With d'Ors the City appears at a convenient level of generality without ever losing the singularity of myth. Capitalized, the term "City" denotes the transition from the common city (or the city of commoners), a place qualitatively differentiated from other places, to the capital city, the city as absolute space. It is the stage on which the law of urban life or "civility" effectively counters the dissolving forces of "nature" embodied by the urban masses. Not coincidentally, a neo-Orphic mythology subtends d'Ors's works in the theme of the struggle of reason against the natural world. However, merely to point out the mythical background of d'Ors's rationalism does not advance our understanding of *noucentisme*'s urban ideal. To move beyond the observation that reason is ideologized by means of the ideal City, we must historicize that ideal.

By 1900 the balance between town and country in Catalonia had tilted definitively toward the town and *noucentisme* expressed the new urban hegemony.[31] D'Ors defined this movement in explicitly urban terms: "In Catalonia *Noucentisme* is qualified by this fact: the city becomes conscious of its cityness" ("La ciutat i les serres," *Obra Catalana* 327–28).[32] For this new intellectual movement, the city becomes the locus of moral, cultural, and political absolutes. Urbanity colonizes the countryside,[33] while in the city the bourgeoisie "civilizes" the working masses. *Noucentisme* gave doctrinal expression to the imperialism of the town over the territory. In its view of things, the city is not merely a concentration of human and material resources that offers multiple opportunities, it is, above all, a civilizing category. Even more than the engine of economic expansion, the polis appears as the privileged site for the articulation of the legal order and, consequently, as the model for the organization of national life.

Turning mountains into architecture, as d'Ors proposed in 1907, anticipating the wildest expressionist visions of a Bruno Taut,[34] meant in practice subjugating, and thus impoverishing, the traditional forms of life and the local economies. With a lofty gesture, d'Ors presented the City not as one space among others but as the only space imaginable from the summits of reason. His "Catalunya-ciutat" (Catalonia-City) names more than a thoroughly urbanized territory. Even from a strictly geographic viewpoint, it is not clear whether, in this city-nation, Catalonia stands in metonymically for Barcelona or whether Catalonia itself is actually imagined as an immense suburb reaching out from its dominant city. In reality, one interpretation implies the other. On the one hand, d'Ors's concept of *civiltat* (cityness) is the inverted image of Barcelona's pathos of growth in the camera obscura of ideology. On the other hand, this growth and the resulting political concentration already announced the vanishing point toward which the countryside was driven at the turn of the twenty-first century. Today Catalonia has been urbanized to such a degree that formerly distinct categories like town and country merge in the ever-expanding suburbia and bedroom communities of the Barcelona conurbation. Traces of the vanished peasant milieu become aesthetic markers in the village homes and beach apartments of urban vacationers. At the same time, Barcelona has regained its status as a capital city, its "capitality," and a certain capacity to organize Catalonia's political space.

Representations of the city as the space of a fully developed citizenship are commonplace in *noucentista* literature. Guerau de Liost, the group's emblematic poet, played with the meanings of "citizenship" in his 1915 "Ciutadania integral" (Integral citizenship). Rather than membership in a state or mere residence in a city, citizenship stands for the integration of nationality, urban life, and a normative code of behavior, all of which are resolved in the concept of capitality. In his account, the City articulates what is spontaneous or instinctual in the nation's existence; thus it "represents the conscious moment of our nationality" (873).[35] Logos conquers bios just as the town triumphed over the country.

This victory of abstraction gives a particular slant to Anderson's notion of imagined community. As a secondary reality subordinated to biological facts, the civil community exists only in the imaginary structures of rational consciousness. Like Anderson's nation, the *noucentista* City is the manifestation of a particular stage in the culture of humanity; therein lies its civilization value. In contrast, the nation exists in habits and reflexes that are transmitted unreflectively and can be genealogically or geographically bounded. Furthermore—and here is another point of contact with Anderson—as long as collective life remains on the national level, it cannot be intuited as a whole. But this impossibility, far from making the nation a ghostly idol, demands the articulation of its sensual aspects in a consciously designed, hence more artificial, social form. In short, the nation's prereflective form of social existence begs to be condensed in an image. Out of this need emerges the City, which, like the ego in the psychic economy, must learn to manage its representations to negotiate a balance between competing demands: "The Nation starts out as an almost material fact and only later, as it articulates and raises itself, looming as a City over its immense expanse and wielding the pacifying trident, does it become a true psychological fact" (873).[36]

Neptune's pacifying trident is not a gratuitous mythological reference. Associated with a deity who holds power over sea currents and tempests, the City—and Barcelona's world-historical ascent was indebted to its status as a seafaring city—appears as a superior agent capable of subduing the modern forms of agitation and engendering a composed social psychology. Thus the very concept of the city is tinged with the classical aesthetics from which *noucentisme* derived its ideal of civil equilibrium. Inheriting the classical role of the city as *imago mundi, noucentista* Barcelona came to represent, or better yet, to image, the Catalonian national space, bringing it into sharp and self-conscious existence.

The aestheticization of the political by *noucentisme* has, in fact, classical roots, the same roots that feed its insistence on imaging the city. As Philippe Lacoue-Labarthe remarks:

> The political (the City) belongs to a form of plastic art, formation and information, *fiction* in the strict sense. This is a deep theme which derives from Plato's politico-pedagogical writings (especially *The Republic*) and reappears in the guise of such concepts as *Gestaltung* (configuration, fashioning) or *Bildung*, a term with a revealingly polysemic character (formation, constitution, organization, education, culture, etc.). The fact that the political is a form of plastic art in no way means that the *polis* is an artificial or conventional for-

mation, but that the political belongs to the sphere of *techne* in the highest sense of the term, that is to say in the sense in which *techne* is conceived as the accomplishment and revelation of *physis* itself. This is why the *polis* is also "natural": it is the "beautiful formation" that has spontaneously sprung from the "genius of a people" (the Greek genius) according to the modern—but in fact very ancient—interpretation of Aristotelian mimetology. (Lacoue-Labarthe 66)

Techné as revelation and highest accomplishment of *physis:* this is exactly what Guerau de Liost holds the City to be when he defines it as the conscious accomplishment of the unreflective, almost material existence of the nation. For him too, the city is a beautiful formation rooted in the natural existence of a people and reflecting its particular character, its "genius." Guerau's organicist view of the city, however, was not shared by the chief intellectual authority of *noucentisme.* D'Ors abhorred the idea of the primacy of nature; consequently, he invokes the city's purported classical origins to justify its superordination to every natural entity, including the "nation." If the city transcends the nation—and d'Ors has no doubts that it does—it is not because it focuses the nation's energies and turns them into self-knowledge. For him the city is not the noblest organ of the national body but a reality of a different order. It originates in sovereign human intervention in the fallen realm of nature. Stemming from the Logos, the city is the form of reason in space. Is it thereby a space of enfranchisement, as medieval townships were? D'Ors suggests it is. Conceiving freedom as a release from nature, he praises the state as the supreme expression of will: "Ceaselessly we must glorify the State—the superb arbitrary creation—and fight the Nation—the fatal yoke" ("Per a la reconstrucció de la ciutat," *Papers* 300).[37] Illuminated by the ratio, the state renders the political field perspicuous. It founds perspective by establishing a center and fixing the proportions of social life.

To tradition, d'Ors opposed the consciously crafted social bond. His city emerges from the destruction of patrimonialism, not as a reborn Phoenix but as a futuristic entity. "The splinters of Thrones will burn in the hearth of the future Republic. From the ruins of Nations we shall build the City" ("Per a la reconstrucció," *Papers* 300).[38] Seen from this perspective, the polis is not a historical creation that grows and changes over time, but a timeless political category. This ideal form reorders a space that was previously constituted by a variety of subjects, reducing historical diversity to virtual homogeneity in an optically dominated telos.

In an early article (1904), he describes the city as the canon of social beauty. "Perhaps you are of immortal lineage. And just as Greek statues have become the definitive mold of human beauty, the city may prove to be the definitive mold of social beauty" ("La casa i la ciutat," *Papers* 285).[39] It is easy to see that d'Ors's aesthetics was parasitic on an ideal of civic harmony, itself contingent on a certain political praxis.[40] In 1918 he gave aphoristic expression to this coercive aesthetic ideal: "There is no salvation away from beauty" ("Towianski, II," *La Vall de Josafat* 70).[41] However, the emphasis on the word "definitive" in the previously quoted passage should not be overlooked. This word places harmony above contingency and thus foresees the final synthesis of an implicit dialectic. But if likening art to politics aestheticizes politics, it also politicizes art. In early twentieth-century Catalonia the postromantic deployment of classicism was unmistakably political. Nowhere is this so evident as in d'Ors's programmatic manifesto of 1911, *La Ben Plantada* (The Elegant Woman), or in the emergence of the poet-politician Jaume Bofill i Mates, alias Guerau de Liost.

A sculptural image of the city presented as canonical space also subtends Guerau's 1918 *La Ciutat d'Ivori* (The City of Ivory), a collection of poems echoing the Platonic vision of the city in *noucentisme*. The first poem, "Pòrtic," evokes an unreal skyline wrought in marble and gold. This implausible image of Barcelona combines classicism with a touch of imperial decadence, though in fact its colors were inspired by the Viennese Sezession and were actually used in *noucentista* buildings (see Bohigas, "L'arquitectura," 15–18; and Bou 131). The City of Ivory is therefore doubly ideological: first because of its chimerical classicism, and second because it generalizes aesthetic practices that emerged under specific conditions.

Yet, more important than the materials deployed is the method that produced the spatial image. Whereas the Rose of Fire named an untamed beauty, the City of Ivory has been "wrought with orderly circumspection" and will, as a consequence, take "the garland of good sense—which is immortal" (Liost 331).[42] Crowned with the Logos, this city reiterates the Greek unity of form and function under modern industrial conditions. Its foundational rationality is supposed to pervade every aspect of life, ordering thought through the rigor and sobriety of the physical layout. Never mind that the final goal is presumed to be at the origin of this space, and the intended social balance is premised on the inaugural "orderly circumspection." Such a space can only be grasped by a balanced mind (this is the meaning of *seny*) capable of rising above the circumstantial. It is absolute space.

In "Ciutadania integral," Guerau de Liost tropes the concept of capitality (and of the capitalized city) by linking it to a figural Athens detached from its geohistorical moorings: "Every Capital is the expansion of an acropolis—and we give a spiritual sense to this word's etymology The acropolis gives it nobility, an urban tone. A city—without this divine unction of the acropolis—would be an impersonal city; it could be a large city, never a Capital" (872).[43]

Guerau allegorizes the etymology of "acropolis," dislocating its original topographic meaning of "upper city." Still, for all the abstraction inherent in this use of the term, the idea that every capital is an expansion of an original acropolis resonates with images of Barcelona's grid. And the association is strengthened by the fact that the Acropolis was originally a citadel, while Barcelona's expansion was advanced by the devolution of its citadel for civilian use as the city's first public park. But, in a stricter reading, the analogy is flawed by the evidence that the core of Barcelona is not an "upper city" but rather stands at sea level. From its original settlement by the shore it could only expand into the hills. The point is clear, however: Guerau's ideal Barcelona is (or ought to be) a summit of civility deserving of capitality, of the right to organize its own national territory. In this pseudo-archaeological image, "acropolis" is merely a figure of speech for the political anointment of a city.

A locality achieves representative value only through a harmonious relation with the territory it subordinates. In practice, however, political centers are generally traversed by tensions with their peripheries or by rivalries with aspiring centers. To check competition and promote the acceptance of their political role, capital cities often resort to the symbolism of universality, of image and reflection. Lefebvre notes that "the town perceives itself in its double, in its repercussions or echo; in self-affirmation, from the height of its towers, its gates and its campaniles, it contemplates itself in the countryside that it has shaped" (*Production* 235). Guerau says it explicitly: "Every capital city or Metropolis represents the elevation of a national value to the level of a universal human category" (Liost 872),[44] an infinitely multiplying image, therefore. Space is rendered absolute in the osmosis of national and urban "matter" through the thin, ideal membrane of the city's image. Yet—Guerau cautions—capitality is not a mixture, not a composite picture of regional diversity but an image distilled from the diffuse, specialized, fragmentary elements that make up national life. These elements, even if complementary and thus necessary to each other, are anecdotal. Tied to their surroundings through the networks of local economies, they can never encompass the national totality. Only the capital comprehends the whole in an integral image.

Consequently, the image of the city, or, for that matter, image-making itself, becomes paramount. D'Ors asserts that Mediterraneans are inherently iconolatrous and live on images. Aesthetics provides the atmosphere in which they breathe, move, and have their being ("Santa eficàcia," *Glosari* 103). And the city is their absolute icon. As a total work of art, it co-opts every skill, turning the collective organization of space into a display of the national spirit: "The city is the first plastic work in which all arts collaborate, from architecture to the lowest craft, in order to make it the monument of a people" (quoted in Peran, Suárez, and Vidal 17).[45] As Lefebvre remarks, absolute space "consecrates, and consecration metaphysically identifies any space with fundamentally holy space" (*Production* 236). The concept of "absolute space"—a term coined by Newton in 1687 and introduced by him into Western physics—is in fact theological, rooted in the two fundamental attributes of the monotheistic God: absolute duration and absolute presence. As Edward Casey explains, for Newton, "God *is* space; He 'constitutes' it through and through; space is thus 'an emanent effect of God'" (Casey 148). Absolute space is therefore infinite; meaning also delocalized, homogeneous, undifferentiated. It can be segmented, but each segment is filled with the same isometric principle, referring the resulting "units of space" to the regularity and homogeneity of the void that absolutized space has become.

Absolute space is ministered to and administrated by a priestly caste of political metaphysicians and image wizards who are capable of generating forms of identification that are at once localizable and generalizable (such as the grid, the acropolis, or the ivory skyline). Consecration is not only a metaphysical performance but also a political one. It presupposes a hierarchical conception of space and an intervention to realize this conception or to preserve it. D'Ors's doctrine of "holy efficacy" arises precisely in this context as a legitimation of the shortest distance between means and end in the production of absolute space. "Efficacy" means both proficiency and effectiveness. It denotes professional mastery (artistic, gnoseological, technical) as well as the integration of the various forms of social labor under the ordering gaze of the authorities. Neither a principle nor exactly an instrument, efficacy is enshrined as an ideological fetish. Raised to a metaphysical category, it drifts into authoritarianism, turning the *noucentista* city into the obverse of the Rose of Fire. In its name d'Ors rejects Maragall's mediating image, opting instead for a Manichaean split between irreconcilable urban and antiurban attitudes: civil and criminal, social and disreputable, the forces that build and those that destroy.

From the point of view of classical regularity, the Tragic Week was exclusively a surge of incivility, of anticity forces that had to be met head-on. This perspective left no room for tolerance or condescension—only for authoritarian control in the name of regularity and form, or even formulas. "The solution cannot be sentimental but civil. It must have a body, a concrete form. It must consist not in forbearance but in action: and not in a suggestion but in a formula. And despite the best of wills, it cannot yet lead to peace but to struggle" ("El problema del mal a Catalunya," *Glosari* 104).[46]

In October 1909, as the executions of those held responsible for the

Tragic Week were under way, the refusal to show leniency had unequivocal implications. Paradoxically, d'Ors's consecration of efficacy cut up the city's common space and violated its inner life, the two aspects of Barcelona on which Maragall predicated its claim to political autonomy. Calling for repressive action, d'Ors implicitly invited state intervention and thus the desecration of a civic sanctuary that Maragall considered prior to, and higher than, the state—hence his choice of the temple as a metonymic image for the city. To Maragall's claim that "the city is a unity engendered by love, and by love it must be ruled" (270),[47] d'Ors opposed an abstract city-idea bereft of living bodies: "May Plato help me to remind you and to remind myself that above the despicable little souls of men there is the great soul of the City. And our City wants to be saved, must be saved. We might fail to turn John Doe and Richard Roe into civil men. But Barcelona, but Catalonia, must win definitive Civility, even if we all die" ("Entre les runes de civiltat," *Glosari* 41).[48]

At the limit of idealism, d'Ors's Barcelona threatens to become a disembodied city where behavioral codes prevail over life. Clearly, this is d'Ors's response to Maragall's dirge "Barcelona deserta, Catalunya desolada," a lamentation triggered by the suspicion that the capital of Catalonia had become an abstract, quantifiable aggregation of interchangeable human units substituting for the distinct collectivity that only a people can represent. In Maragall's late romantic view, the people provide the political reason for the particular status of "place." Through the people Barcelona functions as a metonymic image of Catalonia, seen by Maragall as a sound box for a genius loci (whose voices can be heard in his poem *El comte Arnau*).

Maragall correlates place to the physical body. No soul of the city, no urban culture, exists removed from its national body. This is a far cry from d'Ors's willingness to pay the price of disembodiment for the triumph of an abstract principle, a price that is the corollary of his concept of space. For Maragall the city was a congregation of agents potentially resolvable into a citizenry through mutual exposure and recognition. In contrast, the *noucentista* City of Ivory is a teleological space marshaled from afar by an overruling image. Abstract and dispensed from the summit of power, like Cerdà's expansion, the City of Ivory embodies the exogenous centrality that governs its code. As an aspiring capital, this City organizes the cultural practices and dominant habits that define the nation, yet falls into abject dependence as soon as lofty contemplation gives way to such pressing matters as securing order and repressing revolts.

Maragall's vision of the burned church rebuilt by the arsonists resolved the class conflict idealistically, which is to say, not at all. Still, he was capable of thinking dialectically, resolving the polarity of the class struggle and the tensions between city and state. His appeal to the city's sacrosanct autonomy was a reminder of the instrumentality of the threshold and of the imaginary city gates. The threshold, as distinct from the boundary, invites, but for that reason it must be crossed with circumspection, not trespassed upon. It regulates voluntary association and self-administered socialization, hinging on a necessary degree of spatial agency.

In contrast to Maragall's sentimental appropriation of the city, d'Ors's concept of civility called for the rule of Law. And Law inaugurates a contradiction between, on the one hand, hierarchizing categories like code, concept, archetype, and idea, and, on the other hand, bodies, transgression, localities, materiality, and relativity, all factors that a Foucauldian reading would characterize as modes of "deviance." Insofar as the state is predicated on the rule of Law, or, in more explicitly Hegelian terms, insofar as the state is the manifest embodiment of freedom through the law, its existence engenders a contradiction between rationality and experience, impeding the metaphysical closure of the image. As a result, contradictions that originate at the historical level, that is, at the point of convergence between life and idea, are displaced to the spatial level, where they unravel in the visual simulacrum. Thus the image creates a blind spot in the understanding by *noucentisme* of the social processes it tried to manage. Given the terms with which d'Ors tackled the problem of accommodating the physical structure of Barcelona to fit its social organization and political function, he could not prevent contradictions from emerging in the very space where rationality fuses with politics.

What does it mean to say that space registers contradictions? How do they arise? Above all, what spatial forces come into play? Let me simply indicate the complex intertwining of space with the social processes of image creation. As Lefebvre remarks, contradictions in space imply a dialectic of centrality (*Production* 331). And since the political organization of space in reference to a center gives rise to centralism, ultimately the state's center supplies the power to imagine and the means to implement the city of (bourgeois) order. In d'Ors's less than idealistic account, the role of the state merges with the urban grid, envisioned as a tabula rasa for the deployment of "civility."[49] In the end, the City of Ivory requires the concourse of legislative and executive powers concentrated in the state capital. D'Ors's conviction that the city produces the state in the space left vacant by the demise of nations turns out to guide not just his urban imaginary but his political practice as well.

THE REVOLUTION AS AFTER-IMAGE

Noucentisme's dream of the City of Ivory blossomed during the 1929 World Exposition, which was designed to put an aesthetic face on the brutal state intervention in the space of the city. Shortly thereafter, the demise of the Primo de Rivera dictatorship and the electoral triumph of a reformist social democratic party, the Esquerra Republicana de Catalunya (Republican Left of Catalonia) under the leadership of Francesc Macià inaugurated a hopeful, albeit brief, period in Catalan politics. The Esquerra was the embodiment of Maragall's pleas for an autonomous and inclusive political space that could integrate the popular classes, bestowing symbolic efficacy on their potential creativity. Since this party strove to mediate in the conflict between the city of the bourgeoisie and the revolutionary city, it needed to produce its own urbanistic vision.

A modest though effective scheme for social improvement came with the Macià plan. This new reform of the built environment, devised by the GATCPAC (Grup d'Artistes i Tècnics Catalans per al Progrés de l'Arquitectura Contemporània—Group of Catalan Artists and Technicians for Progress in Modern Architecture), differed from the Eixample in that it was specifically designed for the working classes. Whereas Cerdà had brought the bourgeoisie out of decaying houses on narrow and overcrowded streets and into new apartment buildings in rationally laid-out boulevards and tree-lined streets, the Macià plan was meant to relocate workers from their hovels in the old city and the shanty towns on the industrial outskirts into a new space where urban life coexisted with the elements (air, light, water) of Barcelona's natural setting. This space was expected to satisfy needs and instincts, which, perverted by unregulated industrial development, turned the working class into a desperate, unruly social enemy. In effect, the Macià plan took into account Maragall's plea to redirect social instincts gone awry. Little of that plan was realized, because, as Ray Keenoy observes, "like most of Europe's hopes in the 1930s, it was to disappear under a tide of blood and destruction" (165). Of the Macià plan only a few buildings remain: a tuberculosis clinic, some school buildings and apartment houses, not enough to give an idea of an ambitious project conceived to overshadow the nineteenth-century Eixample, but which was destined to remain sketchy and incomparably less evident in the after-image of the resulting city.

From the early to the mid-1930s, Barcelona, like Catalonia, existed in anticipation of its shape to come, though still in the presence of the physical and economic structures of a dream hatched by centralization, liberal socializing intentions, and unbridled speculation. Keenoy's harsh judgment of Cerdà's Eixample and its political and economic constituency, the Lliga Regionalista, points out real contradictions in the ambitious but irresolute reformism of Barcelona's upper class: "fat bourgeois flesh laid on a democratic skeleton or a modernist chess board filled with medievalist pieces" (Keenoy 162). In the end, neither the Esquerra's political project nor its urbanistic blueprint could vanquish the ivory dream or placate the social violence that made Barcelona a medium for persistent images inspiring revenge and hatred as well as idealizations. The dialectical energy was still at its height, and even as it culminated in the World Exposition, the dream of the City of Ivory was illuminated, proleptically as it were, by the flare-up of the Rose of Fire in the summer of 1936.

Compared to Saint James Day in 1835 and to the Tragic Week, the attacks on churches in 1936 seemed less coordinated and more the action of uncontrolled groups. Syndicalist organizations did not countenance the destruction of Church property or the assassination of priests. Anticlericalism was doubtless a feature of anarchist culture, but in 1936 organized labor knew that its task was to reorganize production and dismantle the bourgeois state, an undertaking which could not go forward by repeating the scenes from 1909.

Eusebi Morell, a worker who served as council director in a collectivized factory during the Civil War, later recalled how, on the evening of July 18, he and fellow anarchists prevented a convent in their neighborhood from being burned down. Morell describes the arsonists as follows: "It was a group of men, women, and children. I can't understand where they came from. Even their clothing was not normal. They looked as if they were disguised as paupers, as indigent people" (Vilanova 412).[50] The question of this group's identity is intriguing. Why was their appearance bizarre by working-class standards? Was it a pose? An instance of conscious image production? An after-image from the past? There might have been a deliberate, though, as it turned out, poorly calculated counterrevolutionary move to exploit the destabilizing power of the after-image. According to historian Raimon Galí, on July 19, the Spanish army, defeated in Catalonia, sought to retaliate by provoking another tragic week. If true, this would explain why the weapons depot of Sant Andreu fell immediately to the lumpen proletariat, preventing organized anarcho-syndicalism from gaining control of the revolutionary situation (Galí). If, rather than spontaneous turbulence, this was a strategy, Galí's thesis would also explain the appearance, already on July 18, of the incendiary groups encountered by Morell.

Although suggestive, this explanation falls short of the mark. The attacks on churches were too widespread throughout Republican Spain and the participation of militiamen is too well documented to allow for a simple delimitation of agency between politically conscious revolutionary labor and the opportunistic riffraff venting its hatred on an obsolete or nugatory enemy. After the failure of the military coup and the flight of the bourgeoisie from Catalonia, the Church remained the visible representative of the reaction, fully enmeshed in the politics of the right-wing parties that had nursed the military rebellion and more exposed than ever by the Spanish bishops' collective statement in support of the fascist "crusade."

Regardless of the immediate political motives, the deployment of an after-image of the Tragic Week in July 1936 had its own logic. It may not be far-fetched to speak of self-parody, of the revolution quoting itself. In the scene recalled by Morell, a class-conscious proletariat confronts an apparently self-conscious lumpen proletariat reenacting its historical precedents. There seems to be a theatrical logic at work, as if, by wrapping themselves in an anachronistic image of a bygone revolution, the arsonists were trying to reassure themselves of their revolutionary legitimacy. Photographs of militiamen and-women jesting with ecclesiastical regalia and liturgical objects eloquently proclaim these people's self-consciousness before the camera. Even the casual, nearly cynical attitude of viewers of the mummies, which were again on display, bespeaks a detachment that can only be explained by the dissipation of every trace of the sublime (fig. 5.6).

Anticlericalism alone does not account for the images of excess from these revolutionary days. Something else must have been at work if churchgoing girls could find amusement in the contemplation of religious corpses. María Ochoa, then thirteen years old, would later remember the spectacle as a welcome diversion for the children:

> They dug up the nuns' corpses, too, and displayed the skeletons and mummies. I found that quite amusing; so did all the kids. When we got bored looking at the same ones in my neighborhood, we'd go to another *barrio* to see the ones they'd dug up there. In the Passeig de Sant Joan, they were exhibited in the street [fig. 5.7]. Not for very long, but long enough for us to go and look. We kids would make comments about the different corpses—how this one was well-preserved, and that one decomposed, this one older; we got a lot of amusement out of it all. (Fraser 152)

Underneath the dogged repetition of the images lies a mesmerizing energy. One way to understand the after-image is as a storage battery for optical and historical meanings that can be activated as mnemonic energy. In the 1920s Aby Warburg saw images charged with potential that could be unconsciously transmitted and turned to creative or deleterious effect by the temperament of a later period (Boyer 199). The comeback of the image, therefore, need not be a matter of deliberate or planned transmission. Outbursts of mnemonic energy elicited under historical pressure explain the phenomenon of transposed images more aptly than does a theory of reflection (inherent in the concept of strategy).

Bourdieu's notion of habitus also helps explain the puzzle of the "spontaneous" reenactment of responses under certain conditions. With Bourdieu what counts is not the reappearance of images defamiliarized by events, but the return of gestures and patterns of behavior that have been incorporated by agents on the basis of past experiences. As a scheme of

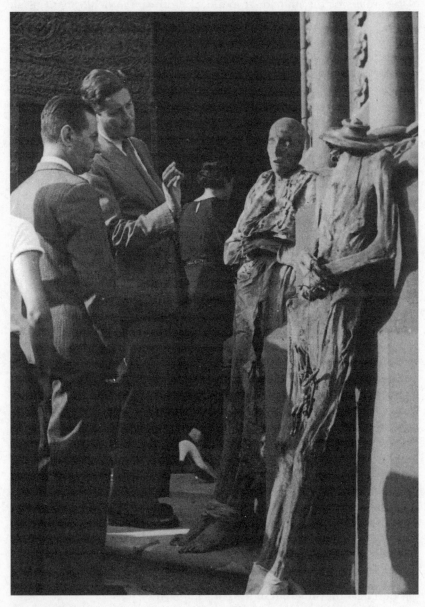

Figure 5.6 Convent of the Salesian Nuns. Mummies exhibited at the entrance of the building. July 18, 1936. Courtesy of the Arxiu Fotogràfic de Barcelona.

Figure 5.7 Mummies exhibited outside the convent of the Salesian Nuns on Passeig de Sant Joan in Barcelona. July 18, 1936. Photo by Pérez de Rozas.

perception and instantaneous evaluation, habitus allow agents to perform without the mediation characteristic of detached, intellectual reflection. Reacting to stimuli with a course of action adjusted to the situation (to its interpretation in light of the incorporated practical knowledge), agents confirm the presuppositions inherent in their roles. Like an actor, "the agent is never completely the subject of his practices" (Bourdieu 138). Thus, the arsonists and the exhumers of July 1936 acted out dispositions that had been incorporated over the course of a century of class struggles and that were called forth (anticipated, as it were) by the immanent tendencies of the response against military aggression, imposing themselves in the urgent situation with the self-evidence of a rote grammar of events.

A capricious thesis? Hardly. One glance at the mummies filmed on July 19 and displayed in Civil War documentaries suffices to emphasize the citational quality of the image. This most notorious "icon" of the Tragic Week, the display of the exhumed corpses of nuns, had been captured by Joan Gaspar in one of the earliest documentary films, *Los sucesos de Barcelona* (1909), and it held fast to the social imaginary. This image haunted the revolution (emerging too in the swift putrefaction of bishops in Dalí's and Buñuel's *L'Age d'Or*) through its elementary understanding of subversion as the breaking of taboos. Since churches had burned and corpses had been exhumed in 1835 and 1909, so again, in 1936, while organized labor stifled a military putsch and conquered Spain's industrial center, churches burned and cadavers of nuns were exposed to public view.[51] This time, however, it all seemed to be happening for the sake of specularity and self-recognition in the image. There was a perverse logic in the fact that these events were captured once more by the camera and a historical irony in the fact that they proved accessible to further decontextualization. Entering the space of technical reproduction, the city's afterimage generated its own dialectic in the world of images by being appropriated and instrumentalized by fascist film (see Resina, "Historical Discourse").

THE PERSISTENCE OF IMAGES

At the close of this third and last stage in the origin of the modern image of the city, the tension between competing identities of the same city was reiterated as a polarity between two different cities. As the purposes competing to define Barcelona's modernity were being torn apart by supreme violence in the name of the state, an archaic polarity that could no longer be represented (and, so to speak, mediated) by a common space took their place. In his pastoral letter, "Las dos ciudades" (The two cities), published a month and a half into the Spanish Civil War, the bishop of Salamanca, Enrique Pla y Deniel, used Saint Augustine's dichotomy between the earthly and celestial cities to exalt the military uprising as a God-serving crusade.

Although far from subtle, the bishop's antimodernism shrewdly displaced the struggle for the image of the modern city. In his pastoral address, the debate over the opposing class-based versions of the secular city was silenced in favor of an opposition between secularism and theocracy, into which a concrete struggle between the larger industrial cities and the small rural towns was tacitly encoded. Pla, himself of Catalan extraction, projects Augustine's dichotomy into social and geographic space, associating the city where temples burn and divine images are defiled—although unnamed, Barcelona is clearly implied—with Cain, the founder of secular cities. On the other side stands the heavenly city of heroic martyrs, ready to take up arms in the struggle between "order" and "anarchy" (Pla y Deniel 271–72; 293). Pla y Deniel also hints at this second city's identity in unmistakable terms. If the anarchist city belongs to the "sons of Cain," the celestial city is in the hands of those the bishop calls his own sons (312).

Hence Salamanca, Franco's government headquarters during the Civil War, is identified with the City of God because it is engaged in a holy crusade against the city of darkness. This antithesis liquidates the earlier contest between images of modernity, giving way to the gray postwar decades of enforced political dependency and urbanistic mediocrity.

Paradoxically, by setting in motion the resistance against fascism, the final revolutionary paroxysm in July 1936 ensured that the space of the city would be violated by a weakened state instrumentalized by exogenous forces capable of more efficient totalization. In May 1937, the revolutionary fires were extinguished by Republican troops sent to Barcelona to comply with the Comintern's counterrevolutionary watchword. The city was coming into an era of political dependence far beyond the influence of the nation and the single state. The embers were put out by Franco's occupation army on January 26, 1939. Reentering with this army the city he had left two decades before, d'Ors witnessed the reconstruction of ideological walls around the city and could see once more a spiritual citadel rising amidst the ruins of the subjugated nation. In the winter of 1939, vacated by thousands, the "saved" city gleamed with a pallor not quite that of ivory. Nor did it look like gold to the coldly ordering gaze.

For decades the fires endured in the collective memory as an afterimage loaded with dialectical potential, and they were literally rekindled as an image in the first film that reclaimed Catalan historical memory at the end of Franco's dictatorship: Antoni Ribas's *La ciutat cremada* (Burned City, 1975). Looking back at the formative years of Catalan nationalism in the aftermath of the Spanish-American War, the revisualization of the fires of the Tragic Week fulfilled a cathartic as well as a monitory role. On the one hand, the film, whose production allegedly began the day after Franco's death, reminded Catalans of their tradition of struggles for their collective rights; on the other, it sounded a warning to the bourgeoisie not to shirk its historical mission as it had in 1909 and, by implication, during the Civil War. In 1976, as Catalans were demanding that their Statute of Autonomy be reinstated, this critique of the upper classes had immediate relevance. Although it was much too early to update the historical record as far as 1936–39, the allusion to this period was apparent in the film's last sequence. The execution of Francesc Ferrer i Guàrdia, founder of the secular Modern School, reverberated with that of Lluís Companys, president of Catalonia during the Civil War and in the first months of his government's exile. Arrested in Paris by the Gestapo at the prompting of the Spanish authorities, Companys was extradited to Spain, summarily court-martialed and brought before a firing squad on October 15, 1940, in the moat of Montjuïc castle, where the executions also take place in the film.

Montjuïc is unquestionably a potent city marker, but also an ambivalent one. Victor Serge begins his novel *Birth of Our Power* (1931) with an image of this fortress and an allusion to the violence with which its stones are grouted:

> A craggy mass of sheer rock—shattering the most beautiful of horizons—towers over this city. . . . We would have loved this rock—which seems at times to protect the city, rising up in the evening, a promontory over the sea (like an outpost of Europe stretching toward tropical lands bathed in oceans one imagines as implacably blue)—this rock from which one can see to infinity. . . . We would have loved it had it not been for those hidden ramparts, those old cannons with their carriages trained low on the city, that mast with its mocking flag, those silent sentries with their olive-drab masks posted at every corner. The mountain was a prison—subjugating, intimidating the city, blocking off its horizon with its dark mass under the most beautiful of suns. (17)

It is no coincidence that the film concludes its historical fresco with the 1909 executions at Montjuïc, since this sequence effectively summarizes a whole decade in the life of Barcelona. Not only is this a statement about the role of political martyrdom in the city's modernization and in its relentless struggle for freedom, but also, by packing into an image of repressive violence the otherwise sequential development and univocal chronology of the film, this shot articulates an important insight about the accumulation of meaning through the transference of cathectic force. Rather than the historical energy flowing from present concerns to past images, the latter (no longer directly available) are invoked through a visual synthesis of different historical events in order to give semantic depth to a present that otherwise risks being arrested in its surface meaning.

J.A. González Casanova made this very point in the prologue to the screenplay, asserting that "as in Eisenstein's best cinema, it is enough to pedagogically invoke the political past in order to understand the present in all its depth" (8). Aside from the excessive epistemological optimism manifested in this assertion, which, under certain circumstances, might serve to undergird the propaganda uses of political film, it remains true that historical film—realist film, says González Casanova—is based on the after-image in the most literal way, namely, in the spatial projection and visual configuration of a temporal and epistemic *différand*.[52] More significantly, however, historical cinema resorts to the dialectics of the after-image in its best instantiations, illuminating the tension-ridden status of the past as well as current struggles to stabilize a desired image of the present. In this respect, an after-image of the past contributes toward visualizing a present that cannot yet muster or master its images.

The end of *Burned City* suggests that the history of Catalan struggles for freedom has proceeded in a staccato manner, punctuated by moments of

Figure 5.8 Montjüic and its military fortress seen from downtown Barcelona at the end of the Tragic Week. From *La ciutat cremada*, directed by Antoni Ribas (1976).

popular defiance followed by fierce repression. Nevertheless, the film does not offer (indeed, does not want to offer) a conclusive statement about the resolution of the dialectic. History is framed by images but is not arrested by them. As the camera cuts from a medium shot of the grim execution scene to a panoramic take of the smoky city watched over by the fortress, the film ends with a powerful after-image of a conflict that had not yet dissipated (fig. 5.8). Two years earlier, in the spring of 1974, the Franco regime had carried out its last political execution in Barcelona, in the person of a young anarchist named Salvador Puig Antich, and the episode was fresh in the memory of the audiences who applauded *Burned City* when it premiered in Barcelona, as was, even after thirty-six years, the shooting of Companys in October 1940.

Throughout 1976, downtown Barcelona was the scene of clashes of workers and students, together reclaiming the city, with a state that asserted, in the words of its secretary of the interior, Manuel Fraga Iribarne, "la calle es mía" (the street belongs to me). The film responded to the subjectivism of autocratic power with the collective strength of historical memory. To this end, Ribas and Miquel Sanz collaborated with professional historians Josep Benet, Josep Termes, and Isidre Molas in a documented script about the state's seizure of the streets. In retrospect, the film seems to have had no anticipatory value, except as a statement of the definitive passing into virtuality of an after-image that in the past had counted on the complicity of the real. In fact, one may wonder if the promotion of Barcelona as a "showcase city" a decade later, culminating in the widely broadcast images of the 1992 Olympics, was not the "posthistorical" fulfillment of the *noucentista* dream of a virtual city, glossier than ever as a result of the mediatic interventions that now convert cities themselves into their own after-images in the specular space of the global village.

CHAPTER SIX

Bees at a Loss: Images of Madrid
(before and) after La colmena

Dieter Ingenschay

INTRODUCTION: TWO MADRIDS

In 1760 Edward Clarke, an English clergyman, and his companion Joseps Baretti attended the public coronation of the new Spanish king, Charles III, in Madrid. Whenever they left the richly decorated Plaza Mayor, they suffered, they complained, "from severe headaches," due to "the horrible stench and foul-smelling exhalations from the mountains of garbage lying everywhere."[1] A few decades later, Alexandre de Laborde, an attendant to Lucien Bonaparte, visited Madrid and found it "the cleanest city in Europe," and "the most beautiful and well-built of all European cities, with the best citizens."[2]

One can also find contradictory and ambiguous judgments of Paris and Berlin; in fact, any formation of city images is characterized by a general tension between a positive reception—the city as a display of culture (in Simmel's sense)—and a negative one—the city as disgusting enemy of human nature.[3] Yet the existence of two antagonistic typologies of a single city is particularly evident in the case of Madrid; this I attribute specifically to the fact that Spain's cultural archaeology is characterized by an immanent dialectics of "two Spains." The notion of "two Spains" refers to the interaction between hegemonic Catholic conservatism and the humanist, enlightened, and democratic periods. This dialectics is superimposed on and broadens the basic dichotomy. In the case of Madrid, each image within the frame of the "two Spains"—at least since the nineteenth century—has acknowledged the other's existence; this leads to unilateral positions such as Mesonero Romanos's formulation of a centralist myth. It also sometimes leads to polemics and to ambiguities such as those found in Larra's problematic role of mediating between proclamations of social reform and disillusionment (see Resina, "Madrid's Palimpsest" 64, and Baker 50–53).

Must we decide that one of the opinions of Madrid—both uttered in the context of nonfictional travel literature at about the same time—was wrong? Was Laborde wrong, since we know from so-called objective sources that the habit of throwing garbage and human excrement out the window was prevalent for decades in the nineteenth century? Or should we assume that the great majority of visitors—including the German Romanist Victor Klemperer in the 1920s—gave negative descriptions? May we postulate that judgments of any city are unreliable, since "readings" of a city are subjective, and that a semiotic approach is therefore dangerous when it claims the unequivocal readability of a city? Yet if it proves impossible to make reliable predications about cities in literature, then the main effect of city literature is that it produces images, which are important in mediating between the city and its literary text. City images are complex because discursive qualities, literary procedures, the search for a style, and so on enter the game of "adequate" description or appropriation. Moreover, even if these images can hardly be fixed by semiotic analysis,[4] they still remain landmarks of reception. As such they coalesce at one precise moment, which might be termed a "degree zero." Prior to this moment the city image is uncertain, oscillating; after it, all new images—in their capacity as after-images—cannot help but refer to that degree zero.

In the case of Madrid, it is particularly difficult to determine this degree zero, because the city's rich literary history lacks the monolithic novels written about cities such as Paris, Berlin, and New York. Undoubtedly, the process of constructing Madrid through literature came to an end a long time ago, which seems evident to writers today: Muñoz Molina quotes Gómez de la Serna's idea of the novelistic character of Spain's capital, and Francisco Nieva, when asked about his recently published Madrid novel, *Carne de murciélago*, said: "Of course, Madrid is a literary invention" (interview with Juan Bonilla in *El Mundo*, September 26, 1998).[5] But what is the starting point beyond when this fact becomes evident? In their anthologies, students of Madrid literature—Baker, Lacarta, Ugarte, Heymann, and Barella—do not reveal any such "degree zero": Baker, because he ends with Galdós, and Lacarta, because the fascination with the Spanish capital seems to be his main objective. Ugarte's intention is to rather analyze literary appropriations of Madrid between the years of Larra's *costumbrismo* (depictions of local or regional customs and manners) and the "modernist" variant of Valle-Inclán and the early Gómez de la Serna.

Ugarte treats the Civil War and Francoism, but it is the following period that would offer much more evidence for what I call the cultural model of two Madrids within two Spains. The main polarization, sharpened by the

Civil War, revolves around the fascist discourse on Madrid. Agustín de Foxá's city novel, *Madrid, de corte a checa* (*Madrid, from Royal Court to Communist Dungeon,* 1938), whose very title documents a split urban society, combines the reconstruction of the historical ambience and cultural gossip with the author's own version of historical development, from the good old days of Alfonsonian Madrid to the horrid years of the republican and proletarian masses. The novel's bourgeois protagonist thus becomes committed to the Falangist cause, praising the fifth column and attacking Red barbarians. The Civil War produced a pathetic indictment of the Republic and an idealization of imperial Madrid by Ernesto Giménez Caballero, a "Spanish Goebbels": it brought forth a curious, pseudo-religious rhetoric, culminating in the apocalyptic vision of José María Pemán's fascist epic, in which "God-the-narrator" looks down on the Civil War being fought in the streets of Madrid and judges the good and the evil. In contrast, quite a few authors in exile (people with good intentions but views narrowed by the exile experience), do not have the same fascist pathos. Nevertheless, they do not adopt the critical stance we might expect; instead, a significant number of them withdraw into a nostalgic continuation of *costumbrismo.* Max Aub, who evolved new forms of experimental discourse, falls back into popular *costumbrismo* in *La calle Valverde.* From his Argentine exile beginning in the 1950s, Gómez de la Serna—who fashioned the modernist aesthetic discourse on Madrid throughout the 1920s and 1930s (see Ugarte 119) between *La viuda blanca y negra* (1917) and *Las tres gracias* (1949)—stylizes the Madrid he longs for as a monolithic rock in a thundering sea, as an enduringly secure point on which he can rely:

> During my last walk through Madrid I found that the present time, unspoiled and complete, was unified in it, that it allowed an identical life, that the young nobleman could walk the same paths and take possession of the city, which increasingly delivered itself to the stroller, a Madrid even more Madrid than the one I was born in, as it was made, at the beginning, from a large mold, according to the classical modern ideal of the Big City. (Gómez de la Serna 11)[6]

Although exiled Spanish authors did not succeed in creating literary documents convincing enough to constitute the great new paradigm of discourse on Madrid, this very project nevertheless received a decisive impetus during the first decades of the Franco regime. Such a "reconstruction of the Democratic City" is described by Manuel Vázquez Montalbán in his recent study, *La literatura en la construcción de la ciudad democrática,* as "the dominent cultural and political project between 1939 and 1982" (Vázquez Montalbán 60), and he concludes: "A historically subtle eye would discover how, like the specter of the Francoist city, the anti-Francoist city began to come together both within and outside the town" (Vázquez Montalbán 60).[7] Perhaps certain later authors can be viewed as contributing considerably toward building this new anti-Madrid. They certainly developed a new literary discourse on the Spanish capital, one that proved strong and convincing enough to represent the prototypical imagery of a "degree zero." The decisive first step in this process was realized in 1951 with Cela's exemplary city novel, *La colmena*.

THE LIFE OF THE BEES AND THE POWER OF A METAPHOR

In proposing Cela's *La colmena* as a crucial stage within the ongoing literary invention of Madrid (instead of, for example, Mesonero Romanos, Baroja, Gómez de la Serna or Umbral), I will concern myself, first, with its "stylistic" handling of the city. Wolfgang Matzat, using Wolfgang Iser's model of subject, horizon, and structure, has shown that the fragmentation of the text does not lead to a multiplicity of horizons and to aestheticization but rather to a limitation of horizons and monotony, thus turning the novel into a "document of alienation" (Matzat). This alienation was not in itself decisive, but the way alienation was realized was, since it was not easy at the time to publish documents of this kind under the conditions of control and censorship. One common strategy was to invent new metaphors. The image of the beehive—quite traditional compared to other urban images, and earlier used by Galdós—was unobjectionable enough, though it could be read critically as a figure for the senselessness and vain activism imposed by fascism. *La colmena* is a "borderline text," constructed at the edge of what Francoist censorship could tolerate (in fact, the regime imposed certain changes) and of what the large contemporary Spanish reading public would still accept. Doña Rosa's first thought, "Let us not lose our perspective" (45)[8] is a clue for the reader, just as it is for all these urban "bees at a loss" in the city. Their horizon is limited and lacks a broad perspective and even a clear view of the streets, since peoples' eyes remain fixed on the ground ("People pass one another hurriedly, no one pays attention to his neighbor, who might be looking downwards" [321]).[9] The metaphor of the beehive is thus turned against Galdós, its inventor, who used it within the context of the traditional panoramic view of the city from above. *La colmena,* and the *novela social* of the 1950s in general, managed to avoid the ridiculous pomp of social realism prevailing elsewhere and to use distinctive imagery, of which the beehive is only one example—the most effective in terms of its reception. *La colmena* is important primarily for the stringent misreadings of it as "realistic," initiated by the author himself, and for a perspective that interprets fragmentation as an expression of the actual post-Civil War situation: Madrilenians as "bees at a loss."

Nevertheless, I would be less enthusiastic in proposing *La colmena* as the degree zero of Madrid imagery if this novel were an isolated phenomenon. It is rather one of a group of texts (written in the 1950s and 1960s, and confirming the aesthetics of the *novela social*) that treat the city similarly, a corpus that includes such novels as Gonzalo Torrente Ballester's *Off-side,* Luis Martín-Santos's *Tiempo de silencio,* and Rafael Sánchez Ferlosio's *El Jarama.* These novels have in common a rejection of both preceding modes: fascist pomp, and a merely nostalgic *costumbrismo* that seeks to bear witness to depression. These new novels emphasize the very existence of the "two Spains." Eighteen years after *La colmena,* Torrente Ballester went far beyond Cela's depiction of the marginalized Madrilenians, and Martín-Santos's *Tiempo de silencio,* even though it revived the single plot line of the conventional novel, both developed a subtle counterpoint to fascist city rhetoric and anticipated new literary tendencies in the appropriation of the city. When the protagonist of *Tiempo de silencio* describes the hovels of the poor, the *chabolas,* as "fortresses of misery," he unmasks a pathetic fascist rhetoric. Comparing this dimension of city life to that of an African tribe, as he does, may not be politically correct, but it is a vigorous counterblast to the self-image of Francoism and its Eurocentric traditionalism. As for anticipating recent tendencies, Martín-Santos is hardly the first to write about the *chabolas* (in fact, his description includes many of the same details as that of Galdós in a passage from *La Desheredada*), but he refrains from depicting them from the perspective of dysphoric realism, going so far as to make an "inappropriate" lyrical gesture, which we find again in Umbral's *Madrid 650* (1995).

The Madrid novels of the 1950s and 1960s, then, as a special form of the *novela social,* however prosaic and conventional they may appear compared to those of Dos Passos and Döblin, should be considered the degree zero on the Spanish scale, not only because they were well received but also because they effectively metaphorize the "two Spains." All together, these novels illustrate Vázquez Montalbán's idea of the reconstruction of the Democratic City and are the first "agglutination" of the anti-Francoist city *intra muros.*

MOVIDA AND THE 1980S

By the time Franco died in 1975, international theories of the city had mapped out a promising approach, adopting an urban semiotics that had had convincing results as long as topography, topology, and mythical creation were at stake. Klaus Scherpe, however, points to the "shift from literal city symbolism and an unequivocal strategy of perception to a semiotic concept of the city's text" (Scherpe 145).[10] The rise of semiotics marked the end of unequivocal recordings of the city. Semiotics, as the theory of reading signs that can never be entirely deciphered, bears within itself an awareness of its own imperfection and is bound, within a contemporary postmodern perspective, to bequeath the legacy of its own failure. This fact is paradigmatically reflected in Baudrillard, who, in *L'échange symbolique et la mort,* searched for a complex semiotic model while capitulating to the "revolt of signs" and their "execution" (see Baudrillard, "Kool Killer"). Roland Barthes offers a parallel when he exchanges the failure of semiotic city analysis for a hedonistic reading of the metropolis (see Barthes, "Sémiologie et urbanisme"). Only recent transsemiotic theory (Michel de Certeau and Marc Augé) gives up the claim to semiotization and sets semiotics free from the "semiocracy" Baudrillard lamented without, however, overcoming it.

By the time Franco died, the younger generation had stopped caring about historical events such as the entry of the victors into Madrid, the fascist seizure of the city that the dictator himself had pathetically evoked thirty-two years earlier in *Raza,* a screenplay he wrote under the pseudonym Jaime de Andrade. Nor could this new generation be moved by the images of the *novela social.* The unreliability of all previous city imagery and of all semiotic interpretations of Madrid can be clearly seen in the new "reading" proposed by the authors of the so-called *movida.* To them, Madrid became the scene of an incomparable aesthetic strike against the past, not only against fascist pathos but also against the documents of alienation proposed by the generation of beekeepers. Although I am unwilling to judge the *movida,*[11] I admit it lacks convincing literary images of Madrid (though not of Barcelona). I would suggest, however, that there is evidence of the power of Madrid to inspire as a "Sleeping Beauty Kissed Awake" by the *movida.* The most eminent representative of the *movida,* Pedro Almodóvar, put an end to fragmented, alienated discourse and returned to stories, placing them in his own central Madrid. He is not ashamed to have cars race up and down the Gran Vía, as if this avenue had never been the symbol of and witness to the fascists' appropriation of the city.

Looking back on the 1970s and 1980s, Almodóvar dares treat with considerable sarcasm the social change in post-Francoist Spain that brought—along with freedom—unemployment and the loss of security. In his essay "La ciudad," his advice to the young unemployed of both sexes arriving from the provinces is to become drug dealers or prostitutes. This cynical advice removes the dualism between the negative conception of the city, frequently linked (since Babylon was designated the Great

Whore) to all forms of prostitution, and a positive conception, insofar as prostitution, regardless of its social implications, is yet another element of modern life, which entails all forms of liberty, including sexual. More important, he establishes a link between Madrid and each of his early films, a relation that is particularly evident in the shots of the urban highway M-30 in *¿Qué he hecho yo para merecer esto?* (What have I done to deserve this?). In his essay "Venir a Madrid," the director explains in detail Madrid's central role in each of his movies, which at least succeeded in forming a new "image" of the city as the center of a new aesthetics of trash and camp. By 1987—the date of *Mujeres al borde de un ataque de nervios* (*Women on the Verge of a Nervous Breakdown*), all Europeans knew that post-Francoist Madrid had become Europe's most exciting city, though the Italian philosopher Gianni Vattimo may have exaggerated when he called Madrid "the capital of the twentieth century as Paris had been of the nineteenth," and a "laboratory of the new postmodern existence."[12] Moreover, with the usual bureaucratic delays, the Spanish central government and the Brussels cultural administration elected the city "Cultural Capital of Europe" in 1992.

At the turn of the 1980s, when every day the *movida* put its own way of life and aesthetics on the urban stage of Barcelona's Rambles and Madrid's Plaza 2 de mayo, postmodern critics, whenever they dealt with city literature, found the metropolis only disorienting and peripheral. While citizens daily experienced bumper-to-bumper downtown traffic (nightly on weekends), theoreticians postulated an empty center (Baudrillard, "L'ascension du vide"), the unimportance and even nonexistence of a single center (Augé, *Non-Places* 70). The Spanish *movida* thus nicely contradicts the critics' observations. Unfortunately, it lacks convincing literary paradigms.

As photographs, the *movida* images of Madrid resemble psychedelic tokens (Warhol and Beatles style), slightly out of fashion, slightly too showy, featuring on the whole one original, Pedro Almodóvar. *Movida* is a form of life in the city, not a literature of the city. The chief importance of its representatives is to have overcome the desperation of the generation of the beekeepers. The *movida* proved to be a short-lived phenomenon, however. One can read Almodóvar's latest films as documents of its definitive end.

POSTMOVIDA MADRID: INTERTEXTS AND NON-PLACES

Let us now turn to the 1990s, to four examples that are, in fact, after-images of Madrid, insofar as they all reject the *movida* madness and the insistence on good intentions of those authors willing to build the Democratic City under Franco. The novels in question are Antonio Muñoz Molina's

Los misterios de Madrid (1992), José Angel Mañas's *Historias del Kronen* (1994), Francisco Umbral's *Madrid 650* (1995), and Mañas's *Ciudad rayada* (1998).

The Intertextuality of Novelistic City Mysteries

Los misterios de Madrid tells of the Madrid experiences of Lorencito Quesada, a young journalist from the Andalusian town of Mágina. One night he receives a call from the most prominent person in town, don Sebastián Guadalimar, "multimillonario y aristócrata," who reports some bad news to Lorencito: the nationally famous statue of San Cristo de la Greña has been stolen from its chapel—and only a week before *Semana santa* (Holy Week). He asks—or rather orders—the journalist to go to Madrid to solve this crime against God, the world, the town, and the *cofradía* (brotherhood). Lorencito reluctantly accepts and sets out for Madrid, where, twenty years earlier, he had attended the second *Festival de la canción salesiana* (Festival of Salesian Song). His Madrid experience prototypically matches a perspective one could call the "peripheral view" (see Buschmann and Ingenschay, *Die andere Stadt*). The main characteristic of Muñoz Molina's tale is humor; predictably, Lorencito's attempts to "read" contemporary Madrid fail, leading him repeatedly into danger. According to one great tradition of the peripheral view, all this serves as a criticism of metropolitan life. Madrid proves to be so central in this novel that the detective story itself appears as a mere pretext.

Lorencito is thrown into the modern post-Francoist metropolis of tourists, skyscrapers of steel and glass, and roaring traffic, with its drugs and sex shops, and, at the same time, into the "Madrid castizo," the traditional inner circle bordered by Castellana and Torre Picasso to the north, Atocha to the south, Plaza de España to the west, and Puerta de Alcalá to the east. The Rastro, Plaza Mayor, and the shady streets north of Gran Vía form a setting that can be found in conventional *costumbrismo*. The protagonist rarely leaves this area. Once, kidnapped and thrown out of a car, he finds himself on a bridge above city highway M 40, confronted with the ugliness and anonymity of the periphery, where a huge sign ironically reads, "Welcome to Madrid, Cultural Capital of Europe" (118),[13] in sharp contrast to this suburban *non-place* of a few miserable *chabolas*, inhabited by pale, zombies without a trace of "European culture." Humor takes the form of a somewhat bitter irony, so it is not surprising that Joan Ramon Resina (insisting that any "reading" of the polis is a political act) refers to this passage in his interpretation of *Los misterios de Madrid* as above all an eminently social critique (see "Madrid's Palimpsest" 81–83). I cannot help but read the novel primarily as a joyful, humorous text, as a postmodern game about city literature, with the shy country hero betraying many signs of a self-portrait of the author. Muñoz Molina's Madrid novel occupies an ambiguous position. There are the critical passing shots wittily analyzed by Resina, but there is also a layer of secret attraction that surfaces whenever Muñoz Molina writes about the "Madrid castizo," whether in this novel or in his newspaper articles.

As an ironic version of a typical city detective novel (with concrete topographical indications on every page: names of streets, places, shops, buildings), *Los misterios de Madrid* is primarily intertextual, beginning with its title, an allusion to Eugène Sue's successful *Mystères de Paris,* and to its many imitators, such as José Nicasio Milà's *Los misterios de Barcelona.* Like his French predecessor, Muñoz Molina combines his depiction of the dark side of the capital with a love story, and while the fallen girl's rescuer in Sue's novel turns out to be a German nobleman, Lorencito's female savior proves to be the daughter of the *marquesa,* whose second husband is don Sebastián, Mágina's boss. But the full impact of this intertextuality manifests itself in the epigraph. It is taken from Ramón Gómez de la Serna's *Nostalgias de Madrid*: "Madrid es tan novelesco que su novela más perfecta es la de lo insucedido" (Madrid is so novelistic that its most perfect novel is one of the events that have never occurred).

This epigraph turns Madrid into a storehouse of stories, turns city life into literary material more novelistic than novels—hardly an innovative procedure. But it seems to me that some personal enthusiasm for the city fuses with the intertextual mode. Whereas Gómez de la Serna turned Madrid into a closed world of projections from the perspective of exile, the Andalusian writer—a citizen of Madrid long before he was elected a member of the Real Academia de la Lengua Española—documents his view of the changes the city has undergone since the demise of Francoism. In this sense, *Los misterios de Madrid* is testimony to the fact that the process of change leading toward modernity has come to an end. And, as a byproduct, Muñoz Molina's novel questions (through the words of its protagonist) semiotic conceptions of the "readability" of the city. Significantly different from his experiences of the (Francoist) city he had gotten to know during his first visit, he now gives up the claim to understand the (postmodern) metropolis: "He decided that Madrid was an incomprehensible city" (47).[14]

The Capital of Dullness and Thrills

José Angel Mañas's *Historias del Kronen,* published in 1994, and Montxo Armendáriz's 1995 film adaptation were sensationally successful in Spain. "El libro se vendió como churros" (The book sold like hotcakes) commented *Tiempo* (May 15, 1995), and *El País* (May 12) wrote: "The 'Kronen Phenomenon' made box office coffers overflow" (for a detailed comparison between the novel and the film, see Ingenschay 1996). Reviews sketched the "urban map of the Kronen-generation" and reaped the "cosecha de los términos" (harvest of expressions). Apparently, Mañas had succeeded for the first time in transposing the feelings of twenty-year-olds into fiction, their hopelessness and inability to establish personal relationships. The book consists of the protagonist Carlos's diary, kept for two weeks during a rather dull vacation. The family context (the protagonist's visit to his grandfather shortly before the latter's death) points to one axis of the novel, the generational conflict. The more essential context, however, is that of the lifestyle of Madrilenian upper middle-class youth, shown in the everyday life of a group of friends, consisting largely of nightly disco visits, casual sexual encounters, and the excessive consumption of drugs: a life without perspective, meaning, or ideals.

Mañas's chief aim is to represent a modern hero who seems devoid of human feelings; his chief innovation is to integrate radical youth slang and to make extensive use of scatological language. The lifestyle of "a Kronen" requires a big city. The movie version begins with a panning shot over Madrid at night, but the novel too underscores the role of the metropolis as the necessary habitat for this sub- or paraculture. The novel shows clearly that the complex space of the inner urban center is not at stake, nor is the contrasting suburban periphery. Neither Cibeles and Plaza Mayor nor the *chabolas* beyond Vallecas are mentioned. The urban map is delimited by bars, discos, and cinemas; the protagonist is no longer the nineteenth-century flâneur but a motorist, and the road most often mentioned is urban highway M-30, the quickest communication line within the urban labyrinth. This fact brings to mind Marc Augé's theory of the contemporary city as a *non-place*; Mañas's Madrid corresponds in its details to Augé's conception of the metropolis as the faceless and finally interchangeable prototype of postmodern life. Consequently, when the protagonist looks at the urban geography in *Historias del Kronen,* the sight stirs no aesthetic feelings. The hero prefers to seek the odd thrill of driving on a highway in the wrong direction. The Kronen-Bar itself has a role that is notably different from the traditional café as center of communication (as in Galdós's *La Fontana de Oro* or Doña Rosa's place in *La colmena*).

Yet *Historias del Kronen* offers a typically Madrilenian setting and reflects the specific self-image of the Spanish capital's young people in the mid-1990s, a fact confirmed by the strong identification young readers have felt. If the novel is preoccupied with marginalized citizens (typical of Cela, Torrente Ballester, and Martín-Santos), it also refrains from creating a substantially new "image" of Madrid and confines itself to a specific after-image. Its intertextual network rejects both preceding paradigms: the 1968 generation of good political intentions and the aesthetically crazy *movida* style. Carlos clearly contrasts the politically leftist "hippie" generation of his father, which was able to cultivate an anti-Francoist position, to the despair of his own group:

> Here we are with the same old sermons. The old people start telling how things were different for them, how they struggled to provide us with what we have. Democracy, liberty, and so on. The well-known '68 pseudo-progressive drivel. The old people possess everything: money and power. They didn't even leave us rebellion: they exhausted it all, these fucking Marxists and hippies of that time.(67)[15]

The feelings of this younger generation are reflected in *Historias del Kronen* through intertexts such as Douglas Coupland's *Generation X* and, above all, through references to Bret Easton Ellis's *American Psycho*, whose protagonist is the only ideal figure for Carlos and his friends, who immerse themselves in a world of movies such as *Clockwork Orange*, *The Silence of the Lambs*, and pornographic snuff films.

These references also point to the growing Americanization of present-day Spain, and they do so more convincingly and quite differently from the touristic views in Torrente's *Off-side*, in Juan Goytisolo's *Señas de identidad*, or in Muñoz Molina's *Los misterios de Madrid*. The Kronen stories question the urban canon by ignoring or neglecting the literary tradition of city perception; they have abandoned the implicit utopia of Vázquez Montalbán's Democratic City and the political vocation of the *novela social*, replacing all traditional city images with the significantly amorphous after-image of a hopeless generation.

Heterotopy as Lyrical Non-Place

Francisco Umbral is a *madrileñista* who—in addition to his study of Gómez de la Serna—wrote a number of essays and novels on the Spanish capital, such as *Nada en el domingo*, his *Madrid Trilogy*, and a collection of costumbristic essays, *Amar en Madrid* and *Madrid 1940: Memorias de un joven fascista*. In 1995 he published his city novel *Madrid 650*, breaking significantly with his own literary past as well as with the literary tradition generally. The epigraph explains that the title is taken from a handbook of geography ("Madrid es una ciudad situada a 650 metros sobre el nivel del mar"; Madrid is a city located 650 meters above sea level), thus referring to the most basic of all geographic aspects of a city. The text, however, cannot claim to be a general predication of Madrid. The fragments of plot take the reader to the periphery, not to a "classical" *chabola*, however, but to a first-class railway coach, standing in the middle of nowhere—not even on the rails—in the absurdly depressing suburb of La Hueva (alluding to the *chabola* agglomeration of El Pozo del Huevo, south of Vallecas). Jerónimo, the occupant of the coach and of the *barrio*, is the most privileged person among its marginalized inhabitants, who support themselves through robbery, drug dealing, prostitution, begging, and grave robbing: a well-organized form of life where unwanted intruders sometimes vanish into the lime pit. Their *barrio* is the center of their lives, whereas central Madrid is reduced to a mere sideshow whose function is to guarantee or facilitate survival. The text preserves the internal social structure of Madrid: rich upper-class girls come from the Salamanca district, and Jerónimo goes to the Legazpi slaughterhouse to settle accounts with an enemy, steals a motorbike near the Nuevos Ministerios, and so on. The text of the novel, however, lacks all descriptive concreteness, and any allusions at all to the canonical city, the "Madrid castizo." The Gran Vía and Callao are mentioned, but they are not invested with significant semiotic power. Madrid remains faceless, of undetermined forms and colors:

> In fact, Jerónimo, seated on top of the wagon many mornings, is not doing transcendental meditation, but instead looking into the distant nothingness, not thinking, looking at the feast of the sun in the distant mountains, where it had arrived like a day-tripper, looking at . . . Madrid on the other side, an enormous mass, pink, extended, endless, infinite, with its own sky, gray and silver and a bit of gold, this place where he goes to rob the stand of a melon merchant, to get a fix, to drink a bottle of whiskey, or to kill a man, depending. (Umbral, *Madrid 650* 11)[16]

As for after-images, the description of the "gray" sky is particularly revealing, since it contradicts the traditional, indeed proverbial, blueness of the Spanish sky, a topos in Madrid literature since the nineteenth century. Thus, Umbral subtly undermines Madrilenian specificity and links his idea of the capital to Augé's "postmodern" conception of the fundamental facelessness of the metropolis: "Jerónimo did not feel the melancholy of great voyages. All cities are the same, he thinks: places to rob, to kill, and to fuck" (42).[17]

Umbral's innovative appropriation, or rather, annihilation, of the city seems to embody a new ("postmodern") conception that found its first expression in Michel Foucault notion of "urban heterotopies" (Foucault, "Des espaces autres"). The places he designates as such—graveyards, prisons, railroad tracks, garbage pits—play a central role in *Madrid 650*. Whereas Foucault's heterotopies ultimately belong to city geography, recent cultural criticism goes beyond this: Marc Augé, within the framework of his theory of the *non-place*, emphasizes the role of junctions, highways, airports, billboards (and—in the future—the worldwide web) in the present-day organization of the city. He goes so far as to deny the existence of the city center even where it is most notorious and best documented by literary history, in Paris ("Paris does not have one center" [*Non-Places*,

70]).[18] If, since the nineteenth century, the urban literary canon has been based on the condition of the city as readable, accessible to semiotic analysis, then *Madrid 650* is an example of a literary text rejecting urban semiotics. Displacing the central action to an amorphous periphery, it denies the central role of the center and overturns the distribution of relevant elements. If postmodern cultural theory stresses the shift between former centers and former peripheries,[19] Umbral offers—within Madrid itself—a postmodern after-image.

Yet the conversion of the periphery into a center remains unreliable, and at the very end of Umbral's lyrical novel, the *chabola* suburb is destroyed by a municipal bulldozer, metaphorized as "a huge one-clawed crab" (248).[20] The protagonist has to flee his territory, to fight his way toward "this red, warm, penetrable, and extended vastness that Madrid is" (253),[21] in search of a new identity. Umbral's fervent *madrileñismo* evidently catches up with him here, but *Madrid 650* goes far beyond the city sketches of *Amar en Madrid,* including the descriptions of the *chabola* and of gypsy life. The novel's elegiac tone does not treat the marginalized inhabitants of La Hueva from the exotic perspective prevalent in Martín-Santos's *Tiempo de silencio,* nor through a mimetic approach (as Mañas does with the slang of the youngsters in *Historias del Kronen*). The discrepancy between the highly poetic language and the crudeness of peripheral life is not the subject, but a by-product, an effect of the text, and nevertheless the main proof of its postmodernity. Another proof is the capsizing of the social hierarchy through language. The social outcasts seem to know how to use metaphors, allegories, and all types of lyrical discourse; they quote Rilke and Lorca, combining the poetic register with the lowest slang—an implicit way to emancipate otherness. As David Harvey postulated: "The idea that all groups have a right to speak for themselves, in their own voice, . . . is essential to the pluralistic stance of postmodernism" (Harvey, *The Condition* 48).

The Home of a Drug Dealer

José Angel Mañas's *Ciudad rayada* (1998) describes the life of a seventeen-year-old Madrid student, nicknamed Kaiser, who makes his living dealing drugs, primarily cocaine. Just as in *Historias del Kronen* (and even more explicitly),[22] the action depends on the metropolis as its indispensable backdrop; Madrid is present throughout the entire text, playing an increasingly significant role in the novel's second part. Kaiser leaves the city limits once to visit his father in the Galician town of Pontevedra, after committing a murder fueled by problems and quarrels in the drug milieu. This trip away from Madrid, however, quickly comes to an end (because of car trouble) in the vicinity of El Escorial, just a few miles from the capital.

On this occasion, Kaiser notices his addiction to Madrid for the first time: "I wanna say that in Madrid I not only know the streets—they're inside my head. It's my city in and out, I don't know if you can understand" (Mañas, *Ciudad rayada* 140).[23] The city with its bars and discotheques is not only the natural ambience for the hero and his friends, it determines his way of life. It is also the source of his aesthetic inspiration insofar as he devotes his free time to techno music, which he—aspiring to a successful job as a deejay—mixes himself. The noises he cuts into his sound tracks, seem to be those best able to represent today's postmodern Madrid myth: the noises of city highway M-30. Here we find something like a hidden leitmotiv of postmodern Madrid, one that has been sounded since Almodóvar,[24] becoming, in the meantime, as typical of this city as the tolling of Big Ben in London. One of the lyrical aphorisms uttered by Kaiser's girlfriend Tula reads: "the M 30 is God's whistling" (111).[25] After being threatened and knocked down in an act of revenge, then abducted to the outskirts to the city, Kaiser finally finds himself in a typical *non-place*, an auto junkyard, with *chabolas* on the horizon. After being released, he runs off at full speed and finally recognizes M-30 (123). The somewhat realistic description of the *chabola* conglomeration that follows proves that this place has quickly lost the exoticism it had in Martín-Santos; it has become familiar, since Kaiser, the postmodern version of Baudelaire's flâneur, recognizes the spot.[26] A gypsy friend of his, Chalo, lives there, and he intends to contact him, realizing how important it is to have friends all over the city: "Like I say, I move around all over Madrid, and it's important to know someone in every district" (128).[27]

Such a celebration of the periphery is characteristic of movements in contemporary culture and in city imagery, according to Salman Rushdie's statement that "marginality thus became an unprecedented source of energy" (Ashcroft et al. 12). Nevertheless, peripheral Madrid is not prominent in *Ciudad rayada* (as it is in Umbral's novel). Whereas the return to the center was a mere episode at the end of *Madrid 650*, Mañas's novel focuses repeatedly on the city center. The *madrileñista* character of the novel is revealed in the chapter "Menudo finde," when the protagonist takes a long walk through "the fucking center of Madrid" (184),[28] from the Cortes to the Retiro, to Puerta de Alcalá, to Plaza de la Independencia, by subway to Banco de España and Cibeles, to the Gran Vía, and finally to Plaza de España, missing very few of Madrid's repertoire of monuments and places. Kaiser's and Tula's affection for their city becomes even more palpable when they move from the non-place of an urban shopping mall (el Centro comercial Arturo Soria) to the hill at Vallecas ("las tetas de Madrid"; the tits of Madrid) from which vantage point Madrid is to be seen "en son ampleur" (in its full expanse), as in Baudelaire's *Petits poèmes en prose.* ("So we went to see the sun set from the tits of Cerro Pío, which are two hills near Vallecas from which you can see all of Madrid" [195]).[29] However conventional a view of a city from a hill may be, the focus of attention is specific, including the significant locations on Kaiser's urban map (including our by-now notorious M-30); and it is innovative in that it creates an individual image, turning the rays of the setting sun into discotheque laser rays. Finally, the young drug dealer takes up the central metaphor that has constituted the degree zero of Madrid literature, Cela's image of *La colmena*:

> It was like a huge beehive of fools—forgetting the group of pot smokers next to us who kept laughing at bad jokes—and we could be above it, controlling the world while the sky caught fire beyond the Azca skyscrapers, coloring everything with a layer of apricot jam. The clouds turned violet, and the last rays of the sun seemed like discotheque lasers. When I saw the Atocha planetarium, M 30, already illuminated, and the Pirulí, the slanted skyscrapers of the Plaza Castilla, I remembered that I once wrecked the TV and I opened it with a screwdriver to see the circuits inside. Awesome. (Mañas *Ciudad rayada* 196)[30]

It is important, however, to notice the difference in the charge of the beehive metaphor in Cela's and in Mañas's novels. Whereas in *La colmena* Cela uses it to express the existential alienation of those "bees at a loss," Mañas (re)gains the view from above as a form of aesthetic, hedonistic appropriation of Madrid, which would be nostalgic if the register actually fit this hero. Mañas, referring to Cela, uses Galdós's device, coloring it with a layer of contemporary city experience. Kaiser, the urban cowboy who found his own strategies of survival, is notably different from the bees in *La colmena*. Although a lack of meaning and orientation undergirds both works, it is now no longer to the result of political oppression but rather of postmodern existence.

Conclusion

In the *posmovida* appropriation of Madrid, the model valid from the nineteenth century until Franco's death, that is, the conception of two antagonistic Madrids, has vanished. We find instead two main lines, one stressing the novelistic character of Madrid (Muñoz Molina's *Misterios de Madrid*, Nieva's *Carne de murciélago*, both of which cast the city as a reservoir of stories), and the other celebrating the capital as a non-place (recall Umbral's statement that all cities are the same: places to fuck and kill). Both conceptions, of the city as an intertextual field and as a faceless non-place—are counterbalanced by a nostalgic turn, especially in the most obviously postmodern novels, Umbral's *Madrid 650* and Mañas's *Ciudad rayada.* In all cases, the dissolution of the metropolis remains relative, and, in the end, the city actually adopts its lost sons. In this sense, the end of Umbral's *Madrid 650* is a rewriting of the end of *La colmena.*

Manuel Vázquez Montalbán, though admitting that Francoist aesthetics have been overcome, remains skeptical about contemporary Spanish achievements and pleads for a new historical consciousness and for a future "global city":

> Spanish literature of this period [i.e. of Postfrancoism], since it bet on the construction of the democratic city and questioned the aesthetic bywords of what Francoism had been, . . . refused . . . to act with a critical discourse on that city, which it had inherited from the period of the transition. . . . Post-modernity, understood as an *impasse* of modernity and not as an ideology, should rehistoricize itself and rediscover that the necessary city of the future . . . is not the definitive skyline of history's last city; that, on the contrary, we must aspire to the different skyline of a future global city, which ought to be at once egalitarian, based on solidarity, and libertarian. (Vázquez Montalbán 95–96)[31]

Notice that Vázquez Montalbán's ideas are not at all confirmed by post-Francoist city literature, which in fact did develop a critical discourse against the Francoist aesthetics and which hardly seems ready to strive for a global city of the future. The most striking result is that Madrid—post-modern and international—is no longer interpreted within the dichotomy of the "two Spains." Combining Augé's conception of the *non-place* with the warmhearted recuperation of a postmodern metropolis, contemporary novels of Madrid have (re)discovered the Democratic City and have exposed an innovative variety of its after-images.

CHAPTER SEVEN

The World in Our Head: Images and After-Images of the City in the Works of Albert Cohen

Ottmar Ette

OF IMAGES AND AFTER-IMAGES

In the preface to the first edition of his *Wanderungen durch die Mark Brandenburg*, dated November 1861, Theodor Fontane speaks of what inspired him to write the book. It began in the Scottish county of Kinross, on Loch Leven, at the heart of which there is an island where the traveler can still find ruins of the once-legendary Loch Leven Castle:

> Then we sailed around the island, directing our boat back to Kinross, but our eyes didn't want to part from the island, on whose gray ruins shone the afternoon sun, with an unnameable melancholic tranquility.
> Now the oars worked quickly, and the island became a strip, finally vanishing. Only the round tower remained before us on the water, a mere form of the imagination, until suddenly our fantasy returned to its own memories, images of the present hour jostled by older ones. These were remembrances of our native land, of an unforgotten day.
> There too lay a sheet of water, yet no stands of willow surrounded the shore; instead, a park and deciduous wood embraced the lake. We set off in a flat boat, and whenever we brushed against the reeds by the shore, it sounded like a hand passing over rustling silk. (Fontane 1)[1]

The intensity of the visual perception of the island on which the traveler's eye is still focused is further increased by the surrounding silence. Because the retinal impact vanishes for a certain time, it is superseded by a "creation of the imagination," until this after-image, too, is suddenly replaced by other after-images produced by the "fantasy" rising from deeper layers of a more distant past. This process of moving silently from retinal images to other, deeper ones reaches a point of consolidation when sound interferes with these almost ghostly images, when visual perceptions are completed by acoustic ones and where both perceptions definitely stabilize the superseding, overlapping scenery. The retina, the place of this superimposition, has not changed: the screen where internal and external images are formed is still located inside the eye.

What do the rather lonely and isolated landscapes of Loch Leven Castle and Schloß Rheinsberg have to do with images and after-images of the city? Fontane's technique of superseding one set of images with another is much more than a literary process. The process of supersession is based on the interplay of identity and difference, self and other; in Fontane's works, the other always serves as both contrast and corrective. The surfaces of the lakes seem to be identical, but (mirrorlike) they are framed by different kinds of vegetation indicating different climatic and cultural contexts. The dissolve results from the identity of the lacustrian surfaces but acquires its depth by differentiating iconic elements. These elements are superimposed in a three-stage process during which the retinal images are modified by the imagination and transformed by preexisting and already-stored images. Hence, an image can be replaced by another without necessarily disappearing completely: *une image peut en cacher une autre.* Thus, currently existing images—including those of the city—do contain an archive of after-images produced by the impact of images stored long ago.

Johann Wolfgang von Goethe, through a series of experiments performed on himself—an important dimension of research in the natural sciences at the turn of the eighteenth century—sought to understand and explain the phenomenon of so-called after-images. In the first part of his *Farbenlehre* (Study on colors), dealing with "Physiological Colors," he observes and measures the production of images and after-images on his own retina, drawing general conclusions that form the basis for the Goethean theory of visual phenomena. Crucial here is his conviction that physiological colors—unlike physical and chemical ones—are intrinsic features of the eye. Goethe describes the eye as an organ possessing its own light, though this *Augenlicht* (eye's light) has the same characteristics as light in general (see Goethe 56). Referring to a text by the German mystic Jakob Böhme, Goethe describes in verse his conviction: "Were not the eye sun-like, / How could we perceive light? / If God's own might lived not in us, / How could Divinity touch us?" (Goethe 57).[2]

These notions of the human eye go far beyond later theorizing on the metaphor of the "eye's light," or *Augenlicht.* Goethe deduces not only that the images we see in our dreams stem from the inner source of life but also that "through our imagination, we are able to produce the brightest images even in darkness" (57). We do not need external light to produce and perceive the most brilliant colors within ourselves, that is, inside the human eye. We can therefore conclude that the eye is not only the camera obscura of the world outside but also the *camera lucida* (see Barthes, *Chambre claire*) of our inner world(s). The conscious as well as unconscious production of our own images, which, according to Goethe, appear on our retina, could be seen as a consequence of this conclusion. In Proust's terms, one could speak of a *mémoire volontaire* and a *mémoire involontaire:* the after-images appearing on our retina as a result of external impulses are not necessarily conscious.

This insight is put to effective use in videos and in the advertising industry. As Goethe put it: "We look from one object to the next, and the succession of images seems pure to us; we are not aware that a bit of the preceding creeps into that which follows" (Goethe 79).[3] According to Goethe, we can perceive only what we already have inside us; and, by analogy to the images produced on our retina by external impulses, we are able to create other images through the imagination, as Theodor Fontane's three-stage process suggests. The succession of images on the retina is launched by external impulses, and is then completed by the imagination (insofar as the eye cannot separate itself from the desired image). It is finally superseded by older images coming from deeper layers of our imaginary.

After-images can even be produced mechanically by closing and opening our eyes: "Such an image, the impression of which is no longer noticed, can be revived on the retina when we open and close our eyes, shifting from excitement to relaxation" (Goethe 72).[4] The effect of these alternating processes is to reactivate after-images thought to be lost, in a way comparable to Freud's legendary *Wunderblock* (mystic writing pad). Of course, these after-images can be formed unconsciously. Goethe continues: "That images, in the case of eye diseases, remain fourteen to seventeen minutes and even longer on the retina, points to the extreme weakness of the organ, to its inability to recover itself, just as recollections of passionately beloved or hated objects point from the sensual to the spiritual sphere" (Goethe 71).[5]

It matters little that Goethe links the persistence of after-images to an organic weakening of the eye. What is more important is that a clear and absolute distinction between images produced by external impulses and those produced by internal sources becomes impossible, and the distinction between consciously and unconsciously produced images cannot be drawn. In other words, the immediate retinal image of a Scottish landscape as described in Fontane's "Preface" cannot be more "real" than after-images, which are at first the result of the eye's desire to remain focused on certain objects. Then, without deliberation, and guided by internal impulses, the eye is referred to after-images of landscapes, distant from Scotland in space and time but close to the subject's home and heart.

How could a clear distinction between external and internal impulses be made at a time when the scientific "development of retina implants for blind humans suffering from various degenerative diseases" seems to be within our reach?[6] According to a new neuroinformatical project launched by the University of Bonn, the retina implant will contain a "retina encoder" placed outside the eye "that will replace the information processing of the retina." It will be accompanied by a "retina stimulator" "implanted adjacent to the retinal ganglion cell layer," connected to a "wireless signal- and energy-transmission system" that will allow communication between the retina encoder and the retina stimulator. Where, then, does the retina end? We know that the retina is a part of our brain, and we now learn that we can connect it directly to a powerful encoder, a small and powerful computer. Where will our images and after-images come from in the future? We will be able to give any visually encodable information to a transmission system that will make no distinction between internal and external data. In a few years, the first generation of retina implants and retina encoders will have been implanted in humans. Our area striata may be linked to a computerized transmission system, and perhaps there will be a slot in our retina encoder for the worldwide web.

The silent fading and overlapping of images cannot be opposed to each other, as *Urbild* and *Abbild,* for example, since it is impossible to banish the ephemeral images to the "Reich der schädlichen Gespenster"(realm of harmful ghosts) (Goethe 63), as theorists had done prior to Goethe's experiments. In Fontane's "Preface," no image is more real or mimetic, more ghostly or more original, than another. In literary texts at least, it is impossible to separate images from after-images: both have the same status and offer the same semantic density to the retina of the reader's intellectual eye. These are images produced by an endless dialogue between identity and difference. The succession of images and after-images creates a kind of cinematographic sequence that a Goethe, fascinated, already described and measured. The retina works as a screen for these projections of our eyesight or "eyelight," even though we now know that the retina remains linked to the virtual screen and to the visual memory of the area striata in our brain. No doubt the world exists inside our brains, somewhere on the data highways between retina and area striata.

APPROACHING THE CITY

How do we approach a city? Which images of a city do we have in our minds before actually seeing it for the first time? What kind of information has shaped our image of it? And which of the many images do we store in our brains and why? Which after-images can we reproduce consciously and voluntarily and which emerge unconsciously from our imaginary; and how can we project them onto our "retina" in the way Goethe postulated? Finally, what national differences influence our approach to a city; what cultural differences mark our images and after-images of cities belonging to our own or to a foreign culture? Néstor García Canclini, a Mexico-based Argentine anthropologist and cultural theorist, has tried to sketch the ways different academic disciplines approach the city. He writes, not without irony:

> The social sciences contribute to this difficulty with their different levels of observation. The anthropologist arrives in the city on foot, the sociologist by car and via the main highway, the communication expert/scientist by plane. Each registers whatever he or she is able to and constructs a distinct and, therefore, partial vision. There is a fourth perspective, that of the historian, which is acquired not by entering but rather by leaving the city, moving from its old center toward its contemporary margins. But the current center of the city is no longer in the past.
>
> Art history, literature, and scientific knowledge have identified repertoires of contents that we have to be familiar with in order to be educated in the modern world. (García Canclini 4)

These different approaches show not only that there are different levels of observation of a city; they also demonstrate that the city as object of research depends on the investigator, his or her specific experiences, academic interests, and individual conditions, which influence the intellectual, ideological, historical, symbolic, and political construction of the space in time called the city. This does not simply mean that a single city is different for each of us. Even though the city can be resolved into an infinite number of perspectives, like the object depicted in a cubist painting, there are still certain laws governing these perspectivizations determined by social, historical, aesthetic, and cultural paradigms. What is the city for the writer and the diplomat, for the Corfu-born Mediterranean and for the Jew, for the asthmatic and aesthete Albert Cohen (1895–1981)—to mention but a few characteristics of the author of *Solal*? But first, a simpler question: How does a writer approach the city?

Roland Barthes asserts that literature is the branch of knowledge that specializes in not being specialized, a claim that obviously links literature to the cultural archive without equating the two. In Barthes's view, then, the writer's approach to the city would be to practice every possible approach, simultaneously or successively. The result would be a juxtaposition of the most diverse images, which would produce, in an ambiguous and multidimensional text, an extreme density of different types of knowledge. Every single image would simultaneously refer to all other images (without necessarily pointing to the "real" city) and, at the same time, would create an archive of images and after-images that the literary text would offer and that the reader could acquire receptively or through hypotyposis. Here again, not only different individual, but also cultural, social, and aesthetic paradigms—including all possible intertextual relationships, from pastiche to parody—come into play, which the author either follows or rejects, imitates or neglects or tries to eliminate from his work. The writer is never able to rid himself completely of these paradigms, which include relationships from a psychoanalytical repression to a multimedia proliferation of images. In other genres as well, even beyond Baedeker-style travel literature, texts of this kind can be found in abundance.

Some might argue that a writer cannot approach a city in any way at all. How ought we to define, then, this "other" relationship between the writer and the object of his writing? Albert Cohen provides an answer in a short text that is of central importance for his entire body of work. In this text, first published in 1945, he adopts the narrative point of view of a ten-year-old Jewish boy:

> When I went to the seashore, I was sure that the Mediterranean Sea I saw could also be found inside my head, not a mere image of the Mediterranean, but the very thing itself, tiny and salted, inside my head in miniature, but real, with all its fish, but very small, with all its waves and a little burning sun, a real sea with its rocks and all its ships complete in my head, with coal and living sailors, each ship with the same captain as the great ship outside, the same captain, but a dwarf one could touch if one had fingers small enough. I was sure that in my head, circus of the world, there was the real world with its woods, all the world's horses, but so tiny, all the kings in flesh and blood, all the dead, the whole sky with its stars and even God, terribly small and nice. And all this I still believe a little bit, but hush. (Cohen, *Jour* 196)[7]

The first-person narrator develops a vision of the world, and even of the universe, in which the real world outside is mirrored by an interior world possessing the same degree of reality and completeness. Each element of the macrocosm is matched by an element of the microcosm, which is both identical and different. Not only all of Creation but also the Creator himself is contained, on an extremely reduced scale, inside the head of the literary creator. There can be no doubt that this vision owes a great deal to the Jewish Cabala and to Christian mysticism. In Cohen's texts, the inversion of the relationship between the Creator and his creation surfaces again and again. The idea of the Creator as puppet in the hands of a playing child can be linked quite easily to the eye as mediator, as the organ that drastically reduces the size of objects in the outer world—perceptible in the "puppet's" pupils—and the organ that transfers them to the observer's inner world. As a result, the infinite space of the external world is contained within the limited space of the internal world, reduced but no less true. The globular shape of the eye is, in a certain way, replaced by the globular shape of the head that houses the circus containing the whole world. The eye and the area striata, opposed as topoi in our heads, determine the diameter of this world. The truth claim of the outside reality is by no means of higher authority since its objects and creatures are contained within the child's head. "Only the similar can recognize the similar," Goethe explained, alluding to the wisdom of the Ionic School (Goethe 56). This idea must have been familiar to Albert Cohen who, born on the island of Corfu, had his hero Solal be born on the small island of Cephalonia in the Ionic Sea. Cohen, however, radicalizes the idea by transforming the two-dimensionality of the retina into the three-dimensional inner space of his "circus of the world." The dimension makes possible the diverse hermeneutic viewpoints characterizing his protagonists.[8] Goethe's retinal after-images have materialized in Cohen's texts. In his texts, then, Cohen is not approaching the city; the city has always been within him, and he has always been inside the city. This writer's world is the world in our heads.

The City as Inner Space — Inner Space as City

It is not without reason that the crucial passage from Cohen's key text "Jour de mes dix ans" refers to a Mediterranean scene. Born in Corfu's Jewish ghetto, Cohen held Ottoman citizenship until he became a Swiss citizen (and added an "h" to his name) in October 1919, just one month before marrying his first wife, Elisabeth Brocher, in Geneva. It was the Jewish ghetto that he invoked so warmly in his autobiographical writings and in his novels. There is, in fact, an intimate correspondence between the relative isolation of the ghetto as a self-contained entity, which the family decided to leave because of the tensions and imminent pogroms in 1900, and the far greater isolation of the interior spaces of Cohen's novels. This isolation (*Abgeschlossenheit*) seems to be a leitmotiv in the almost six decades of his writing and in his private life, connecting his condition as a Jew to his existence as a writer. It was not by coincidence that his biographer, Gérard Valbert, compared Cohen's apartment in Geneva to a fortress.[9] Cohen's third wife, Bella, mentioned the couple's secluded lifestyle several times.[10] Cohen's rare excursions to the city could provoke attacks of fever, which Bella and Albert attributed to his physical weakness.[11] Even in the Jewish writer's last book, *Carnets 1978*, there is a twofold reflection on this isolation: on the one hand, the Geneva-based narrator looks back on his past life; on the other, the young boy depicted in the narrative, growing up in Marseilles, where the family had moved after leaving Corfu, reflects on his own isolation. In this southern French seaport, where antisemitism, influenced by the Dreyfus affair, grew stronger every day, and where Jewish parents escorted their children home from school or tried to find Catholic institutions to protect them better, young Albert Cohen was time and again exposed to teasing and persecution. In *Carnets 1978,* depictions of interiors prevail over the attractive but always dangerous outside world. The transition from inner world to outer urban space is made possible by the figure of the mother: her smiles and kisses made this transition possible by culturally encoding it:

> She combs my hair, brushes it, gives me a franc, tells me not to buy french fries or fritters, for the Gentiles don't wash their hands before cooking. And not to go to the roller coasters, for that is a pastime for brainless pagans, she tells me. I look at her as she opens the door in front of me. Yes, she is a bit stout, but that doesn't matter, it's nice. The angels be with you, look carefully both ways before crossing, she tells me, and she kisses me, smiling. (Cohen, *Carnets* 1122)[12]

In a text first published in 1922, after Albert Cohen had moved to Geneva, confronted there with a motherless town and a world of distractions frequented by Gentiles and pagans, an exterior space far from the Jewish ghetto seems to prevail. In his "Projections ou après-minuit à Genève," published in the prestigious *Nouvelle Revue Française,* the young writer develops another exterior world marked exclusively by interiors. The incipit—by no means accidentally—highlights the transition to a world of internal spaces. "The lighthouses violate with cold rage the locality screaming with immensity against the door I push" (Cohen, *Projections* 414).[13] The next thirty-three pages are a highly fragmented depiction of precise movements and observations, a succession of scenes in which the characters are illuminated as if standing in the dazzling light of spotlights; after they are given a chance to speak, they disappear into the darkness of the *vie nocturne.* From the very beginning, the I-narrator traces the image of a world subject to an unstoppable decadence. In a few lines of the second fragment, he sketches the life of one of the main characters:

> My gardener's daughter has become a whore, her old face of twenty years bearing the nobility of a wicked life.
> Pauline with her hair parted on the side argues, showing proudly the vivid rubies of her tongue. She shakes the ashes, laughing with the musty nose of the cocaine addict. She pulls the smoke into her mouth with mechanical charm. The yellow water Pauline drinks tells me of the stinking end of her loves. (Cohen, *Projections* 414)[14]

The concentration of drugs and alcohol, the cut-up bodies with their sharply illuminated fragments, the still shots of stereotypical movements form a world of images that is rudimentarily perceived subjectively, reminding us, in spite of its colors, of the old silent pictures. The cuts and explicit allusions to the cinematographic world link this internal space of nightclubs to the configuration of images projected in darkened rooms and accompanied by orchestras. This scene, it seems at first glance, could have taken place in almost any metropolitan space in the Western hemisphere.

The title, however, suggests that the projections take place after midnight in Geneva, where the writer took up residence in 1914. How does the text itself, clearly influenced by the literary procedures of the (historical) avant-garde, manage to link the nightclub scenes to the city of Geneva? At the end of "Projections," the I-narrator returns early one morning to his luxurious hotel, whose name is well known, and not only to the taxi driver. From inside the car, the narrator sees the lights flickering on the French lakeshore (*Projections* 441). These few elements, especially the mention of such well-known places as the hotel Beau Rivage, constitute the fundamental literary procedures Cohen uses to situate a text in a particular city. The city of Geneva is identified only by a few markers; it appears to be presented almost exclusively from an internal perspective. After leaving the dance hall, the narrator immediately takes a taxi, and it is from the inside of this moving, protective vehicle that the identity markers of the urban space are perceived, before the narrator reaches the interiors of his hotel, whose staff seems to be used to the caprices of spoiled guests. A tired porter is there to ease the transition from outside to inside.

Nevertheless, *local color* is taken into the internal spaces. It is the representation of the Geneva of the recently founded League of Nations, explicitly mentioned in the text, the Geneva of a multicultural society that neglects the intercultural relations that are supposed to bring the nations together. Patrons of nightclubs, both men and women, coming together from distant parts of the world, are unable to create an authentic dialogue between different cultures, races, and sexes. Cohen's "Projections" is a first sketch of the city whose epic portrait is further developed in his novel *Belle du Seigneur*, a project begun in the early 1930s and finally published in 1968. The people in the nightclub meet and engage in brief relationships without really taking care of one another. Geneva has become a city with an international flair, but nothing more. As in "Projections," the rules of this game continue to be those of a Western city.

In "Projections," a succession of incoherent actions unfold, their causes beyond the observer's understanding. It is not astonishing, therefore, that Prospero, a jazz musician and the narrator's friend, has been making his living moving furniture from one internal space to another. Nonetheless, these movements and interiors allow brief glimpses of the times: Prospero tells us about organizing the moving of Russian students where the name Trotsky is mentioned. The Swiss prelude to the Russian Revolution (the name Lenin would have been more historically precise), together with numerous other historical elements, is projected inside the text. These elements form the historical background of Cohen's narrative experiment, written in a period later called the *entre-deux-guerres* (interwar period). From the midnight projections of Geneva a portrait of a city emerges whose different aspects are developed only in fragmentary form in the darkroom. It is up to the reader to complete these fragments to create an image of Geneva at the time of the League of Nations. For the implied reader, any other European city could stand in for Geneva. Geneva seems to possess no specific qualifications for this political role. Argentines and Americans, Russians and Japanese, British lords and Swiss servants compose the portrait of a city, and there is no need for the writer or the reader to approach it systematically. The city is simply there, and is invoked by its name and its numerous identity markers. Despite their uniqueness, these are easily exchangeable, and, in fact, Cohen did slightly change the location of various scenes in his novels. For Cohen, the city as such is secondary. Its image is supposed to be known. The projections bring forth images already stored in the reader's memory (either literary images or images produced by external impulses), which, as after-images, fill in the gaps of Cohen's fragmented city portraits. The movement initiated in this process is twofold: on the one hand, the city appears as an internal space. In the case of "Projections ou après-minuit à Genève," it is an immense, darkened dance hall artificially illuminated by spotlights, where men from all over the world come to have a good time with their wives and other women. On the other hand, the internal space itself is transformed into a city insofar as it contains the people who give the urban atmosphere its shape. Once more, the interior can be seen as a *circus of the world* in Cohen's sense. As a result, the room into which these sequences of images (formed by continuous dissolves) are projected enters into a metonymic relationship with the city. Simultaneously, the city itself is metaphorically transformed into an internal space that can be compared to a dance floor on which couples and individuals move. The feeling of solitude and isolation not only dominates in Cohen's later autobiographical narrative, it is already present in the world of these crowded nightclubs. Thus, one of the protagonists, called "L'Isolé" (The Loner), remarks: "I create a small world of my own, where my persecutors see bad times! This is philosophy. Metaphysics, to be more exact. Or rather a sort of religion. It's all pretty complicated, and I can't explain my system to you in just a few minutes" (Cohen, *Projections* 425).[15] By analogy, Albert Cohen's "vistas" of the city are not a physics but a metaphysics, not images but after-images of the city. This, however, does not mean we are dealing with static images.

THE STRUGGLE OF IMAGES

The second chapter of Albert Cohen's novel *Mangeclous* (Gallimard, 1938), presents the active street life of the Jewish ghetto in Cephalonia, where five friends, the "Valeureux de France," meet. In some parts of the chapter, merchants and businessmen dominate the scene, in others, students of the Talmud pray while rabbis debate certain passages in detail. Mangeclous, perhaps the most grotesque character in Cohen's works, tries to annoy and provoke these men of religion by proclaiming there is no God. His opponents react by covering their ears with their hands. Mangeclous, who—as the narrator tells us—actually believes in God "quite frequently" but loves to be taken for an *esprit moderne*, now tries a different approach: "'A pretty naked woman!' he cried all of a sudden, full of malice, at the most devout of the law students, a pale young man with blue shadows around his eyes, who immediately thinks how repulsive this impudent lady would be if one were to skin her alive" (Cohen, *Mangeclous* 377).[16] Mangeclous's insidious attack is directed at a vulnerable place. Because the Jews cover their ears, his words cannot reach them. They could have also closed their eyes to avoid any excitation of their retinas that might have interrupted their religious worship. That is why the cunning Mangeclous resorts to a ruse. With a few words he tries to make an impact on his preferred enemy, forcing him to project an image within himself, one that goes counter to his religious convictions. Mangeclous's words function as an external impulse, setting off a complicated mechanism that inevitably, and independently of the victim's will, leads the religious man to construct an attractive nude before his "inner" eye.

The ancient rhetoricians already knew the power of hypotyposis, which Albert Cohen tries to illuminate in this passage. The projection of an image evoked by rhetoric is realized deep within the listener, who cannot escape it. But the reaction of the pale young man is highly instructive. In trying to neutralize its erotic impact, he manipulates the image of the "impudent lady" in his imagination. This procedure once more uses the interplay between identity and difference: the young lady stays the same but her nudity is radicalized by a series of consciously created after-images of her skinned alive.

How is the transformation of the image of an erotic female body into an extremely cruel and sadistic sight useful in recovering one's religious devotion? There is no doubt that the images projected within us exert power over us and that there is a decisive struggle between images and counter-images to dominate the internal spaces and of the human imaginary. Furthermore, it is obvious that a political dimension is involved, of which Albert Cohen was very conscious. The mechanisms of antisemitism are based to a significant extent on the struggle between the different images of the other which people have internalized. In this scene, which may seem harmless and of secondary importance, it becomes clear that an impulse coming from the outside does not have to strike the retina to initiate this struggle. As a matter of fact, after-images can also be invoked in more mediated ways and can be produced on our retina or, we might say, in the complex data transmission system around our area striata. After-images are not invoked by mechanically closing and opening the eyes; rather, the words of the other stimulate a hypotyposis. The details of these after-images in the listener's mind (such as the hair or skin color of Mangeclous's naked woman) result from our own experiences or desires, and are of secondary importance. For these unconsciously projected after-images to make a strong impact, it is far more efficient to leave their details to the listener's visual archives, consisting of both "true" and "imaginary" images. The persuasive power and authenticity of the after-images created by hypotyposis depend precisely on individually significant details and even on a great number of superfluous aspects that produce the desired *effet de réel* (reality effect), in Roland Barthes's sense.

Cohen's texts make use of a great number of archival images and counterimages. The economy of his writing may even be founded on the production of diametrically opposed images. These binary oppositions—such as internal versus external spaces, Judaism versus Christianity, men and women, life and death—introduced at the very beginning, are worked through as the text develops without the basic binary structure being completely eliminated. Transgressions of boundaries formed by antinomic structures give new strength to these polarities, as in the case of the complex femininity (or should we say the femininity complex) of the male Solal, his life after death, the Jewish essence of Christianity, and the presence of external spaces on the inside, to mention but a few examples. This bipolarity is only partly transformed into ambiguity, and never resolves itself into complete indifference.[17] This, and not the moralizing tendencies of Cohen's narrators, may be the reason Albert Cohen's writing, despite the sometimes extreme self-reflexive ness of his texts, is clearly situated within the paradigm of a modern aesthetics not yet radicalized by postmodern writing strategies.

IMAGES AND COUNTERIMAGES OF THE CITY

How do the oppositions in Cohen's texts influence his creation of images and after-images of the city? On a wonderful April morning in 1936, on the lovely Greek island of Cephalonia, little Salomon Solal, probably the most lovely character in Albert Cohen's novels, is exercising, making swimming motions on his balcony. He talks to himself, as he often does:

"'April in Cephalonia,' said the solitary swimmer, 'is nicer and milder than July in Berlin! Certainly. But why in heaven's name do they all build their capitals in such cold, sad places, and why do they put them along black rivers? I think they are wrong. But in the end, they know better than I do'" (Cohen, *Mangeclous* 366).[18]

The capitals that play a major role in Cohen's novels, with the exception of Berlin, also played an important role in his life. Indeed, they are located, at least in comparison to the Greek archipelago, in the dark regions of the "cold," with rivers that may hardly be called "black" but that also do not display the bright colors of Cephalonia. Who would deny the climatic difference in climate between the Ionic Sea and Paris, Berlin, London, or even Geneva? But the north-south contrast, highlighted by Salomon, reminds us of a basic opposition that structures Cohen's work in its totality, the polarity between light and darkness. This polarity seems almost as irreconcilable as the opposition between the first-person singular and the third-person plural, in Salomon's language. This opposition is finally undermined in the cycle of Cohen's novels. Solal, the tetralogy's central figure, has become a man of the north who is still closely connected to the Mediterranean south. Unlike him, the Valeureux are loyal inhabitants of the Jewish ghetto on their island, who nevertheless have great esteem for the major cities of the north, and for the values represented by France, Great Britain, and Switzerland. In this case, Germany embodies the European counterimage. Solal's farewell to his father, Gamaliel, who does not want to leave the world of his Jewish ghetto around the Ruelle d'Or and under the protection of the citadel, and, even more, his farewell to his uncle Saltiel, a mediator between the different cultural worlds emerging in the novel, is contrasted with the arrival of the Valeureux in the capitals of "froidure," as Salomon would put it. Their arrival in Paris opens chapter 18 of Cohen's first novel, *Solal* (1930):

> At first, leaving the compartment, Uncle Saltiel felt he had to greet the City of Light with a great wave of his cap. . . . Mangeclous stopped sometimes, addressing the mocking spectators. . . . Then the Valeureux went into Paris with the sole aim of greeting the statues of the benefactors of mankind.
> At seven o'clock in the evening, these naive people stood in front of the Ministry of Foreign Affairs, removing their hats before the tricolor banner. (Cohen, *Solal* 226)[19]

Paris is called the *Ville lumière*, City of Light, the cradle of human rights. By symbolically greeting the French flag and by visiting the statues of major benefactors of mankind, the five Jews try to invoke these values. At this point, the dark side of this city of light is still invisible to them. The same ritual is enacted by Saltiel and Salomon as they walk through the streets of Geneva. On their way, they pay a visit not only to the university (where Cohen himself once studied law) but also to the statues of the great Reformers[20] representing, like the statues in Paris, dimensions of mankind that transcend national concerns. In these scenes, stereotypes are consolidated through personal "experience" and visual impressions, even though—as in the passage cited above—the inhabitants of the praised cities do not hesitate to discriminate against strangers who have recently arrived from the Orient, using the same images as the Valeureux de France and vice versa. The conscious and explicit use of this "struggle of images" may be the main reason Cohen insisted, at the performance of his play *Ezéchiel* at the Comédie Française in 1933 (i.e., the year of the Nazi takeover), on projecting antisemitic images and stereotypes onstage. This decision shocked many Parisian theater critics and spectators at the time. Cohen was not willing to accept the fact that the moment for these projections was badly chosen: what counted for him was the struggle of images and counterimages, a battle that (in the case of the 1933 theater production) he could never win. Not surprisingly, Cohen turned away from the stage forever and tried to put forward his cosmos of images in his narratives. In the 1930s and later, in complete independence from the chosen literary genres, he analyzed the clichés the word "Jew" evoked by hypotyposis in a European readership. Starting with the projection of after-images that can easily be re-created in a thoroughly antisemitic Europe, Cohen wanted to provoke changes in the visual archives of his audience and readership. In the end, it did not matter whether these images were produced by external impulses on the retina, as was the case in his plays, or—as in his narratives—by inner impulses on the "screen" of the area striata. Still, his preference for the "inner" images is completely coherent.

Once again, the interaction between identity and difference is decisive, insofar as the mere projection of a counterimage would not have been sufficient. Cohen first introduces positive images of a city in order to submit these after-images, in a second stage, to deliberate changes. This is the case in those traumatic scenes of Geneva and Paris, where Solal, the incarnation of the "wandering Jew," roams through the streets exactly as the young boy had suffered in the streets of Marseilles on his tenth birthday ("Jour de mes dix ans"). Because of his commitment to the German Jews, Solal is stripped of his French citizenship and simultaneously expelled from his important position in the League of Nations. Momentarily liberated from the sufferings of his "chemically pure" love for Ariane, he roams through a Paris whose walls bear the slogan "Mort aux Juifs!" (Death to the Jews!), transforming him into a "chemically pure" Jew. The streets and locales of Paris, mentioned as identity markers, also allow the reader to follow Solal through the city on a map. But the "Mort aux Juifs!" that constantly drives him back to the "petit ghetto, notre petit ghetto"

(Cohen, *Seigneur* 849) of his hotel room links together all the cities of Christianity, all the major Western cities, wiping out their differences in spite of the proliferation of names invoking well-known Parisian places and streets: "Such a desire for 'Death to the Jews' in these cities of brotherly love" (Cohen, *Seigneur* 852).[21] Beyond the differences between these cities, an identity emerges that leads from the proliferation of heterogeneous street names back to the unity of a homogeneous death wish: "Death to the Jews. Everywhere, in all lands, the same words" (861).[22] Thus, it is not surprising that, in the following chapter, Cohen transfers Solal from the streets of Paris to the streets of Geneva, a wandering Jew searching in vain for a place in the society of nations, in the League of Nations. In a long letter to Ariane, written almost without punctuation and in a deliberate stream-of-consciousness style, Solal reflects on his situation and the alternatives he faces:

> Outside I walked through the streets, trailing my unhappiness, wishing oh to see Uncle Saltiel again to live with him but no impossible he would be so unhappy to see me so haggard I cannot make him suffer stopping in front of the lake ripping to pieces the two letters my two nice inventions my grand hopes throwing them into the lake watching the current take them away, the streets the streets thinking of liberating you from me of leaving you all my dollars putting them for you into a bank account me going to live with them in the cellar, I was tired I had not eaten anything bent over my typewriter. (875)[23]

For Solal, there are only three alternatives to wandering at length through the streets of Paris and Geneva, an activity that also profoundly marks *Belle du Seigneur* and Cohen's other novels. First, he can return to his uncle Saltiel and his native ghetto, a possibility Solal immediately rejects. Second, he can commit suicide, physically eliminate the Jew, leave behind all his possessions, a "solution" that comes close to the Nazis' plan of genocide. Finally, he can choose a life underground, in "the cellar," a choice made in a variety of Cohen's texts. These alternatives would "liberate" the wandering Jew from roaming the cities of the West. But none of them really offers him a way out, and his death therefore corresponds to the novel's ambiguous conclusion. A fourth possibility, Zionism and the founding of the state of Israel, which would allow Jews to join the League of Nations, is only briefly alluded to in the novel. This question is related to the problem of reterritorialization, which I have analyzed elsewhere (Ette). In this context, the possible physical elimination of the Jews, the images of various European cities almost merge. The identity markers remain on the surface; underneath, the differences between them fade away. In the struggle of images, the City of Light and the statues of the benefactors of mankind stand opposed to an underground city where Jewish characters, banned from the surface, reach epic proportions. Underneath the surface of the city of light, which Cohen had to escape because of the imminent danger of the Nazi occupation, another city emerges.

THE CITY OF THE UNDERGROUND

The Valeureux, arriving in Geneva or Paris as if from another world, knew exactly where to find the city's spiritual center, its nucleus. There is no such center any longer for Solal, who has been banned from European society. He wanders around cities that are not intentionally decentered but whose original center has been lost. The lost nucleus of the city can be counterbalanced by the more or less protected internal space of the "ghetto," whether it takes the form of a hotel room or a chalet Solal shares with his lover, carefully separated from the world outside.

The ghetto takes yet another form. In Cohen's first novel, Solal, occupying a powerful social position, buys a medieval palace where he lives with Aude, a beautiful young lady he first met in Cephalonia during his youth. It is only by chance that she discovers his secret purchase of the Commanderie. This name is one of the frequent allusions to Marcel Proust's *A la recherche du temps perdu*.[24] The Jew Solal buys a symbolic part of the old Christian tradition and transforms it into a Jewish microcosm. Aude notices that her lover keeps escaping through a secret door into the immense, catacomblike basement from which she believes she heard voices earlier. Solal had temporarily broken off relations with his father, Gamaliel, and with Jewish culture because of his love for Aude and, perhaps even more, for the West. When taken by surprise, he confesses he has reconciled with his father and explains the consequences:

> I went to throw myself on my knees before my lord and father, and that merciful man pardoned me. He ordered me to make a secret home in my European home. I obeyed. In his wisdom, he understands that I must continue my Western life. I asked the Solals to come, those from Cephalonia, and those from elsewhere. A biblical city swarms beneath His Excellency's house. During the day, the ministry, home, party meetings. And by night, I go to my own country. Both day and night, I am sad, so sad. (Cohen, *Solal* 290–91)[25]

The Western, surface world is opposed to a non-Western world below— a "biblical city" invisible to outsiders. The protagonist's split between day and night, the "Western" and "Jewish" worlds, corresponds to the city's own split between a "Christian" surface and a "Jewish" underground. For the first time in Albert Cohen's writings, the two distant poles dominating the image of the city come together in space. The Jewish ghetto of Cephalonia is projected into a closed space inside the Western city. In this process, a tension between the two spaces is created and cannot be eliminated. Aude forces her lover to choose between the two worlds, the two cities. When he refuses, she leaves him, simultaneously excluding him from the *City of Light*. After a time, Solal loses all his official duties, consequently losing his powerful position in Western society. The tension between the two poles was already present and almost irresolvable in 1930, when *Solal* was published. After the Nazi takeover in Germany, however, it increased so dramatically that one city tried to destroy the other—the Jewish city. On the first pages of *Mangeclous*, Salomon, still protected by a certain distance, fearfully mentions the terrible pogroms against the Jews in Germany. In *Belle du Seigneur*, Solal's visit to Berlin in the mid-1930s becomes a journey into the night, via a city almost swallowed up by horror. Only by chance can he escape from the approaching Nazi hordes into a basement, where the dwarf Rachel has become a central figure in a Jewish world radically threatened in its existence. Albert Cohen presents Berlin as a *biblical city*, a sometimes absurd or grotesque counterworld of the external urban space, the Western world, dominated by the logic of murder. From the darkness of the basements, the external world can be perceived only acoustically. But, even on this level, a sharp contrast emerges:

> Suddenly there was another loud noise outside, and at the same time, when the hammering of the boots echoed the German song, song of wickedness, song of German joy, joy of the blood of Israel spurting under the German knives, *Wenn Judenblut unter'm Messer spritzt*, sang the young hopes of the German nation, whereas from the cellar next door another song rose up, song to the Eternal, a heavy song of love, emerging from the fount of ages, the song of my King David. (Cohen, *Seigneur* 514)[26]

The dissonance between these two worlds culminates in the chant, where sound replaces image, the ear replaces the eye, as we frequently observe in Cohen's representations of religious devotion.[27] Blindness, then, corresponds to insight. Visual images are replaced by sound images, making the reader aware for the last time of the unrepresentable, articulated in a foreign language as spurting blood. In the course of Cohen's novels, images of the city become increasingly obscure. They can also be considered after-images in the sense that they are images of the city after the experience of a radicalized antisemitism, after the Holocaust. These after-images, *Nachbilder*, turn into *Nachtbilder*, images of the night(mare) that descended on Germany and Europe, which had been so marvelously civilized on the surface. We move from a retinal perception of the city to a series of fading and overlapping stereotypes and after-images of different cities, and finally, to a situation where differences lose their impact and homogeneous spatial structures appear, where the footsteps of the wan-

dering Jew fade away. The projection of the city into the interior is followed by its expansion into inner spaces that become increasingly dark
under the burden of history. It is easy to relate this last darkened interior,
constantly surrounded and threatened by death, to those images (or so we
might think) of the romantic tradition invoked by Albert Cohen in his
Carnets 1978. There as well, the aimless movements of the "I" in the streets
of Marseilles gradually come to an almost complete standstill under the
surface. The transition from the city of life to the city of death is captured
in fast motion:

> Back at the Canebière, I cast down my eyes while walking, biting my lips to
> keep from crying. "Tired of living," I write with my finger in the air. Then I
> write the word "catalepsis." I read this word in a book, and I learned from the
> dictionary that it means you cannot move any longer, as though you were
> dead. With any luck, they will not bury me alive, by mistake. Then I would
> awake in my coffin, and cry out, and hear the steps of the living passing
> through the graveyard, I'd cry out to them to come and rescue me, but they
> wouldn't hear, and I'd cry, and implore, suffocating, the boards of the coffin
> in front of my living nose. Back at home, I'll ask Mother to make sure I am re-
> ally dead, when I die, I'll ask her to stab me in the heart for safety. But
> enough: no more thoughts of catalepsis. (Cohen, *Carnets* 1129)[28]

AFTER-IMAGES OF THE CITY AFTER THE SHOAH

Albert Cohen's texts show a continuous deterritorialization linking a
persecuted Jewish culture, and his own writing, to internal spaces, even
though they are not locally grounded. The resulting images of the city are
eventually conceived from an inner perspective. This means that these images become increasingly indistinguishable, that their identity markers no
longer refer to substantial differences. These images are integrated into a
series of easily interchangeable after-images. The continuous overlapping
of different structures of images transforms every image in response to
previously represented structures. Thus, a concrete image of a certain city
already contains after-images of other cities. Cohen's texts configure a
highly sensitive literary retina that differs from a simple screen or canvas
in its ability to store successive exposures. This is why there are different
"nerve endings" on the surface of this (literary) retina. Images of one city
always contain the after-images of the others. The "succession of images"
may seem "pure," but, as Goethe put it, some elements of the preceding
images are secretly maintained in the succeeding ones: "daß sich von dem
vorhergehenden etwas ins nachfolgende hinüberschleicht" (Goethe 69).
The textual image of the city still refers to a preexisting intertextuality.
Cohen's images of the city may sometimes seem stereotypical—and this

might be why, as far as I know, no detailed study of his images has been undertaken thus far. But the dynamics and variety of these images is expanded in that retinal network created by the complex relationship among them.

We can now understand how much the inner perspective of urban spaces owes to the Jewish condition of Cohen's writing. The marginalization of his protagonist's perspective, already present in *Solal* and radically increased in *Belle du Seigneur*, including the view from the basements, may clarify the inhuman way the ghettoization of the Jews was pursued in the twentieth century, a process that led to the concentration camps of the Third Reich. It is not surprising that the camps have been ubiquitous as a structural element in Cohen's novels since 1945. The vision of Berlin from the basement darkens the image of the city, increasingly replacing it with a world of noises that is all the more threatening in that it announces the mechanisms of destruction and genocide.

No doubt, after the Shoah, Europe's major cities are now different. From this point of view, the current debates around the revitalization of the German capital of the so-called Roaring Twenties seem somehow ridiculous: there could have been no Roaring Twenties without the Jews. Berlin has to play both a very specific and a paradigmatic role. How can we write about such cities? We know that, even after Adorno's famous and controversial statement that there can be no poetry after Auschwitz, poetic writing has continued. In the same way, the city has returned as a literary theme in post-Shoah European literature, of even greater importance, perhaps, than it was before 1933. The deterritorialization of the city developed differently from Cohen's model. Literature and the fine arts give us new images of cities proliferating on the surfaces (and not in the "depths"). This may represent a new sensitivity toward the (post)modern city whose urban spaces are dominated by surface (not to say superficial) structures, without a center in the proper sense, and characterized by aimless and nomadic movements.[29] The French philosopher and cultural theorist Jean Baudrillard approached U.S. cities in the second half of the twentieth century the way sociologists (to follow Néstor García Canclini's statement) once used highways and freeways. Perceiving cities from this perspective in his travel book *Amérique,* Baudrillard established metonymic relationships between the vast urban spaces and the even greater deserts in North America (see Baudrillard, *Amérique,* part 1). As we know, the desert, like Baudrillard's cities, is defined as a "depth problem," a lack of water: as a result, one of its major characteristics is a physiognomy of surfaces. Is it possible that the otherness of European cities, already noticed by Baudrillard through the windows of an airplane[30] and still observable, is the result of processes of marginalization and destruction unparalleled in the history of mankind? How do European cities remember or commemorate their dark past? Is the destruction of (historical) depth reflected in the (contemporary) surface? Or do the surfaces of contemporary cities produce depth only to simulate historical continuity and to ignore the fractures? What about the traces of absence? Certainly, it would be too simple to answer this question by arguing for a Holocaust monument in Berlin. The images of the city from the dominant inner perspective, as created by Cohen, seem to have been almost forgotten. Their after-images grew increasingly weak, not least because of Cohen's powerful images of love. Nevertheless, it would have been impossible for Solal not to have "seen" the streets of Marseilles, Paris, and other cities as he walked through Geneva.

Rather than build a monument of any kind, it might be more important (to refer to Goethe one last time) to recall as a literary and artistic presence the faded after-images of the city that began as projections on our retina. If we close our eyes and open them again, we may see, inside the images of our proliferating cities, the caves beyond the surface, the cities below our cities, as after-images we can constantly adapt to the new contexts of our rapidly changing urban spaces. Unlike photographs, these after-images are hypotypotic creations that may appear, in the midst of our retinal perceptions, as products of reminiscences that go far beyond our personal experiences. Then we can imagine the after-images stored in other images, which Albert Cohen has created to accompany us and illustrate the most cruelly antisemitic decades of the last millennium.

CHAPTER EIGHT

Tijuana: Shadowtext for the Future

Debra Castillo

In August 1997 the mayor of Tijuana, José Guadalupe Osuna Milán, received the following communication from the head of the city's justice department, as the final statement in a series of municipal discussions and negotiations that had been going on for months, much to the consternation and bemusement of the local press:

> Attendant upon the instructions generated at that point and having concluded the transaction, I append to this document the original copy of the Title of Trademark Registration number 555863, file number 300027 of the Mexican Institute for Industrial Property, under class 35, nominative, the term "TIJUANA" which protects publicity and business, circulation of publicity materials, brochures, prospectuses, printed matter, samples, films, novels, videotapes, and documentaries on behalf of the Municipal Government of Tijuana.[1]

The mayor's office clarified that under no circumstances would the office charge royalties for the use of this newly registered term, and that the purpose of the legislation was purely to protect "the word 'Tijuana' so as to avoid its misuse."[2] The elected officials' concern for the good name of Tijuana inevitably reminds us of the city's less than pristine reputation; indeed, such legislation can only be imagined in the context of the considerable adverse publicity that has made "Tijuana" a byword for the worst stereotypes of excess associated with Mexico's northern border: Americanized inhabitants, tacky businesses, bad food, sleazy sex joints. This stereotype, conceptualized somewhat differently in the two dominant cultures (United States and central Mexico), combines with the anxious rage in Tijuana itself of being caught helplessly between two giant propaganda machines. The resulting volatile mixture constitutes what Jorge Busta-mante calls, in another context, the "síndrome de Tijuana"—which, after August 1997, would have to be called the Tijuana® Syndrome—the hap-less feeling of living on the wrong side of the defining edge of national culture while at the same time persisting as an obsessive object of dis-course.

The region seems almost fatally predisposed for such obsessions, given the lucky or unlucky circumstance of its hyperdetermined geographical location, its always-already liminality to traditionally sanctioned discus-sions of national power and gender rights, long before the small settle-ment on the United States/Mexico border became a boom town and in-ternational sin city at the beginning of the twentieth century. In 1535, Hernán Cortés wrote the name "California" on a map, identifying a strip of land on the western edge of New Spain and paying tribute to one of the more intriguing mythic sites invented for the immensely popular chivalric romance cycle dedicated to the adventures of Amadís de Gaula and his progeny, in this case, Garci Rodríguez de Montalvo's *Las sergas de Esp-landián*: "On the right-hand side of the Indies there was an island called California, which was very close to the region of the Earthly Paradise. This island was inhabited by black women, and there were no males among them at all" (457).[3] Montalvo's California, therefore, before being specifi-cally located geographically—to the left of the West Indies, but indeed, from a global perspective, on the right hand of the fabled East Indies—was already marked out as a fabulous and incomprehensible site, fiercely guarded, ruled by women, liminally paradisiacal, racially differentiated.

Louis XIV of France's court geographer, Sanson d'Abbeville, warns in the introduction to his description of California that the reports of re-turned travelers and knights should not always be accepted at face value: "These opposite descriptions about these areas show us how dangerous it is to trust those who return from far away. We should not be deceived by people who make such claims, regardless of how well dressed these people may be, or regardless of how well they speak, or of how good-look-ing they are. We should not trust them even if they give much assurance of the truth" (Sanson d'Abbeville 55). In the concluding paragraph of this little book, the geographer gives one example of such inaccurate report-ing. It seems that people believed for many years that California was a peninsula; however, d'Abbeville has privileged information from a Dutch ship, which had captured a Spanish ship, which had complete charts showing that California was an island after all (65). Interestingly enough, Montalvo had already presciently foreseen this fact in *Esplandián*—and it is worth noting parenthetically that the French also read Spanish chivalric novels, which were the best-sellers of the time, and were almost immediately translated into the major European languages. The place name "California," then, evokes a temporal, spatial, gender-marked anomaly outside the normative domestication of the American wilderness as a (male) conquerable space. It is a markedly, uneasily feminine space, unusually subject to the superimposition of, or veering between, dystopian and utopian visions, reactionary and avant-garde political and social perspectives, nostalgia for an invented past and anticipation of an imagined future.

Even in current discussions, the remoteness and relative isolation of California from the two contemporary dominant national discourses (Mexico, the United States) offer intriguing opportunities for speculative projection from both the Distrito Federal and the District of Columbia. As political interest in the border region grows, Debbie Nathan asks, "Does such a turnabout then mean that life on the *frontera* is actually the avant-garde of our larger cosmopolitan *mañana?*" Nathan's comment is a tongue-in-cheek question about the modalities increasingly associated with modern late-capitalist production, and as such, puts its finger on an issue that is only beginning to be addressed seriously. In addition, one of the things I particularly like about her form of expression is that it offers a paradigmatic instance of a highly self-conscious border discourse at play, one in which a French-derived high art literary term ("avant-garde") jostles with colloquial expressions from both sides of the linguistic and political border, implicitly calling into question the cultural assumptions about cosmopolitan (implicitly U.S.) and *mañana* (Mexican) cultures.

Much of the discourse of/from the *frontera* in general, and about Tijuana in particular, has this shadowtext quality, that is, it issues from a space ambiguously inside/outside dominant discourse(s) and it echoes the issues that both societies uneasily abject or repress. On the one hand, dominant discourse about the *frontera* tends to look like the dark side, to display a hidden attachment to a discourse otherwise cast in bright light. Sometimes this play of light and shadow is overtly described. "Mexican cynicism is an aspect of the Mexican habit of always seeking the shade," says Richard Rodriguez in his discussion of Tijuana, "In Athens Once," and continues: "Americans distrust Mexican shading. The genius of American culture and its integrity come from fidelity to the light" (88). On the other hand, the shadowtext provides contours, if only in a dangerous, phallic, and fetishized manner. Here I am thinking of Ortega y Gasset's much-cited definition of the polis in his 1930 *Revolt of the Masses*: "The most accurate definition of the *urbs* and the *polis* is very like the comic definition of a cannon. You take a hole, wrap some steel wire tightly around it" (151). Analogously, in the border text, you would take a whole and wrap a steel fence along it.

The military metaphor for this dark space is particularly apt, not only in terms of the United States' language of the "war" on drugs and against undocumented aliens, but also in its evocation of a space that is both contained and associated, from the moment of its invented origin, with an othered bellicose nature. This latent violence is echoed even in the U.S. tourist's imagination, where Tijuana frequently figures as a sort of cinematic Wild West outpost, and in centrist Mexican conceptions, where it persists as a convenient trope for the provincial city full of violent men (Tijuana was where Party of the Institutionalized Revolution (PRI) presidential candidate Luis Donaldo Colosio was famously assassinated) and lawless women (its infamous place in the centrist imagination as a ratty prostitute of a town).

Tijuana border writing—and here I intentionally confuse writing *on* with writing *from*—is, furthermore, a peculiar kind of shadowtext, one projected simultaneously into an anticipated future: "avant-garde," "cosmopolitan *mañana*," says Nathan, which is at the same time a refused past. The term "refuse" can function as both a noun and a verb (Trinh Minh-ha [6] has already pointed this out in another context) and can connote an inadequate suturing: re-fuse, fusing together two disparate materials that continually come unstuck. The Tijuana Syndrome reflects the stereotypes about itself that each society has refused, while readmitting the stereotypes about the refused other; it also reflects the border as a well-known site of refusal—the literal and figural dump for each society's urban, industrial, toxic, and sexual waste. In one such formulation, Tijuana is described as an "inedible city" where "street vendors offer unclean enchantments" (Rodriguez 92), capturing in this manner the image of a sexualized abundance of things and people (women) to chew and suck, which nevertheless must be refused. And yet, because the refused (repressed) always returns in some future moment, because the refuse is inextricably linked to the most personal and private details of modern life, the refusal by the dominant culture is doomed to shadow itself, in the past and in the future. Trinh says: "If, despite their location, noun and verb inhabit the two very different and well-located worlds of designated and designator, the space between them remains a surreptitious site of movement and passage whose open, communal character makes exclusive belonging and long-term residence undesirable, if not impossible" (6). Who can live on a waste dump? Or in a cannon's mouth? Is it not the lure of "unclean enchantment" that draws a significant portion of Tijuana's tourist industry to the city?

The metaphors for Tijuana continue to proliferate, but curiously, follow similar lines of thought, presenting variations on the theme of an abjected shadow other as a projected future self. Writing from the U.S. side, Richard Rodriguez posits that "Tijuana is where Mexico comes to an end." Immediately after this statement he summarizes what he considers the Mexican centrist view of the northern border city: "People in Mexico City will tell you, if they have anything at all to say about Tijuana, that Tijuana is a city without history, a city without architecture, an American city" (83), and he concludes that "taken as one, Tijuana and San Diego form the most fascinating new city in the world, a city of world-class irony" (106). For Rodriguez, then, Tijuana is at one and the same time "the end" (of Mexico) and the beginning of something else. Furthermore, Rodriguez does not dissent from the view of Tijuana he puts in the anonymous mouths of Mexico City's inhabitants, but he shadows and elaborates on it in relation to his own peculiar take as the English-favoring, United States–identified son of a Mexican father. From that point of view, in some respects like Rodriguez and his father, Tijuana is the shadow that defines Mexican national character by antinomy—unlike Mexico City with its long historical trajectory, its pyramids and skyscrapers, its absolute hegemony as the site of national culture, Tijuana has no history, no architecture, no claim on the national imagination. Rodriguez takes this catalog of negatives and turns it into a positive attribute. Tijuana–San Diego (like the gay American son of the macho Mexican man) is the model for a transcultured, transexualized identity: the city as rhetorical trope, the heartlands of po-mo irony.

Writing from Mexico City, Néstor García Canclini posits two different models of Tijuana, both of which enter into dialogue with Rodriguez, as one dominant culture again shadows itself and its dominant culture counterpart in the bordertext. For García Canclini, Tijuana, along with New York City, represents "one of the biggest laboratories of postmodernity" (233).[4] In an alternative metaphor, it is "everyone's house." Here too, as in Rodriguez's text, Tijuana is both exceptional and paradigmatic, both not-Mexico and globally transcendent. Tijuana is everyone's house in this formulation precisely because it is not a symbolic house at all, but rather a huge laboratory for aesthetic contemplation from the outside, where scientists can go to do fieldwork in postmodern reality effects. I suspect that Welchman would place García Canclini's version of a border theory in the same category as the position he aligns with the Baudrillardian spectacle in which "'home' is thus evaporated" and the "'borderama' is vaunted . . . as the governing trope of the postmodern" (175). Note Welchman's appropriately San Diegan quotation marks, ironic commentaries on this archetypal First World po-mo position—like Nathan, and unlike Rodriguez and García Canclini, he lives in the waste heap of Western civ, in the can[n]on's mouth, with all its attendant shadow rites and responsibilities.

Baudrillard, along with Lyotard and other luminaries of French high theory, whose travels in America figure prominently in their analyses of the (post)modern condition, hold a significant place in García Canclini's discussion of the Tijuana borderlands as a privileged site of postmodern production. His conceptualization of the region centers on the term "deterritorialization" (borrowed from Deleuze and Guattari, though unattributed); it is elaborated through references to Certeau, finds support in Gómez Peña, turns to seminal passages from Baudrillard and Lyotard, and concludes with reference to "May '68 in Paris (also in Berlin, Rome, Mexico City, Berkeley)" (249–50).[5]

It is worth exploring briefly a few typical instances of this citational practice to more fully understand the implications of textual shadowing. As Mexican border scholar María-Socorro Tabuenca Córdoba writes, for scholars working in Mexico, "it is difficult to conceive of the border simply as a metaphor at the very moment in which we are seeking conceptual frameworks for the analysis of border literature. And if border literary expression in Mexico is someday reduced to simply being a metaphor, it will be necessary for us to find out the direction of such metaphor" (151). In the conjunction of, for example, Néstor García Canclini (an Argentine scholar living in Mexico City), Michel de Certeau (a French scholar who has relocated to San Diego), and Guillermo Gómez Peña (a Mexico City artist working in Tijuana), we can readily see the complicities and alliances among various dominant cultural discursive practices and politics that determine the valences ascribed to particular cultural modes.

BORDER CONTAMINATION

A quotation from Certeau, "life consists of constantly crossing borders,"[6] introduces García Canclini's assertion that Tijuana, along with New York City, is one of the two great laboratories of postmodernity. The essay from which García Canclini took the Certeau line, "Californie, un théâtre de passants," is an ambiguously located travel narrative in which text shadows text to an unusual degree. Written for a French audience on Certeau's return to France and French after two and a half years in San Diego, the article describes the author's Californian writing block and the release from that inability to write once back in his home country, and does so by positioning itself with reference to yet another text, a poem in which California becomes an imaginary space (he might just as accurately have evoked Montalvo's splendid description of California in *Esplandián*):

> I have been in California for two and a half years. Up to this point I have abstained from writing about it. Back there, the sentences get lost in the waves of the Pacific. On returning to France I have the impression that the lunar country from which I come cannot be introduced or spoken about in the closed text of my Parisian villages. . . . Perhaps California must be described as a dream, in the style of Edgar Morin, in his *California Journal*, the poem of an imaginary country.[7]

Interestingly enough, Certeau can write about California only from France, for a French audience that is incapable of understanding a place so foreign, and can approach it only metaphorically through a poem in which California becomes an imaginary country. If, as Tabuenca Córdoba asserts, it is important to discover the direction of the guiding metaphor in construction border theory, then Certeau's orientation is clearly eastward, back toward Paris, where writing can occur, rather than toward the too-real California that swallows up his commentary. Furthermore, he can write about California only as a certain kind of fictional effect, filtered through the metaphorical appropriations of poetic expression. It is also interesting to note that the dominant image he chooses to organize this discussion, "théâtre de passants" (theater of passersby) evokes the most famous and stereotypical association of U.S. California with a certain Hollywood-style theatricalized play of identity, alongside the stereotypical association of Mexican California with illegal emigrants, who, in their efforts to avoid the border patrol, not only attempt surreptitious border crossings but also hope to "pass" as U.S. nationals. Certainly, it is this multitextually shadowed French appropriation of an imaginary country that García Canclini finds so postmodernly productive in his own reading of the border area. In this context, it is not surprising that the Argentine critic located in Mexico City comes to Tijuana through the French thinker and ends up, discursively at least, in Paris (or Berlin or Berkeley) in May 1968.

If Certeau is one of the signally important validating authorities in the theoretical appropriation of the border as text, García Canclini confirms this validation when he cites Guillermo Gómez Peña as Tijuana's native-informant intellectual. Other critics have succinctly pointed out how the choice of this particular performance artist, considered, in the border area, an outsider to Tijuana's cultural circles, has created the conditions for conjoining dominant cultural discursive practices that define "hybridity" and determine the value ascribed to his project in the metaphorized community to which both authors refer. For example, Eduardo Barrera writes, "Gómez Peña fabricates his border by drinking from the same theoretical watering holes as the academics who test their arguments with his texts. . . . Gómez Peña's border turns into the Border of García Canclini and Homi Bhabha" (16); and Tabuenca Córdoba adds: "It is ironic to note how hegemonic critics such as García Canclini validate Gómez Peña by accepting the latter as 'the fronterizo' while presenting Tijuana as the representation of 'the' hybrid space" (153). I do not wish to act as an anthropologist or ethnographer in search of a locatable authentic fronterizo (artist/thinker) who might serve as an elided shade haunting the dominant shadowings of the border as text,[8] but rather to signal the processes by which border theorization seems to require a transcultural dialogue between the dominant cultural discourses in which the border culture is invented, projected as an imaginary space, and reread in the engagement between shadow texts. To speak of the border in such a context is, as Ortega y Gasset's metaphor suggests, to empty it out, retaining the projected residue of a refused and powerful violence. As Certeau quite rightly recognized, it also "brings us back to a ubiquitous problem. . . . *Where does one speak? What can be said?* But also, in the end: Where do *we* speak? This makes the problem directly political, because it makes an issue of the social—in other words, primarily repressive—function of learned culture" (*Heterologies* 135). Tijuana can be both a battleground for this will to knowledge in its most traditional formulations and a place from which to speak otherwise (e.g., in a postmodern ironic mode); in either case, as Certeau intuits, the competing models of discourse both operate from the premise that they speak from or against the time and place of a dominant culture.

"How does one depict the history of so unmonumental a city?" asks Richard Rodriguez early in the chapter of *Days of Obligation* that focuses on Tijuana (86). Implicitly, we are asked to agree with the postulate that the terms "city," "history," and "monument" are all inextricably connected. And yet it is clear that the absence of monumental architecture in this most visited of cities is a liability primarily for those visitors for whom tourism necessarily includes prescribed doses of culture to assuage the nagging guilt that travel does not broaden one's knowledge, as it is supposed to do. The reinforcement of this connection between travel and history lessons and the assuagement of tourist guilt readily leaps to the fore in the five-cities-in-seven-days tours of Europe, for example, or in group trips to central Mexico. In each case, "seeing the city" primarily involves instantly forgettable canned guides of large public structures. Yet, contradictorily, Tijuana is a heavily tourist-oriented city—though clearly not suitable for the ideologically and ethically correct, monumental-historical tours. What to do?

Since there are no monuments to catch the eye, entrepreneurs construct a false nostalgic idea of "old Mexico" for tourists, as this Tijuanan quoted by García Canclini indicates: "Faced with the lack of other types of things, as there are in the south where there are pyramids, there is none of that here . . . as if something had to be invented for the gringos. . . . It also refers to the myth that North Americans bring with them, that has something to do with crossing the border into the past, into the wilderness, into the idea of being able to ride horseback" (236).[9] As this businessman recognizes, tourists come to Tijuana not to see another, othered (monumental) history, but rather to travel into their own imaginary past, where—implicitly—men were white, women were cantina whores, and Mexico was the place evil bandidos hid out from Wild West cowboys. This past, in turn, is projected into the nostalgic superiority of past-as-future where, for instance, on the famous Revolución strip, gringos and gringas can take turns being photographed with zebra-painted donkeys so they can go home and tell all their friends about the truly tacky things contemporary Mexicans try to sell to savvy North Americans.

In Tijuana's notorious "zona norte," the Adelita Club (now with its own website!) stands in for the internet-aware sex clients as the handiest representation of this kind of created authentic Mexicanness; that is, of a living culture read as if it were a movie set invented to respond to U.S. consumer dreams of the picturesque. One internet "researcher" into the region calls Adelita "pure South of the Border," and another client elaborates: "When the taxi dropped us off . . . we knew we weren't in Kansas anymore. This was the Mexico of the movies . . . steamy streets, food vendors everywhere, ladies more then [*sic*] everywhere." Still another writer describes it as "like walking into a brothel in some old Western." Interestingly enough, Adelita's clientele is divided between Mexican and U.S. residents, and if, for the U.S. client, the bar evokes the imaginary Wild West, for the Mexican client it creates a parallel but different image of a revolutionary past ("Adelita" is one of the most instantly recognizable ballads of the Mexican Revolution, and one that specifically highlights the exploits of a famous *soldadera*).

The Mexican Revolution is one of the unrecognized and unstated backdrops to a fair amount of Wild West footage, just as the revolutionary general Pancho Villa is the unnamed villain whenever Mexican bandidos appear to disturb the peace. In the shadowing of text upon text, the Wild West cowboy is an anglicized version of the Mexican immigrant *vaquero* (why else would blond men in movies live on a diet of beans and run around "lassooing" cows, horses, bad guys, and women?), back-projected onto a Tijuana that looks to U.S. tourists like a run-down version of a Hollywood film set.

Writing from Mexico City, culture critic Carlos Monsiváis reminds us that in traditional centrist discourse, not only is national identity firmly located in central Mexico, so too is the imaginary projection of that identity. Thus, the capital city is associated both with the authentic repository of Mexico's past and with the progressive conception of its future, and the provinces become the repositories of unassimilated, chaotic partial identities along with a rejected, and implicitly inauthentic, past. Nevertheless, while Mexico City is somewhat insulated by virtue of its geographical location, the northern border states "debate on a daily basis the limitations of localism and of the national. In the border states the similarities are intense: culture shock to some degree compensated by the relative abundance of employment, the certified absence of regional traditions, and the fact that the 'typical northerner' derives directly from cultural industry, the opportunistic and commercial use of nationalism" (Monsiváis 202).[10] Still, in this mobile and constantly changing border definition of the national future lies precisely those elements of national restructuring that central Mexico needs to refuse to maintain the primacy of its own vision of national identity: "The manager of one assembly plant by the airport predicts that all of Mexico will soon look like Tijuana. . . . Tijuana is an industrial park on the outskirts of Minneapolis" (Rodriguez 94). Uncannily, it is some version of Minneapolis that crystallizes Mexico City's technocratic imaginings about the centrist-based progressive future, but according to that dominant discourse both industrial Tijuana and the Midwestern United States need to be carefully expelled.

Michel de Certeau, writing from the other side of another border (across the line, across the Rockies and the deserts, in France) highlights the metaphor of migration as the dominant strand in his elaboration of Californian identity. In his case, however, and despite his recent stay in San Diego, the metaphor of migration and movement clearly focuses on the migration from east to west rather than south to north. He emphasizes the role of cars, job mobility, and secondhand books in defining the Californian *passant*, singles out credit cards and driver's licenses as replacements for the familiar French *carte d'identité*, and highlights jogging (rather than, say, stoop work in the fields) as his favored image of the physical side of migration: "One never ceases passing from one history to another, from one language to another, and from one region to another. The entire society is passing. In this respect, jogging is only the physical metaphor of a daily activity. . . . But immigration is a more internal experience, one that characterizes Californian socializing" (Certeau, "Californie" 11, 14).[11]

Once again, it is Richard Rodriguez who crystallizes this modality, transferring one of the most readily available images of commercialized utopia from one side of the border to the other: "It is more fun, perhaps, to approach Revolución with adolescent preconceptions of lurid possibility. Marrakesh. Bangkok. . . . A quick shot of the foreign. Unmetered taxis. Ultramontane tongue. Disney Calcutta" (Rodriguez 82). There is an unintended irony or a bilingual pun in the conjunction of fun-revolution-possibility. Rodriguez theatricalizes a trip to Mexico as a journey from staid normality (and middle-class morality) into a revolutionary realm of a degraded utopian potential. Like the Wild West film set, Rodriguez's Disney Calcutta is an artificial and contained space, though the film set is a trip to one's own imaginary past whereas Disneyland is a commercialized dream of the future. In each case, U.S. popular culture dreams are exoticized and projected onto another and foreign space, one that reaches out to enable them through skewed and commercialized shadowings of its own: Disney, but reimagined in Calcutta.

Michel de Certeau also evokes Disney as a metaphor for understanding his Californian theater. Combining two large public spaces, he says of Disneyland and supermarkets: "These are the spaces that tend to make one believe that the rest of Californian life is not a fiction" (Certeau, "Californie" 17).[12] This curious turn of phrase suggests once again that California itself and life in California are, in fact, irremediably fictitious, and that only encounters with hyperreal public commercial utopias dispel this pervasive imaginary quality. Although he recognizes and underlines the utopian quality of the Disneyland experience—and remember, he includes California supermarkets as a kind of Disneyland—the primary function of this real pseudo-utopia in de Certeau's analysis is not to secularize a semireligious attachment to the idea of California as Earthly Paradise, but rather to signal commodification as its central and most significant mode of operation.

Both García Canclini and Monsiváis seek methodologies for associating popular culture with national identity formation. Both writers also signal the danger and opportunity involved in the material and commercial deployment of certain theatricalized roles as salable iconic representations: what Olalquiaga, in her essay "Vulture Culture" calls "the displacement of referentiality by simulation" and the "valorization of surface, immediate gratification, and highly iconographic codes over the tradition of depth, contemplation, and symbolic abstraction" (92, 94). Both García Canclini and Monsiváis record and discuss the dominant Mexican culture's concern that a contaminated, Disneyfied version of popular culture will block access to real national culture and stifle progress. Among the oppositions these authors set up between Mexico and the First World are the still-current debates centering on colonizer versus colonized and cosmopolitanism versus nationalism. In a parallel manner, Monsiváis elaborates on the binary oppositions still undergirding official national understandings of the conflict between central Mexico and the provinces. In this view, the conflict between capital city and provinces carries with it the baggage of civilization versus barbarism, culture versus desolation, national consolidation versus aborted history. New complicating factors make these dichotomies increasingly difficult to maintain; both authors point to the population explosion, industrial development extending into formerly isolated zones, the influence of the mass media, creeping Americanization—"so feared by the ingenuous and so sacralized from the point of view of consumption" (Monsiváis 201)[13]—and, in more general terms, "the delocalization of symbolic products by electronics and telematics, and the use of satellites and computers in cultural diffusion" (García Canclini 229).[14]

Briefly, then, Tijuana becomes the space where popular culture icons of Mexicanness can be reified, refried, and sold, so long as these iconic representations also concatenate with U.S. cultural stereotypes of Mexican identity in their Disneyfied variations. Mexican centrist culture fears border contamination; Tijuana becomes the realm of fearful possibility and rejected affinities. Tourists, on the other hand, want cross the border to see the "real" Mexico, as long as the real Mexico looks and sounds like a down-market Speedy González cartoon.

Yet, by holding in abeyance these two texts and their shadow others, by representing for both cultures the place of opportunity and the site of refusal, Tijuana also slips outside the norming processes of popular culture absorption. As Michel de Certeau notes, "'Popular culture' presupposes an unavowed operation. Before being studied, it had to be censored. Only after its danger had been eliminated did it become an object of interest" (*Heterologies* 119). He concludes: "This takes us to the root of the problem: popular culture can only be grasped in the process of vanishing.... These blank spots outline a geography of the *forgotten.* They trace the negative silhouette of the problematics displayed in black and white in scholarly books" (131). California, no matter how imaginarily constructed, no matter how Disneyfied in the popular and official imaginations, never quite disappears entirely; its geography is, and has been from the beginning, blurred, though always located on the maps.

Tijuana almost too neatly conflates the symbolic, geographical, and moral exclusions from the healthy body of the state. From both sides of the border, the city represents that tacky, vile, and threatening thing that middle-class morality must resist and cannot stop talking about. Most potently, Tijuana becomes a powerful shadowtext defining the whole of Mexico as a passive whore to be fucked over: "Mexico lay down and the gringo paid in the morning" (Rodriguez 88). Rodriguez's phrase succinctly captures a U.S. male fantasy grounded in racist misogyny and reinforced in a gendered structural inequality between nations, while at the same time echoing a Mexican inferiority complex about its relation to the United States, most strikingly captured in the Mexican misogyny toward traitorous females who sleep with conquerors—even though payback time eventually rolls around.

In her discussion of the sexual interface of colonial encounters, Ann Laura Stoler offers a helpful starting point for an analysis of this trope. Her work focuses on what she calls the "analytic slippage between the sexual symbols of power and the politics of sex," and asks: "Was sexuality merely a graphic substantiation of who was, so to speak, on the top? Was the medium the message, or did sexual relations always 'mean' something else, stand in for other relations, evoke the sense of *other* . . . desires?" (346). Control and manipulation of the sexualized trope, despite, or perhaps because of its shocking physicality, serve both the central Mexican and the U.S. dominant discourses as a salient instrument of textual authority for constructing and controlling discussions about the dangerous attractions of a degraded Tijuanan reality.

There is a strong note of (postmodern?) ironic *ubi sunt* in Richard Rodriguez's account of his arrival in Tijuana. Although he imagines the city as "a metropolis crouched behind a hootchy-kootch curtain," (81) his trip through the *zona norte* fails to live up to its advance billing: "Mexican men loiter outside the doors of open bars. From within come stale blasts of American rock. Is this all that is left of the fleshpots of T.J.? We are a generation removed from that other city, . . . a succubus that could take [American men] as far as they wanted to go. At the turn of the century . . . there were whores and there was gambling and there was drink" (87). Strikingly enough, Rodriguez's complaint involves both Mexican men and U.S. rock, which have presumably and unforgivably replaced U.S. men and Mexican whores. García Canclini marks a similar change, and dates the reformation of the old image to a recent shift in public perception: "From the beginning of the century until fifteen years ago, Tijuana was known for a casino . . . , cabarets, dance halls, and liquor stores where North Americans came to elude their country's prohibitions on sex" (234).[15] In each case, the illicit relations between U.S. men and Tijuanan women are relegated to the past. Furthermore, regardless of the industrialization and modernization that have changed the face of the city, both Rodriguez and García Canclini find it necessary to remind their readers of the recent past, if only to tell us that this past is no longer representative of contemporary reality. In effect, then, both writers have found an answer to Rodriguez's question about how to write the history of so unmonumental a city; they set up a contrast between the distanced and romanticized calumny overlaid on the city through images of the past as a depraved female and the macho image of modern industry. The ratty or vampiric whore becomes the rejected image that must be obsessively called to memory, along with the abjuration that such an image is no longer accurate or adequate.

Interestingly enough, in this manner the "unhistorical" Tijuana stands as a prominent example of the operations of centrist historical discourse that have been so ably dissected by Benedict Anderson, though Anderson's work develops without paying attention to that history's gender politics: "Having to 'have already forgotten' tragedies of which one needs unceasingly to be 'reminded' turns out to be a characteristic device in the later construction of national genealogies" (201). Unsurprisingly, in the context of Anderson's observation, Rodriguez's other metaphors for Tijuana also bring up remembered/forgotten peoples who also founded national genealogical projects: Tijuana is "silent as a Trojan horse, inevitable as a flotilla of boat people" (Rodriguez 106).

Stoler would add a reminder about the significance of gender politics in the construction of these historical models. When we turn back to the border with these insights in mind, it is striking how consistently, in discussions of Tijuana, images of sneaky invading hordes are linked to phobias about female sexuality and disguised in the dominant culture's fear and celebration of social change. Welchman's admirable overview of the "philosophical brothel" in Western thought brings some of these imaginary overlays together:

> Remembering Derrida's etymological association of the border, the plank, and brothel, Picasso's image [Les *demoiselles d'Avignon*] can be read as an arrest and incarnation of the non-processional border, the purest moment of modernist border fetishism. This brothel/border is a place of violence and consumption which objectifies and consumes both women and others. It is this *bordello* that is the scene of the masculinist metaphorics of war and combat, of the appropriative transplantation of so-called primitive faces onto the already fractured bodies of the so-seen deviant women. It is here that the western fantasies of philosophy, the non-western other, and sexual violence converge on the territory of the border. ("Philosophical Brothel" 180)

Tijuana speaks most allegorically, and most clearly, to its old image as an abjected feminine presence, and it is the continuing resonance of this image, which must not and cannot be forgotten, that has motivated José Guadalupe Osuna Milán and the other members of the Tijuana municipal council to take the extraordinary step of attempting to register "Tijuana" as a trademark. Like the Wild West image, the vampiric whore meets barely articulated needs coming from outside the municipal limits, U.S. pornographic fantasies that can be safely projected across the border onto an exoticized other. Tijuana has "a more graceful sense of universal corruption," says Rodriguez (90); and though graft is a painful reality for Mexican nationals struggling day after day to live and raise their families, "graceful universal corruption" has an exotic and erotic attraction for the gringo tourist. In the good old/bad old days evoked by both Rodriguez and García Canclini, there were plenty of whores/succubi to trap and victimize innocent U.S. men into the sinful fleshpots of an entire city given over to decadence; now, in contrast, and in a pathetic devolution, Mexican men are corrupted by U.S. rock—a point also made by García Canclini in his lucid reading of the ambiguities infesting the street sign proclaiming, "rock in your language on Thursdays" (237). There is a loss of poetic resonance and erotic force in the shift from fleshpots to U.S. rock, from elegant whores to loitering Mexican men.

Objectively speaking, of course, the closing of the Agua Caliente casino during the Lázaro Cárdenas administration brought only a symbolic end to all that glamorous corruption. In Tijuana today there are an estimated fifteen thousand women working as prostitutes, on the streets in some sectors, and in 210 nightclub/brothels (Castillo et al.). In the bars and streets of Tijuana at least two dominant (U.S., Mexican) and two marginalized (underclass) versions of male and female stereotypes meet as various sets of cultural mores grate against one another. When we try to understand the concrete situation of real women in that city, we are thrown back on ambiguously framed narratives about lives that implicitly or explicitly rub up against all these social, theoretical, cultural, and historical frames in a sometimes complicitous, often contentious manner. Tijuana involves a complex history in which all these magic signs, discourses, practices, and struggles are filtered through a particular border site with its own metaphorical overlay of feminization and abjection, its own legal history, its own racially inflected past and present, its own biculturally determined exchanges.

TIJUANA IN FICTION

Traditional fictional representations of Tijuana also echo these themes obsessively. Let us consider two representative texts from different genres and perspectives: Cheech Marín's English-language film *Born in East L.A.* (1987); and Regina Swain's collection of short stories *La señorita Superman y otras danzas.*

Cheech Marín's film opened to mixed reviews in the United States, but that same year became the first Chicano film to win several major awards at the New Latin American Cinema Festival in Havana, Cuba (Noriega 17; Fregoso 264). It has also been very favorably received by U.S. Latino scholars, who interpret it as an important contribution to the growing Chicano film industry and a significant commentary on Chicano identity in this country. Of particular interest to such scholars is Cheech Marín's script, inspired by reports of U.S. citizens being accidentally deported to Mexico. Cheech Marín intensifies the jazzy ironic-parodic edge of *Born in East L.A.* by musically framing the film with his version of Bruce Springsteen's xenophobic rock hit, "Born in the USA" at the beginning, and Neil Diamond's "America" at the end.

In the film, Rudy, an English-speaking Chicano from East L.A., is illegally deported to Mexico when he is accidentally caught up in an Immigration and Naturalization Service sweep. Arriving penniless in Tijuana, Rudy does a series of odd jobs for a seedy U.S. businessman located in that city, and finally beats the Migra and wins his way back home. When a fellow deportee in a truck en route to Tijuana calls Rudy "a pocho, and a pocho pendejo at that," we are expected to laugh, and to share in the Mexican's evaluation of Rudy's willful ignorance about the politics of race in the United States. This movie is, in some sense, Rudy's bildungsroman, and the deportation to Tijuana plays an essential role in forcing him to grow up and take on responsibilities consistent with his adult years.

One analysis interprets the story through the biblical Book of Exodus; after his capture by evil immigration officers, "like Moses, Rudy is subsequently banished to the desert where he struggles with his identity and ultimately his destiny," before emerging to lead his people to the Promised Land (Tafoya 124–5).[16] What is striking about Tafoya's analysis is that it unironically embraces the United States' dominant understanding of itself as the Promised Land, in contrast to the undesirable desert across the border.

Another reading focuses on the concatenation of images of nation and gender. Chon Noriega links the film's strong ideological questioning of the ephemeral basis of Latino citizenship in the United States to a commentary on the gender-specific representations of hearth and home played out in the film: "The French woman is the whore to Dolores's Madonna. The film also conflates the sexual dichotomy with cultural nationalism, so that the whore also tempts Rudy with assimilation, while the Madonna ensures cultural affirmation" (Noriega 18). The first woman is foreign and, at the same time, quintessentially American; she is the material girl that the cultural sellout Rudy longs to possess. After suffering in the character-building crucible of Tijuana, he returns to L.A. with Dolores, the domestic woman (she cooks and waits on her man) from, significantly, El Salvador, a woman who, punningly, saves him from his worst instincts and brings him to his cultural, national, and personal home.

Fregoso's lucid analysis captures the cultural balancing act of the border artist, who plays one style against another, in a continual awareness of differential, even contradictory readings that such a parodic practice may generate:

> It is important to resist the . . . temptation to label Cheech Marín's experimental style as one more manifestation of the "postmodernist" trend in culture. The film is in fact reflective of the "crossover phenomenon," or interest on the part of dominant culture . . . in the subject matter of marginal groups. Yet what may be considered "modernist" formal revision or "postmodernist" innovation for the dominant culture may, on the other hand, simply be common fare for "popular" groups like Chicana/os. (Fregoso 268–69)

Fregoso emphasizes that those elements of the "crossover" drama that attract mainstream audiences in this country, the outsider's appropriation of or puzzlement about Marín's work, tend to organize themselves neatly around theoretical concerns that may be alien to or inconsistent with Marín's own discursive and cultural roots. As she notes, Chicano popular culture, as received by the avant-garde and uprooted from its own heritage, can be read as postmodern. But this reading is a distortion.

At the same time, reading from the other side of the border, a critic of the film might note that although the Chicano reality is given aesthetic complexity and nuance, the filmmaker, in playing U.S. dominant culture against its stereotypes of Chicano life and presenting hilarious parodic skits based on Chicano understandings of its own popular culture, allows stereotypes about Tijuana to stand untouched. Cheech Marín's film indubitably yearns north. Los Angeles is largely shot during the day, and the cityscape is filled with sunlight and bright colors, whereas Tijuana is a nighttime city, characterized by neon signs and dangerously underilluminated back streets. Los Angeles has industry and regular work hours; Tijuana has sex joints where barkers shill for commissions. In Los Angeles, foolish or jolly law enforcement officers bumble around; in Tijuana, sinister punks extort bribes from hapless prisoners and run a creepy Mafia peopled with grunting thugs, hypocritical born-again Christians, and deranged effeminate homosexual rapists.

Rudy's most significant guide to this nightmare town is a blond U.S. businessman with a mysterious past. To Rudy's question, "What are you doing in TJ?" Jimmy reminds Rudy of their shared cultural context, the idealized Wild West of Hollywood: "It's kind of like in those cowboy movies. . . . [Two guys on the run tell each other:] If we can make it to the Mexican border we can make it." Jimmy has certainly "made it" south across the border, where he reigns in a sleazy underworld, his multiple commercial tentacles including a prostitution bar, a pool hall, and border-crossing scams. At the same time, Jimmy's assertion, "If we can make it to the Mexican border we can make it," is just as forceful when applied north to south as south to north; that is, while for Jimmy Tijuana is the lawless place to which he has escaped and in which he has been able to "make it," for Rudy, for his batch of successful Cholo-Chinese-Indian-or-whatever students, and for the masses of Mexicans struggling to cross the border to the United States each day, making it to the border means crossing to the other direction into the Promised Land of Opportunity.

The U.S. rock music framing the movie sets up the dominant musical theme, even in Tijuana, where local musicians struggle with requests from drunken compatriots to play such classics as "Summertime Blues." One of the signs that Rudy too is "making it" in this foreign context is signaled by his connection to a trio of street musicians. His suggestion to the band is along the same lines as the cultural cross-fertilization (or contamination) that García Canclini elucidates in his reading of the "rock en tu idioma" sign. Rudy tells the other members of the band, "We have to do something different" to increase their income. His first idea—"If we put rock with this kind of music"—cuts to the next scene, where "Rudy and the New Huevos Rancheros" try to play a Mexican mixed hard rock number, blow out the lights, and fail to attract an audience. In the next scene, the group is back on the streets, but Rudy's softer version of the cross-cultural musical number works marvelously well; norteña music blends into the German polka, "Rosamunda"—and the band earns a hundred-dollar tip from an enthusiastic German couple passing by on the street.

Back in Los Angeles, Dolores, Rudy, and Rudy's students surface from a manhole on a sunny afternoon immediately under the festive Mexican music of the annual Cinco de Mayo parade. When Dolores asks, "What's the Cinco de Mayo?" Rudy responds: "I don't know, but we have a parade every year." Rudy may have become domesticated as a result of his trip to Tijuana and his association with Dolores, but he has by no means become a cultural nationalist, and his Tijuana-based reflections on his identity and on the nature of Americanness have not provided him many opportunities for illuminating insights into his own heritage. In an ironic palimpsest, what Rudy does not know, and clearly *ought* to know—the meaning of the Cinco de Mayo celebration—reflects an ignorance the film would expect the dominant culture crossover audience to share, and about which they would be equally unconcerned. At the same time, savvy members of the audience familiar with Chicano popular culture know that the Cinco de Mayo in the United States is an important holiday, a reminder of Mexican heritage and a celebration of freedom on a par with the Fourth of July. That Rudy, an East L.A.–born Chicano, does not know this history is, at this level, an index of his reprehensible assimilation to the dominant culture.

Curiously, the Mexican dominant culture audience might find the celebration a bit puzzling as well, since, though May 5 is a national holiday in that country, commemorating the poorly armed Mexican army's victory over the French forces in the Battle of Puebla, it is lower key (somewhat more like Memorial Day) than the retooled Cinco de Mayo celebrations in northern California, and the day celebrated as Independence Day in Mexico is September 16—a distinction that in Chicano popular culture is often fuzzy. Thus, interestingly enough, what Rudy does not know reflects information not available in the repertoire of either dominant culture's vocabulary and yet very familiar to the informed Chicano audience. To get the joke, even uninformed members of the audience need only the film's rich visual cues to make the independence day association, and then we too are insiders to that celebration. At the same time, from another point of view, this "correct" interpretation involves a prior "error," by which Chicanos celebrate Mexicanness while forgetting the official, dominant cultural context.

While U.S. and Mexican dominant cultural discourses carry different weight in Marín's Chicano contestation and appropriation of them, in each case Tijuana and its remembered/forgotten shadows objectifies the conflict, propels the narrative into existence, and clarifies the ideological, cultural, and ethical stakes. Even in the fictional context, Tijuana serves as a textual backdrop for reality-as-simulation: a real-life Wild West, a real Disneyland. Like Ortega y Gasset's city-as-cannon metaphor, Tijuana offers a contentless explosive violence that needs to be contained, because the simulated fiction-reality is sometimes too real, too Third World, too aesthetically contaminated, too unpleasantly disruptive. At the same time, it is this simulated, contaminated, Third World disruptiveness that is Tijuana's major selling point, and the main assurance of its authenticity for the gringo tourist who crosses the border to purchase a piece of the "real Mexico" instead of taking the family to Disneyland farther north. Sleaze sells in a way that one more northern California mall or supermarket would not.

Marín's film is highly sensitive to these two dominant cultural discourses—that of the United States and that of central Mexico—and to the most common stereotypes that each of these dominant cultures has created about the other. As these discourses and stereotypes interact with each other, they shadow each other with varying degrees of intensity, in their discussions of the discursive equivalent of the no-man's-land: the fetishized and abjected border other. Thus, for example, Gronk's comment that "borders don't apply now. East L.A. is everywhere" (quoted in Fregoso 273) resonates on the same cultural register as Richard Rodriguez's "Mexico will soon look like Tijuana. . . . Tijuana is an industrial park on the outskirts of Minneapolis." In each case, the real border is blurred into the shadow of a preferred dominant culture construct. Furthermore, in each of these discussions—whether philosophical, anthropological, critical, or fictional—there are typical themes or narrative tics: the flexible geography that makes Tijuana both an island and an analogue for the postmodern condition, the theme of the city as a Hollywood set for a Wild West movie, the puzzlement over how to understand the role of the *maquiladoras* and the area's industrial boom, the awareness of a vast movement of people both north and south at this busiest of the world's borders, the uneasy concern that Tijuana is both a pop culture commercial construct and a degraded utopia, and a persistent and nagging phobia about feminization and female sexuality.

Regina Swain's collection of short stories, *La señorita Superman y otras danzas* (Miss Superman and other dances) provides an explicitly border Mexican, explicitly female take on these issues. If the metaphor of the city as cannon helps us understand Marín's take on this subject, Swain's practice requires a different metaphor, perhaps (with apologies to Quetzil Castañeda) an aesthetics of the doughnut hole. As Castañeda notes, "This uncanny pastry is a presence defined as an absence and an absence materialized as a presence" (26). The similarity between Swain's narratives and a fatty, yeasty confection with a paradoxical name is borne out in the history of traditional discursive encrustings that project onto Tijuana a no-culture imaginary presence: from the U.S. side, an illusory reality as the Third World's three-dimensional concretization of a Hollywood dream of the real Mexico; and from the Mexican side, as a sinister place without culture that nevertheless serves as the site of cultural contamination from the United States that must be contained. In other words, Tijuana is scandalous from two cultural points of view because it is an absence (a no-culture culture) and an overdetermined presence (an excessively two-cultured culture, in which the dominance of one culture over the other is precisely calibrated from the opposite space: Mexico for the United States; the United States for Mexico).

In these brief stories, Swain traces critical nodes in these contradictory and complementary discourses, recovering their concealed or forgotten genealogies and setting them side by side in a text where everything and everyone is dangerously, disruptively, out of place. Like the doughnut hole, a fatty presence and nominal absence, her stories are both overly allusive and vaguely ungrounded. A doughnut hole aesthetics has some of the qualities Judith Butler ascribed to the performance of realness in drag balls: "the contest (which we might read as a 'contesting of realness') involves the phantasmatic attempt to approximate realness [or, alternatively, merely to 'do' realness], but it also exposes the norms that regulate realness as *themselves* phantasmatically instituted and sustained" (130). It is precisely this phantasmatic quality that regulates the gap between "Miss" and "Superman" in the collection's title, with its evocation of other staged rituals of performative femininity such as beauty contests, and with its grating gender transgression (this is explicitly *not* about Supergirl, the comic book's cop-out confection of a cousin for the Man of Steel). It is also this phantasmatic quality that supports the text's contestation of the dual set of institutional norms that undergird its textual practice.

The city is never named, though it is said to be located in California, which both the Amazon Calafia's letter to the conquistador Balboa (Swain 57–58),[17] and an implicitly more contemporary resiting identify as an island: "The Border is still the same Free Trade Zone ever since it was only a small island named California" (Swain 23).[18] The city, like Tijuana, is subject to floods in the downtown area (Swain 18), has a suburb called "Playas" (29), and is described as "an enormous and capricious city, whose inhabitants lived on the knife edge of two distinct but similar worlds" with "houses constructed all along a barbed wire fence"(18).[19] It is fundamentally a "nocturnal city" (18) inhabited by "nocturnal creatures" (52). Contemporary inhabitants of this unnamed city include a troop of García

Márquezian gypsies, the "wolfmen" and "Clairol blondes" who hang out in the bars, and the Amazon queen Calafia herself, along with a special guest appearance by "la negra Angustias," who has stepped out of the pages of Rojas Gónzalez's eponymous novel to do a striptease in the Aloha bar.

In these unauthorized juxtapositions, Swain's short stories economically provide a parodic displacement of both "authentic" (i.e., noncommodified, precapitalist) Mexican culture and its postmodern ironic shadowtext supplement. Here too Swain offers allusive sketches of alternative histories involving unachieved potential and loss. In a punning allusion to Lázaro Cárdenas's closing of the famous Agua Caliente casino, Señorita Superman gets up one morning only to discover "THERE IS NO HOT WATER [NO HAY AGUA CALIENTE]" (51). In another story, referring to the colonial period, the Amazon Calafia writes a letter to Balboa:

> In this Northern Empire, the afternoons are still disheveled in the water's reflection. Nothing bothers them. . . . Here the palm trees rock borders that remain reachable; here the reflection of dreams remains the same, regardless of entrances and exits. Here, wandering knight, the conquerer is still conquered by the large eyes of the women of my race. Women made of desire and metal, of skin and flame. (57–58)[20]

In each case, a feminine voice remembers/forgets a preexisting dominant cultural discourse. In the first case, a controversial (and from some perspectives, hypocritical) moralizing action by one of Mexico's greatest presidents is domesticated in a punning overlay with a young woman's frustration at not being able to take a hot shower in the morning. In the second case, Calafia responds in writing to the chivalric novels that in some sense provided a discursive context for narratives of the colonial encounter and to the Spanish colonial chronicles themselves. Calafia's letter describes the imagined utopia of the Californian island, where conquerors' dreams are reflected in a common pool, and at the same time hints at the duplicity of such encounters between a fictitious wandering knight and a dream lover. These women represent the reachable dream, insofar as it serves both conqueror and conqueror's woman as they imagine a traditionally lyric space; yet these seductive, large-eyed women have a cybernetic dissonance that interrupts the island idyll. They are women of desire, skin, flame—and metal.

Even as these brief texts serve as counternarratives to an established discourse, they contest it in a specifically female-centered way. Swain uses her brief tales as a medium to bring sharp clarity to the idea that traditional dominant texts, like the ones to which she alludes, are irremediably male-centered constructions. Thus, she ironically presents the border woman as consumer and as consumer product, in her home, and, even more particularly, in bars, where eroticism is most strictly understood in terms of commodity culture. Here, for example, the great lyric theme of love is reimagined through the metaphor of a can of Nestlé's condensed milk: "love, my Love, is a can of Nestlé's condensed milk, that's why it sweetens you up and then, after the third spoonful, the poor can of love always ends up in the garbage."[21] In a later story, one of the characters muses that "Nestlé's divides up culture and one throws oneself into living a latex love through the demands of canned sex."[22] In Swain's world, Campbell's soup and Nestlé's love are equally instantaneous, equally disposable commodities.

Read together, Calafia's letter and Señorita Superman's meditations speak powerfully to each other and help the reader grasp an edgy, feminine, bordered discursive context for Swain's work. Calafia's Amazon women live in a prefabricated (male) paradise where traditional lyric dreams jar with visions of metal women. In this world, the abandoned Nestlé's can provides another context for imagining the subtext to Calafia's seductive cybernetic scene; it points to the canned sex, the throwaway love that defines commercialized sexual relations between local women and visiting conquerors. It is no wonder that Señorita Superman comments that "wrinkles have appeared in her soul."[23] In contrast to Richard Rodriguez's lament for the lost *putas* of yesteryear, Swain's narrator complains to the archetypal "madrerreina" (motherqueen):

> But, instant soup, mother, and the dog-eat-dog race to get a job? . . . Where do I put away the prostitutes from the North Zone, mom, where do I put the anguish? . . . And the threat of AIDS, mother, and the colored condoms, and the drunk on the corner, where, where can I place them? . . . Where do I save the pressure from work and the deaths of the migrants, and the woman from the assembly plant? They don't fit on the shelf with the Barbie dolls!
>
> And the thing is that we live in a generation of instant soup and instant love that doesn't last longer than four drinks.[24]

Swain captures well the cost of living in a site of contested meanings, specifically those deriving from both dominant discourses, which perceive the border as a place of no culture. Nevertheless, Nestlé's milk, instant soups, Barbie dolls, and other material analogues of U.S. cultural influence are understood even in this supposedly no-culture context as scandalous contaminations that do not fit in with and cannot be appropriately placed in the proper Mexican house. At the same time, while these products allegorize a perceived scandal, they are already entirely naturalized in Swain's world; Nestlé's is a metaphor for love, and Barbies already have their assigned place in the girl's room: the problem remaining for the narrator of the story is how to incorporate other, homegrown scandals. In effect, then, Swain points to the intricacies of regional politics, which traditionally decry a superficial scandal while ignoring a profound one.

In his discussion of the workings of cultural imperialism in the Mexican Yucatán, Quetzil Castañeda uses Coca-Cola as a convenient shorthand for this unequal form of transculturation: "Because Coke has become a synecdoche for a specific culture, this situation is often nostalgically or angrily lamented by some culture-bearers of the metropolitan core as cultural loss or cultural rape. . . . The analogy is not that Coke is Culture, but that Culture is like Coke." Castañeda extends this conclusion, and asks his readers to imagine "the invention of Culture whether locally or globally as if it were Coca-cola," what he calls "the Coke theory of culture," that is, culture as "a heterogeneous entity constituted in and through the contested crisscrossings of borrowings across boundaries forged by such transcultural traffic" (37). Castañeda's point is that Coke (taken as a symbolic marker) has a conventional cultural association in U.S. dominant culture *and* in U.S. cultural commentaries of contestation, while in other sites it has been infused with other significations. In Swain's stories too, imported consumer products are infused with new meaning. Like Nestlé's condensed milk, Coca-Cola plays a small but important role in these fictions, where it too becomes a synecdochic marker for a scandalously naturalized cultural product.

In Swain's collection of short stories, the tale of the Amazon Queen of California, Calafia, is told twice; once in the pseudo-colonial letter, and a second time in the final story of the volume, a pseudo-folktale entitled "On How the Amazon River Was Created, or, Don't Back Down Calafia!"[25] In the second version of the story, the island utopia gives way to the modern border city and the protagonist has a much harder life. This Calafia was named after the bus on which she was born, and her mother's fellow passengers "called her 'queen' because she would never become a princess" (i.e. beauty queen).[26] While growing up, Calafia buys her treats in the Chinese grocery, "where, despite being located far from the marvelous kingdoms of the North, she could find Diet Coke, Cherry Coke, and Coca-Cola Classic."[27] If, in the earlier story, the conqueror Balboa serves as an organizing center for the narration, in this more contemporary story of Calafia, a cultural context is built from missed connections and reassigned significations: Calafia's name comes from a public transport bus; she is nicknamed "queen" as a consolation for her lack of beauty; her palace is the corner grocery; riches mean being able to choose among the various Coke products. Here, Swain economically alludes to the conventional meanings of such cultural signifiers as (concretely) Coca-Cola and (abstractly) the myth of the Little Princess, and at the same time exposes the constructedness of these conventional meanings, reinfusing them with alternative discursive contexts.

The first Calafia, Esplandián's and Balboa's Calafia, is an Amazon queen; this latter-day Calafia becomes a fortune-teller. Each of the women loves and is abandoned by a foreign man; in each case they mistake a brief conqueror's visit for true love, exchange drunken imaginings for solid human bodies, transpose genealogies and cultural mappings, and bring together the foreign man and the Californian woman. "Know this, conqueror Balboa," says the first Calafia at the end of her letter, "that the black woman in white you called Evohe is none other than the Amazon Calafia."[28] The second Calafia invests the attribute *amazona* with a new connotation: "Aprendió a querer a Homobono por zonas," says the narrator, and, when he leaves her: "She learned to love Homobono by zones. . . . She cried so much that her tears made a stream . . . called AMA-ZON [LOVE-ZONES] in honor of the fabled map of Homobono's anatomy."[29] Cortés honored Montalvo by giving the name "California" to a distant western province of New Spain; Swain picks up on this old misappelation and gives it her own twist. Montalvo's liminally paradisiacal island is the home of legendary warrior women who live without men. In Swain's version of this legend, the women, discarded metal cans of Nestlé's love, must also make do without men, and their suffering is comically, hyperbolically transmuted into a flood of tears that turns the Río Tijuana into the Amazon.

Finally, one of the qualities of the doughnut hole and its perfect nutritional partner, Coca-Cola, is to fill us up with empty calories. Swain's doughnut-hole-and-Coke aesthetics continually evokes its stagy no-culture culture backdrop, often through references to another controversial U.S. export: Hollywood movies. One character is described as "muy James Bond" (24); a certain bar is "simply a Capra film" (30);[30] another character explains her inability to sustain a relationship thus: "I prefer *TV Guide* to television and the trailers in the movie theater to the films" (37).[31] Swain's narrative is full of similarly parodic cinematographic references: "Suddenly, as in Warner Brothers films, we can enjoy a flashback" (52).[32] If one of the modalities for inventing Tijuana in modern U.S. and Mexican dominant culture discourses is to do a bad imitation of second-rate Hollywood movies, Swain's response would be to explore the implications of such overlays through a textual shadowing that overdetermines them. In shadowing the shadowtext, Swain's female-centered narratives do not pretend to step outside dominant culture—an impossible enterprise—but to shake up conventional attributions of signification and hint at the unrecognized premises upon which such discourses have been grounded.

CHAPTER NINE

After-Images of the "New" New York and the Alfred Stieglitz Circle

Mary N. Woods

The concept of after-image, as articulated by Joan Ramon Resina in this volume, is especially suggestive when considering how Alfred Stieglitz and his circle of photographers visualized New York as the modern metropolis during the early decades of the twentieth century. First, the photographic process itself (involving exposure, development, and printing of the still or moving image at separate and discrete moments in time) is what Resina characterizes as an after-image at its most basic level, "a visual sensation that lingers after the stimulus that provoked it has disappeared."[1] By exposing a visual stimulus to light-sensitive chemicals, the photographer creates a negative on paper, on a glass plate, or on celluloid film. But the Stieglitz circle photographers engage the question of after-image on a much more profound level. Their photographs of the "new" New York, a city of skyscrapers, also involve the temporal dimensions Resina discovers in after-image, i.e., they open up "the idea of 'image' to a cluster of theoretical possibilities based on temporal displacement, sequentiality, supersession, and engagement." The experience and comprehension of time articulated in Resina's conceptualization of the after-image are crucial not only for the forms and compositions of these photographs but also for the processes of their making, presentation, and interpretation.

Critics and historians of photography have long celebrated William Henry Fox Talbot's invention of the first negative in 1839. Unlike Louis Daguerre's unique images on silvered plates (the daguerreotype named for its inventor), Talbot's paper negative had a "latent image" with the potential to "fix" fugitive visual impressions again and again. It could be used to create multiple prints from a single exposure (Gernsheim and Gernsheim 26–31). Now photography was no longer a unique object but a medium full of possibilities for repetition and reinterpretation. "The magical quality of that momentous event," the curator and historian Maria Morris Hambourg writes of Talbot's invention,

> is today almost impossible to grasp; it was as if one of the thousands of images that flicker across the eye had alighted like a butterfly on a sheet of paper. Just as the retina receives light and forms images in the mind, so it seemed, Talbot's astonishing optical and chemical process allowed the sun to draw pictures on paper. (3)

Photography was, in Talbot's words, "the pencil of nature" (n.p.).

This seemingly magical power to fix the transitory moment has haunted photography throughout its history, driving the development of ever faster lenses and films. According to the photographer Henri Cartier-Bresson, freezing the "decisive moment" in the flow of sensations was the basis for both knowledge and aesthetics. Writing in 1952, Cartier-Bresson explained this moment in photography as "the simultaneous recognition in the fraction of a second, of the significance of an event as well as of a precise organization of forms which gave that event its proper expression" (n.p.).

Inherent in Cartier-Bresson's "decisive moment" is the idea that the photograph can be both an archival document and an artistic masterpiece. Photographic representations, he asserts, are about capturing ever-changing moments and rendering them definitive and, if the photographer is also an artist, transcendent. Time appears to be arrested. And the photograph is iconic in the sense that its accuracy or artistry has become, like a Byzantine icon, an object of devotion. Although postmodern theory has dismantled Cartier-Bresson's claims for photography as archival document or universal expression, the romance of the decisive moment lingers in the criticism, history, exhibition, and collection of photographs. The digital editing and enhancement of photographs disturb us, as if these processes somehow defaced an iconic image. Exhibitions, publications, and art market prices continue to be driven by vintage prints, i.e., photographs developed and printed under the artist's supervision. Such a view of photography is as limiting as a definition of the after-image as only a flickering visual sensation on the retina. It arrests photography at a single point in what is actually a complex and protracted process involving machinery, chemistry, memory, and imagination. For photographers such as Alfred Stieglitz and his protégés Alvin Langdon Coburn, Edward Steichen, Paul Strand, and Charles Sheeler, photography was not a linear process but an iterative one that circled back on itself. The Stieglitz circle's images of the "new" New York are best understood as after-images. Their art is truly what Resina calls "the provisional stabilization of visual effect" achieved through "mental [and] technical editing" rather than "a timeless Platonic entity . . . [or] a concurrence of presences linking the subject to the object."

ALFRED STIEGLITZ AND SKYSCRAPER PHOTOGRAPHY

Alfred Stieglitz (1864–1946) was an artist, critic, editor, impresario, and mentor of the avant-garde in the United States. His passion was photography, and he saw himself as its savior, redeeming the medium from the degrading commercialism of George Eastman's "point and shoot" Kodak cameras and recasting it as the preeminent art form of modern life. Wealthy, educated, and refined amateurs like himself, he contended in his publications *American Amateur Photographer* (1893–96), *Camera Notes* (1897–1902), and *Camera Work* (1903–17), were key to the rejuvenation of photography as a fine art. He exhibited photographs alongside paintings, sculptures, and works on paper in his gallery, located at 291 Fifth Avenue in New York City. But Stieglitz was also a master of the science of photography. He took his first photographs while studying mechanical engineering in Berlin. There he also explored the physics and chemistry of the medium with scientists such as H.W. Vogel. Returning to the United States in 1890, he became a master printer, working in a photoengraving business where his father had purchased a partnership for him. Charles Caffin, a critic and friend, wrote that "Stieglitz's prominent characteristic is the balanced interest which he feels in science as well as art" (39).

Stieglitz introduced Americans to successive waves of the European avant-garde: Auguste Rodin and Paul Cézanne, then Pablo Picasso and Henri Matisse, and finally, Francis Picabia and Marcel Duchamp. But he was committed to a distinctly American modernism, promoting the works of Edward Steichen, Alvin Langdon Coburn, Marsden Hartley, John Marin, Georgia O'Keeffe, and Paul Strand. In 1914 Steichen wrote that progress at 291 was due "not to a gradual process of evolution but to sudden and brusque changes caused by eager receptivity to the unforeseen" (63). Stieglitz's own work reflected these "sudden and brusque changes." Reinventing his photographic persona, Stieglitz moved away from intimate portraits and precious landscapes to scenes of modern urban life and the machine age (fig. 9.1). Eventually, a new style accompanied this change of subject matter as Stieglitz abandoned pictorialism with its blurred forms, subtle tones, and painterly surfaces in favor of the crisp focus, high contrast, and abstracted forms of so-called straight or new vision photography before 1910 (fig. 9.2) (Schleier 41–68; Kiefer, *Art Criticism* 3; Szarkowski 74).

Stieglitz was the key figure in developing both the techniques and aes-

Figure 9.1 Alfred Stieglitz, *Flatiron*, 1902; photogravure, 1910.
Courtesy National Gallery of Art, Washington, D.C., Alfred
Stieglitz Collection.

Figure 9.2 Alfred Stieglitz, *Old and New New York*, 1910; photogravure on Japanese tissue mounted on paperboard before 1913. Courtesy National Gallery of Art, Washington, D. C., Alfred Stieglitz Collection.

thetics of photographing New York skyscrapers and the vertical city they created. His photographs of the Flatiron Building and the Manhattan skyline from the early 1900s influenced the imagery of the modern metropolis that his protégés Alvin Langdon Coburn, Edward Steichen, Paul Strand, and Charles Sheeler later developed. Committed to an aesthetic infused with life, Stieglitz photographed New York by day and by night (Stieglitz 183). He depicted the city in fog, rain, and snow, becoming one of the first photographers to overcome the difficulties of working in low light and inclement weather. To photograph a stagecoach struggling up Fifth Avenue in the blizzard of 1893, Stieglitz stood in the storm for three hours, waiting with his handheld camera for the "moment in which everything is in balance" (183). But his photography was about moments after the shutter was released and the negative exposed. "This incident," Stieglitz wrote about photographing the blizzard, "goes to prove that the making of the negative alone is not the making of the picture. My hand camera negatives are all made with the express purpose of enlargement, and it is but rarely that I use more than part of the original shot" (183). Interpreting and reinterpreting the "latent image" on his negatives, Stieglitz grasped that the photographic process was essentially about creating after-images.

TIME AND PHOTOGRAPHY

The relation of time to art photography was a question that absorbed the Stieglitz circle during the early 1900s. Alvin Langdon Coburn explored it in a 1911 article written for *Camera Work*, which Stieglitz edited and published. Coburn (1882–1966), whom Stieglitz mentored, was a wealthy amateur devoted to the pictorialist movement in photography. An American expatriate living in London, he became the most ardent photographer of New York skyscrapers in the Stieglitz circle. Inspired by Stieglitz's photographs of the Flatiron Building, Coburn photographed it and the skyscrapers of lower Manhattan beginning in 1905 (Coburn, *Autobiography* 11–18, 86; Weaver 33–42).

Coburn begins his 1911 essay, "The Relation of Time to Art," by describing his experiences of two distinct but interrelated modern environments, the suburb and the city: "After living constantly for two years in the quiet and seclusion of a London suburb, and then suddenly being plunged into the rush and turmoil of New York, *where time and space are of more value than in any other part of our world,* this consideration of the relation of time to art has been forced upon me" (72). Contrast and dislocation in time and space were key to Coburn's visualization of the "new" New York. Time was also critical in defining photography as "the most modern of arts." The difference between photography and the "the older art of painting," Coburn continues, "is not so much a mechanical one of brushes and pigments as compared with lens and dry plates, but rather a mental one of a slow, gradual, usual building up, as compared with an instantaneous, concentrated mental impulse, followed by a longer period of fruition." Speed was of the essence as he struggled to expose his negatives, but developing and printing involved another displacement in time and space:

> It has been said of me . . . that I work too quickly, and that I attempt to photograph all New York in a week. Now to me New York is a vision that rises out of the sea as I come up the harbor on my Atlantic liner, and which glimmers for a while in the sun for the first of my stay amidst its pinnacles; but which vanishes, but for fragmentary glimpses, as I become one of the grey creatures that crawl about like ants, at the bottom of its gloomy caverns. My apparently unseemly hurry has for its object my burning desire to record, translate, create, if you like, these visions of mine before they fade. I can do the creative part of photography, the making of the negative, with the fire of enthusiasm burning at the white heat; but the final stage, the print, requires quiet contemplation, time, in fact, for its fullest expression. *That is why my best work is from American negatives printed in England.* (72)

THE FLATIRON BUILDING: SKYSCRAPER AS ICON AND AFTER-IMAGE

Photography, Coburn also wrote, was "born of this age of steel [and] seems to have naturally adapted itself to the necessarily unusual requirements of an art that must live in skyscrapers" ("Relation of Time," 72). Stieglitz and his circle had firsthand experience of the skyscraper. The Flatiron Building across from Madison Square at Broadway and Twenty-third Street was in the midst of the brownstone neighborhoods where these photographers worked and exhibited. This area was and still is the New York "photo district" of studios, camera stores, and processing labs.

Rising from a triangular site (hence its nickname "Flatiron") created by the collision of old, meandering Broadway with the grid of Fifth Avenue and Twenty-third Street, the Flatiron Building stood apart from the dense urban fabric of four- and five-story buildings. At twenty-one stories, it was the tallest skyscraper north of the financial district in lower Manhattan (Landau and Condit 301–3002).[2] It became celebrated in American popular culture because of its distinctive prismatic form; but its completion in 1903 fortuitously coincided with the rise of movies and picture postcards, modern media that could disseminate its image (Woody 16, 42).

The Flatiron defied the monotonous streetscapes created by the relentless geometry of the grid. While its narrow, prismatic form posed problems of framing for its structural engineers and quandaries of planning for its occupants, it was an exceptional opportunity for urban photographers. It literally broke free from the plat of nineteenth-century Manhattan. Surrounding buildings did not impinge on the Flatiron Building; there was a view of the entire building silhouetted against the sky from Broadway or Madison Square. Photographers could celebrate what architect Louis Sullivan defined as the skyscraper's essence, "every inch a proud and soaring thing" (Sullivan 340–41), in their images of the Flatiron Building.

Commercial photographers exploited the figure/ground compositions made possible by the Flatiron's unique position in the urban grid. Crisply outlined and detailed, their photographs cast the skyscraper as an inert icon of the "new" New York (fig. 9.3). But Stieglitz felt the Flatiron was moving toward him up Broadway, like the "bow of a monster ocean liner," bearing down on the old brownstone city where he lived and worked. It was, Stieglitz later proclaimed, "a picture of the new America in the making" (quoted in Norman 45).

The challenge to Stieglitz as a photographer was to make visible the collision of the present with the past and future in a two-dimensional medium. He and his protégés Steichen and Coburn did so by abstracting the building and absorbing it into fugitive effects. In their images, the Flatiron was neither inert nor fixed; it partook of the contingencies of time, weather, light, and shadow. Stieglitz found a way to depict the building as becoming, not simply as being (fig. 9.1). When he photographed the Flatiron soon after its completion, he evoked its *natural rhythms*, emphasizing a particular time, a particular light, and a particular season. Steichen and Coburn were equally explicit in their images. They both chose to photograph the Flatiron at twilight on rain-slicked streets (figs. 9.4 and 9.5). This moment, poised between day and night, is known as the "magic hour" to photographers and cinematographers. Because the light level changes so quickly, it is notoriously difficult to photograph then, but the magic hour is aesthetically prized for the subtle tonal effects created as light fades from the night sky (Abraben 125; McGrath 183, 186).

Although a contemporary critic's contention that Stieglitz reduced the Flatiron Building to a "column of smoke"(Corbin 261) seems exaggerated, he did create an image of transitory and ephemeral effects from the stone and steel of the skyscraper. In his photograph and those of Steichen and Coburn, the skyscraper is poised between lightness and solidity; it is emerging and dissolving; natural and man-made; modern and timeless. The Flatiron seemed to pose a particular challenge for Stieglitz, attracting him again and again. In the early 1900s he cropped his image to produce a long and narrow photogravure. The dimensions of this print, along with the asymmetry and strong contrasts, are reminiscent of the Japanese

Figure 9.3 Flatiron postcards, 1900s, author's personal collection.

Figure 9.4 Edward Steichen, *Flatiron-Evening*, 1909; greenish-blue pigment gum-bichromate over platium print from 1904 negative, The Metropolitan Museum of Art, Alfred Stieglitz Collection, 1933. (33.43.43)

Figure 9.5 Alvin Langdon Coburn, *Flat Iron Building*, 1912, gelatin silver print, Courtesy George Eastman House.

woodblock prints favored by fin de siècle artists and collectors. In designing such a format, Stieglitz echoed the Flatiron's narrowness and verticality in the two-dimensional space of his print (fig. 9.1). Between 1924 and
1932 he returned to this image again when he embarked on another
major study of the "new" New York. Reproducing it now as a gelatin silver
print rather than a photogravure, Stieglitz gave the image a harder edge,
recasting his earlier pictorialist interpretation of the Flatiron into a
straight or new vision photograph. Printing the full negative, he increased
the width of the image, giving more emphasis to the surroundings and
more space for the skyscraper to breathe (fig. 9.6) (Smith, "Cityscapes"
322). Stieglitz's imagery of the Flatiron was unfixed and unstable, matching his perception of the skyscraper slicing through the grid and moving
up Broadway.

The potential for multiple identities inherent in photography also
intrigued and challenged Steichen. Born in Luxembourg, Steichen
(1879–1973) first worked as a painter and lithographer, later bringing
these media to bear on his photography. He made three distinctive prints
of the Flatiron from a single negative by overprinting the image two or
three times with different pigments. Beginning with a platinum print
taken from the negative, Steichen created a soft, textured image by allowing platinum metals to be absorbed by the paper fibers. He then brushed
on blue-green and orange watercolors, mixed with potassium bichromate
and gum arabic, superimposing discrete layers and points in time as he
built up the image. The translucent layers of color of this gum bichromate
print float over the pentimento of the platinum print. Like the old master
painters he admired, Steichen created, in the words of one critic, a vision
of "Baroque splendor," in contrast to Stieglitz's "stripped down formal
perfection" (Smith, *Steichen* 24). These three prints were as unique as
paintings. Stieglitz, however, recognized their potential as after-images,
exhibiting them together for the first time when he donated them to the
Metropolitan Museum of Art years later (*Steichen* 24). They became, then,
not the timeless Platonic entities that Steichen seemed to value, but after-
images about temporal displacement, sequentiality, supersession, and engagement. This was part of Stieglitz's growing fascination with the filmic,
still images made to move, in the 1920s and 1930s. Photography was never
the pencil of nature for Stieglitz; it did not fix elusive shadows but rather
destabilized and defamiliarized images in the camera, darkroom, gallery,
and interpretive spaces.

Yet the Flatiron photographs of the Stieglitz circle still alluded, however
elliptically, to the painterly surfaces and figure/ground compositions of
iconic images. By 1910 Stieglitz was seeking more purely photographic
means to capture the juxtapositions, displacements, and contingencies
that he experienced in the "new" New York as he moved from pictorial to

Figure 9.6 Alfred Stieglitz, *The Flatiron*, 1902; gelatin silver print, 1924–1932. Courtesy National Gallery of Art, Washington, D.C., Alfred Stieglitz Collection.

straight photography. His friend Charles Caffin defined Stieglitz's straight photography as working "chiefly in the open air, with rapid exposure, leaving models to pose for themselves, and relying for results upon means strictly photographic" (39). The precious painterly effects Steichen devised on site, smearing oil over the lens, or performed in the darkroom, brushing the print with watercolors (which Stieglitz had never really embraced even in his pictorial phase), Stieglitz now definitively rejected as alien to the true nature of photography.

Images like Stieglitz's 1910 *Old and New New York* directly register his experience of urban transformation and the printmaking process (fig. 9.2). Now the skeletal frame of a skyscraper under construction attracts him, rather than the stone and terra cotta veneer of the completed Flatiron. Stieglitz seems more fully engrossed in the city; he does not observe it filtered through the trees of Madison Square. He photographs not a deserted space after a snowfall brings the city to a halt but the workaday rhythms of pedestrians and trolleys. Poised on the curb, a man in a white fedora gazes upward, in a gesture that emphasizes the reorientation of New York from the horizontal to the vertical axis. Skyscrapers like the one Stieglitz shows under construction made New York sui generis. It no longer depended on Parisian ideas of modernity based on the horizontality of boulevards, parks, squares, and uniform cornice lines. The new city was now about verticality, and New Yorkers, like the man in the white fedora and Stieglitz, were learning to see a uniquely American modernity (Bender and Taylor 186, 191). Stieglitz's perceptions of New York in 1910, like Resina's of Madrid in 1976, unfolded in an interzone, one that was "strongly imprinted with the past, but a past already worn around the edges." The old New York of brownstone solidity collided with the steel filigree of skyscrapers, creating, in Resina's words, "moments in a lengthy and ongoing effort to determine the symbolic status of that 'place.'"

In this image of transformation, photographed in Stieglitz's own Madison Square neighborhood, the past, present, and future come together. Berenice Abbott, who made this changing New York the focus of her documentary photography during the 1930s, marveled at just this power of photography to depict "how the past jostles the present" and "what the past left you and what you are going to leave the future" in the space of a two-dimensional print (quoted in McEuen 266, 269). In 1910 Stieglitz had found in the city that surrounded him a changing New York, both old and new. His subjects now brimmed with temporal slippages that could be visualized within the space of a two-dimensional print.

Modernity and Modernism

As the city grew skyward, photographers left the street for different vantage points on the "new" New York, viewing skyscrapers from rooftops, balconies, and rooms. Like Roland Barthes's Eiffel Tower, New York skyscrapers transgressed the "separation, this habitual divorce of seeing and being seen." Towers and skyscrapers were active and passive, having "both sexes of sight," as subject and object (Barthes, "Eiffel Tower" 5). Here Coburn seemed to be teaching his mentor Stieglitz. Ascending the Singer Tower on lower Broadway, Coburn photographed the new vertical city that it and other skyscrapers were creating at the southern tip of Manhattan. After photographing from atop Mount Wilson and on the Grand Canyon rim, Coburn was eager to depict "the manmade views from the top of New York skyscrapers" when he returned to the city (Coburn, *Autobiography* 84). Focusing his camera on New York from the observation balcony of the Singer Tower, then the world's tallest building, he collapsed both the past and the future into his photographs of the present. In his 1912 *The House of a Thousand Windows*, he peered down on Liberty Tower, a skyscraper now dwarfed by the Singer Tower. Looking northward, Coburn photographed the Woolworth Building under construction, producing a print in 1911–12. When completed a year later, this neo-Gothic skyscraper would overtake the Singer Tower as the tallest building in the world.

Coburn saw not only the vertical city the skyscrapers created on lower Broadway but the dense urban fabric they wove above the Manhattan grid. His 1910 *Park Row Building* reveals a cubist collage created by the overheated and unregulated real estate market (fig. 9.7). He was later explicit about this "organic" or natural cubism, subtitling *The House of a Thousand Windows* a "cubist fantasy." Coburn found abstraction by focusing on the Park Row's unadorned rear walls and light courts rising above the darker buildings below. The forms of the Park Row continue skyward, unconstrained by the frame of his image. Averting his gaze from the neoclassical facade facing Broadway, Coburn discovered a complex geometrical composition in the skyscraper's backside. In 1903 Sadakichi Hartmann, a critic close to the Stieglitz circle, encouraged artists to look at the rear walls of skyscrapers. Here, Hartmann wrote in Stieglitz's *Camera Work*, "the laws of proportion, the comparative relation of large flat surfaces, broken by rows of windows, create the esthetical impression" ("Flat-iron Building" 39). Seven years after Hartmann's essay appeared, Coburn clearly saw the dense collage of buildings being formed at the tip of Manhattan as a vernacular cubism. Just as the Liberty Tower was the Singer Tower's past and the Woolworth Building its future, Coburn believed, his image of the Park Row Building anticipated a radically abstracted architecture. Yet this modern architecture barely existed either in European or American cities in 1910. Only Frank Lloyd Wright's organic modernism, seen in his Larkin Building and Unity Temple of 1904 and 1906 respectively, equaled Coburn's vision of abstract and dynamic forms expressive of a new America. In Coburn's photograph of the Park Row Building, New York is an organism, developing to the rhythms of the market. It grows through what

Figure 9.7 Alvin Langdon Coburn, *Park Row Building*, New York Portfolio, 1910, photogravure, Courtesy George Eastman House.

the historian Max Page has called creative destruction, devouring an existing urban form to re-create itself again and again (251–60).

The nocturnal city artificially illuminated, first by gas and then by electricity, was another aspect of modernity that attracted the Stieglitz circle. U.S. cities, the historian David Nye writes, were "discordant environments, indiscriminately mixing a great variety of styles, juxtaposing new towers with two-story buildings and squalid apartments." Electricity "edited, simplified and dramatized" New York after dark (*Electrifying* 47, 58). Night reduced the buildings Stieglitz saw from the rear window of his Fifth Avenue gallery to ghostly, skeletal frames. Old tenements and brownstones, along with new towers, are reduced to a common geometrical essence in his 1915–16(?) print (fig. 9.8). Lights flare harshly from doorways and windows, and an illuminated garland crowns the cornice of the Vanderbilt Hotel. It is an austere cubist composition, relieved by the electric swags that function rather like curvaceous wine glasses or café tabletops in the Picasso and Braque still lifes that Stieglitz exhibited at his gallery. Unlike the gentle nocturnes the Flatiron Building inspired in the early 1900s, Stieglitz's view from his rear window now has an urban edginess. It exemplifies what Hartmann called a "new style in night photography," dealing "almost exclusively with the bewildering confusion of light as seen from high viewpoints . . . perhaps less pictorial than a deserted street or church in the moonlight, but which are more realistically true of the restless flimmer and flare, the blaze of radiance, of nocturnal life" ("Night Photography" 130–31).

In this image Stieglitz combined the modernism of abstraction with the modernity of the performative nocturnal city. Here Janet Wolff's distinction between modernity, "specific historical experiences," and modernism, "particular practices and ideologies of representation," is crucial (57). Electrified Manhattan offered a nightly performance where reassuringly solid and permanent skyscrapers were transformed into luminous columns of light. This "architecture of the night" (Neumann)[3] was an alternative modernism, not of austere abstraction, but of evanescent spectacle. Although inert forms governed by gravity, buildings took on new identities governed by temporality. Lighting designers, who had honed their craft illuminating the ephemeral architecture of international expositions, now outlined skyscrapers like the Singer Tower and Woolworth Building with thousands of electric bulbs and then bathed them in colored floodlights (Bacon 225–30; Cochrane 8). New York was now a twenty-four-hour city and illuminated skyscrapers became, in the architect Rem Koolhaas's words, "landlocked lighthouses" (Koolhaas, *Delirious* 23, 28), beckoning travelers toward the artificial nature that was Manhattan. Contemporary designers have recently returned to this alternative mod-

Figure 9.8 Alfred Stieglitz, *From the Window of 291*, 1915–1916?, platinum print. Courtesy National Gallery of Art, Washington, D.C., Alfred Stieglitz Collection.

ernism, the architecture of the night. A computerized lighting program transforms the facade of Platt, Dovell, and Byard's New 42nd Street Studios into a kaleidoscope of colored lights each night (Goldberger 90–93). Yet the building by day becomes a rather self-effacing grid of glass and steel. The architects Elizabeth Diller and Ricardo Scofidio use thousands of high-pressure nozzles to form a three-hundred-foot-long cloud around a steel structure at the edge of a Swiss lake (Marks 1, 4). When one enters the mists and vapors the two architects call *Blur,* one discovers an "architecture" of transient effects that recalls the changing weather in which the Stieglitz circle enveloped the Flatiron Building.

MAKING THE CITY MOVE

New York as performer was at the heart of *Manhatta,* a 1920 film shot and edited by Paul Strand (1890–1976) and Charles Sheeler (1883–1965), in and above the financial district, from Battery Park to Trinity Place. Trained by the documentary photographer Lewis Hine, Strand depicted the life of New York's streets and skyscrapers in images that Stieglitz extolled as "pure photography" in the last issue of *Camera Work* (1917). Sheeler, who had originally studied painting with American impressionist William Merritt Chase, made his living as a commercial photographer. This work led to his fascination with the modern vernaculars of the "new" New York. It was Sheeler who asked Strand to explore filming the city with him (Horak 98; Handy 45–46). Now the change and dynamism implied in the still photographs of the Stieglitz circle became real. Space was collapsed into time through the viewfinder of Sheeler's Akeley movie camera.

Manhatta has no conventional narrative or characters. It inaugurated the genre of "city symphony" in avant-garde cinema. The film is structured around a day in the life of Manhattan, beginning with the views of Manhattan towers that morning commuters have from the Staten Island ferry and concluding with the sun setting over the Hudson River, as seen from atop a skyscraper. There are four movements in this symphony, separated by intertitles with excerpts from Walt Whitman's poetic celebration of Manhattan. The images of lower Manhattan are incomplete, splintered, the modern pedestrian's experience of the new vertical city. As the film historian Jan-Christopher Horak notes, Strand and Sheeler shot more than half the film frames by either tilting the camera up and down the skyscrapers or by panning across the horizon of the vertical city now at the southern tip of Manhattan (85, 88). Fascinated by the steam clouds vented by the skyscrapers, Strand and Sheeler choreographed a striptease, veils of smoke alternately cloaking and revealing the tall buildings.

But there is no one star performer in *Manhatta.* The dense collages of cubist forms that Coburn and Stieglitz distilled from the city profoundly influenced Strand and Sheeler's film. The Woolworth Building appears in the second movement of the symphony (fig. 9.9). But it is almost unrecognizable because Strand and Sheeler behead it, tilting their camera downward at the point just below the Woolworth Building's distinctive py-

Figure 9.9 Paul Strand and Charles Sheeler, frame enlargement from Woolworth Building sequence, *Manhatta*, 1920. Courtesy of Aperture Foundation, Inc., Paul Strand Archive.

ramidal crown. Perversely denying us the thrill of soaring up the building's facade, the camera moves downward until the Woolworth Building disappears from view. Looking decidedly grimy only seven years after its completion, Frank W. Woolworth's monument is now embedded in a tightly compressed space, exaggerated by the long focal length of the camera lens. Here buildings collapse into one another, creating flattened, abstract patterns. No longer an iconic form, the Woolworth Building is enfolded in Strand and Sheeler's cinematic vision of the claustrophobic spaces of lower Manhattan. The photographers suppress the horizon line, giving the viewer no point of orientation in the sequence. The filmic processes (tilting, panning, compressing, cutting, and editing) become the very image of the city. *Manhatta* is Resina's after-image, "brimming with the history of its production."

Just as Coburn's images of lower Manhattan influenced Strand and Sheeler, their *Manhatta* affected Stieglitz's imagery of the city. After decades of promoting American modernism by mentoring younger artists like Strand, John Marin, and Georgia O'Keeffe in his galleries, Stieglitz returned to photographing the city in the 1920s and 1930s. He was now in his sixties, and the more then ninety views of midtown skyscrapers he made from his gallery and the apartment he shared with his wife, O'Keeffe, were to be his last hurrah as a photographer. Shot at different times of the day and night, these images document the transformation of midtown Manhattan from a brownstone neighborhood of shops and homes to a skyscraper city of hotels, apartments, and office buildings. The creative destruction of Manhattan that had so fascinated Stieglitz in his Madison Square neighborhood continued to appeal to him as he followed the movement of the new city to midtown. Intended to be exhibited and published in groups, these photographs seem to be single frames in a film Stieglitz created by juxtaposing still images shot over time from the same vantage points. Yet the dense collages he created by looking west from his apartment in the high-rise Shelton Hotel toward the RCA Building at Rockefeller Center, the first planned skyscraper city, also circle back to his first images of the "new" New York, the Flatiron Building (figs. 9.1 and 9.10).

Stieglitz situates the RCA Building within the fugitive effects of time and weather. He shoots it at the notoriously tricky "magic hour," when the building is silhouetted against the last light of day. Soberly illuminated across its shaft by floodlights, the RCA Building is dark at its crown.[4] The skyscraper seems to be a dying star, going black from its crown downward. It is an elegiac image for both the skyscraper and the photographer, yet it is an after-image of the "new" New York that Stieglitz had been photographing for thirty years.

AMBIVALENCE AND THE CITY

Critics and historians have been ambivalent about the skyscraper imagery of the Stieglitz circle, often regarding it as modernity without modernism. Stieglitz and his protégés seem to occupy two different spaces in their photography of the "new" New York. While exhilarated by this modern city, they filter it through the tonality, symbolism, and aestheticism of the fin de siècle. They "have their feet in two worlds," the art historian Wanda Corn wrote in 1976, establishing a "new iconography . . . clothed in yesterday's fashions" (Corn, "The 'New' New York" 60–61). More recently, Corn has written that these photographers in their pictorialist phase "saw the new in the context of the old," casting New York "in terms of a Grand Tour mentality and gentility" (*Great American* 163). The representational conventions of the seascape or landscape seem to shape their views of New York. These were, Corn and others argue, traditional and comforting tropes of American identity and aesthetics dating from the rise of the Hudson River School, the first national school of painting, in the early nineteenth century (*Great American* 163; Solomon-Godeau 21–22). Even the Stieglitz circle's move from pictorialist to straight photography around

Figure 9.10 Alfred Stieglitz, *From the Shelton*, gelatin silver print, 1933/1935. Courtesy National Gallery of Art, Washington, D.C., Alfred Stieglitz Collection.

1910, evident in his *Old and New New York* and Coburn's *Park Row Building*, and then continuing in Strand and Sheeler's *Manhatta*, is dismissed as a romantic's longing to harmonize nature and technology in the city (Horak 80). Indeed, the critic Lewis Mumford, an intimate of Stieglitz's, wrote in 1934 that the Stieglitz circle's New York photographs were always about "nature in its most simple form, the wonder of the morning and the night," the "sky in the cracks between buildings," and the trees "in the surviving cracks of the pavement" (Mumford 48, 49). The American avant-garde that Stieglitz nurtured seems fundamentally romantic and traditional, clinging to Jeffersonian concepts of a national identity rooted in nature. Struggling to fuse two unique identities of landscape and skyscraper, they supposedly fail to grasp the potential of twentieth-century New York. While European modernists such as Marcel Duchamp and Francis Picabia reveled in the popular culture of jazz, movies, advertising, and Coney Island, the Stieglitz circle disapproved, appalled by its vulgarity and materialism. Collage and abstraction were common to both the European and American artistic movements in the early twentieth century. But the avant-garde around Stieglitz, Corn writes, conceived of them as a "healing vocabulary of organic lines, sensuous forms, and orbs of light . . . to redeem America from its spiritual bankruptcy" (*Great American* xvi), just as the landscape supposedly cleansed the national soul.

The Stieglitz circle photographers were undeniably ambivalent about New York City. It was the reason they ventured out to photograph at night and in inclement weather. At that time, the crowds of office workers were gone and the usually traffic-choked streets were deserted. Ice, darkness, overcast skies, and fallen snow all served to edit and dramatize the city, obscuring the visual clutter and architectural cacophony of commerce. These photographers shunned the other nocturnal New York of Coney Island and the Great White Way. The attraction of the Flatiron Building was, in part, that its neoclassical shaft had replaced what they surely considered an eyesore, a forty-five-foot-long pickle made of green lightbulbs against an orange background, advertising H.J. Heinz's fifty-seven varieties of condiments (Nye, *Electrifying* 50).

In withdrawing from city streets as their working space, the photographers also displayed an ambivalence about the "new" New York. They saw the city from a distance, from roofs, balconies, and rear windows. But such a strategic retreat was also empowering. As Michel de Certeau has written, to view New York from the World Trade Center Towers was "to be lifted out of the city's grasp. . . . When ones goes up there, he leaves behind the mass that carries off and mixes up in itself any identity of authors or spectators. . . . It allows one to read it [the city], to be a Solar Eye, looking down like a god" (Certeau, *Practice* 92). Writing to the playwright Sherwood Anderson about living in the Shelton Hotel, Stieglitz ruminated on the city in 1925:

New York is madder than ever. The pace ever increasing—But Georgia and I somehow don't seem to be of New York—nor of anywhere. We can live high up in the Shelton Hotel. . . . We feel as if we are out at midocean. All is so quiet, except the wind—and the trembling and shaking hulk of steel in which we live—It's a wonderful place (quoted in Greenough, *Alfred Stieglitz* 214)

Here Stieglitz circles back to his first experience of the skyscraper, the Flatiron as an ocean liner tossed by gale winds. Now inside the skyscraper, Stieglitz is still displaced in time and space. He is not a part of New York or of anywhere else. Protected within the steel-framed and brick-veneered skyscraper of the present, he is still rootless and adrift. Yet he is not fearful but exhilarated by this "wonderful place," quiet, solitary, and yet alive. It recalls the frontier where nature ruled. Stieglitz is certainly nostalgic here, but it is what Svetlana Boym has termed a "reflective nostalgia," a nostalgia of irony, wistfulness, and ambivalence (i–ix). Stieglitz may long to possess a home, to be rooted, but he also seems to recognize that no home can ever be fully satisfactory in either time or space (Boym).

Thus the Stieglitz circle photographers are never completely at home in either the nineteenth or the twentieth century. Stieglitz may have felt about New York as Resina did about the Madrid of 1976, that it was a "non-place . . . that re-places the image, restores it to place by infusing it with time and change." This understanding of the after-image as a non-place transformed into place by time and change may explain the attraction of landscape for the Stieglitz circle as they visualized the "new" New York. Change is what infuses and animates the landscape as well as the New York Stieglitz and his protégés knew and photographed. As David Nye has observed about purportedly "natural" landscapes like the New England foliage created from cleared pastures and planted with native and imported trees,

> Landscape is thus defined not as natural but as cultural. It is not static, but part of an evolving set of relationships. Landscapes are part of the infrastructure of existence, and they are inseparable from the technologies that people have used to shape them. . . . Human beings have repeatedly shaped the land to new uses and pleasures, and what appears natural to one generation often is the end result of a previous generation. (*Technologies and Landscapes* 3)

When Stieglitz and his circle invoked nature and landscape as metaphors and processes in their urban imagery, they were not trying to stop time and escape into an Edenic America. Instead, they saw analogies between the juxtapositions, displacements, and sequentiality of the American landscape and the "new" New York. New York intermingled forms and experiences of the present with the past and future. In their photographs New York was about the after-image rather than inert icons beyond time and space. They were ambivalent about this "new" New York, but it was an ambivalence that Marshall Berman has characterized as absolutely essential to experiences of modernity for both the artist and ordinary person: "To be modern is to live a life of paradox and contradiction. . . . It is to be both revolutionary and conservative . . . longing to create and to hold onto something real even as everything melts. We might even say to be modern is to be anti-modern" (13–14).

AN ART LOCATED ON THE HYPHEN OF THE AFTER-IMAGE

Critics and historians have contested the "place" of the Stieglitz circle photographers in modern art. The first historians saw them as unjustly ignored modernists, forgotten because of Eurocentric critics, scholars, and curators (Norman; Homer; Naef). Postmodernist scholars have viewed the Stieglitz circle as Americans unable to embrace the machine age, retreating into late nineteenth-century symbolism and aestheticism (Solomon-Godeau). Recently, a few claim a special place in American identity for them, an identity that has unified the art of this country over the centuries (O'Connor; Kornhauser; Corn, *Great American Thing*). I would argue that we need to reposition them apart from issues of style, periodization, and nationalism in the gap separating "after" from "image." After-image weaves time and change back into the two-dimensional spaces that the Stieglitz circle photographers created from the "new" New York. After-image is at the heart of their ideas about subject, process, and presentation methods. They focused their cameras on the creative destruction and reinvention of Manhattan, the provisional spaces of a city driven by market forces. They understood photography's equally provisional character, inherent in the latent images contained on their negatives. Stieglitz and his followers photographed the same subjects at different times and seasons. They reduced, enlarged, and reconfigured the prints they developed and printed; they experimented with different papers and printing techniques; they reprinted from negatives years after they had first exposed them; they exhibited images in series rather than as unique prints; and they created the first nonnarrative film about the modern city.

All this engages what Resina sees as the nonsynchronicity of the after-image. Their photographs, like his after-images, are "tension-ridden, mutation-oriented, and temporally determined". They manifest an ambivalence about modernism, skyscrapers, modern cities, and national identity. But, all too often, critics, curators, and historians interpret and theorize these photographs as simply static constructions, icons that are triumphs or failures of modernism or special cases of national identity. Understanding them as after-images of modernity offers us a more subtle, dynamic, and multivalent reading of the Stieglitz circle's photography and film. It is paradoxically when poised in the non-place, on the hyphen between "after" and "image," that these still and moving images seem most at ease.

Nevertheless, the need to fix them as icons is powerful. As the critic Adam Gopnik has written about such unlikely New York landmarks as the Pepsi-Cola sign and El Teddy's Mexican restaurant, we fight tenaciously for the "right to symbolize, to think expansively and metaphorically in a city given to thinking economically about nearly everything" (34). Yet our dreams and symbols seem to fixate on the icon rather than the after-image. The need to erase the hyphen between "after" and "image" is also deeply rooted.

CHAPTER TEN

The City Vanishes

Tom Conley

Cultural studies have become a commanding discipline in the liberal arts. Much of their analytical energy is devoted to close analysis of material of the kind that fills the sections of *USA Today* devoted to "Life" (signaled by a block of violet surrounding the word) and "Sports" (the word in white inscribed in a box colored blood red). Readers of that daily know it is formatted to resemble television, combining news, athletic events, infotainment, talk shows, and dramas such as *E.R.*, *Law and Order*, and *West Wing*. In general, television's mix of prose and pictures, coupled with the aftereffects of other images, constitute, in a weak sense of the concept, "events" that give viewers a vague sense of community, a community without geographical or genealogical boundaries. The material sparks conversation among viewers who watch collective spectacles such as football or basketball games. The communal event of people watching television together is already co-opted in our minds by memories of beer commercials that show handsome souls with broad smiles, who eat and drink together in front of a television set.

A community defined by the aftereffects of a television spectacle or of a commercial can be sensed immediately in the endless chatter of "call-in talk shows" that rehash news items and, especially, sports events, by having the public—armed with cell phones in their cars—contribute their reflections. Our impression of the reality of urban centers seems to be increasingly created by mediated participation in local events. Through "talk" and "discussion" by telephone, on websites, or via e-mail, we gain a sense of belonging to a common space.

The "imagined community," to borrow Benedict Anderson's celebrated concept, is surely of interest in the areas of cultural studies devoted to television images and their aftereffects. Community, allegory, ritual, and the electronic transmission of images engender illusory events that produce civic consciousness, a sense of identity in relation to a given space, and a rapport that ties collectivities to the cities where they are located. Any number of items could be chosen and would probably lead to similar conclusions. For the sake of simplicity, let us choose a sports event, Monday Night Football, now commemorated and immortalized on a thirty-four-cent U.S. postage stamp, the World Series, or the National Basketball Association playoffs. In this angle of approach, the event itself and the rules of the game are less important than how the transmission of the event constructs an "urban community" to be consumed, assimilated, and forgotten. The effect produced is what I should like to call the *vanishing city*, that is, the way urban spaces are strategized, constructed, and negotiated on television.

The term "vanishing city" points to how visual representations of cities impose and simultaneously take away a sense of identity and belonging on a vast and anonymous public. Insofar as one of the axioms grounding subjectivity is that *no one belongs anywhere in the world*, and that a sense of belonging is the result of a complex fiction emerging from psychogenesis (Aulagnier 14 and passim), the media gain credibility when they succeed in making their readers and viewers feel they are part of a space delineated by the name of a city. For the media, it is important to craft a public that will affiliate itself with the urban images they project. Viewers are invited to identify with these images, but, as a corollary, in a quasi-dialectical fashion, the identification is felt only with the disappearance of city views. The sense of "vanishment" entrances, but it also inspires disillusionment and frustration—two vital elements of subjectivity—whenever the observer is inclined to imagine that a given city may be an origin, a site of a particular "lifestyle," or that it may provide an illusion of rootedness. Media effects that ratify a city dweller's affiliation also tend to take it away.

Urban images, which we encounter everywhere in everyday life—in magazine advertisements, in grainy pictures on websites, on placards in buses and subways, in television commercials, in almost every Hollywood feature film, but especially on televised sports events, and the illusory sense of belonging they build—have to do with what Joan Ramon Resina calls "after-effects" or "after-images." They belong to agencies that colonize the imagination and use a politics of place to situate subjectivity. Yet, at the same time, the after-effect itself, like a dream, never entirely corresponds to what an image maker might want it to be. The vigilant reader of media images will find in their after-effects (that is, in the interstices between their disappearance and the emergence of new images) rich areas of contradiction. In their liminal and generally fleeting quality, these spaces are not always controlled by the strategists and editors of television programming for the simple reason that the imagination can turn them against themselves and yield new and different practices.[1] When the imagination makes strong use of the aftereffects of images, it can even be said to construct new *events* from the most common assemblages of impressions that strike the eye.[2]

Media images of cities have impact less in their emission than in their evanescence. While they persist in the imagination, as the eye and other faculties are absorbing new material, they seep into memory. They belong to the misprisions and associative divagations of the psychopathology of everyday life. In their haziness, they can acquire an idealizing or even "auratic" quality since they contain contradictions. In Walter Benjamin's writings on Paris during Baudelaire's time, the German translator and flâneur of the City of Light stresses how images seduce when they disappear. The poem in *Les fleurs du mal* dedicated to a woman passerby ("A une passante") describes the everyday rush that, in our day, subway riders may feel when they spot, ambling into a train, an alluring body that radiates an instantaneous aura and then disappears. All of a sudden, the rider ruminating on the travails of the day and of life in general, of "relations" with parents, children, spouse, would-be-significant-others, or with the daily dilemma of keeping schedules and making ends meet, is arrested and mesmerized. Thought turns to fantasy and stands still, before the push and pull of pedestrian traffic makes the mind move elsewhere. The most obvious aftereffects attesting to the force of these images are seen in the personal ads of tabloid newspapers. The anonymous writers in search of the name of the spectral beauty who slipped out of the Essex Street Station of the F train near Delancey on a hot mid-August day, wish to "capture" an event whose essence was to trigger a fantasy.[3]

In most televised sporting events an image of the city presents the stadium and plots its position with respect to the urban environs and tourist sites. In the basketball playoffs of 1999, the camera moved around the top of the Statue of Liberty, below the torch in her grasp, suggesting that the lady who had welcomed millions of immigrants was now practicing a set shot from an imaginary foul line. In the images taken from blimps and helicopters, the city is presented as barely accessible to those mired in it: the establishing shots bathe us in an aura that, because it is an aura, has to vanish. Now, when the Goodyear blimp floats in the sky over the stadium, the sky is less a visual effect than a background for a cavalcade of logos. These logos collapse the depth and flatten the spatial aura by reminding us that the image, seen to be remembered, figures in an archaic practice of baiting and badgering. What is proximate and welcomed, as a spirit of sweltering community that seems to live in the pores of concrete or to be exuded from the heat of the asphalt in the hot afternoon, is placed beyond reach. The city and its so-called community become a commercial image. It might be said that intimate proximity is what televised broadcasts of metropolitan sports events construct in order to exacerbate conflict. In the media, the task entails producing an effect of a community seen now from afar, now from close by, first in establishing shots, then in close-ups in which the image of the city disappears.[4] In this montage the city becomes an object of speculation, seen as a series of familiar sites occluded by fetish objects and emblems.

It is said that stockbrokers bite their nails when the baseball, football, or basketball season draws to a close. Far more money is to be made on identifiably "big" cities whose signature images will attract investment and wagers. In 2000 the "October classic" (which almost extended into November), the fabled subway series between the New York Yankees and the New York Mets, which had on its side the historical rivalry from the early 1950s between the Bronx Bombers and the Brooklyn Dodgers, was a good deal for the investors along the eastern corridor. But it was a bust for the media, which might otherwise have capitalized on viewers from Los Angeles or San Francisco. The basketball playoffs of 1999 had, possibly for allegorical reasons, enough resilience to become more than what they had promised. San Antonio, a city in its adolescence, was staked against the veteran Gotham of grime. In the overall production of images, neither Latrell Sprewell nor Tim Duncan, who, along with Marcus Canby (a tattooed stand-in for Patrick Ewing) and other designated dramatis personae of the championships, really drove the allegory of rivalrous cities in conflict to its just end.

Cutaway shots contrasted a young and anonymous public in a new arena to an audience of familiar faces of New Yorkers. Entertainers in Manhattan were contrasted to a public "out there." The figure who emblazoned the city and its vanishment was Spike Lee. Pacing nervously around the Knicks' bench, he was the black incarnation of bad boy Jack Nicholson, the self-designated mascot of the "Lakers" from arid Los Angeles (the history of the team's name is almost entirely unknown to most basketball fans under fifty) in the halcyon days of Magic Johnson. He was the reminder as well for the former Lew Alcindor, known in the 1960s as a New York kid from Power Memorial High who went west to the eucalyptus groves surrounding the basketball courts at UCLA, the solemn giant who changed his named to Kareem Abdul-Jabbar, and for Jamal Wilkes, Kurt Rambis, and other so-called immortals that memory now strains to recall. Spike had to pick up Jack's baton. In the language of icons heralding the power of cities, Lee was "New York" where Nicholson had been "L.A."

In 1999 it was up to Lee to make New Yorkers forget Hollywood and be done with the memory of Celtic warriors. He did so by shaking a white towel to cheer the Team of the City to victory. He was chosen to be the man *between* the basketball players and the public; *between* his specialty, mediated images, and "life itself." The latter was authenticated by the squeaks and slaps of rubber soles on the parquet. One could almost smell the musky sweat of struggle dotting black and white skin. And surely the lines of colors in the effects of electronic streaks following the quick movements of the players were like retinal aftereffects when the swish-pans of the cameras registered fast breaks and jump balls. In the midst of the spectacle on the floor Lee stood *between* a white establishment of corporate spectators and the "people" of Bedford-Stuyvesant and Harlem watching the game on television. He was *between* the men who handled the money that paid for Lee's Swoosh spots during time-outs and the people who were fantasizing the action in their half-court games on sooty city lots. A mediator in the space and time of the playoffs, Spike Lee was a trickster, a thief, a Hermes, an incarnation of the god of thieves and merchants who paced on the edge of the varnished floors of New York's Madison Square Garden. The role he had been designated to play in 1999 can no doubt be attributed to two causes. The first, which has accreted through a growing body of films associated with his name, affiliates him with the black man chosen to represent mimetically (that is, convey veraciously but also displace) the populace of New York. A heavy burden of images follows every one of his movements. A New York filmmaker who came out of New York University, he depicts New York locales from Bed-Sty barbershops to blues bars. He blends New York basketball with the texture his films would consider New York Life. In the media war in which he finds himself with other cities, especially Boston (an urban arch-rival for many historical reasons), in order further to underscore the rivalry and exacerbate the social contradictions, he estivates on Martha's Vineyard. All this material belongs to the Lee effect and figures in the image of the city conveyed by the playoffs.

In 1999 Lee was responsible for bringing to the public at large the intensity of the game that only he and others at courtside could feel in all its immediacy. As a result, in this role he had the additional asset of being a man "sensitive" to social contradiction, a man with the talent and wherewithal to convey to other, higher echelons the ferocity and pride of the lower orders who live in and for their city. He has thus been the underling New Yorker's counterpart to Woody Allen. Where Allen's Horatian wit plays on the neurosis that comes with the confines of urban life among New Yorkers rich enough to afford the talking cure, Spike Lee's mix of reflective ease and social awareness makes the City appear habitable for less fortunate strata of the population. Allen is Jewish, neurotic, an uptown dweller, a virtual client of Zabar's and of the psychoanalytical establishment on the west side, while Lee is black, hard-working, self-made, a New York University graduate, a man from the margins, the figure who lets film, sport, and music cure everything therapy cannot. Together, two great Knick fans, Allen and Lee, could be incorporated into something of a dream team. But in 1999, when cutaway shots caught Allen, in the press of the game, somewhat behind the bench, his presence was noted only to give way to Lee, the proclaimed leader of the Knickerbocker nation.

The second cause can be attributed to the opposite quality, Lee's inaccessibility. The playoffs announcers, who feigned neutrality by equally praising the virtues of San Antonio and of New York, had to admit that tickets were cheaper in the city of the Alamo. In fact, they avowed, almost no one from "the street" could gain admission to Madison Square Garden: prices were in the range of one hundred dollars minimum per seat and available only for the rich and famous. The cutaway shots of the final three games, then, were less a report on New York and its basketball than a haphazard occasion for stargazing. Thus Spike Lee, wearing the togs of his team, flailed a towel to emerge from the anonymity of a sovereign mass as the man of the people. Even if the fans were obscenely rich, when Spike melded into the images of the city, he was the man of the people *all the same*, the man who could make the contradiction of a popular game, the glue of leisure, of everyday life, of conversation—of all social interaction in the environs of New York—palatable for each one of his acolytes, for the well-to-do and the poor alike.

For people influenced by French literature, something reminiscent of Alfred de Vigny's "Moïse" marked Lee's character. His cheers, like the cry of Moses when he raises his fist in the battle for romantic supremacy, would bring the City to the threshold of the Promised Land. For the aristocrat Vigny in the age of the July Monarchy, the task of leading the people devolved on whatever poet and genius possessed vision, invention, and alexandrines epic enough to stir national consciousness to a new fervor. But with Spike Lee, the difference was that, as a black Moses, he would be in a rivalry with Patrick Ewing, a more likely candidate because a thoughtful and muscular giant. Ewing was the man of size and torso, recalling Charlton Heston in Cecil B. De Mille's film *The Ten Commandments*. Insofar as the media call any playoff team that will "take them to the promised land" the team of destiny, by most measures Lee could be a younger and bleaker version of the arch-villain Edward J. Robinson, the actor from gangster and noir films, whom De Mille consigned to worship the golden calf.

But Lee *had* to be seen in the cutaway shots leading the people, at once among the rich crowd in Madison Square Garden and in sympathy with viewers of the broadcasts, whom market researchers had determined to hail from the eastern seaboard and who were all leaning toward the underdog Knicks. Lee could be doubly effective, even if his commitment to the nouveaux dot-com riches and to New Yorkers was being translated into the pose of an authentic and faithful Knick fan. In the spin the networks gave to his image, Lee could leave no one watching indifferent. His miniature Mosaic figure was a ready-made abstraction that served, on one level, first to inspire everyone following the championships and then to call into question the ideological machinery in which he figured so prominently. On another level, in the world of the vanishing city, his image evoked an invisible tessellation of investments and multicorporate interests, which seemed, like New York itself, far from what was being broadcast but pervasive in every aspect of urban life.

In a broader historical context, the city of New York visible to television viewers of the playoffs was seen in a manner somewhat comparable to how it had been represented to the curious readers of city views in the early modern age. In the bird's-eye or three-quarters views presented in many editions of Braun and Hogenburg's *Civitates orbis terrarum* from the late sixteenth and early seventeenth centuries, city images were fashioned to promote spaces where the hustle and bustle of commerce were the order of the day. All the activities of the city, seen from above and without pedestrian interference, can be comprehended in the blink of an eye. Yet spectators are included in the images. Usually a man and a woman stand on a hillock in the foreground, their backs to the viewer, contemplating the landscape before our eyes. Their view duplicates our own. Following this model, different cities are contrasted to one another and their singularities recorded. Designated tourists in the image wear the "typical" dress of the city and bear sartorial signs of commercial success. With the flick of a hand, readers can move from folio page to folio page, from a picture of one urban center to another, in an order prescribed as much by chance as by an implicit narrative. The image of one urban center comes into view, only to disappear when another takes its place. The early atlas carries the logic of evanescence and reappearance in the design that places the folio maps on *guards,* strips that hold the pages to the binding.

The shots of New York seen before the basketball finals bear a resemblance to the innovations of these sixteenth-century city views. An ideal is constructed from a composite image of buildings superimposed on land and water, which arc slightly, almost imperceptibly, congruent with the curvature of the earth's surface. The city is seen from a point where the eyes can reach to the eastern and western horizons (looking north). It is the view that a sovereign or deity of a city would take as his or her own. Such is the stuff inspiring touristic desire; it is what the television broadcasters so carefully reproduce in the liminal moments between advertisements and the games themselves.

Where the viewer of the *Civitates* looked at the city from an eminence in the foreground, the Knicks enthusiast was taken up to the sky to see the enclosure concealing the contest in the dazzle of Manhattan beneath the Goodyear blimp. The spectators, far from the city itself, could peer down into the slits of its streets; they could partake of a fantasy summed up in

Foucault's term "panopticism." Michel de Certeau describes this feeling of ravishment, when, in the guise of a tourist, he suddenly felt himself rivaling God while looking at Manhattan from the observation deck of the World Trade Center towers. In his assessment of the mystical experience he called a "fiction given to the eye," he conveyed the feeling of the ancient mystic looking at the world from afar, in rapture, before descending into the streets and alleys of the city (Certeau, *The Practice* 22).

That strange effect was cast as mystical love in the plot of the film *An Affair to Remember* and resurfaced in the computer-generated images of intercontinental space stippled with stars in *Sleepless in Seattle*. The blimp shots of the city by night made New York as conspicuously out of reach as any city depicted in the woodcuts or copperplates of the *Civitates*. Yet, just after the city was seen from afar, the game was glimpsed in extreme close-up. Succeeding shots focused on the hoop of the glass-backed basket on which Latrell Sprewell's eyes were fixed. The media spectacle performed a Leibnizian feat, combining two contrasting views, one infinitely small, the other infinitely large. Both were taken to be views of entirely closed hermetic spaces inaccessible to the everyday world. The combination of the blimp's-eye view and the close-ups shown by an army of steady cam operators milling around on the floor produced the aftereffect of an event, because it was both close and far away, seemingly located in the interstice between inside and outside. Because the visual scheme belonged to an order analogous to the Spike Lee effect, connected to a web of social forces, the real site of the event, the city, seemed to disappear.

Each quarter of every playoff game began with a bird's-eye view of the city. The cityscape was seen through various superimposed emblems to identify what and who was the efficient cause of the program. The logos of Budweiser, Miller Beer, Merrill-Lynch, and so on, were both impediments and vital components of the image of the City. The Chevrolet escutcheon was set above the slogan "the heartbeat of America." Together, the heraldic sign and its legend were placed over the cartography obtained by the blimp. So too was the enigmatic monosyllable "bud" from the sound bite "this bud's for you," confusing a brand of beer with the tip of a flower in spring. By way of asyndeton the name of the beer was whispered into the space of Gotham.

Most striking in the cavalcade was the strange icon that, for lack of a better name (not quite the ogee or waving curve defining the decorative patterns of later medieval flamboyant architecture) is called a "Swoosh," the logo for Nike sportswear and shoes, winging its way across the Manhattan sky. It was an approximation of a wing that might have been on Mercury's sandal, or perhaps an Icarian reminder warning the blimp not to aspire to reach the stratosphere. No matter what it meant or implied, the Swoosh, like "bud" and "the heartbeat of America," were applied like decals to the image of the City, seen either from afar, from the air blimp, or from within the arena, from the viewpoint of agitated handlers of cameras at courtside. New York came to function as an advertisement, as would any other city view in the emblematic configuration heralding each portion of the telecast.

The genius (or the obscenity) of the mechanism in the Knickerbocker finals lay in the presence of the director of the Nike spots, Spike Lee himself. Both Lee and his Swoosh became multilocal. Lee was at the game, in the game, but he was also, during the showing of the Nike commercial, in its margins. Through the feat of the logo, he came to epitomize professional basketball. He just "did it." He *was* the game, at once the signifier and the signified, the modus vivendi of basketball, the negotiator of images that reaped and unequally distributed the profits; and, in turn, he *was* the City itself as it could be dreamed of, a place of equal opportunity, the site of the success of the democratic-consumerist ideal. By virtue of editing technology, the combination of Lee and his product confirmed that the signs of the merchandise displayed were equally intended to be sold. They figured in a more general rhetoric in which signs circulate in collusion with what is seen in and about them, in their emergence and evanescence, whether in the form of the athletic rite supposed to make the image of the city cohere, or in that of other signs and advertisements that belong to what one critic calls "any-place-whatsoever" (Deleuze *Cinéma 1* 284) and another, "non-places" (Augé *Non-Places*).[5] In the broadcast, the net effect was a muffled disappointment or frustration, a queasy feeling that may indeed, because of fatigue or overkill, prompt a dull impulsion to keep purchasing and consuming. In this process, so common to television in general, the image of the city must be put forward as a community that cannot quite be discerned.

If some of the classical hypotheses about the nature of ritual are applied to the telecasting of sports, the identity of a city and its public are woven in the montages of images prepared for consumers. The sports event is traditionally a rite rivaling religion. National Football League games are broadcast on Sunday afternoons and thus stand as either a replacement for or a supplement to the rituals of the Christian Church. The celebrated "Thanksgiving" games have become part of one of the most sacred holidays on the U.S. calendar, so much so that programmers have taken care to exclude the Washington "Redskins" from the contest on a day when colonizers and Native Americans were said to have shared some of the natural wealth of the New World (turkey, cranberries, potatoes, pumpkin). Unlike the Redskins, the Detroit Lions and Green Bay Packers bear emblems that do not interfere with that history. In a broader way, a television event has the character of a rite when a group organizes its activities around the broadcast. According to Claude Lévi-Strauss, a rite simplifies the givens of a cultural process through its theatrical display of a small number of social codes. It succeeds in erasing social contradiction and class conflict, but only for the time the broadcast lasts (Lévi-Strauss 610). When attendance and participation are mediated through telecasting, there is little need to make the collective body "cohere." From the point of view of the broader economic complex, it is better to invite the viewer to feel—and perhaps realize—that he or she is superfluous.

In the sphere of marketing, a collective feeling of superfluousness seems to be the logical outcome of "imagined communities," In his book by that title, Benedict Anderson observes that, for countless human beings, "the last question asked is their nationality" (Anderson 205). If we substitute a city affiliation for a nationality, the present and future of the urban complex can be discerned. Like the nuclear family pulverized within the sphere of flexible capitalism,[6] the sense of belonging to an urban space counts only within an arsenal of stratagems used to emphasize further exclusion and dissociation.

In a compelling first-person account of one day in the life of an anthropologist in Paris, Marc Augé remarks that athletic ritual is the glue of urban consciousness, especially in Paris, where talk of cycling and soccer is on the tips of many tongues (Augé *La traversée* 180–81). To a degree, he reiterates one of Jacques Barzun's observations, made in the 1950s and aimed at Europeans, from whom the Columbia University professor of comparative literature had proudly broken his ties. Barzun noted that anyone who wants to learn about U.S. culture would do well to study baseball. Augé repeats that reflection from European shores by calling into question the pragmatics of Allen Guttman's *From Ritual to Record* (1978), in which the author argues that sports have become a grid of statistics denoting achievement, in other words, a surface of ciphers all but eradicating the honest communicative function of ritual in games of years past.

After reflecting on the way the Tour de France can provide fodder for speculation or theories—about collective sports events as both "the opium of the people" and "the instrument of a heightened awareness of class consciousness" (182)—Augé notes that the circulation of signs has flattened out what had formerly been distinct social spaces. The implication is that the great lines of demarcation between city and country and between different locales within French urban areas are becoming increasingly blurred.[7] The ritual athletic event seen on television is symptomatic of the trend. "It is because sports are increasingly and ostensibly something other than sports that they contribute toward inserting more and more of those whose gaze they capture into a world where signs are everything, a world where every sign would refer only to another sign, were it not simultaneously for every spectator the sign of others, the proof that others are making signs and that the spectator is not alone" (184–85). A semiology of the circulation of signs has become an antidote of sorts to opiates.

Augé wants to see whether a communitarian ideology, like that which is written into the design of many urban maps, can be built from the imagination of sporting events. Despite the forms of control exerted by the media to dissociate the Tour de France or the World Cup from ritual, he implies they are not entirely impervious to cultural uses or practices other than the circulation of signs within the channels of consumerism. One of the practices available might be that by which a community produces a sense of urban space by refusing to believe in any ritual that includes icons and logos cemented to geographical images. Two paradoxical examples may serve as test cases. In the early 1980s, in Minneapolis, numerous groups of concerned citizens—all sports fans, and all communitarians— lobbied *not* to have a domed stadium built adjacent to the business district for year-round entertainment. It became glaringly clear that commercial interests in the urban center wanted the stadium constructed. Corporate power won out over the people. The old outdoor Memorial Stadium in Bloomington retained an aura both because of a spatial intimacy its design shared with that of Wrigley Field and Fenway Park and because the ghosts of the champion "Twins" of 1965—Tony Oliva, Harmon Killebrew, Jim Kaat, Mudcat Grant, and Bob Allison—seemed to inhabit the place. It was also in that stadium that, in the fall and early winter months between 1961 and 1984, Bud Grant built a signature football team that used the bitter cold as part of its offensive arsenal (to the sadistic extreme that visiting teams were not given heated benches on which to rest their frozen bottoms). Outside the stadium citizens invented "tailgating," a genial, if indeed bourgeois, invention that turned a non-place of asphalt into a space of communal invention. The surrounding lots were used for a festive mode of parking, not merely for the temporary storage of motor vehicles. The Bloomington stadium, a non-place that a populace turned into a festive space from its beginnings until 1984, was razed, and the Mall of America was erected on the site where baseball and football had been played since 1961.

Since 1991 Minneapolis has been unable to muster revenues from the media coverage of professional sports to rival those raised by larger urban centers. Baseball fans have slowly abandoned the sport played in an enclosed space and have reinvented it, now practicing it in new ways. Fans have shirked the air-conditioned nightmare of the Metro Dome and have affiliated themselves vociferously with a minor league team, a member of the Northern League, that plays in an outdoor park in Saint Paul. Attendance has swelled so much that, in 1999, in a nationally televised commercial for Norelco razors, the minor league park was seen from an aerial view, followed by simulated interviews with the faithful fans of the Saint

Paul Saints. In this instance, the media were a step behind the fans, who had constructed different spaces with what was available.

A related event took place on a national scale on July 13, 1999, in the moments before the All-Star baseball game. Ted Williams, who had a tunnel in Boston named after him to immortalize his career, which stretched from 1939 to 1960, returned to Fenway Park to toss the ritual ball onto the playing field. The victim of a stroke, he arrived in a golf cart (in reality, an electric wheelchair), hobbled out, was buttressed by fellow players, and threw the inaugural ball to Carlton Fisk, a former catcher and hero of the 1975 World Series, on this occasion the official overseer of the game. The pitch was broadcast throughout the world. But before Williams raised his arm to aim the ball, the players surrounded the hero and gave him an ovation that so disrupted the schedule of events that loudspeakers implored the stars pressing around the hero to return to their dugouts immediately. The timing of the commercials and of the sponsors on the field was, for a minuscule moment, disrupted. The following day, reporters for the Boston papers, those whom Williams used to call "the knights of keyboard," wrote of an "immortal and moving" moment in the history of the team and its city, a moment that had not quite been preempted or co-opted by the television order.

As in the moments that went "awry" at public tortures and murders before the French Revolution, as described by Michel Foucault (*Surveiller* 64–65), something happened amid the usual torpor of an all-star game on a mid-summer Tuesday.[8] An unexpected throng around Williams produced, in a flash, the illusion of a cohesive history and a commemoration reaching back sixty years, among players for whom the hero was more legend (for hitting .406 in 1941) than person, for the simple reason that he had retired from the game (after hitting a home run against the Yankees in Fenway Park in 1960) long before any of the players had been born. If Williams's welcome indeed exceeded the frame the media had assigned to it, then it qualified as an *event*: it did not disappear in a lap-dissolve under the more enduring overlay of a logo, nor was it scripted to produce the illusion of a local community. It did not blur into an aftereffect associated with the technology of commercial fade-outs, which would have made the stadium or the city an emblem of urban space as a field of mediated representation.

By contrast, in the days following the championship matches between the Knickerbockers and the Spurs, Spike Lee marketed his most recent feature, a film commemorating the heat of New York City between June and August 1977. In the guise of a priest of the basketball ritual in Madison Square Garden, Lee blended his fabled identification with the city and his unmitigated adherence to its professional basketball team with his new historical persona as a chronicler of Gotham's recent past. New York was one of the signs that went with the Swoosh, his emblem, and with Spike Lee enterprises. In the medley of commercials from which the Lee spot provided some relief, "New York" and its network of professional sports teams came forward as a sign, put into circulation in the midst of other signs and images, intended to make the city recede and disappear. The preparations for the film witnessed in the playoffs and seen in the following weeks may have qualified as a calculated anticipation of an aftereffect. If indeed an event is considered a "nexus of prehensions" and an anticipation that supplants an intended effect, then the production of the city that vanishes into commercial imagery—to be retained on collective memory screens—cannot qualify as an event. Yet the world of televised sports remains a place where events, in spite of a complex and refined system of montage and mediated controls, can nonetheless take place.

Now and again, but rarely, events take place in the thousands of tiny perceptions of things that do not quite comply with the rhetoric of vanishment, in which a televised broadcast, its advertisers, and the site of its emission coalesce and disappear. A miniature "politics" in the field of cultural studies, where the bane of professional sports serves as a topic of reflection, can therefore be developed. One of its principal stakes is to work in the margins of consumerism. No political action could have occurred at the National Basketball playoffs of 1999 through a fan's identification with the dramatis personae next to the bench where the Knickerbockers sat with towels draped over their shoulders. It could only have begun with attention to the composite effect of the attraction produced by the mediated confusion between a city and its so-called team. The same confusion would be an aftereffect or an after-image in which the city vanishes.

The paragraphs above were written long before the events of September 11, 2001. Somehow the title can now refer only to the destruction of the World Trade Center towers and must return as a lugubrious aftereffect or unyielding reminder of death and chaos. A part of the city vanished, not in the aura of the media but literally before our eyes, in and through the media. And the media, with their stress on their own power and their identification with the architecture of power, were implicated in what caused the events. Those of us still fortunate to be alive, who relive the events through the relentless repetition of the collision, the fire, the implosion, and the collapse of the towers, saw the televised images bathed in the crisp sunshine of an early autumn morning. Slowly falling debris, smoke and atomized matter—steel, paper, flesh, reinforced concrete—turned lower Manhattan into a smoky haze. In the space of a few hours, when the fires abated, air occupied the space that had been filled by two oblong megaliths. In the weeks following the events, people in the streets of lower Manhattan still smelled the strange odor of decaying flesh mixed with burnt metal.

The olfactory and visual effects remained so overwhelming that the first impressions, which made the event resemble something in a film, made it a reincarnation of *The Towering Inferno*, lost their validity, despite the agony of seeing them constantly replayed on the national networks. Once or twice was enough; more than that, and they came to resemble a commercial. For once and, after the brute fact of the report, we had had enough of the media. At its worst, the eyewitness account became pornography; at its best, it showed that the images were wholly inadequate to what they broadcast. The stunning spectacle, worthy of the best crapulous "special effects" of contemporary cinema, expressed the reality of vanishment that inhabits all our thoughts every day and night of our lives: the reality of the demise of every passenger in the airplanes that struck the Pentagon, the Trade Center towers, and the ground east of Pittsburgh; of the feelings of the poor souls who had to decide whether to burn alive or splatter on the asphalt far below them; of office workers who had been staring at computer terminals, suddenly startled and blitzed when the collision occurred; of firefighters climbing stairwells that suddenly gave way and crushed them beneath burning rubble. And so on. With these thousands of victims we try to share a collective tragedy. The reality of their demise and, now, their vanishment, cannot be represented by any image.

If any solace is to be gained from the events, it might be that we now are better equipped to see through representations of our so-called return to normal life and everyday activities. In the context of representations of professional sports events, an affirmation of life seemed to come, albeit slowly, with the Sunday spectacle of football played, as Jean-Luc Godard said of images produced in the aftermath of the Holocaust and Chernobyl, "nonetheless," in the awareness that their fragility is indeed their substance. Some of the unsettling after-images thus came in television commercials, no doubt overlooked by editors and broadcasters, in which the skyline of New York prior to September 11 was seen as the background to the logos of beer manufacturers. The perception of death, vital to the strategies of advertising, was too stark.

In the sports events that followed, the World Series, the beginnings of the National Basketball season, and the early going of the National Football League, lay the images of cities and lives that really do vanish. The fervor we witnessed in the victories of the New York Yankees in the three games played in their stadium in October seemed to be an abreaction to the destruction in lower Manhattan and a celebration of a community coping with collective anguish. When the Giants played the Saints in the Meadowlands, the usual shots of Manhattan from the New Jersey shoreline were attenuated, as were those made from blimps, no doubt because they represented a would-be terrorist's point of view, as if from an aircraft aimed to crash into a stadium filled with eighty thousand people. The image of Spike Lee near the Knickerbocker bench suddenly appeared real because, all of a sudden, he was, like the rest of us, merely a fan, like many of our friends who died in the events and like ourselves, who bear the responsibility of living for them. Like us, Lee now has to live with the reactions the events have precipitated all over the globe. Like Lee, we too can enjoy the silly but vital pleasures of organizing our lives to the rhythm of the fates and fortune of teams that mean everything and nothing to us. The grip of the media is loosened and the relation of the events of September to these other events, however innocuous and senseless, is strengthened. Hail to inhabitants of cities who refuse the images that would cause them to vanish.

Notes

CHAPTER 1. THE CONCEPT OF AFTER-IMAGE AND THE SCOPIC APPREHENSION OF THE CITY

1. I mean, of course, that I coined the hyphenated form, whose conceptual scope I discuss in the following pages. Many years ago, E. H. Gombrich used this form once in his book, *Art and Illusion,* but the passage in question makes clear that he uses the term exclusively in the traditional sense of an abiding retinal impression, precisely that which can be stimulated by a stroboscope (Gombrich 229). Elsewhere in his book he uses the nonhyphenated form.

2. Unbeknownst to me, Walter Prigge used the term "Vor-Bild" in a book that appeared at roughly the time I proposed "after-image" and its German translation, "Nach-Bild." Prigge's term, though suggestive of the temporality of the image, moves in a very different sphere, that of architectural typology and of a new (avant-garde) architectural "technology of sight," which, paradoxically, shies away from visual or photographic recognition and thus leaves behind the typological models (Prigge 107, 110–11).

3. As is the term "after-image," which began to circulate in spring 1996, during the period leading up to the international conference "After-Images of the City," held at Cornell University on October 16–17, 1998. The papers presented at this conference constituted the preliminary stage for the materials published in this book. Within a few months, the term seemed to have caught on. The *New York Times Book Review* of February 7, 1999, announced the publication later that year of a book by James E. Young in a review titled "After-Image: A Rising tide?" Young's book, *At Memory's Edge: After-images of the Holocaust in Contemporary Art and Architecture* was published in 2000. The same year, Christopher Gogwilt published *The Fiction of Geopolitics: Afterimages of Culture from Wilkie Collins to Alfred Hitchcock.* A coincidence? In any case, the term "after-image" was publicized in widely distributed conference fliers and on the internet beginning in late August 1998, and the concept has been discussed in public lectures, seminars, and conferences for several years. In the meantime, the present book, conceived in

the months leading up to the Cornell conference, was delayed by unavoidable circumstances.

CHAPTER 2. CITY FUTURE IN CITY PAST

1. Apparently, Marx was a great admirer of this novella and he too resolutely prevented everyone (even Engels) from having access to volumes 2 and 3 of *Capital.* After Marx's death, however, Engels did not find Marx's writings devoid of content. See Prawer 367.

2. On this theme, see L. Marx 164; K. Marx, *Grundrisse* 524–39; Harvey, *The Condition,* part 3.

3. For an excellent account of globalization in Balzac's lifetime, see Marx and Engels, *The Manifesto of the Communist Party* 46–47.

4. Lynch's arguments also play a role in Jameson's *Postmodernism.*

CHAPTER 3. LONDON

1. See Sinclair *Lights Out;* excerpts from the most important reviews are reproduced on the back cover.

2. For "thick description," see Geertz *Interpretation* 10.

3. Lynch 9–12; for a critique of Lynch's approach see Gottdiener and Lagopoulos 6–7.

CHAPTER 4. BERLIN 2000

1. The surreal estate of the postwar city made visible everywhere "the ruins of uncanny life": "A room cut in half sways at a height above the abyss of a courtyard filled with rubble; hopelessly isolated in the wasteland of rubble of an executed quarter, with a table, piano, sofa, chairs, and both walls hung with pictures. . . . From behind the curtains of this deserted world, a woman emerges from an invisible backdoor on to the stage, groping along the table . . . borne aloft for a moment." In this state of suspension there is "something artificial about such preservation amid the general devastation, like something put together for an exhibition" (Johannes R. Becher, "Deutsches Beckenntnis," quoted in Schivelbusch, "Cold Crater" 19, 21).

2. See *The Phantom Public Sphere,* ed. Bruce Robbins. On some of the risks involved in endorsing the spectral and radically open *tout court* (that is, in endorsing a politics of the de-signifier), see note 3 below.

3. The opening of bodies and persons to public experience is perhaps intimated in the very notion of the public sphere as *Öffentlichkeit,* openness (the etymological root of Habermas's word for the public sphere). But I have in mind something other than the overly hasty theorization of "openness" that has governed some recent work on the culture and politics of the urban scene, for instance, Edward Soja's formulaic reiteration of a democratizing "radical openness," or Rosalyn Deutsche's compelling, Lefortian theorization of a logic of eviction, which yet similarly lapses in the direction of a general and "radical openness" (see

Soja; Deutsche, *Evictions* 324–27). It may be that the democratic invention posits a politics without foundation. But if the democratic invention is without foundation—if it is of necessity uncertainly premised on the openness of an empty place—an abstracted antifoundationalism does not equal democracy. The (pop) deconstructive turn here, from the object to its theorization, risks the petrification of the idea of democracy—its congealed idealization—in the name of just the opposite, a radical openness. That is, the defetishizing groundlessness of the democratic invention is itself fetishized, congealed and idealized by way of a simple logic of equivalence between openness and democracy. (Hence it becomes necessary, for example, for Michael Sorkin, in the introduction to a recent collection of essays on the "politics of propinquity," to issue a reminder that "it is most likely because public space is so often and so readily conceived as dependent on a decorporealization of its citizenry—a demotion and even denigration of the particular and the physical—that the notion of public space has become so *abstract*, so divorced from any theorization of physical locations" (Sorkin 9). The irreducibility of the public sphere to physical place does not mean that place simply gives ground to a rhetoric of groundlessness.) This is in effect to evict the democratic invention by way of endorsing democracy as eviction tout court.

4. I am drawing here on Baudrillard, *The Perfect Crime* 131–41.

5. The first position is epitomized by the work of Jean Baudrillard, the second by the earlier work of Rem Koolhaas (see, for example, Koolhaas, "'Life in the Metropolis' or 'The Culture of Congestion'"). But Koolhaas, who began by writing about the Berlin Wall as architecture, has recently renovated his account of "orphaned" public space:

> Instead of public life, Public Space™: what remains of the city once the unpredictable has been removed . . . space for "honoring," "sharing," "caring," "grieving," and "healing" . . . civility imposed by an overdose of serif. . . . In the Third Millennium, Junkspace will assume responsibility for pleasure and religion, exposure and intimacy, public life and privacy. Inevitably, the death of God (and the author) has spawned orphaned space; Junkspace is authorless, yet surprisingly authoritarian. (Koolhaas, "Junkspace" 426)

There is no richer representation of the radical entanglement of these positions, and of their architectural idiom, than the fiction of J. G. Ballard, from the 1970s novel *High-Rise* to the recent *Cocaine Nights*. As Ballard puts it in *High-Rise*, tracing these alternating currents of the real: "A new social type was being created by the apartment building, a cool, unemotional personality impervious to the psychological pressures of high-rise life, with minimal needs for privacy, who thrived like an advanced species of machine in the neutral atmosphere. . . . Alternatively, their real needs might emerge later. . . . In many ways, the high-rise was a model of all that technology had done to make possible the expression of a truly 'free' psychopathology."

6. See the essays in the exhibition catalog, *Wounds: Between Democracy and Redemption in Contemporary Art.* For the exhibition curator, David Elliott, the singularity or "autonomy" of the wound represents the "individual path" that counters modern "collectivism": "Wounds, it could be argued, result from the incompatibility of democracy with individual freedom or redemption" (Elliott 10–16). This is exactly to mistake what I have been describing as the sociality of the wound in contemporary culture—the *convening* of the public around sites of damage and violation. (or, as Bataille puts it, "Human beings are never united with each other ex-

cept through tears and wounds" [quoted in Hollier 67–68]). A similar case is made in Nancy Spector's contribution to the catalog (89–93), which explicitly draws on the notion of a "wound culture" I have been elaborating.

7. The condition of referred intimacy and referred belief might also be seen to structure a good deal of the style of commentary that relays these culture scenes. Hence Rugoff, in "More than Meets the Eye" (*Scene of the Crime*), repeats the notion that in the face of such art "one's reassuring belief in a moral and rationally ordered universe was rudely imperiled" (68); that it produces a "violent disruption of conventional 'reality'"; that this art image is "no longer a mere container . . . no longer simply looked at . . . no longer an ideal viewing position" (72–73). Hence Arthur Danto, in a review of "Sensation," writes: "Body, menace, death, shit, murder . . . already we are able to sense the agenda of the young British artists. They are probing certain boundaries it had never occurred to us to think about" (26).

One rediscovers here something more than the lingua franca of the recent art scene and also something like the mimesis of belief and the mimesis of publicness that is the contemporary condition of belief, intimacy, and publicness. For, what exactly does it mean to appeal to the disruption of a conventional reality when that disruption *is* the conventional reality? What exactly does this *no-longer-ism* posit, other than something like the historical sense of, say, MTV's *House of Style*? And what does it mean to posit that it has never occurred to "us" to think about the only things the art scene (in the faux-sensation of the Sensation show, for example) has been thinking about, its clichés du jour? The point is that this referred sensation and referred belief is here exactly the condition of sensation and belief. (This is not merely because such clichés cannot be reduced to "mere" cliché—precisely in that the cliché is the voice of the community at its purest.) It is not quite accurate to say that the speakers of such beliefs—"disrupts our conventional expectations," "no longer simple . . . no longer ideal," "never occurred to us to think about," etc.—believe them. They simply believe that everyone believes them. That is, they believe through the citation to others and to an elsewhere—to a public without a place. They believe, in effect, through the other, which means, by extension, that the other can believe for them. This is the structure and appeal, for example, of "public opinion" and "popular psychology." And it is the structure of the mimesis of publicness: belief by way of the detour of believing a fiction about what *other* people *elsewhere* believe, while we may stay skeptical ourselves. The mimesis of belief cannot be separated from a sort of *collective transitivism*. That is, one believes through the opinions or feelings of *no one in particular,* through the opinion or feeling of *everyone else,* an opinion or feeling one can then cite, feel, and believe as *one's own*. Or, as Michel de Certeau puts it, "the 'real' is what, in a given place, reference to another place makes people believe in" ("Practice" 188). For an extended account of the structure of referred belief, its technologies, and its centering place in the pathological public sphere, see my "True Crime," forthcoming.

CHAPTER 5. FROM ROSE OF FIRE TO CITY OF IVORY

1. On the relation between visuality and concealment, see Bull 165–77.
2. Unless otherwise indicated, translations of quoted passages are my own.

3. On June 23, 1768, a *Real Cédula* of Charles III made Spanish compulsory in the schools, religious institutions, and courts of the Catalan regions.

4. "La justicia demanda, exige, impone esa uniformidad e igualdad que los necios llaman *monotonía*. La justicia es siempre y para todos igual y uniforme; y en este sentido no hay en el mundo monotonía mayor que la igualdad ante la ley"

5. For a study of this architectural loss, see Bassegoda Nonell.

6. I use the term in the sense popularized by Bataille, who mentions the burning of entire villages in the northwestern United States as a way of humiliating a competing social group (32–33). I am aware, however, that the term and the sense given to it by Franz Boas and later by Bataille have been criticized as a colonial invention (see Bracken, especially 162–65). Nevertheless, since the term, in this meaning, is a European construction, it may not be entirely out of place in an analysis of pure expenditure among European populations.

7. In 1854, another revolutionary action, also in mid-July, was marked by generalized arson. This time, however, it was not religious property that burned but textile factories, especially those where automated production (the so-called self-acting looms) had been introduced. The Luddites had been encouraged by the optimistic expectations raised by a liberal *pronunciamiento*.

8. "L'aspect de Barcelona ressemble à Marseille, et le type espagnol n'y est presque plus sensible. . . . Barcelone a un air un peu guindé et un peu roide, comme toutes les villes lacées trop dru dans un justaucorps de fortifications."

9. "Au sortir de ces villes étouffées et étouffantes . . . une grande ville, enfin! la seule d'Espagne!"

10. In 1845, Richard Ford remarked that "Barcelona possesses more European establishments than most Spanish cities, and they are better conducted. The merchants, by travelling abroad in search of machinery and new inventions, have imported also some parcels of the sensual civilization of the foreigner" (2: 724).

11. "El dia de Sant Jaume—de l'any trenta-cinc/hi va haver gran broma—dintre del torin;/van sortir set toros—tots van ser dolents:/això va ser la causa—de cremar els convents" (quoted Tasis 316).

12. Intriguingly, Ford never mentions the convent burnings, although he insists time and again on the alleged ferocity and brutality of Catalans.

13. "En medio de esta confusión la ciudad estaba tranquila: todas las azoteas estaban llenas de espectadores, los vecinos conversaban risueños por los balcones, en las puertas de las tiendas y en las mismas calles. Otros más curiosos recorrían con calma y serenidad los lugares incendiados, y se congratulaban al oír el horroroso estrépito de las bóvedas que se desplomaban, considerando que aquel y no otro era el único medio de acabar de una vez con la roedora carcoma de los enclaustrados, que tantos males han traído a la humanidad. Hombres, mujeres y niños con semblante risueño se volvían a sus casas satisfechos sobre manera al considerar que de entonces en más ya no habría frailes."

14. "Enfondint la divisió entre carlins i liberals, deixava la burgesia al costat d'aquests darrers, compartint . . . la joia 'de ver suprimidas las instituciones monásticas.'"

15. "El medio violento que para ello se había empleado."

16. In 1871 the Marseillaise was translated into Catalan by Josep Anselm Clavé, a musician committed to working-class republicanism.

17. Barrachina gives the number of convents existing in Barcelona in 1909 as 348 (118). That number seems exceedingly high. Later on, he says that a total of

eighty religious buildings were burned down, representing half of all those existing in Barcelona (121).

18. The first building to burn was the Workers' Circle of Saint Joseph, run by the Marist Brothers.

19. "No l'hi torneu a prendre reedificant-la; no vullau alçar-ne les parets més fortes, ni la volta més ben closa, ni hi poseu portes millor forrades de ferro, que no està en això la seva mellor defensa . . . i tornaríeu a adormí'us-hi; ni tampoc demaneu més protecció de l'Estat per ella, que massa semblava ja una oficina als ulls del poble en certs aspectes, ni vullau gaires diners dels rics per refer-la, que els pobres no puguen pensar que és cosa de l'altra banda i rebin amb recel el benefici. Que se la refacin ells si la volen: aixís podrà ésser al seu modo, i sols aixís se l'estimaran."

I quote from Benet's complete rendition of the original manuscript. This version had to be censored slightly before it could appear in *La Veu de Catalunya,* and also differs from Maragall's revision for his *Collected Works.*

20. "Tiene barrios donde, en el fondo de una miseria pintoresca, late el odio destructor; y otros en que la frivolidad descansa muellemente en el lujo con insolencia desdeñosa. Y de repente veis un rayo de piedad estremecer a ambos por igual y hacerlos hermanos."

21. "Puede haber un estado político que las rija y combine [a las ciudades] bien o mal para fines más o menos generales; pero su vida interna es sagrada e inviolable, porque es el espíritu vivo de un mundo que es mundo por sí anterior y superior al Estado y a todas sus combinaciones externas.

Por esto toda acción que viniendo de fuera de la ciudad y de su espíritu intenta dirigir su vida interna, es una profanación; y el instrumento de ella ha de ser repelido como elemento extraño y dañino. Todo lo que dentro de ella se pone al servicio de aquellas combinaciones exteriores sacrificando su espíritu es una traición que ha de ser descubierta y castigada. Todo lo que en ella es odio, o egoísmo personal, o germen de destrucción infecunda, ha de ser extirpado y aventado."

22. "A veces la ciudad se congestiona, se amotina gritando horriblemente: choca el odio calenturiento con la fuerza fría y feroz, y el terror cunde y la sangre corre por el arroyo de sus vías agitadas . . . ; y cuando las sombras obscurecen aquella plazoleta ya solitaria, en las vías que fueron campo de batalla la gente circula en paz como súbitamente desemborrachada de su reciente odio, y acude olvidada de todo a los palacios del placer brillantemente iluminados, en cuyo fondo tal vez trabajan obscuramente los gérmenes de terribles catástrofes."

23. "Heus aquí una gran conglomeració d'energies individuals que no ha pogut crear un organisme social proporcionat a la seva massa."

24. "La bomba i el renec són, sobretot, una mateixa cosa: un desfogament destructor de la impotència per crear."

25. "Això, que en el descontent de la vida és odi, i en el content, egoisme: tot plegat lo mateix, falta d'amor; i l'amor és el primer 'perquè' social, i el regenerador d'organismes, i la potència: l'única."

26. "L'altra turba . . . conservadora."

27. "Al mirar Barcelona deserta, Catalunya desolada, qualsevulga viatger podria dir: Aquí hi hagué potser una gran població; però per cert que mai hi ha hagut un poble."

28. "Symptome für die Unmöglichkeit, die neuen sozialen Wirklichkeiten aus der Perspektive der überkommenen Intellektuellen-Rollen zu erfahren."

29. "Vager Bezug auf die 'Unterschichten' . . . der neue Gedanke vom 'Volk als Souverän.' "

30. "Les multituds que ja no són Caos, s'organitzaran, millor, es *vertebraran* definitivament en ciutat."

31. Between 1857 and 1900, the population living in towns of more than ten thousand grew from 28.4 percent to 42 percent (see Espinet and Tresserras).

32. "El Noucentisme es caracteritza a Catalunya per aquest fet: la ciutat adquireix consciència que és ciutat."

33. Examples in d'Ors abound. See, for example, *Oceanografia del tedi*.

34. "L'arrenjament de les Muntanyes" (*Glosari* 47–48).

35. "Representa el moment conscient de la nostra nacionalitat."

36. "La Nació comença essent un fet gairebé material i només quan s'articula i redreça i, arborada en Ciutat sobre la immensitat de la seva estesa, empunya el trident apaivagador, arriba a ser un veritable fet psicològic."

37. "Caldrà glorificar, una darrera altra hora, l'Estat—la superba creació arbitrària—i combatre la Nació—el jou fatal."

38. "Les estelles dels Tronos cremaran en la llar de la República futura. Amb les runes de les Nacions edificarem la Ciutat."

39. "Acàs sies de mena immortal. I, talment aixís com les estàtues gregues han arribat a constituir el motllo definitiu de la bellesa plàstica humana, constitueixi aquella el motllo definitiu de la bellesa social."

40. Four years later, d'Ors used this metaphor again in his "gloss," "Estètica de les eleccions," March 7, 1907). Here too the image of Greek statuary places us in the presence of an archetype (*Glosari* 42).

41. "Lluny de la bellesa, cap salvació."

42. "Laborada amb ordenat esment . . . la palma del seny—que és immortal."

43. "Tota Capital és l'expandiment d'una acròpoli—i donem a l'etimologia d'aquesta paraula un sentit espiritual—. L'acròpoli li dóna la nobilitat, l'aire ciutadà. Una ciutat—resum, sense aquesta unció divina de l'acròpoli—fóra una ciutat impersonal; podria arribar a ser una ciutat gran, mai una Capital."

44. "Tota capital o Metròpoli és l'elevació d'un valor nacional a categoria universal humana."

45. "La ciutat és la primera obra plàstica on col·laboren totes les arts, des de l'arquitectura fins el darrer ofici, per a fer-ne el monument de la raça."

46. "La solució no pot ser sentimental, sino civil. Cal que tingui un cos, una forma concreta. Cal que es xifri, no en una resignació, sino en una acció: i no en una suggestió, sino en una fórmula. I no pot dur, malgrat el millor desig, una pau encara, sinó una lluita."

47. "La ciudad es una unidad producida por el amor, y por el amor ha de ser regida."

48. "Plató em valgui, per a recordar-vos i per a recordar-me, com per sobre les animetes miserables dels homes, hi ha la gran ànima de la Ciutat. I la Ciutat nostra vol ser salvada, ha de salvar-se. Podrem no convertir en Pau, en Pere, en Berenguera en homes civils. Però Barcelona, però Catalunya, han de guanyar Civiltat definitiva, així ens morim tots."

49. Admiration for the absolute state is a constant in his thought. His dissertation for the Master of Law, defended in 1905, was *Genealogía ideal del imperialismo (Teoría del Estado-héroe)* [The ideal genealogy of imperialism (Theory of the hero-state)].

50. "Era un grup d'homes, dones i nens que no entenc d'on van sortir. Fins i tot la indumentària no era normal, era com si s'haguessin disfressat de pobres, miserables."

51. Even in December George Orwell still saw workmen demolishing gutted churches all over the city (4).

52. From "différance," a term coined by Jacques Derrida, meaning both "to differ" and "to defer." A "différand," in this context, depends on its relation to other images to which it refers for its meaning, but also differs from them. In Derrida's sense, this difference is also a deferral that suspends the determination of meaning.

CHAPTER 6. BEES AT A LOSS

1. Llamazares 52. (All translations are mine, unless otherwise specified.)

2. Llamazares 89. On the question of the cleanliness of Madrid see also Ugarte 55.

3. On disgusting city imagery from Nietzsche to Gehlen, Spengler, and Lévi-Strauss, see Kuhnle. The construction of a "utopically positive" appropriation of Berlin in the late 1920s, when Isherwood and Döblin attested to the rise of Nazism, is to be found in Jean Giraudoux's *Rues et visages de Berlin;* see Hassauer.

4. Concerning the effects, limits, and history of urban semiotics, see Buschmann and Ingenschay, *Die andere Stadt.*

5. "Por supuesto, Madrid es una invención literaria."

6. "En mi último repaso por Madrid comprobé que está unificado en él el presente, indeteriorado, cabal, permitiendo idéntica vida, pudiendo el hidalgo pasearse por sus mismas sendas, tomando posesión de la ciudad que más se entrega al paseante, un Madrid más Madrid que cuando yo nací, pues estuvo hecho, desde el principio, con un molde grande, de acuerdo con el ideal clásico-moderno de gran ciudad."

7. "Una retina históricamente sutil descubriría que como sombra de la ciudad franquista empezaba a aglutinarse, intra y extramuros, la ciudad antifranquista."

8. "No perdamos la perspectiva."

9. "Las gentes se cruzan, presurosas. Nadie piensa en el de al lado, en ese hombre que a lo mejor va mirando al suelo."

10. "Kein Ende und keine Endlösung des Konflikts zeichnet sich ab, sondern eine Umschichtung der wortwörtlichen Stadtsymbolik und eindeutigen Wahrnehmungsstrategie in eine semiotische Auffassung vom Text der Stadt."

11. Again, there are varying judgments of the *movida* and its social impact. Whereas Vilarós paints a rather negative picture, accusing the movement primarily of a lack of political innovation, other authors (Gallero; Ingenschay "Movida et la fin") stress instead its innovative power.

12. Quoted in Bou and Soria Olmedo 399.

13. "Bienvenidos a Madrid, capital europea de la cultura."

14. "Decidió que Madrid era una ciudad incomprensible."

15. "Ya estamos con el sermón de siempre. El viejo comienza a hablar de cómo ellos lo tenían todo mucho más difícil, y de cómo han luchado para darnos todo lo que tenemos. La democracia, la libertad, etcétera, etcétera. El rollo sesentaiochista pseudoprogre de siempre. Son los viejos los que lo tienen todo: la guita

y el poder. Ni siquiera nos han dejado la rebeldía: ya la agotaron toda los putos marxistas y los putos jipis de su época."

16. "En realidad, más que meditación trascendental, lo que Jerónimo hace sentado encima del vagón, muchas mañanas, es mirar las distancias de la nada y no pensar, mirar la fiesta del sol en las remotas montañas, a las que ha llegado como un excursionista, mirar . . . Madrid para el otro lado, una masa inmensa, rosa, extendida, interminable, infinita, con su cielo propio, gris y plata y un poco de oro, ese sitio adonde él baja a robar el puesto de un melonero, pegarse un pico, pispar una botella de jotabé o matar a un hombre, según."

17. "Jerónimo no siente la melancolía de los grandes viajes. Todas las ciudades son iguales, se dice: un sitio donde robar, matar y follar."

18. On Paris as the most evident paradigm of city literature, see Stierle.

19. See the programmatic title of the (still) most important discussion of postcolonial literary culture, Ashcroft et al., *The Empire Writes Back*.

20. "El Gran Cangrejo de una pata."

21. "Ese resplandor rojo y tibio, penetrable y extenso que es Madrid."

22. Together with *Mensaka* (1995) and the recently published *Sonko 95. Autorretrato con negro de fondo* (1999), *Historias del Kronen* and *Ciudad rayada* form part of what Mañas's publisher now calls "the Kronen tetralogy"; the connections between these novels, however, are rather loose.

23. "Kiero decir ke en Madrid no sólo konozco las kalles, es ke están en mi kabeza. Es mi ciudad por fuera y por dentro, no sé si me expliko."

24. Relating each of his films to Madrid, the movie director states: "La desolación del barrio de la Concepción y ese mar sin fondo que es la M-30, en ®*Qué he hecho yo*" (The desolation of the Concepción suburb and this groundless sea which is M-30, in *What Have I Done to deserve this?* [Almodóvar, "La ciudad" 1991: 110]).

25. "La Emetreinta es el silbido de Dios" (111).

26. "Siempre me ha alucinado eso de Madrid, sabes, que en cuanto sales un poquito te encuentras con chabolas por todos lados. Y te creerás que los gitanos viven mal. Pues tú pregúntale a cualquier heroinómano de la ciudad dónde está la mejor droga de Madrid. Yo conocía alguno de estos poblados a través del Chalo, y sabía dónde debía estar hoy, así que después de pensarlo un poco decidí ir a buscarle." (What always shocks me about Madrid is that whenever you get out a bit you find yourself in the middle of the *chabolas*. Now you may think that the gypsies live in poverty. But just ask any junkie where to find the best stuff in town. I knew some of these villages through Chalo, and I knew where he would be today, so after thinking it over a little, I decided to look for him [Mañas, *Ciudad* 124]).

27. "Ya digo que yo me muevo por todo Madrid y es importante tener siempre algún conocido en cada barrio."

28. "El puto centro de Madrid."

29. "Así que nos fuimos a ver la puesta del sol a las Tetas del Cerro Pío, que son dos montículos por ahí por Vallecas, desde donde se puede ver todo Madrid."

30. "Era como si aquello fuera una gran colmena de locos, y nosotros—olvidando la panda de fumetas de al lado que no hacían más que reírse con chistes apestosos—estuviésemos por encima, controlando el mundo mientras el cielo prendía fuego detrás de las torres de Azca, untando todo con una capa de mermelada de albaricoque. Las nubes se volvían moradas, y los últimos rayos de sol parecían láseres de discoteca. Viendo el planetario de Atocha, y la Emetreinta, ya iluminada, y el Pirulí, y las torres inclinadas de Plaza Castilla, me acordé de una

vez que jodí la tele y la abrí con un destornillador para ver las placas de circuitos de dentro. Molaba."

31. "La literatura española de este período, desde apostar por la construcción de esa ciudad democrática, cuestionando las claves estéticas de lo que había sido el franquismo, . . . ha rechazado . . . el intervenir con un discurso crítico sobre esa ciudad que había heredado de la etapa de la transición. . . . La postmodernidad, asumida como situación de *impasse* de la modernidad y no como ideología, tendría que volver a rehistorificarse y redescubrir que la necesaria ciudad del futuro . . . no es el *skyline* definitivo de la última ciudad de la historia, sino que hay que aspirar a otro *skyline*, el de una ciudad global, futura, que a la vez sea igualitaria, solidaria y libertaria."

CHAPTER 7. THE WORLD IN OUR HEAD

1. "Dann umfuhren wir die Insel und lenkten unser Boot nach Kinross zurück, aber das Auge mochte sich nicht trennen von der Insel, auf deren Trümmergrau die Nachmittagssonne und eine wehmütig-unnennbare Stille lag.

Nun griffen die Ruder rasch ein, die Insel wurd ein Streifen, endlich schwand sie ganz, und nur als ein Gebilde der Einbildungskraft stand eine Zeitlang noch der Rundturm vor uns auf dem Wasser, bis plötzlich unsre Phantasie weiter in ihre Erinnerungen zurückgriff und ältere Bilder vor die Bilder dieser Stunde schob. Es waren Erinnerungen aus der Heimat, ein unvergessener Tag.

Auch eine Wasserfläche war es; aber nicht Weidengestrüpp faßte da Ufer ein, sondern ein Park und ein Laubholzwald nahmen den See in ihren Arm. Im Flachboot stießen wir ab, und sooft wir das Schilf am Ufer streiften, klang es, wie wenn eine Hand über knisternde Seide fährt" (unless otherwise indicated, translations are my own).

2. "Wär' nicht das Auge sonnenhaft, / Wie könnten wir das Licht erblicken? / Lebt' nicht in uns des Gottes eigne Kraft, / Wie könnt' uns Göttliches entzücken?"

3. "Wir blicken von einem Gegenstand auf den anderen, die Sukzession der Bilder scheint uns rein, wir werden nicht gewahr, daß sich von dem vorhergehenden etwas ins nachfolgende hinüberschleicht."

4. "Ein solches Bild, dessen Eindruck nicht mehr bemerklich ist, läßt sich auf der Retina gleichsam wieder beleben, wenn wir die Augen öffnen und schließen und mit Erregung und Schonung abwechseln."

5. "Daß Bilder sich bei Augenkrankheiten vierzehn bis siebzehn Minuten, ja länger auf der Retina erhielten, deutet auf äußerste Schwäche des Organs, auf dessen Unfähigkeit, sich wiederherzustellen, so wie das Vorschweben leidenschaftlich geliebter oder verhaßter Gegenstände aus dem Sinnlichen ins Geistige deutet."

6. See "Welcome to Retina Implant News in Bonn," (http://www.nero.uni-bonn.de/ri/retina-en.html).

7. "Si j'allais au bord de la mer, j'étais sûr que cette Méditerrannée que je voyais se trouvait aussi dans ma tête, pas l'image de la Méditerrannée mais cette Méditerrannée elle-même, minuscule et salée, dans ma tête, en miniature mais vraie et avec tous ses poissons, mais tout petits, avec toutes ses vagues et un petit soleil brûlant, une vraie mer avec tous ses rochers et tous ses bateaux absolument complets dans ma tête, avec charbon et matelots vivants, chaque bateau avec le

même capitaine que le grand bateau du dehors, le même capitaine mais très nain et qu'on pourrait toucher si on avait des doigts assez fins et petits. J'étais sûr que dans ma tête, cirque du monde, il y avait la terre vraie avec ses forêts, tous les chevaux de la terre mais si petits, tous les rois en chair et en os, tous les morts, tout le ciel avec ses étoiles et même Dieu extrêmement petit et mignon. Et tout cela, je le crois encore un peu, mais chut." The poetological importance of this passage for all Cohen's texts is highlighted by the fact that in 1954 the author incorporated a slightly modified version of it into his *Le livre de ma mère*, see *Oeuvres* 714.

8. For an analysis of the hermeneutic movements in Albert Cohen's works, see Ette.

9. "Les verrous de sa porte donnaient à croire que son appartement du neuvième étage du numéro 7 de l'avenue Krieg, à Genève, était une forteresse. On ne venait pas chez lui sans s'annoncer et la ponctualité au rendez-vous était obligation" (The locks on his door convinced you that his apartment, on the ninth floor of no. 7 Krieg Avenue in Geneva, was a fortress. You never went to see him without giving notice, and punctuality at the meeting was an obligation [see Valbert 12]).

10. "J'ai partagé la vie d'Albert Cohen pendant trente-quatre ans. Durant la plus grande partie de ce temps, nous avons vécu repliés sur nous-mêmes, presque en marge, ne sortant que rarement, ne voyant que des amis intimes" (I shared Albert Cohen's life for thirty-four years. Most of this time we lived our own secluded life, almost at the margins, going out but rarely, meeting only close friends [Bella Cohen, "Albert Cohen" xlv]). See also Bella Cohen, *Autour*.

11. "Albert Cohen nous fournit la clef de l'l'énigme lorsqu'il dit un jour: 'Je suis physiquement vulnérable. Il me faut vivre préservé.' Il était en effet d'une grande fragilité physique. Même lorsqu'il était encore relativement jeune—bien avant la soixantaine—la fatigue d'un dîner en ville, d'où il rentrait pourtant avant minuit, pouvait provoquer chez lui une forte poussée de fièvre" (Albert Cohen furnished the key to the enigma one day when he said: "I am physically vulnerable. I must live in a well-protected way." In fact, he was of a great physical fragility. Even when he was relatively young—before his sixties—the fatigue caused by a dinner in town from which he nevertheless returned before midnight, could provoke in him a strong attack of fever [Bella Cohen, "Albert Cohen" xlvii]).

12. "Elle me recoiffe, me brosse, me donne un franc, me recommande de n'acheter ni pommes frites, ni beignets, car les Gentils font la cuisine sans se laver les mains auparavant. Et ne va pas non plus sur les montagnes russes, ce sont divertissements de païens sans cervelle, me dit-elle. Je la regarde qui ouvre la porte devant moi. Oui, elle est un peu forte, ça ne fait rien, c'est mignon. Les anges avec toi, regarde bien des deux côtés avant de traverser, me dit-elle, et elle m'embrasse, me sourit" (Cohen, *Carnets* 1122). Just a few pages later, the narrator remarks: "Chaque sourire d'elle est une protection" (each of her smiles is a protection), linking to this ritual of transition the act of writing itself, though it is still writing in the air: "'Maman chérie,' écris-je avec mon doigt sur de l'air, tout en descendant l'escalier" ("Beloved mom," I wrote with my finger into the air, while going down the stairs [1128]).

13. "Les phares violent de froides colères la salle hurlant immensément contre la porte que je pousse."

14. "La fille de mon jardinier est devenue putain, et sur sa vieille face de vingt ans s'achève la noblesse de la vie noceuse.

Pauline à la raie de côté discute, montrant avec fierté les agiles rubis de sa langue. Elle secoue le cendre et rit au nez moisi du cocaïnomane. Elle lance la fumée vers la bouche qui s'étire en charme mécanique. L'eau jaune que boit Pauline me dit la fin puante de ses amours."

15. "Je me crée un petit monde bien à moi, où mes persécuteurs passent de mauvais quarts d'heure! C'est de la philosophie. De la métaphysique, pour être plus exact. Ou plutôt une sorte de religion. Tout cela est assez compliqué; et je ne peux pas, en quelques minutes, vous exposer mon système."

16. "'Une belle femme nue!' cria-t-il soudain par pure méchanceté au plus pieux des étudiants de la Loi, un pâle jeune homme aux yeux cernés qui aussitôt se représenta combien cette dame impudique serait répugnante si on l'écorchait vive."

17. For the concepts of ambiguity, ambivalence, and indifference see Zima, chap. 4.

18. "'L'avril de Céphalonie,' énonça le solitaire nageur, 'est plus beau et plus doux que le juillet de Berlin! Sûrement. Mais pourquoi diable mettent-ils tous leurs capitales en des endroits de froidure et de tristesse et pourquoi les posent-ils tous sur des fleuves noirs? Il me semble qu'ils ont tort. Enfin ils savent mieux que moi.'"

19. "Et tout d'abord, en descendant du compartiment, l'oncle Saltiel crut devoir saluer la Ville lumière d'un geste large de sa toque. . . . Mangeclous s'arrêtait parfois, interpellait les badauds qui se moquaient. . . . Ensuite, les Valeureux sortirent dans Paris à seule fin de saluer les statues des bienfaiteurs de l'humanité.

A sept heures du soir, ces naïfs stationnaient devant le ministère des Affaires étrangères, se découvraient devant le drapeau tricolore."

20. "Après, nous sommes allés voir le Mur de la Réformation qui est magnifique. Nous nous sommes découverts devant les quatre grands Réformateurs et nous avons observé une minute de silence parce que le protestantisme est une noble religion, et d'ailleurs les protestants sont très honnêtes, très corrects, c'est connu" (After that, we went to look at the Wall of Reformation, which is marvelous. We took off our hats in front of the four great reformers, and we remained silent for a minute, because Protestantism is a noble religion, and, moreover, the Protestants are very honorable, very correct, as we know [Cohen, *Seigneur* 132]). Like the visit to Paris, the Valeureux's visit to Geneva is counterbalanced by the mention of inhabitants of the admired city who are far from displaying the spirit of tolerance and correctness invoked in this passage.

21. "Que de souhaits de mort aux Juifs dans ces villes de l'amour du prochain."

22. "Mort aux Juifs. Partout, dans tous les pays, les mêmes mots."

23. "Dehors j'ai marché dans les rues traînant mon malheur désirant l'oncle Saltiel oh le revoir vivre avec lui mais non impossible il serait si malheureux de me voir déchu je ne peux pas le faire souffrir m'arrêtant devant le lac déchirant les deux lettres mes deux belles inventions mes grandes espérances les jetant dans le lac les regardant emportées par le courant, les rues les rues les rues pensant à te débarasser de moi à te laisser tous mes dollars les déposer pour toi dans une banque moi allant vivre dans la cave avec eux, j'étais fatigué je n'avais rien mangé penché sur ma machine à écrire."

24. The numerous allusions to Proust begin with the very first words in his first novel, *Solal*: "L'oncle Saltiel s'était réveillé de bonne heure" (Uncle Saltiel had got up early) *Un incipit peut en cacher un autre*.

25. "Je suis allé me jeter aux genoux de mon seigneur père et cet homme mis-

éricordieux m'a pardonné. Il m'a donné l'ordre de faire une demeure secrète dans ma demeure d'Europe. J'ai obéi. Il est sage et il comprend que j'ai ma vie occidentale à continuer. J'ai fait venir des Solal, ceux de Céphalonie et ceux d'ailleurs. Une ville biblique grouille sous la demeure de Son Excellence. Le jour au ministère, à la chambre, aux réunions du parti. Et la nuit, je vais dans mon pays. Et de jour et de nuit, je suis triste, si triste."

26. "Soudain, il y eut de nouveau une grande rumeur dehors, et en même temps que le martèlement des bottes retentit le chant allemand, chant de méchanceté, chant de la joie allemande, joie du sang d'Israël giclant sous les couteaux allemands. *Wenn Judenblut unter'm Messer spritzt,* chantaient les jeunes espoirs de la nation allemande, tandis que de la cave voisine s'élevait un autre chant, chant à l'Eternel, grave chant d'amour, surgi du fond des siècles, chant de mon roi David."

27. This is clear, for example, in his last book, *Carnets 1978.*

28. "De retour à la Canebière, je baisse les yeux en marchant, et je mords ma lèvre pour ne pas pleurer. 'Fatigué de vivre,' écris-je avec mon doigt sur de l'air. Ensuite, j'écris le mot 'catalepsie.' C'est un mot que j'ai lu dans un livre, et j'ai appris par le dictionnaire qu'il signifie qu'on ne bouge plus, qu'on est comme mort. Pourvu qu'on ne m'enterre pas vivant, par erreur. Je me réveillerai dans mon cercueil, et je crierai et j'entendrai les pas des vivants qui passeront dans le cimetière et je crierai qu'ils viennent me délivrer, mais ils ne m'entendront pas et je crierai, je supplierai, j'étoufferai, la planche du cercueil contre mon nez vivant. En rentrant, je demanderai à Maman qu'elle s'assure que je suis vraiment mort, si je viens à mourir, et qu'elle me donne un coup de couteau dans le coeur, pour plus de sûreté. Assez, ne plus penser à la catalepsie."

29. See the remarkable essay by Brissac Peixoto, 29–32.

30. According to García Canclini, this is the favorite perspective of a communications expert.

CHAPTER 8. TIJUANA

1. "Atendiendo la instrucción girada en su momento y habiéndose concluido el trámite, anexo al presente me permito acompañar original del Título de Registración de Marca número 555863, expediente 300027 por el Instituto Mexicano de la Propiedad Industrial, bajo la clase 35, nominativa, vocablo 'TIJUANA' que protege publicidad y negocios, difusión de material publicitario, folletos, prospectos, impresos, muestras, películas, novelas, videograbaciones y documentales, a favor del Ayuntamiento de Tijuana" (unless otherwise indicated, translations of quotations are mine).

2. "El vocablo Tijuana para evitar su mal uso."

3. "A la diestra mano de las Indias hubo una Isla, llamada California, muy llegada á la parte del Paraíso Terrenal, la cual fué poblada de mujeres negras, sin que algun varon entre ellas hubiese."

4. "Uno de los mayores laboratorios de la posmodernidad."

5. "Mayo del 68 en París (también en Berlín, Roma, México, Berkeley)."

6. "La vie consiste à passer constamment des frontières."

7. "Voici deux ans et demi que je suis en Californie. Jusqu'ici je me suis abstenu d'en écrire. Là-bas, les phrases se perdent dans les rouleaux du Pacifique. . . . De

retour en France, j'ai l'impression que le pays lunaire d'où je viens ne peut pas s'introduire ni se dire dans le texte serré de mes villages parisiens. . . . Peut-être faudrait-il décrire la Californie comme un songe, à la manière d'Edgar Morin dans son *Journal de Californie*, poème d'un pays imaginaire."

8. If I were to engage in such a search, I would consider at least two issues. First, there is the displacement of writers *from* the border—whose works are subject to small press runs and inadequate distribution and who are less well known and tend to be associated with "regional" themes—by centrist writers *about* the border (Carlos Fuentes's *Frontera de cristal* is a salient recent example) whose work is widely read and distributed, and which also fits more neatly into dominant culture constructions/inventions of borderness. This displacement of Mexican border writers is borne out in the series of conferences on border literature that take place every two years on the border, with the participation (primarily) of writers from central Mexico and well-known Chicano authors and critics. Second, there is the Border Art Workshop/Taller de Arte Fronterizo (BAW/TAF). It was founded in 1984 by Guillermo Gómez Peña to bring together Mexican and U.S. border artists, Chicanos and non-Chicanos, but many of the Mexican nationals dropped out. Explains Chicano artist David Avalos: "Some resistance to the BAW/TAF came from Tijuana artists. They said, hey, we don't think that the border is this wonderful place of exchange. We can't dispense with our nationality, so we can't join the parade. . . . The BAW/TAF has the perspective of the USA, as do so many of the notions of border that we consume" (198).

9. "Ante la falta de otro tipo de cosas, como en el sur, que hay pirámides, aquí no hay nada de eso . . . como que algo hay que inventarle a los gringos. . . . también remite a este mito que traen los norteamericanos, que tiene que ver con cruzar la frontera hacia el pasado, hacia lo salvaje, hacia la onda de poder montar."

10. "Refrenda[n] a diario las limitaciones del localismo y de lo nacional. En los estados fronterizos las semejanzas son intensas: el *shock* cultural en algo compensado por la relativa abundancia de empleos; la ausencia certificada de tradiciones regionales y el hecho de que 'lo norteño típico' deriva directamente de la industria cultural; el uso oportunista y comercial del nacionalismo."

11. "On ne cesse de passer d'une histoire à l'autre, d'une langue à l'autre et d'une region à une autre. La société entière est passante. A cet égard, le *jogging* n'est qu'une métaphore physique de l'activité journalière. . . . Mais l'immigration est une expérience plus intérieure, qui caractérise la socialité californienne."

12. "Ce sont des espaces qui tendent à faire croire que le reste de la vie californienne n'est pas une fiction."

13. "Tan temida desde la ingenuidad y tan sacralizada desde el consumo."

14. "Deslocalización de los productos simbólicos por la electrónica y la telemática, el uso de satélites y computadoras en la difusión cultural."

15. "Desde principios de siglo hasta hace unos quince años, Tijuana había sido conocida por un casino . . . , cabarets, dancing halls, liquor stores a donde los norteamericanos llegaban para eludir las prohibiciones sexuales."

16. I have one quibble with Tafoya's analogy; given the circumstances, the appropriate redemption tale might more accurately be that of Joseph bringing his family to join him in Egypt.

17. This letter is an explicit allusion to *Esplandián* and to the Spanish conquistadores' appropriation of mythic exploits as models for their own conquest of the

Americas. As in Swain's text, in Montalvo's earlier novel, the inhabitants of the island California are black-skinned Amazons, ruled by Queen Calafia (Montalvo, 539–40, 456–60).

18. "La Frontera sigue siendo la misma, Zona Libre desde que era sólo una pequeña isla llamada California."

19. "Una ciudad enorme y caprichosa, cuyos pobladores vivían al filo de dos mundos distintos pero similares" with "casas construidas a lo largo de alambre de púas."

20. "En este Imperio de Norte, las tardes aún se despeinan sobre el reflejo del agua. Nada las perturba. . . . Aquí las palmas mecen fronteras que siguen siendo alcanzables; aquí, el reflejo de los sueños sigue siendo igual, no importan salidas o llegadas. Aquí, caballero errante, el conquistador sigue siendo conquistado por los ojos grandes de las de mi raza. Mujeres hechas de deseo y metal, de piel y llama."

21. "El amor, Amor, es una lata Nestlé de leche condensada, por eso te empalaga y luego, después de la tercera cucharada, la pobre lata de amor termina siempre en la basura.'

22. "La Nestlé reparte la cultura. . . . y se lanza a vivir un amor látex a fuerza de sexo enlatado."

23. "Le han salido arrugas en el alma."

24. "Pero, ¿y las sopas instantáneas, madre, y las carreras de perro por conseguir trabajo? . . . ¿Dónde guardo las prostitutas de la Zona, mamá, dónde pongo las angustias? . . . ¿Y la amenaza del SIDA, madre, y los condones de colores, y el borracho de la esquina, dónde, dónde colocarlos? . . . ¿Dónde guardo la presión del trabajo, y las muertes de migrantes, la mujer de la maquila? ¡Ya no caben con las Barbis!"

Y es que vivimos en una generación de sopas instantáneas y amores instantáneos que no duran más de cuatro copas."

25. "De cómo se creó el río Amazonas (o ¡Ay, Calafia, no te rajes!)"

26. "La llamaron reina porque jamás llegaría a princesa."

27. "El Palacio" (the palace), "donde, a pesar de encontrarse alejado de los maravillosos reinos del Norte, se podía encontrar *diet coke, cherry coke* y coca-cola clásica."

28. "Sepa usted, Conquistador Balboa que aquella negra en blanco a quien llamó Evohé, no ha sido otra que la amazona Calafia."

29. "Lloró tanto que sus lágrimas hicieron un riachuelo . . . que se llamó AMAZONAS en honor al mapa fabuloso de la anatomía de Homobono."

30. "Simplemente una película de Capra."

31. "Yo prefiero el *TV-Guide* a la televisión y los cortos en cine a las películas."

32. "De pronto, como en las películas de Warner Brothers, podemos apreciar una escena retrospectiva."

CHAPTER 9. AFTER-IMAGES OF THE "NEW" NEW YORK AND THE ALFRED STIEGLITZ CIRCLE

1. All quotes from Resina are from chapter 1 of this book, "Concept of After-Image."

2. Designed by Daniel Burnham's Chicago firm, the Flatiron Building was the headquarters for the George A. Fuller Company, developer of the building and a

leading contractor. The skyscraper's official name was the Fuller Company Building.

3. The Art Deco architect Raymond Hood, who designed such buildings as the American Radiator Building in the 1920s, coined the term "architecture of the night" for these illuminated skyscrapers.

4. Professor Dietrich Neumann explained, however, that the RCA Building's darkened crown was part of the lighting design created for the skyscraper. It was not an effect Stieglitz created in his darkroom. See Neumann.

CHAPTER 10. THE CITY VANISHES

1. In *The Practice of Everyday Life*, Michel de Certeau distinguishes a "strategy" from a "tactic" in the same way that he draws a line of demarcation between "place" and "space." A strategy is conceived by a dominant order as a way of profiting from the dominated population. A tactic is an anonymous, often imperceptible practice fashioned to work against a strategy but still within it. Likewise, a place is a geographical site that a subject is given to believe is simply there. A space is a tactical practice of place insofar as a subject "uses" it within and against what it is given to be. Certeau's definitions can be compared to Roland Barthes's distinction in *Mythologies*, his early work in cultural studies between nature and history. A strategist will "naturalize" a space by calling it a place; a tactician will "historicize" a place by recalling how it changes over time and for what reason. For that reason, history has great potential for strategic use.

2. To the question, "What Is an Event?" which inaugurates chap. 9 of *Le Pli: Leibniz et le Baroque*, Gilles Deleuze responds that it may be a "nexus of prehensions," or even a "prehension of prehensions" that both captures and releases sensations and impressions of varying quality. For Leibniz, the event is experienced in the paradox of a closed system of impressions that pass through a *crible*, or mesh, whereas, for Alfred North Whitehead, a close reader of Leibniz's *Monadology* and *Theodicy*, it continually opens and follows different lines and is self–re-creating. It is worth comparing Deleuze's work on the event to Francis Wolf's *Dire le monde*, where events are defined in a similar manner but open consciousness to the question of where and how one exists in the world. For Wolf, issues of place and relationships emerge from speech acts, which displace the speaker and thus correlate identity to a loss of place. The logical aftereffect of an event is a heightened awareness of a world in which space has become problematic. That is also what media effects of vanishment bring forward.

3. Baudelaire's *passante* transmogrifies into the figures Marc Augé takes up in his pages on solitude in *Un ethnologue dans le métro*, chap. 2. Augé is amused by the prose of these anonymous writers who put messages of desire into bottles before corking them and tossing them into the sea of the classifieds. In light of the events we are considering here as an anticipation of an aftereffect, the message may be that which seeks to deny what has taken place; but, in its printed version, it may be an avowal of a space experienced within the commotion of the city.

4. Through a close study of Benjamin, Samuel Weber's "The Virtuality of the Media" treats the dialectical process of mediated images. The latter, Weber notes, ignite "in the now of cognizability." The apparition of such images "disappears in appearing," "takes leave in arriving," and hence "becomes the epitome of medial-

ity in the later texts of Benjamin" (312) and, we shall add, in televised mixtures of sports events, city views, and advertising.

5. See also Deleuze, *Cimémа1: L'image-mouvement* 290ff on the *lieu quelconque* of postwar cities in ruin, especially in Rossellini's *Païsa* (episode 4).

6. In David Harvey's *The Condition of Post-Modernity,* a historical parabola shows that the compression of time and space since the advent of capitalism has tended to fracture familial units. This finding has been confirmed in studies released through the major media (*New York Times,* May 14, 2001), which showed that the number of single parents has risen dramatically over the past two decades in North America. Hence the replacement of the extended family by the nuclear family during the Industrial Revolution has now been paralleled, in the growth of global and flexible capitalism, by the dissolution of the nuclear family in favor of the single-parent family.

7. In chap. 4 (90–107), based on research on neorural movements in France in the 1970s, Augé shows that the migration from the city belongs to a deeper affiliation with urban space and to a persistently romantic trope, which, he studies through research on middle-class "country homes" in *Domaines et châteaux,* especially 68–72, in reference to advertisements. We might add that television and televised sports events mediate and ritualize the fabled distinction between urban and rural spaces.

8. Foucault notes that the effect of public executions became difficult to predict. Sometimes they held their audience captive, while at other times fanatical disruptions ensued.

Works Cited

Abraben, E. Manny. *Point of View: The Art of Architectural Photography.* New York: Van Nostrand Reinhold, 1994.

Almodóvar, Pedro. "La ciudad." In *Patty Diphusa y otros textos.* Barcelona: Anagrama, 1991: 154–60. First published in *Diario 16* (1985).

——. "Venir a Madrid." In *Patty Diphusa y otros textos.* Barcelona: Anagrama, 1991: 106–10. First published in *Diario 16* (1989).

Amicis, Edmundo de. *Spain.* Trans. Wilhelmina W. Cady. New York: G.P. Putnam's Sons, 1881.

Anderson, Benedict. *Imagined Communities: Reflections on the Origin and Spread of Nationalism.* Rev. ed. London: Verso, 1991.

Anguera, Pere. *Els precedents del catalanisme: Catalanitat i anticentralisme: 1808–1868.* Barcelona: Empúries, 2000.

Ashcroft, Bill, Gareth Griffiths, and Helen Tiffin, eds. *The Empire Writes Back. Theory and Practice in Post-colonial Literatures.* London: Routledge, 1989.

Atkins, Marc, and Iain Sinclair. *Liquid City.* London: Reaktion Books, 1999.

Augé, Marc. *An Anthropology for Contemporaneous Worlds.* Trans. Amy Jacobs. Stanford: Stanford University Press, 1999.

——. *Domaines et châteaux.* Paris: Seuil, 1989.

——. *Un ethnologue dans le métro.* Paris: Hachette, 1985.

——. *Non-Places: Introduction to an Anthropology of Supermodernity.* Trans. John Howe. London: Verso, 1995.

——. *La traversée du Luxembourg: Ethno-roman d'une journée française considérée sous l'angle des moeurs de la théorie et du bonheur.* Paris: Hachette, 1984.

Aulagnier, Piera. *Un interprète en quête du sens.* Paris: Ramsey, 1987.

Avalos, David, and John C. Welchman. "Response to the Philosophical Brothel." In *Rethinking Borders,* ed. John C. Welchman. Minneapolis: University of Minnesota Press, 1996, 187–99.

Bachelard, Gaston. *Poetics of Space.* Trans. Maria Jolas. Boston: Beacon Press, 1969.

Bacon, Mardges. *Ernest Flagg.* New York: Architectural History Foundation, 1986.

Baixeras, Angel Josep. *Proyecto de reforma de la ciudad de Barcelona.* Arxiu Administratiu de l'Ajuntament de Barcelona, doc. 1, Memoria descriptiva, 1881.

Baker, Edward. *Materiales para escribir Madrid. Literatura y espacio urbano de Moratín a Galdós.* Madrid: Siglo XXI, 1992.

Ballard, J. G. *Cocaine Nights.* London: Flamingo, 1996.

——. *High-Rise.* New York: Henry Holt, 1997.

Balzac, Honoré de. *Cousin Bette.* Trans. Marion Crawford. Harmondsworth, England: Penguin, 1965.

——. *Cousin Pons.* Trans. Herbert Hunt. Harmondsworth, England: Penguin, 1968.

——. *Eugenie Grandet.* Trans. Marion Crawford. Harmondsworth, England: Penguin, 1955.

——. *A Harlot High and Low.* Trans. Rayner Heppenstall. Harmondsworth, England: Penguin, 1970.

——. *History of the Thirteen.* Trans. Herbert Hunt. Harmondsworth, England: Penguin, 1974.

——. *Old Goriot.* Trans. Marion Crawford. Harmondsworth, England: Penguin, 1951.

——. *The Quest of the Absolute.* Trans. Ellen Marriage. New York: Hippocrene, 1989.

——. "The Unknown Masterpiece." In *Selected Short Stories,* ed. and trans. Stanley Appelbaum. Mineola, N.Y.: Dover, 2000: 88–133.

Barella, Julia. *Madrid en la novela.* Vol. 1. Madrid: Comunidad de Madrid, 1992.

Barrachina, Jordi. "Crónica de la Semana Trágica." In *Barcelona, 1888–1929: Modernidad, ambición y conflictos de una ciudad soñada,* ed. Alejandro Sánchez. Madrid: Alianza Editorial, 1994: 113–23.

Barrera, Eduardo. "Apropiación y tutelaje de la frontera norte." *Puentelibre, Revista de Cultura* 4 (1995): 13–17.

Barthes, Roland. *La chambre claire. Note sur la photographie.* Paris: Gallimard–Seuil, 1980.

——. "The Eiffel Tower." In *The Eiffel Tower and Other Mythologies.* New York: Hill and Wang, 1979: 3–17.

——. *Mythologies.* Paris: Seuil, 1956.

——. "Rhetoric of the Image." In *Image-Music-Text,* ed. and trans. Stephen Heath. New York: Hill and Wang, 1977: 32–51.

——. "Sémiologie et urbanisme." In *L'aventure sémiologique.* Paris: Seuil, 1985: 261–71.

Bassegoda Nonell, Juan. *La arquitectura profanada.* Barcelona: Mare Nostrum, 1990.

Bataille, Georges. *La part maudite.* Paris: Minuit, 1967.

Baudrillard, Jean. *Amérique.* Paris: Grasset-Fasquelle, 1986.

——. "L'ascension du vide vers la périphérie." In *L'illusion de la fin ou La grève des événements.* Paris: Galilée, 1992: 29–38.

——. *L'échange symbolique et la mort.* Paris: Gallimard, 1976.

——. "Kool Killer oder Der Aufstand der Zeichen." In *Aisthesis. Wahrnehmung heute oder Perspektiven einer anderen Ästhetik,* ed. Karlheinz Barck. Leipzig: Reclam, 1990: 214–28.

——. *The Perfect Crime.* Trans. Chris Turner. London: Verso, 1996.

Bender, Thomas, and William R. Taylor. "Culture and Architecture: Some Aesthetic Tensions in the Shaping of Modern New York." In *Visions of the Modern*

City, ed. William Sharpe and Leonard Wallock. New York: Columbia University Heyman Center for the Humanities, 1983: 185–217.

Benet, Josep. *Maragall i la Setmana Tràgica*. Barcelona: Edicions 62, 1964.

Benjamin, Walter. "Surrealism." In *Reflections*, trans. Edmund Jephcott. New York: Schocken, 1978.

——. "Theses on the Philosophy of History." In *Illuminations*, ed. Hannah Arendt, trans. Harry Zohn. New York: Schocken, 1969: 253–64.

——. "The Work of Art in the Age of Mechanical Reproduction." In *Illuminations*, ed. Hannah Arendt, trans. Harry Zohn. New York: Schocken, 1969: 217–51.

Berman, Marshall. *All That Is Solid Melts into Air: The Experience of Modernity*. New York: Simon and Schuster, 1982.

Beyme, Klaus von. *Hauptstadtsuche: Hauptstadtfunktionen im Interessenkonflikt zwischen Bonn und Berlin*. Frankfurt am Main: Suhrkamp, 1991.

Bierce, Ambrose. *Letters*. Ed. Bertha Clark Pope. 1922. Rpt. New York: Gordian, 1967.

Bofill, Ricardo, and Nicolas Véron. *L'architecture des villes*. Paris: Éditions Odile Jacob, 1995.

Bohigas, Oriol. "L'arquitectura, Noucentisme i 'Novecento.'" *Serra d'Or*, 6, no. 8 (1964): 15–18.

——. *Combat d'incerteses. Dietari de records*. Barcelona: Edicions 62, 1989.

Bou, Enric. *La poesia de Guerau de Liost: Natura, amor, humor*. Barcelona: Edicions 62, 1985.

Bou, Enric, and Andrés Soria Olmedo. "Postmodernity and Literature in Spain." In *International Postmodernism: Theory and Literary Practice*, ed. Hans Bertens and Douwe Fokkema. Amsterdam: J. Benjamins, 1997: 397–403.

Bourdieu, Pierre. *Pascalian Meditations*, trans. Richard Nice. Stanford: Stanford University Press, 2000.

Boyer, M. Christine. *The City of Collective Memory: Its Historical Imagery and Architectural Entertainments*. Cambridge: MIT Press, 1994.

Boym, Svetlana. *The Future of Nostalgia*. New York: Basic Books, 2001.

Bracken, Christopher. *The Potlatch Papers: A Colonial Case History*. Chicago: University of Chicago Press, 1997.

Brissac Peixoto, Nelson. "Periphere Modernen." In *Die anderen Modernen. Zeitgenössische Kunst aus Afrika, Asien und Lateinamerika*, ed. Haus der Kulturen der Welt. Heidelberg: Edition Braus, 1997: 29–32.

Bull, Malcolm. *Seeing Things Hidden: Apocalypse, Vision and Totality*. London: Verso, 1999.

Burgin, Victor. *Some Cities*. Berkeley: University of California Press, 1996.

Buschmann, Albrecht, and Dieter Ingenschay, eds. *Die andere Stadt. Gro;dsstadtbilder in der Perspektive des peripheren Blicks*. Würzburg: Königshausen und Neumann, 2000.

Butler, Judith. *Bodies That Matter: On the Discursive Limits of "Sex."* London: Routledge, 1993.

Cacho Viu, Vicente. *Revisión de Eugenio d'Ors (1902–1930)*. Barcelona: Quaderns Crema, 1997.

Caffin, Charles. *Photography as Fine Art*. New York: Doubleday, 1901.

Carroll, David. *French Literary Fascism: Nationalism, Anti-Semitism, and the Ideology of Culture*. Princeton: Princeton University Press, 1995.

Cartier-Bresson, Henri. *The Decisive Moment*. New York: Simon and Schuster, 1952.

Casey, Edward S. *The Fate of Place: A Philosophical History.* Berkeley: University of California Press, 1997.

Castañeda, Quetzil E. *In the Museum of Maya Culture: Touring Chichén Itzá.* Minneapolis: University of Minnesota Press, 1996.

Castillo, Debra A., María Gudelia Rangel Gómez, and Bonnie Delgado. "Border Lives: Prostitute Women in Tijuana." *Signs* (forthcoming).

Castillo y Mayone, Joaquín del. *Las Bullangas de Barcelona o Sacudimientos de un pueblo oprimido por el Despotismo Ilustrado.* 1837. Repr. Vic: Eumo Editorial, 1994.

Cela, Camilo José. *La colmena,* ed. J. Urrutia. 1951. Repr. Madrid: Cátedra, 1996.

Cerdà, Ildefonso. *Las cinco bases de la teoría general de la urbanización.* Ed. Arturo Soria y Puig. Barcelona: Fundació Catalana per a la Recerca, 1996.

———. *Teoría general de la urbanización y aplicación de sus principios y doctrinas a la reforma y ensanche de Barcelona.* Vol. 1. Madrid: Instituto de Estudios Fiscales, 1968.

Certeau, Michel de. "Californie, un théâtre de passants." *Autrement* 31 (1981): 10–18.

———. *Culture in the Plural.* Edited and with an introduction by Luce Giard, trans. Tom Conley. Minneapolis: University of Minnesota Press, 1997.

———. *Heterologies: Discourse on the Other.* Trans. Brian Massumi. Foreword by Wlad Godzich. Minneapolis: University of Minnesota Press, 1986.

———. *The Practice of Everyday Life.* Trans. Steven Rendall. Berkeley: University of California Press, 1984.

Chevalier, Louis. "La Comedie Humaine: A Historical Document?" Trans. Martin Kanes. In *Critical Essays on Honore de Balzac,* ed. Martin Kanes. Boston: G.K. Hall, 1984: 170–76.

Clark, T.J. *The Painting of Modern Life: Paris in the Art of Manet and His Followers.* London: Thames and Hudson, 1985.

Clay, Grady. *Close-Up: How to Read the American City.* Chicago: University of Chicago Press, 1973.

Coburn, Alvin Langdon. *An Autobiography.* Ed. Helmut and Alison Gernsheim. New York: Dover Books, 1978.

———. "The Relation of Time to Art." *Camera Work* 36 (1911): 72–73.

Cochrane, Edwin. "The Cathedral of Commerce." In *The Cathedral of Commerce.* New York: Broadway Park Place Company, 1917: 7–31.

Cohen, Albert. *Belle du Seigneur.* Ed. Christel Peyrefitte and Bella Cohen. Paris: Gallimard, 1986.

———. *Carnets 1978.* In *Oeuvres,* ed. Christel Peyrefitte and Bella Cohen. Paris: Gallimard, 1993.

———. "Jour de mes dix ans." *La France libre* (London) (July 16, 1945): 193–200 (part 1) and (August 15, 1945): 287–94 (part 2).

———. *Le livre de ma mère.* In *Oeuvres,* ed. Christel Peyrefitte and Bella Cohen. Paris: Gallimard, 1993

———. *Mangeclous.* In *Oeuvres,* ed. Christel Peyrefitte and Bella Cohen. Paris: Gallimard, 1993.

———. "Projections ou après-minuit à Genève." *Nouvelle Revue Française* 19 (1922): 414.

———. *Solal.* In *Oeuvres,* ed. Christel Peyrefitte and Bella Cohen. Paris: Gallimard, 1993.

Cohen, Bella. "Albert Cohen." In *Belle du Seigneur,* by Albert Cohen, ed. Christel Peyrefitte and Bella Cohen. Paris: Gallimard, 1986.

——. *Autour d'Albert Cohen.* Paris: Gallimard, 1990.

Colquhoun, Alan, Manfredo Tafuri, Joan Ockmann et al. "Theory and Praxis: Berlin." In *Architecture, Criticism, Ideology.* Princeton: Princeton Architectural Press, 1985.

Corbin, John. "The Twentieth Century City." *Scribner's* 33 (1903): 259–72.

Corn, Wanda. *The Great American Thing.* Berkeley: University of California Press, 1999.

——. "The 'New' New York." *Art in America* 61 (1976): 58–65.

Coromines, Pere. *De la Solidaritat al catorze d'abril.* Vol. 2 of *Diaris i records.* Barcelona: Curial, 1974.

Cortada, James W. *A City in War: American Views on Barcelona and the Spanish Civil War, 1936–39.* Wilmington, Del.: Scholarly Resources Inc., 1985.

Damisch, Hubert. *Skyline: The Narcissistic City.* Trans. John Goodman. Stanford: Stanford University Press, 2001.

Danto, Arthur. " 'Sensation' in Brooklyn." *Nation* (Nov. 1, 1999): 26.

D'Arcy Wood, Gillen. *The Shock of the Real: Romanticism and Visual Culture, 1760–1860.* New York: Palgrave, 2001.

Davis, Mike. "Berlin's Skeleton in Utah's Closet." *Grand Street* 69 (issue on Berlin): 92–105.

——. "Beyond *Blade Runner.* Urban Control—the Ecology of Fear." *Open Magazine Pamphlet Series* 23 (1992).

——. "Urban Renaissance and the Spirit of Postmodernism." In *Postmodernism and Its Discontents: Theories, Practices,* ed. E. Ann Kaplan. London: Verso, 1988.

Deleuze, Gilles. *Cinéma 1: L'image-mouvement.* Paris: Minuit, 1983.

——. *Le pli: Leibniz et le baroque.* Paris: Minuit, 1988.

Deleuze, Gilles, and Felix Guattari. *A Thousand Plateaus.* Trans. Brian Massumi. Minneapolis: University of Minnesota Press, 1987.

Deutsche, Rosalyn. "Architecture of the Evicted." *Strategies* 3 (1990): 176.

——. *Evictions: Art and Spatial Politics.* Cambridge: MIT Press, 1996.

Doel, Marcus A., and David B. Clarke. "From Ramble City to the Screening of the Eye: *Blade Runner,* Death and Symbolic Exchange." In *The Cinematic City,* ed. David B. Clarke. London: Routledge, 1997: 140–67.

Domínguez, Christopher. Review of *Peregrinos de Aztlán. Vuelta* (Aug. 1989): 88.

Donald, James. "The City, the Cinema: Modern Spaces." In *Visual Culture,* ed. Chris Jenks. London: Routledge, 1995: 77–95.

——. *Imagining the Modern City.* Minneapolis: University of Minnesota Press, 1999.

D'Ors, Eugeni. *Glosari.* Ed. Josep Murgades. Barcelona: Edicions 62, 1982.

——. *Obra catalana completa. Glosari 1906–1910.* Barcelona: Selecta, 1950.

——. *Oceanografia del tedi.* 1916. Repr. Barcelona: Selecta, 1948.

——. *Papers anteriors al Glosari.* Ed. Jordi Castellanos. Barcelona: Quaderns Crema, 1994.

——. *La vall de Josafat.* Ed. Josep Muragades. Barcelona: Quaderns. Crema, 1987.

Durth, Werner. *Deutsche Architekten: Biographische Verflechtungen 1900–1920.* Braunschweig: Friedrich Vieweg, 1986.

Elliott, David. "No Pain No Gain." In *Wounds: Between Democracy and Redemption in Contemporary Art.* Ex. cat. no. 268, Moderna Museet Stockholm, 1998: 10–16.

Elsaesser, Thomas. "Subject Positions. Speaking Positions: From *Holocaust, Our Hitler,* and *Heimat* to *Shoah* and *Schindler's List.*" In *The Persistence of History: Cinema, Television, and the Modern Event,* ed. Vivian Sobchack. London: Routledge, 1996: 145–83.

Engels, Friedrich. "Die Bakunisten an der Arbeit." Vol. 18, *Werke,* by Karl Marx and Friedrich Engels. 1873. Repr. Berlin: Dietz Verlag, 1962: 476–93.

Espinet, Francesc and J.M. Tresserras. *La gènesi de la societat de masses a Catalunya, 1888–1939.* Bellaterra: Servei de Publicacions de la Universitat Autònoma de Barcelona, 1999.

Ette, Ottmar. "Albert Cohen: *Jour de mes dix ans:* Räume und Bewegungen interkultureller Begegnung." In *Dulce et decorum est philologiam colere. Festschrift für Dietrich Briesemeister,* ed. Sybille Gro;dse and Axel Schönberger. Vol. 2. Berlin: Domus Editoria Europea, 1999: 1295–1322.

Fishman, Robert. *Urban Utopias in the Twentieth Century.* Cambridge: MIT Press, 1982.

Fontane, Theodor. *Wanderungen durch die Mark Brandenburg. Erster Teil: Die Grafschaft Ruppin.* Ed. Gotthard Erler and Rudolf Mingau. Berlin: Aufbau Verlag, 1997.

Ford, Richard. *A Handbook for Travellers to Spain and Readers at Home.* 3 vols. 1845. Repr. Carbondale: Southern Illinois University Press, 1966.

Foucault, Michel. "Des espaces autres." In *Architecture, Mouvement, Continuité,* Paris: Société des architectes diplômés par le gouvernement, 1984: 46–49.

——. *Surveiller et punir.* Paris: Gallimard, 1975.

Fraser, Ronald. *Blood of Spain: An Oral History of the Spanish Civil War.* New York: Pantheon, 1979.

Fregoso, Rosa Linda. *"Born in East L.A.* and the Politics of Representation." *Culture Studies* 4, no. 3 (1990): 264–80.

Galí, Raimon. "1939: La caiguda de Catalunya." *AVUI* (Feb. 12, 1999).

Gallero, José L. *Sólo se vive una vez. Esplendor y ruina de la movida madrileña.* Madrid: Ed. Ardora, 1991.

García Canclini, Néstor. *Culturas híbridas: Estrategias para entrar y salir de la modernidad.* Mexico City: Grijalbo, 1989. English translation: *Hybrid Cultures: Strategies for Entering and Leaving Modernity,* trans. Christopher Chiappari and Silvia L. López. Minneapolis: University of Minnesota Press, 1995.

Gautier, Théophile. *Voyage en Espagne.* Paris: G. Charpentier, 1881.

Geertz, Clifford. *The Interpretation of Cultures.* London: Fontana Press, 1993.

——. *Local Knowledge: Further Essays in Interpretative Anthropology.* New York: Basic Books, 1983.

Gernsheim, Helmut, and Alison Gernsheim. *The Concise History of Photography.* New York: Grosset and Dunlap, 1965.

Gilloch, Graeme. *Myth and Metropolis: Walter Benjamin and the City.* Cambridge: Polity Press, 1996.

Goethe, Johann Wolfgang. *Farbenlehre.* With an introduction and commentaries by Rudolf Steiner, ed. Gerhard Ott and Heinrich O. Proskauer. Stuttgart: Verlag Freies Geistesleben, 1979.

Goldberger, Paul. "Busy Buildings: New Skyscrapers in Times Square." *New Yorker* (Sept. 4, 2000): 90–93.

Gombrich, E.H. *Art and Illusion. A Study in the Psychology of Pictorial Representation.* Princeton.: Princeton University Press, 1969.

Gómez de la Serna, Ramón. *Nostalgias de Madrid.* Madrid: Espasa Calpe, 1966.

González Casanova, J.A. "Prologue." In *La ciutat cremada: De 1899 a la Setmana Tràgica,* by Antoni Ribas and Miquel Sanz, trans. Maria Antònia Oliver. Barcelona: Laia, 1976.

Gopnik, Adam. "Just a Bar: What Makes a Landmark?" *New Yorker* (April 16, 2001): 34–39.

Gottdiener, M., and Alexandros Lagopoulos, eds. *The City and the Sign*. New York: Columbia University Press, 1986.

Gramsci, Antonio. *Prison Notebooks*. Ed. and trans. Quintin Hoare and Geoffrey Nowell Smith. London: Lawrence and Wishart, 1971.

Gumbrecht, Hans Ulrich. *"Eine" Geschichte der spanischen Literatur*. 2 vols. Frankfurt am Main: Suhrkamp, 1990.

Guttman, Allen. *From Ritual to Record*. New York: Columbia University Press, 1978.

Halbwachs, Maurice. *On Collective Memory*. Ed. and trans. Lewis A. Coser. Chicago: University of Chicago Press, 1992.

Hall, Stuart. "Popular-Democratic vs. Authoritarian Populism: Two Ways of Taking Democracy Seriously." In *The Hard Road to Renewal: Thatcherism and the Crisis of the Left*. London: Verso, 1998: 123–49.

Hambourg, Maria Morris. "Picturing Victorian Britain." In *The Waking Dream: Photography's First Century*, by Maria Morris Hambourg et al. New York: Harry N. Abrams, Inc., 1993: 3–41.

Handy, Ellen. "The Idea and the Fact: Painting, Photography, Film, Precisionists, and the Real World." In *Precisionism in America 1915–1941: Reordering Reality*, ed. Gail Stavitsky. New York: Harry N. Abrams, 1995: 40–51.

Harley, Brian. "Maps, Knowledge, and Power." In *The Iconography of Landscape*, ed. Denis Cosgrove and Stephen Daniels. Cambridge: Cambridge University Press, 1988: 277–312.

Hartmann, Sadakichi. "Recent Conquests in Night Photography." 1909. In *Valiant Knights of Daguerre: The Writings of Sadakichi Hartmann*, ed. Harry Lawton and George Know. Berkeley: University of California Press, 1978: 127–31.

——. "The Flat-iron Building: As Esthetical Dissertation." *Camera Work* 1 (Oct. 1903): 36–40.

Harvey, David. *The Condition of Postmodernity*. Oxford: Blackwell, 1989.

——. *Consciousness and the Urban Experience*. Baltimore: Johns Hopkins University Press, 1985.

——. "Contested Cities: Social Process and Spatial Form. In *Transforming Cities: Contested Governance and New Spatial Divisions*, ed. Nick Jewson and Susanne MacGregor. London: Routledge, 1997: 19–27.

——. *Spaces of Hope*. Berkeley: University of California Press, 2000.

Hassauer, Friederike. "Stadtersatz Berlin 1930. Jean Giraudoux: *Rues et visages de Berlin*." In *Die andere Stadt: Großstadtbilder in der Perspektive des peripheren Blicks*, ed. Albrecht Buschmann and Dieter Ingenschay. Würzburg: Königshausen und Neumann, 2000: 72–88.

Hays, K. Michael, ed. *Architecture Theory since 1968*. Cambridge: MIT Press, 1998.

Hollier, Denis. *Against Architecture: The Writings of George Bataille*. Trans. Betsy Wing. Cambridge: Harvard University Press, 1992.

Homer, William I. *Alfred Stieglitz and the American Avant-Garde*. Boston: New York Graphic Society, 1977.

Horak, Jan-Christopher. *Making Images Move: Photographers and Avant-Garde Cinema*. Washington, D.C.: Smithsonian Institution Press, 1997.

Huyssen, Andreas. *After the Great Divide: Modernism, Mass Culture, Postmodernism*. Bloomington: Indiana University Press, 1986.

Iglesias Prieto, Norma. *Beautiful Flowers of the Maquiladora: Life Histories of Women*

Workers in Tijuana. Trans. Michael Stone with Gabrielle Winker. Foreword by Henry Selby. Austin: University of Texas Press, 1997.

Ingenschay, Dieter. "Großstadtaneignung in der Perspektive des 'peripheren Blicks.'" In *Die andere Stadt: Großstadtbilder in der Perspektive des peripheren Blicks,* ed. Albrecht Buschmann and Dieter Ingenschay. Würzburg: Königshausen und Neumann, 2000: 7–19.

——. "José Angel Mañas, *Historias del Kronen.* La 'Generación Kronen': La novela, la película y la estética desesperada de la posmovida." In *La dulce mentira de la ficción. Ensayos sobre Literatura española actual,* ed. Hans Felten and Agustín Valcárcel. Vol. 2. Bonn: Romanistischer Verlag, 1996: 151–66.

——. "Movida et la fin de la discussion du passé." In *Le roman espagnol face à l'histoire,* ed. Marie-Linda Ortega. Paris: ENS, 1996: 149–67.

Jackson, John Brinckerhoff. *The Necessity for Ruins and Other Topics.* Amherst: University of Massachusetts Press, 1980.

Jameson, Fredric. *The Political Unconscious.* London: Methuen, 1981.

——. *Postmodernism, or the Cultural Logic of Late Capitalism.* Durham: Duke University Press, 1991.

Jenks, Chris. "Watching Your Step: The History and Practice of the Flâneur." In *Visual Culture,* ed. Chris Jenks. London: Routledge, 1995: 142–60.

Karatani, K. *Architecture as Metaphor: Language, Number, Money.* Cambridge: MIT Press, 1995.

Keenoy, Ray. "Barcelona-Utopia: The Social Archaeology of a City." *Critique of Anthropology* 10 (1990): 159–78.

Kiefer, Geraldine Wojno. "Alfred Stieglitz, *Camera Work,* and Cultural Radicalism." *Art Criticism* 7 (1992): 1–20.

——. *Alfred Stieglitz: Scientist, Photographer, and Avatar of Modernism.* New York: Garland Press, 1991.

Kittler, Friedrich. "Unconditional Surrender." In *Materialities of Communication,* ed. Hans Ulrich Gumbrecht and K. Ludwig Pfeiffer. Stanford: Stanford University Press, 1994.

Koolhaas, Rem. *Delirious New York.* New York: Oxford University Press, 1978.

——. "Junkspace." In *Harvard Design School Guide to Shopping: Project on the City 2,* ed. Chuihua Judy Chung, Jeffrey Inaba, Rem Koolhaas, Sze Tung Leong. Cologne: Taschen, 2001: 408–22.

——. "'Life in the Metropolis' or 'The Culture of Congestion.'" In *Architecture Theory since 1968,* ed. K. Michael Hays. Cambridge: MIT Press, 1998: 323–30.

——. "On the Current Urban Reconstruction in Berlin," interview by Hans Ulrich Obrist, *Feed* (http://www.feedmag.com), posted 1998.

Kornhauser, Elizabeth et al. *Stieglitz, O'Keeffe, and American Modernism.* Hartford, Conn.: Wadsworth Athenaeum, 1999.

Kracauer, Siegfried. *From Caligari to Hitler: A Psychological History of the German Film.* Princeton: Princeton University Press, 1947.

——. "The Hotel Lobby." In *The Mass Ornament: Weimarer Essays,* trans. Thomas Y. Levin. Cambridge: Harvard University Press, 1995.

Kuhnle, Till R. "Ekelhafte Stadtansichten." In *Die andere Stadt: Großstadtbilder in der Perspektive des peripheren Blicks,* ed. Albrecht Buschmann and Dieter Ingenschay. Würzburg: Königshausen und Neumann, 2000: 144–56.

Lacarta, Manuel. *Madrid y sus literaturas. De la Generación del 98 a la posguerra.* Madrid: Avapiés, 1986.

Lacoue-Labarthe, Philippe. *Heidegger, Art, and Politics: The Fiction of the Political.* Trans. Chris Turner. Oxford: Blackwell, 1990.

Ladd, Brian. *The Ghosts of Berlin: Confronting German History in the Urban Landscape.* Chicago: University of Chicago Press, 1997.

Landau, Sarah, and Carl Condit. *Rise of the New York Skyscraper 1865–1913.* New Haven: Yale University Press, 1996.

Lapsley, Rob. "Mainly in Cities and at Night: Some Notes on Cities and Film." In *The Cinematic City,* ed. David B. Clarke. London: Routledge, 1997: 186–208.

Lefebvre, Henri. *The Explosion: Marxism and the French Revolution.* Trans. Alfred Ehrenfeld. New York: Monthly Review Press, 1969.

———. *The Production of Space.* Trans. Donald Nicholson-Smith. Oxford: Blackwell, 1991.

Lefort, Claude. "'The Logic of Totalitarianism.' The Political Forms of Modern Society:Bureaucracy, Democracy." In *Democracy and Political Theory.* Minneapolis: University of Minnesota Press, 1988.

———. "The Question of Democracy." In *Democracy and Political Theory.* Minneapolis: University of Minnesota Press, 1988.

Leonard, Mark. *Britain.* London: Demos, 1997.

Lévi-Strauss, Claude. *Mythologiques 4: L'homme nu.* Paris: Plon, 1971.

Lincoln, Bruce. *Discourse and the Construction of Society: Comparative Studies of Myth, Ritual, and Classification.* Oxford: Oxford University Press, 1989.

Link-Heer, Ursula. "Versuch über das Makabre: Bilder vor und nach Auschwitz." In *Kunst und Literatur nach Auschwitz,* edited by Manuel Köppen in collaboration with Gerhard Bauer and Rüdiger Steinlein. Berlin: Erich Schmidt Verlag, 1993: 83–96.

Liost, Guerau de. *Obra poética completa.* Barcelona: Selecta, 1983.

Llamazares, Julio. *Los viajeros de Madrid.* Madrid: Ollero y Ramos, 1998.

Llates, Rossend. *30 Anys de Vida Catalana.* Barcelona: Aedos, 1969.

Llobera, Josep Ramon. "The Role of Historical Memory in Catalan National Identity." *Social Anthropology* 6 (1998): 331–42.

Lüdtke, Jens. "Indiengesetze in den katalanischen Ländern. Zur Sprachpolitik Karls III." *Neue Romania* 10 (1991): 135–46.

Lynch, Kevin. *The Image of the City.* Cambridge: MIT Press, 1969.

Lyotard, Jean-François. *The Postmodern Condition: A Report on Knowledge.* Trans. Geoff Bennington and Brian Massumi. Minneapolis: University of Minnesota Press, 1984.

Maier, Charles. "A Surfeit of Memory? Reflections on History, Melancholy and Denial." *History and Memory* 5 (1993): 136–52.

Mañas, José Ángel. *Ciudad rayada.* Madrid: Espasa, 1998.

———. *Historias del Kronen.* Barcelona: Destino, 1994.

———. *Mensaka.* Barcelona: Destino, 1995.

———. *Sonko 95. Autorretrato con negro de fondo.* Barcelona: Destino, 1999.

Maragall, Joan. "La ciudad." In *Obres completes.* 2 vols. Barcelona: Selecta, 1981: 269–70.

Marcus, Sharon. *Apartment Stories.* Berkeley: University of California Press, 1999.

Marks, Peter. "Diller and Scofidio: Architects Building Castles in the Clouds." *New York Times,* May 23, 2001.

Marx, Karl. *Grundrisse.* Trans. Marin Nicolaus. New York: Viking, 1973.

———. *Capital.* Vol. 1. Trans. Samuel Moore and Edward Aveling. New York: International Publishers, 1967.

——. *A Contribution to the Critique of Political Economy*. Translated by S.W. Ryazanskaya with an introduction by Maurice Dobb. New York: International Publishers, 1970.

——. *The Eighteenth Brumaire of Louis Bonaparte*. Trans. Karl Marx. New York: International Publishers, 1963.

Marx, Karl, and Friedrich Engels. *The Manifesto of the Communist Party*. Trans. Samuel Moore. Moscow: Progress Publishers, 1952.

Marx, Leo. *The Machine in the Garden*. Oxford: Oxford University Press, 1964.

Martín-Santos, Luis. *Tiempo de silencio*. 1961. Repr. Barcelona: Seix Barral, 1980.

Matzat, Wolfgang. "Die Modellierung der Großstadterfahrung in C.J. Celas *La colmena*." *Romanistisches Jahrbuch* 35 (1984): 278–302.

Mazzoleni, Donatella. "The City and the Imaginary." Trans. John Koumantarakis. In *Space and Place: Theories of Identity and Location*, ed. Erica Carter, James Donald, and Judith Squires. London: Lawrence and Wishart, 1993: 285–301.

McClintock, Anne, Aamir Mufti, and Ella Shohat, eds. *Dangerous Liaisons: Gender, Nation, and Postcolonial Perspectives*. Minneapolis: University of Minnesota Press, 1997.

McDonogh, Gary. "Discourses of the City: Policy and Response in Post-Transitional Barcelona." In *Theorizing the City: The New Urban Anthropology Reader*, ed. Setha M. Low. New Brunswick: Rutgers University Press, 1999: 342–76.

McEuen, Melissa. *Seeing America: Women Photographers between the Wars*. Lexington: University of Kentucky Press, 2000.

McGrath, Norman. *Photographing Buildings Inside and Out*. New York: Whitney Library of Design, 1993.

Mitchell, W.J.T. *Iconology: Image, Text, Ideology*. Chicago: University of Chicago Press, 1986.

Monsiváis, Carlos. "De la cultura mexicana en vísperas del TLC." In *La educación y la cultura ante el tratado de libre comercio*, ed. Gilberto Guevara Niebla and Néstor García Canalini. Mexico City: Nueva imagen, 1992.

Montalvo, Garci Rodríguez de. *Las sergas de Esplandián*. In *Libros de caballerías*, vol. 40 of *Biblioteca de autores españoles*, ed. Pascual De Gyangos y Arce. Madrid: Real academia española, 1950. English translation: *The Labors of the Very Brave Knight Esplandián*, trans. William Thomas Little. Binghamton, N.Y.: Renaissance and Medieval Texts and Studies, 1992.

Montherlant, Henry de. *La petite Infante de Castille*. Paris: Grasset, 1929.

Morris, Meghan. "Great Moments in Social Climbing: King Kong and the Human Fly." In *Sexuality and Space*, ed. Beatriz Colomina. Princeton: Princeton University Press, 1992: 1–52.

Mumford Lewis, "Metropolitan Milieu." In *America and Alfred Stieglitz: A Collective Portrait*, by Waldo Frank et al. Garden City, N.Y.: Doubleday, Doran, and Company, 1934: 33–58.

Muñoz Molina, Antonio. *Los misterios de Madrid*. Barcelona: Seix Barral, 1992.

Naef, Weston. *The Collection of Alfred Stieglitz: Fifty Pioneers of Modernism*. New York: Viking Press, 1978.

Nathan, Debbie. *Women and Other Aliens: Essays from the U.S. Mexico Border*. El Paso, Tex.: Cinco Puntos, 1991.

Neumann, Dietrich. "Architecture of the Night." Lecture, Collins/Kaufmann Colloquium, Columbia University, March 21, 2001.

Nicholson, Geoff. *Bleeding London*. London: Indigo, 1998.

Nieva, Francisco. *Carne de murciélago. Cuento de Madrid.* Barcelona: Plaza y Janés, 1998.

Noriega, Chon. "Café Orale: Narrative Structure in *Born in East L.A.*" *Tonantzin* 8, no. 1 (1991): 17–18.

Norman, Dorothy. *Alfred Stieglitz: An American Seer.* 1960. Repr. New York: Random House, 1973.

Nye, David. *Electrifying America: The Social Meanings of a New Technology.* Cambridge: MIT Press, 1990.

——. Introduction to *Technologies and Landscape: From Reaping to Recycling,* ed. David Nye. Amherst: University of Massachusetts Press, 1999: 3–17.

O'Connor, Celeste. *Democratic Visions: Art and the Theory of the Stieglitz Circle, 1924–1934.* Berkeley: University of California Press, 2001.

Olalquiaga, Celeste. "Vulture Culture." In *Rethinking Borders,* ed. John C. Welchman. Minneapolis: University of Minnesota Press, 1996: 85–100.

Ortega y Gasset, José. *The Revolt of the Masses.* New York: W. W. Norton, 1957.

Orwell, George. *Homage to Catalonia.* Boston: Beacon Press, 1952.

Ossorio y Gallardo, Angel. *Barcelona, Julio de 1909: Declaración de un testigo.* Madrid: R. Rojas, 1910.

Page, Max. *The Creative Destruction of Manhattan.* Chicago: University of Chicago Press, 1999.

Park, Robert. *On Social Control and Collective Behavior.* Chicago: Chicago University Press, 1967.

Peran, Martí, Alícia Suàrez, and Mercè Vidal. "Noucentisme i Ciutat." In *Noucentisme i Ciutat,* ed Martí Peran, Alícia Suàrez, and Mercè Vidal. Madrid: Electa, 1994: 9–31.

Pike, Burton. *The Image of the City in Modern Literature.* Princeton: Princeton University Press, 1981.

Pla y Deniel, Enrique. "Las dos ciudades." *Boletín Oficial del Obispado de Salamanca* 10 (Sept. 30, 1936): 265–314.

Poulet, George. *The Interior Distance.* Trans. Elliott Coleman. Ann Arbor: University of Michigan Press, 1964.

Prawer, S. *Karl Marx and World Literature.* Oxford: Oxford University Press, 1976.

Prigge, Walter. *Urbanität und Intellektualität im 20. Jahrhundert. Wien 1900, Frankfurt 1930. Paris 1960.* Frankfurt and New York: Campus, 1996.

Pynchon, Thomas. *Gravity's Rainbow.* New York: Vintage, 1973.

Raban, Jonathan. *Soft City.* 1974. Repr. London: Harvill Press, 1998.

Rabinow, Paul. *French Modern.* Cambridge: MIT Press, 1989.

Resina, Joan Ramon. "Historical Discourse and the Propaganda Film (Reporting the Revolution in Barcelona)." *New Literary History* 29 (1) (Winter 1988) 67–84.

——. "Madrid's Palimpsest: Reading the Capital against the Grain." In *Iberian Cities,* ed. Joan Ramon Resina. London: Routledge, 2001: 56–92.

Ribas, Antoni. *La ciutat cremada.* Barcelona: Leo Films/P.C. Teide, 1975.

Robbins, Bruce, ed. *The Phantom Public Sphere.* Minneapolis: University of Minnesota Press, 1993.

Robins, Kevin. "Prisoner of the City: Whatever Could a Postmodern City Be?" In *Space and Place: Theories of Identity and Location,* ed. Erica Carter, James Donald, and Judith Squires. London: Lawrence and Wishart, 1993: 303–30.

Roca, Francesc. "Ildefons Cerdà, 'el hombre algebraico.'" In *Barcelona,*

1888–1929: Modernidad, ambición y conflictos de una ciudad soñada, ed. Alejandro Sánchez. Madrid: Alianza Editorial, 1994: 155–65.

Rodriguez, Richard. *Days of Obligation: An Argument with My Mexican Father.* New York: Viking, 1992.

Rodríguez del Pino, Salvador. *La novela chicana escrita en español: Cinco autores comprometidos.* Ypsilanti, Mich: Bilingual Press, 1982.

Rogers, Richard. *Cities for a Small Planet.* Ed. Philip Gumuchdjian. London: Faber and Faber, 1997.

Romero Maura, Joaquín. *La Rosa de Fuego: Republicanos y anarquistas: La política de los obreros barceloneses entre el desastre colonial y la Semana Trágica, 1899–1909.* Barcelona: Grijalbo, 1975.

Ronan, Ruth. *Possible Worlds in Literary Theory.* Cambridge: Cambridge University Press, 1994.

Rossi, Aldo. *The Architecture of the City.* Trans. Diane Ghirardo and John Ockman. Cambridge: MIT Press, 1982.

Rugoff, Ralph. "Introduction" and "More than Meets the Eye." In *Scene of the Crime.* Cambridge: MIT Press, 1997: 12–22, 59–108.

Sánchez Ferlosio, Rafael. *El Jarama.* 1955. Repr. Barcelona: Destino, 1991.

Sánchez de Juan, Joan-Anton. "La 'destrucción creadora': El lenguaje de la reforma urbana en tres ciudades de la Europa mediterránea a finales del siglo XIX (Marsella, Nápoles y Barcelona)." *Scripta Nova* 63 (May 1, 2000). http:www.ub.es/geocrit/sn-63.htm.

Sanson d'Abbeville, Nicolas. *America 1667.* Trans. Pauline Carson Bloch and Robert Martinon. Ed. Louis M. Bloch, Jr. Cleveland: Bloch and Company, 1959.

Scherpe, Klaus, ed. *Die Unwirklichkeit der Städte. Großstadtdarstellungen zwischen Moderne und Postmoderne.* Hamburg: Rowohlt, 1988.

Schivelbusch, Wolfgang. *In a Cold Crater: Cultural and Intellectual Life in Berlin, 1945–48.* Trans. Kelly Berry. Berkeley: University of California Press, 1998.

———. *The Railway Journey: The Industrialization of Time and Space in the Nineteenth Century.* Berkeley: University of California Press, 1986.

Schleier, Merrill. *The Skyscraper in American Art, 1890–1931.* New York: Da Capo Press, 1986.

Schreiber, Mathias. "Selbstdarstellung der Bundesrepublik Deutschland." In *Staatsrepräsentation,* ed. Jörg-Dieter Gauger and Justin Stagl. Berlin: Dietrich Reimer Verlag, 1992.

Schumacher, Thomas. "Guiseppe Terragni: Political and Other Allegories." In *The Architecture of Politics: 1910–1940,* ed. Samuel C. Kendall. Miami Beach: Wolfsonian Foundation, 1995.

Schumpeter, Joseph. *The Theory of Economic Development.* Cambridge: Harvard University Press, 1934.

Seltzer, Mark. *Serial Killers: Death and Life in America's Wound Culture.* New York and London: Routledge, 1998.

Sennett, Richard. *The Conscience of the Eye: The Design and Social Life of Cities.* New York: Alfred A. Knopf, 1990.

Serge, Victor. *Birth of Our Power.* Trans. Richard Greeman. London: Victor Gollancz, 1968.

Shattuck, Roger. *The Innocent Eye.* New York: Washington Square Press, 1986.

Sieverts, Thomas. "Bild und Berechnung im Städtebau." In *Information und Imagination.* München: Piper, 1973: 85–119.

Simmel, Georg. "The Metropolis and Mental Life." 1903. Trans. Edward A. Shils. In *On Individuality and Social Forms,* ed. Donald N. Levine. Chicago: University of Chicago Press, 1971: 324–39.

Sinclair, Iain. *Lights Out for the Territory.* London: Granta Publications, 1997.

———. *Sorry Meniscus: Excursions to the Millennium Dome.* London: Profile Books, 1999.

Smith, Joel. *Edward Steichen: The Early Years.* Princeton: Princeton University Press, 1999.

———. "How Stieglitz Came to Photograph Cityscapes." *History of Photography* 20 (1996): 320–31.

Sobrequés i Callicó, Jaume. "La ciutat mediterrània de l'Edat Mitjana a la Revolució Industrial: El cas de Barcelona." In *Les ciutats catalanes en el marc de la Mediterrània,* by Carles Miralles et al. Barcelona: Edicions de la Magrana, 1984: 69–109.

Soja, Edward W. *Thirdspace: Journeys to Los Angeles and Other Real and Imagined Places.* Oxford: Oxford University Press, 1996.

Solà-Morales, Ignasi de. "Los locos arquitectos de una ciudad soñada." In *Barcelona, 1888–1929: Modernidad, ambición y conflictos de una ciudad soñada,* ed. Alejandro Sánchez. Madrid: Alianza Editorial, 1994: 141–54.

Solomon-Godeau, Abigail. "Back to Basics: The Return of Alfred Stieglitz." *Afterimage* 12 (1984): 21–25.

Sorkin, Michael. "Introduction: Traffic Democracy." In *Giving Ground: The Politics of Propinquity,* ed. Joan Copjec and Michael Sorkin. New York: Verso, 1999.

Spector, Nancy. "Subtle Bodies." In *Wounds: Between Democracy and Redemption in Contemporary Art.* Ex. cat. no. 268, Moderna Museet Stockholm, 1998:89–93.

Steichen, Edward. "291." *Camera Work* 47 (1914): 63.

Stieglitz, Alfred. "The Hand Camera—Its Present Importance." 1897. In *Alfred Stieglitz: Photographs and Writings,* ed. Sarah Greenough and Juan Hamilton. Washington, D.C.: National Gallery of Art, 1983: 182–84.

Stierle, Karlheinz. *Der Mythos von Paris. Zeichen und Bewußtsein der Stadt.* Munich: Hanser, 1993.

Stoler, Ann Laura. "Making Empire Respectable: The Politics of Race and Sexual Morality in Twentieth-Century Colonial Cultures." In *Dangerous Liaisons: Gender, Nation, and Postcolonial Perspectives,* ed. Anne McClintock, Aamir Mufti, and Ella Shohat. Minneapolis: University of Minnesota Press, 1997.: 344–73.

Sullivan, Louis. "The Tall Building Artistically Considered." In *America Builds,* ed. Leland Roth. New York: Harper and Row, 1983: 340–46.

Swain, Regina. *La señorita Superman y otras danzas.* Mexico City: Fondo editorial tierra adentro, 1993.

Szarkowski, John. "Alfred Stieglitz." In *Looking at Photographs,* ed. John Szarkowsi. New York: Museum of Modern Art, 1973: 74.

Tabuenca Córdoba, María-Socorro. "Viewing the Border: Perspectives from 'The Open Wound.'" *Discourse* 18 (1995–96): 146–68.

Tafoya, Eddie. "*Born in East L.A.*: Cheech as the Chicano Moses." *Journal of Popular Culture* 26, no. 4 (1993): 123–29.

Tafuri, Manfredo. "Toward a Critique of Architectural Ideology." In *Architecture Theory since 1968,* ed. K. Michael Hays. Cambridge: MIT Press, 1998: 2–35.

———. "U.S.S.R.—Berlin 1922: From Populism to 'Constructivist International'." In *Architecture, Criticism, Ideology,* ed. Joan Ockman (Princeton: Princeton Architectural Press, 1985).

Talbot, William Henry Fox. *The Pencil of Nature*. 1844–46. Repr. New York: Da Capo Press, 1969.

Tasis, Rafael. *Barcelona: Imatge i Història d'una ciutat.* Barcelona: Rafael Dalmau, 1961.

Taylor, Keith. *The Political Ideas of the Utopian Socialists.* London: Frank Cass, 1982.

Telotte, J.P. "The Seductive Text of *Metropolis.*" *South Atlantic Review* 55, no. 4 (1990): 49–60.

Torrente Ballester, Gonzalo. *Off-side.* 1969. Repr. Barcelona: Destinolibro, 1981.

Trillo de Leyva, Manuel. "La exposición 'Cerdà. Ciudad y Territorio' en Andalucía: Las ciudades andaluzas del siglo XIX." In *Cerdà: Ciudad y Territorio. Catálogo para la exposición en Andalucía.* Seville: Consejería de Obras Públicas y Transportes de la Junta de Andalucía, 1996: 9–30.

Trinh, T. Minh-ha. "An Acoustic Journey." In *Rethinking Borders,* ed. John C. Welchman. Minneapolis: University of Minnesota Press, 1996: 1–17.

Turner, Victor. *The Ritual Process: Structure and Anti-Structure.* Chicago: Aldine, 1969.

Ugarte, Michael. *Madrid 1900. The Capital as Cradle of Literature and Culture.* University Park, P.A.: Pennsylvania State University Press, 1996.

Ullman, Joan Connelly. *The Tragic Week. A Study of Anticlericalism in Spain, 1875–1912.* Cambridge: Harvard University Press, 1968.

Umbral, Francisco. *Amar en Madrid.* Barcelona: Destino, 1991.

———. *Madrid 1940. Memorias de un joven fascista.* Barcelona: Planeta, 1993.

———. *Madrid 650.* Barcelona: Planeta, 1995.

———. *Trilogía de Madrid.* Barcelona: Planeta, 1996.

Valbert, Gérard. *Albert Cohen, le seigneur.* Paris: Grasset, 1990.

Vázquez Montalbán, Manuel. *La literatura en la construcción de la ciudad democrática.* Barcelona: Crítica Grijalbo Mondadori, 1998.

Vicens i Vives, Jaume. *Industrials i polítics del segle XIX.* Barcelona: Teide, 1958.

Vilanova, Mercedes. *Les majories invisibles. Explotació fabril, revolució i repressió.* Barcelona: Icaria, 1995.

Vilarós, Teresa. *El mono del desencanto. Una crítica cultural de la transición española (1973–1993).* Madrid: Siglo XXI, 1998.

Virilio, Paul. *The Vision Machine.* Trans. Julie Rose. London: British Film Institute, 1994.

Wark, McKenzie. *Virtual Geography: Living with Global Media Events.* Bloomington: Indiana University Press, 1994.

Weaver, Mike. *Alvin Langdon Coburn: Symbolist Photographer 1882–1966.* New York: Aperture and Eastman House, 1986.

Weber, Samuel. "The Virtuality of the Media." *Sites* 4, no. 2 (2000): 297–318.

Welchman, John C. "The Philosophical Brothel." In *Rethinking Borders,* ed. John C. Welchman. Minneapolis: University of Minneapolis Press, 1996: 160–86.

———, ed. *Rethinking Borders.* Minneapolis: University of Minnesota Press, 1996.

"Welcome to Retina Implant News in Bonn" (http://www.nero.uni-bonn.de/ri/retina-en.html).

Wise, Michael Z. *Capital Dilemma: Germany's Search for a New Architecture of Democracy.* Princeton: Princeton University Press, 1998.

Wittgenstein, Ludwig. *Philosophical Investigations.* Trans. G.E.M. Anscombe. 2d ed. New York: Macmillan, 1958.

Wolf, Francis. *Dire le monde.* Paris: Presses Universitaires de France, 1997.

Wolff, Janet. "Feminism and Modernism." In *Feminine Sentences,* ed. Janet Wolff. Berkeley: University of California Press, 1990: 34–50.

Woody, Howard. "International Postcards: Their History, Production, and Distribution." In *Delivering Views: Distant Cultures and Early Postcards,* ed. Christraud M. Geary and Virginia Lee-Webb. Washington, D.C.: Smithsonian Institution Press, 1998: 14–43.

Wounds: Between Democracy and Redemption in Contemporary Art. Ex. cat. no. 268, Moderna Museet Stockholm, 1998.

Wright, Patrick. *A Journey through Ruins.* London: Harper Collins, 1992.

Zima, Peter V. *Moderne/Postmoderne. Gesellschaft, Literatur, Philosophie.* Tübingen: Francke (UTB), 1997.

Contributors

DEBRA A. CASTILLO is Stephen H. Weiss Presidential Fellow and Professor of Romance Studies and Comparative Literature at Cornell University, where she also serves as director of the Latin American Studies Program. She specializes in contemporary narrative from the Spanish-speaking world, women's studies, and cultural theory. She is the author of several books, including *The Translated World: A Postmodern Tour of Libraries in Literature* (1984), *Talking Back: Strategies for a Latin American Feminist Literary Criticism* (1992), and *Easy Women: Sex and Gender in Modern Mexican Fiction* (1998). She is also the translator of Federico Campbell's *Tijuana: Stories on the Border* (1994), and coeditor of various volumes of essays. Her most recent book (cowritten with María Socorro Tabuenca Córdoba) is *Border Shorts: Theory in Practice* (forthcoming from the University of Minnesota Press).

TOM CONLEY is Professor of Romance Studies at Harvard University. He is the author, recently, of *L'inconscient graphique: Essai sur la lettre de la Renaissance* (2000) and *The Self-Made Map: Cartographic Writing in Early Modern France* (1996). Forthcoming translations include Marc Augé's *An Ethnologist in the Subway* (2001) and Christian Jacob's *The Sovereign Map* (2001).

OTTMAR ETTE is Professor for Romance Literatures at Potsdam University. His publications include monographs on José Martí (1991), Reinaldo Arenas (1992), and Roland Barthes (1998), *Literatur in Bewegung* (2001). He has published numerous articles on literary theory, travel literature, and French and Hispanic literatures of the eighteenth, nineteenth, and twentieth centuries. His edition of Alexander von Humboldt's *Relation historique* received the Heinz-Maier-Leibnitz Award.

DAVID HARVEY is Professor of Cultural Anthropology at the Graduate Center of the City University of New York, Senior Research Fellow at St. Peter's College, Oxford, and Miliband Visiting Fellow at The London School of Economics and Political Science. He has held teaching positions at the Johns Hopkins University and at the University of Bristol and Oxford University. He has been the recipient of numerous awards, including a Guggenheim Fellowship (1976), the Gill Memorial Prize of the Royal Geographical Society (London) in 1972 and the Outstanding Contributor Award of the Association of American Geographers in 1980. He was awarded the Anders Retzius Gold Medal of the Swedish Society of Anthropology and Geography in 1989, the Patron's Medal of the Royal Geographical Society of London in 1995, and the Vautrin Lud International Prize for Geography, also in 1995. He holds honorary doctorates from the University of Buenos Aires, Argentina, and the University of Roskilde, Denmark. In addition to numerous essays in journals or contributed volumes, he has published the following books: *Explanation in Geography* (1969), *Social Justice and the City* (1973), *The Limits to Capital* (1982), *The Urbanization of Capital* (1985), *Consciousness and the Urban Experience* (1985), *The Condition of Postmodernity* (1989), *Justice, Nature and the Geography of Difference* (1996), and, most recently, *Spaces of Hope* (2000).

DIETER INGENSCHAY is Professor of Hispanic Literatures at the Humboldt University, Berlin. He is currently the president of the Deutscher Hispanistenverband. His main areas of interest are contemporary Hispanic literatures, city literature, gender and gay studies, and the relations between literature and anthropology. He is the author of *Alltagswelt und Selbsterfahrung: Ballade und Testament bei Deschamps und Villon* (Munich: Wilhelm Fink Verlag, 1986) and coeditor of the following books: *Abriendo caminos. La literatura española desde 1975* (Barcelona: Lumen, 1994); *La novela española actual. Autores y tendencias* (Kassel: Reichenberger, 1995); *Werk und Diskurs. Karlheinz Stierle zum 60. Geburtstag* (München: Wilhelm Fink Verlag, 1999); *Proust und die Kritik* (Frankfurt am Main: Insel Verlag, 2000); and *Die andere Stadt. Großstadtbilder in der Perspektive des peripheren Blicks* (Würzburg: Königshausen & Neumann 2000).

JOAN RAMON RESINA is Professor of Romance Studies and Comparative Literature at Cornell University. He has taught at various U.S. and European universities. He is the editor of *Diacritics* and the author of *La búsqueda del Grial* (Barcelona: Anthropos, 1988); *Un sueño de piedra: Ensayos sobre la literatura del modernismo europeo* (Barcelona: Anthropos, 1990); *Los usos del clásico* (Barcelona: Anthropos, 1991); *El cadáver en la cocina. La novela policiaca en la cultura del desencanto* (Barcelona: Anthropos, 1997). He has edited four volumes: *Mythopoesis: Literatura, totalidad, ideología* (Barcelona:

Anthropos, 1992); *El aeroplano y la estrella: El movimiento de vanguardia en los Países Catalanes (1904–1936)* (Amsterdam: Rodopi, 1997); *Disremembering the Dictatorship: The Politics of Memory in the Spanish Transition to Democracy* (Amsterdam: Rodopi, 2001); and *Iberian Cities* (New York: Routledge, 2001).

JÜRGEN SCHLAEGER is Professor of British Literature and Culture and director of the Centre for British Studies at the Humboldt University, Berlin. He has published widely on English literature, literary criticism in Britain and the United States, on diaries and autobiographies, and on representations of emotions. He is the author of *Imitatio und Realisation* (1974) and *Grenzen der Moderne: Gertrude Steins Prosa* (1978), and the editor of the following books: *Kritik in der Krise* (1986); *The Anthropological Turn in Literary Studies* (1996); *The Media Debate* (1997); *Representations of Emotions* (1999), with G. Stedman; and *Representations of Emotional Excess* (2000).

MARK SELTZER is Professor of English and American Studies at the University of California Los Angeles. He has taught at Cornell University and at the Humboldt University and the Free University in Berlin. His publications include *Henry James and the Art of Power*, *Bodies and Machines*, and, most recently, *Serial Killers: Death and Life in America's Wound Culture*, as well as numerous articles in literary and cultural studies.

MARY N. WOODS is Associate Professor of Urban and Architectural History at Cornell University. Her interests include architectural education and practice and the intersections of photography and film with the built environment. Recent and upcoming publications include: *From Craft to Profession* (1999), a study of architectural practice in the nineteenth-century United States; *Cass Gilbert: A Life* (2001), on avant-garde photography of the Woolworth Building; and *Architecture of the Night* (2002), on photography of the urban night. She is currently at work on books dealing with documentary photography in the southern United States and imagery of New York City skyscrapers.

Index